States and Sovereignty in the Global Economy

States and Sovereignty in the Global Economy challenges several points of "conventional wisdom," including the extent to which globalization is truly new, the claim that there is an inevitable decline of the state, and the argument that the global economy dictates a common fate for all states. Rather than emphasizing state sovereignty and globalization as opposing forces, this volume reveals that certain powerful states have played a pivotal role in the creation of institutions of contemporary global capitalism. Anti-state popular images – which stress the need to reduce state spending and cut social welfare – have strong ideological roots but distort historical and contemporary reality. Overall, the chapters in this collection highlight that *how* states matter depends upon their differing roles in the global economy and geopolitical system, distinct history, varying resource bases and the nature of their domestic class relations.

Globalization and the role of the state are issues at the forefront of contemporary debates: this volume presents an unconventional and radical perspective which reveals that states do still matter despite the vigor of international capital flows and the omnipresence of the global marketplace.

David A. Smith is Associate Professor of Sociology and Urban Planning; he is the author of *Third World Cities in Global Perspective*, and co-editor of *A New World Order? Global Transformations in the Late Twentieth Century*. **Dorothy J. Solinger** is Professor of Politics and Society. She is the author of five books on contemporary China including *China's Transition from Socialism* and *Contesting Citizenship in Urban China*. **Steven C. Topik** is Professor and Chair of the Department of History. He is the author of four books focusing on Brazil including *Trade and Gunboats* and *The Second Conquest of Latin America*. All three are based at the University of California, Irvine.

States and Sovereignty
in the Global Economy

Edited by David A. Smith,
Dorothy J. Solinger and
Steven C. Topik

This project was co-sponsored by the University of
California Institute on Global Conflict and Cooperation

London and New York

First published 1999
by Routledge
11 New Fetter Lane, London EC4P 4EE

Simultaneously published in the USA and Canada
by Routledge
29 West 35th Street, New York, NY 10001

Routledge is an imprint of the Taylor & Francis Group

Typeset in Baskerville by Routledge
Printed and bound in Great Britain by TJ International Ltd,
Padstow, Cornwall

British Library Cataloguing in Publication Data
A catalogue record for this book is available from the British Library

Library of Congress Cataloging in Publication Data
States and Sovereignty in the Global Economy / edited by David A.
Smith, Dorothy J. Solinger and Steven C. Topik.
p. cm
Co-sponsored by the University of California Institute on Global Conflict
and Cooperation
Includes bibliographical references and index.
1. International economic relations. 2. Capitalism. 3. Sovereignty. 4. State,
the. 5. Competition, International. 6. Economic History 1945– I. Smith,
David A., II. Solinger, Dorothy J.,III. Topik, Steven C. IV. University of
California Institute on Global Conflict and Cooperation.
HF1359.S734 1999

ISBN 0–415–20119–5 (hbk)
ISBN 0–415–20120–9 (pbk)

Contents

Notes on contributors

Giovanni Arrighi is Professor of Sociology at the Johns Hopkins University, Baltimore. His latest books are *The Long Twentieth Century* (1994) and *Chaos and Governance in the Modern World System*, with B. J. Silver *et al.* (1999).

József Böröcz is Associate Professor of Sociology and Director of the Institute for Hungarian Studies at Rutgers University. His books include *Leisure Migration: A Sociological Comparison* (1996) and (with David A. Smith, eds) *A New World Order? Global Transformations in the Late Twentieth Century* (1995).

William Gervase Clarence-Smith is Reader in the Economic History of Asia and Africa at the School of Oriental and African Studies, University of London. He teaches comparative colonialism in the Early Modern and Modern periods, and his research interests cover the impact of diasporas and agricultural systems, especially in the lands bordering the Indian Ocean and the South China Sea.

Edward Friedman, the Hawkins Chair Professor of Political Science at the University of Wisconsin, Madison is a specialist in the international political economy of Asia. His most recent books are *Chinese Village, Socialist State* (Yale, 1991), *The Politics Of Democratization: Generalizing East Asian Experiences* (Westview, 1994) and *National Identity and Democratic Prospects in Socialist China* (Sharpe, 1995).

Eric Helleiner is an Associate Professor in the Department of Political Studies, Trent University (Peterborough, Ont., Canada, ehelleiner@trentu.ca). He is author of *States and the Reemergence of Global Finance: From Bretton Woods to the 1990s* (Ithaca: Cornell University Press, 1994), editor of *The World of Money: The Political Economy of International Capital Mobility* (a special issue of *Policy Sciences*, 1994), co-editor of *Nation-States and Money: The Past, Present and Future of National Currencies* (London: Routledge, forthcoming), as well as author of many articles on issues relating to international finance and international political economy.

Stephen D. Krasner is the Graham H. Stuart Professor of International Relations and a Senior Fellow at the Institute for International Studies at

Stanford. He received his BA from Cornell, MA from Columbia, and Ph.D. from Harvard. Before coming to Stanford in 1981, he taught at Harvard and UCLA. He was the Chair of the Political Science Department from 1984 until 1991 and editor of International Organization from 1986 to 1992. His publications include *Defending the National Interest: Raw Materials Investment and American Foreign Policy* (1978), *International Regimes* (ed.) (1983), *Structural Conflict: The Third World Against Global Liberalism* (1985), *International Organization: Exploration and Contestation in the Study of World Politics* (1998) co-editor, and *Sovereignty: Organized Hypocrisy* (1999). Professor Krasner is a Fellow of the American Academy of Arts and Sciences and a Member of the Council on Foreign Relations.

Colin M. Lewis is Senior Lecturer in Latin American Economic History at the London School of Economics and Political Science, and an Associate Fellow of the Institute of Latin American Studies, University of London. His recent publications include *The New Institutional Economics and Third World Development* (edited with John Harriss and Janet Hunter) (London: Routledge, 1997) and *Latin America: The State and Economic Imperialism* (edited with Christopher Abel) (London: Athlone, 1993). He is currently working on Latin American economic and social policy in the post-1920s period and will shortly publish a study of the history of social insurance in the Argentine.

Julius E. Nyang'oro is Professor and Chairman of African and Afro-American Studies at the University of North Carolina at Chapel Hill. He has published widely in the field of African political economy. His publications include *The State and Capitalist Development in Africa*. He is currently working on a manuscript on political transition in Africa.

Dr Manuel Pastor is Chair of Latin American and Latino Studies at UC Santa Cruz. An economics Ph.D. from the University of Massachusetts, Amherst, his research on Latin American issues has concentrated on the political economy of macroeconomic stabilization and income distribution and has been published in journals such as *International Organization, World Development, Journal of Development Economics, Journal of Latin American Studies,* and *Latin American Research Review*. He is currently working on a comparative project involving Mexico and Argentina, and on the dynamics of reform in contemporary Cuba.

Kenneth Pomeranz is Associate Professor of History and East Asian Languages at the University of California, Irvine. He is the author of *The Making of a Hinterland: State, Society and Economy in Inland North China, 1853–1937* (University of California Press), which won the John K. Fairbank Prize from the American Historical Association; *A Great Divergence: China, Europe, and the Global Environment of the Industrial Revolution* (Princeton University Press, forthcoming); and (with Steven Topik) *The World That Trade Created* (M. E. Sharpe, 1999).

Saskia Sassen is Professor of Sociology at the University of Chicago and Centennial Visiting Professor at the London School of Economics. Her most recent books include *Globalization and its Discontents: Selected Essays* (New York: New Press, 1998) and *Losing Control? Sovereignty in an Age of Globalization* (Columbia University Press, 1996). Her books have been translated into nine languages. She directs the project "Cities and their Crossborder Networks," sponsored by the United Nations University and continues to work on her project "Governance and Accountability in a Global Economy." She is a member of the Council on Foreign Relations and a Fellow of the American Bar Foundation.

Vivien A. Schmidt is Professor of International Relations at Boston University. She received her BA from Bryn Mawr College, her MA and Ph.D. from the University of Chicago, and attended the Institut d'Etudes Politiques, Paris. She was formerly Professor of Political Science at the University of Massachusetts, where she served as Director of the European Studies Program and Director of the Center for Democracy and Development of the McCormack Institute for Public Affairs. Professor Schmidt has published widely in the areas of European political economy and public policy. Her books include *From State to Market? The Transformation of French Business and Government* (Cambridge University Press, 1996) and *Democratizing France* (Cambridge University Press, 1990). Recent articles have appeared in such journals as *Daedalus*, *Governance*, *Journal of European Public Policy*, *Journal of Common Market Studies*, and *Comparative Politics*. Currently, Professor Schmidt is completing a book on the impact of European integration and globalization on economics, institutions, and discourse in France, Britain, and Germany. She is also co-directing a project at the Max Planck Institute for the Study of Societies in Cologne on the adjustment of the welfare state to international economic pressures.

Richard Stubbs is Professor of Political Science and Chair of the Department of Political Science, McMaster University, Canada. He is author and coeditor of a number of books, the most recent of which is (with Geoffrey Underhill) the second edition of *Political Economy and the Changing Global Order* (Toronto: Oxford University Press, 1999). As well as contributing to edited collections, he has published articles on the political economy and security of East and Southeast Asia in leading journals.

Immanuel Wallerstein is Distinguished Professor of Sociology and Director of the Fernand Braudel Center at Binghamton University. Author of *The Modern World-System*, 3 vols; *Historical Capitalism, with Capitalist Civilization*; *Unthinking Social Science*; *After Liberalism*; and, most recently, *Utopistics, or Historical Choices of the 21st Century*.

Preface

This volume is, first of all, the product of many years of joint collaboration between the co-editors, beginning with our formation of a study group in early 1987 focused on the formation, historical growth, and range of roles taken on by the contemporary state, as it is and has historically been manifested globally.

When our study group began to consider issues of state formation and the articulation of the state with civil society in 1987, we were reacting to the growth of multinational corporations, which appeared ready to challenge nation-states as the principal actors in the international political economy. Steeped in theories of development, including dependency and world systems analysis, and familiar with positive possibilities in state socialism, we saw states as crucial agents of social reform.

By 1995, when we originally conceived the conference that gave birth to this volume, neoliberalism was asserting hegemony, both in scholarly circles and in the public mind. Then we were told that history, as well as the Cold War, had already ended. We had entered a completely novel historical epoch, it was said, so that one could learn no lessons from the past. Market society, it appeared, had so completely triumphed that state tutelage and guidance were no longer necessary. The private sector alone, many contended, would ensure "efficiency" and maximize returns, which seemed to be all that really mattered.

In the short year and a half since the conference convened in February 1997, world events spiraled off in a totally different direction and with a dizzying speed. A global financial crisis passed from Thailand, Malaysia, and Indonesia to Russia, Korea, and Brazil. The high priests of *laissez-faire* became belated converts to some level of statism. Even the World Bank recognized that the market alone cannot guarantee productivity and keep the global economy – or even domestic ones – in a sure equilibrium. The events we have witnessed have reconfirmed our belief in the key role of states in market economies and in the global economy as well.

Over time, we have accumulated many debts. At first, we were joined in our study group by a number of faculty and graduate students across several disciplines in the social sciences and history, whose intellectual friendship inspired our endeavor. These people included Frank Cancian, Angela Crowly, David Easton,

Creel Froman, Zhengyuan Fu, James Given, Ping-ti Ho, Edward Kaskla, Robert Moeller, Patricia O'Brien, Ricardo Ovalle, Kenneth Pomeranz, Mark Petracca, Matthew Shugart, Timothy Tackett, Ginger Walker, Carole Wise, and R. Bin Wong.

Over a decade, as the group expanded and deepened its purpose, it matured from a reading group whose refreshments were funded by the Dean of the School of Social Sciences, William Schonfield, to one that won funding from the University of California, Irvine campus in the form of a Focused Research Program (FRP). That funding enabled the members to design colloquia featuring invited outside speakers, to hold a graduate student conference, and to finance some of their own research. We thank the Dean and the campus-wide Committee on Research for their support of our early endeavors.

In mid-1995, we learned that we had more funding in our FRP budget than we realized, and determined to use that money as a foundation in applying for grants to hold a large international conference on "State and Sovereignty in the World Economy." During the year and a half between the time of our decision and the convening of the meeting in February 1997 in Laguna Beach, California, all of our applications were successful.

This means that we are fortunate to be able to thank the following institutions and units for the financial assistance that made our conference possible: the University of California Institute for Global Conflict and Cooperation; the University of California, Irvine Program for Global Peace and Conflict Studies; the University of California, Irvine Center for the Study of Democracy; the University of California Office of Research and Graduate Studies; the University of California Program for Collaborative Research in the Humanities; and the University of California School of Social Sciences.

It took more than funding to make this conference possible. Without the superb, very professional and painstakingly attentive administrative management of Lykke Anderson of the School of Social Sciences and Kristen Maher (then a graduate student in Politics & Society), no amount of money would have been enough. We take this opportunity to express our gratitude to the two of them who produced not only a successful meeting, but an elegant and exceedingly smooth and efficient one as well. Mindy Han in the Department of History and Estela Mendez in the School of Social Studies also deserve a special thanks.

We appreciate, too, the intellectual input we received from our six outstanding discussants at the meeting: James Given, Peter J. Katzenstein, Su-Hoon Lee, Wayne Sandholtz, Barbara Stallings, and R. Bin Wong. Their comments provided insights that contributed significantly to the ultimate shape that the volume took. We are also grateful for the high degree of cheerful and prompt cooperation we got from our authors at every stage of the project. They were willing to undergo several revisions and (almost always!) met all of their deadlines.

At the press, Victoria Smith lent her enthusiastic support from the very early stages of planning the conference and at a number of points along the way. Patrick Proctor helped to shepherd the volume through the review process, and James Whiting also was available for help at several junctures. At the production stage, Elizabeth Gant, Mark Majurey and Eve Daintith all supplied their assistance. To all of them, many thanks.

Finally, the three of us each thank the other two for unfailing comradeship, intellectual stimulation, and mutual effort that absolutely never broke down.

Introduction

David A. Smith, Dorothy J. Solinger, and Steven C. Topik

The end of the twentieth century is a time of tumultuous change: not only is our world becoming increasingly interdependent, but the nature of fundamental relationships between its parts are changing – and at an increasing pace. The unprecedented volume and velocity of international flows of trade, investment, information, cultural exchanges, and human migrations are creating a new, more tightly integrated, world and one that seems to be in the throes of some fundamental restructuring.

A wide range of commentators, from journalists, to politicians, to scholars from a range of disciplines, have attempted to describe and analyze this phenomenon. The pictures they paint vary greatly in terms of their institutional foci, level of sophistication, ideological predilections. But they tend to agree that "globalization," along with the end of the Cold War, has radically changed the basic "rules of the game" for a variety of key actors, particularly states.

This volume investigates how much of this is new and what the impacts are in a range of states. We ask three large questions. In the current processes of "globalization," are states confronting a fundamentally new phenomenon? What are the structural forces – new technologies, discourses, geopolitical contexts – with which today's states must contend? And how do individual states vary in their response to these forces? We conclude that the generic "state" persists as a crucial actor in the world economy, but that individual states operate in changing contexts and have made new choices that, in turn, have saddled their officials with new problems and necessitated the assumption of new functions and roles. To reach that conclusion, we inquire what, precisely, is the niche of, or the stamp of the state today, and how does that vary among different kinds of states; what is the frame within which they must now operate? And we place this inquiry within a broad historical context.

Specifically, we ask how states situate themselves in an era of rapid capital mobility and massive and rapid resource flows. Why do national leaders choose to move toward greater integration into the global economy, and how do a variety of domestic motives across the globe reflect the weight of the past in different places? In short, we seek to reveal the ways in which states, from the perspective of a long-term historical framework, still matter. Further, we probe the extent of states' sovereign powers in contemporary times in light of claims (sometimes disputed) about the heightened international economic involvement of national governments now, as compared with the past.

The concept of the "state" has been the object of much scholarly discussion. Classical social theorists variously situated the state's essence in its exclusive control over legitimate force within a specified territory (Weber 1978: 902, 904), in its character as a site for the formulation of ideas and policies for the collectivity (Durkheim, in Giddens 1978: 192), or in its utility as an instrument of class domination (Marx ([1872]1972: 337). Contemporary commentators also approach the state from a plethora of perspectives. For instance, some highlight the state's possession of centralized authority, authorship of codified law, and power to make decisions (Hall 1984: 1–2), its role in resource mobilization (Nettl 1968: 564), its identity as a bureaucratic apparatus and institutionalized legal order (Krasner 1984: 224), its posture as a goal pursuing organization and configuration of institutionalized interests (Skocpol 1985: 28), its function as a policing organ (Thomson 1995: 226), or its provision, within a particular space, of a focus for popular allegiance (Jackson and James 1993: 17).

While not denying the importance of any of these ideas, this volume addresses two dimensions of states in particular: their dependence upon the consent of the governed (the domain of "legitimacy") and their capacity to act. Capacity for our purposes is comprised of three chief ingredients: resource endowment, the quality of leadership and political institutions, and historical legacies (including traditions of rule, national culture, and past policy decisions).

We are also interested in what forms "sovereignty" takes in disparate countries. Sovereignty is also a term that scholars have cast in different ways. Some, concentrating on its domestic configuration, see it simply as "the state's supreme power" as exercised within set, territorial boundaries (Hall 1984: 17–18), as "constitutional independence" (Jackson and James 1993: 19), as "self-help and territoriality" (Krasner 1993: 301), or "as a claim to the exclusive right to make rules" and to "intervene coercively within its territory" (Thomson 1995: 219, 223). Others place more emphasis on the state's situation as a member of a global community, as in Giddens' (1981) stress on the dependence of sovereignty on a "reflexibly monitored set of relations between states" (pp. 263, 282) or Ruggie's (1983) focus on the time-bound ordering of global politics unique to the modern state system.

The discussion of sovereignty in this volume is framed by Stephen Krasner's fourfold categorization of general meanings of this term: (1) control or independence sovereignty; (2) domestic sovereignty; (3) Westphalian sovereignty; and (4) international recognition or international legal sovereignty (see Chapter 2). Throughout the chapters, authors were urged to refer to the concept along these dimensions, standardizing their terminology (despite *not* always agreeing on issues of substance).

A key problem in the present era is the perceived need of national leaders to navigate between the demands of acquiring and maintaining internal legitimacy, on the one hand, and the necessity of securing and ensuring financial backing that appears – in a time of enhanced global interaction among states – to underwrite that legitimacy, on the other. What, we ask, do leaders today (given currently popular ideologies and practices) believe they need to create and sustain domestic legitimacy? What is the character of the context in which they act? And what shapes policy choice in various kinds of states and regions?

We are primarily concerned, then, not with all dimensions or definitions of the state, but with the style of international economic integration of different states, changes that happen once they enter into this involvement, and the range of choices that politicians in particular places can retain. This is a matter of the interaction between the (contested) degree of sovereign power of various states, on the one hand, and global economic forces, on the other. This means that we consider involvement in the world economy as a result of decision-making – in large part in response to leadership concerns with domestic consent and legitimation – but a choice that is constrained by state capacity and contemporary global structures and processes.

The word "globalization" is familiar to anyone who reads newspapers or watches television newscasts, and is rapidly emerging as the favorite mantra of political leaders all around the world. It is clearly one of those faddish neologisms that is frequently invoked but rarely defined (and, in this case, freighted with ideological implications). It refers to what they consider major transformations in the global system that have occurred in the past two or three decades. For instance, two recent books, William Greider's (1997) *One World, Ready or Not* and Dani Rodrik's (1997) *Has Globalization Gone Too Far?*, proceed from very different assumptions, are written in divergent styles, and come to conflicting conclusions. Yet both books agree that there is something fundamentally distinct about the current period that poses basic challenges to contemporary societies. (Some prominent analysts argue that the term is fundamentally misleading, and that what is called "globalization" is not really new or novel (Schwartz 1994; Cox 1996; Panitch 1996; see also Wallerstein (Chapter 1) and Arrighi (Chapter 3) in this volume); others eschew it because they find its usage hopelessly vague (Strange 1996: xiii).)

Although many people agree that we live in a world that has recently been transformed by "globalization," just what that expression means is less clear, and often left conveniently undefined. Fully exploring what globalization means is not the central project of this volume (for this, see Smith and Böröcz 1995 or Mittelman 1996a). But some grasp of the basic characteristics of today's "new world order" is necessary as a context for investigating the role of states. Minimalist definitions of globalization emphasize increases in "international economic integration" (Rodrik 1997), sometimes invoking ideas related to "a new international division of labor" (Frobel *et al.* 1980) and the rise of "the global assemblyline" (Feuntes and Ehrenriech 1984), or the functional integration of national economies within the circuits of industrial and financial capital (Rhodes 1996). Somewhat broader definitions begin with ideas about economic changes where "(t)he chain of causality runs from the spatial reorganization of production to international trade and to the integration of financial markets" on to demographic, political and cultural changes (Mittelman 1996a: 3). Other authors take an even more generic view that de-links globalization from economic transformations, preferring to conceptualize it as a melange of diverse phenomena, driven by improvements in technology and communications that have brought the world closer together (see Krasner, Chapter 2, this volume). Yet others, in a more economistic vein, prefer the term "internationalization," which they define as processes generated by underlying shifts in transaction costs that produce observable flows of goods, services and capital (Milner and Keohane, 1996a).

We choose to remain agnostic about the advantages of inclusive or exclusive definitions of globalization (and are sympathetic to historically grounded arguments that insist it may not be new). But there are two particular insightful arguments in discussions of contemporary globalization that we would underline. First, is the notion that a basic dimension of the current global economy is an increasing "time–space compression" in which the sheer velocity of exchanges rapidly multiplies (Mittelman 1996a; Arrighi, Chapter 3, this volume). For example, Robert Wade, who claims that the extent to which most economic activity is truly globalized is exaggerated, none the less describes "liquid capital ricocheting across the foreign exchanges" as the volume of currency exchange accelerates to astronomical levels ($900 billion a day as of September 1992) (Wade 1996: 64). This enormous acceleration of transactions profoundly affects contemporary global political economy, including the roles states play in it. Second, we maintain that many images of globalization are deeply imbued with an ideology, promoted by conservative theorists, large corporations, and wealthy individuals and foundations, that claims that forces like deregulation and "marketization" are "inevitable" ("there is no alternative") and "in the long run beneficent, at least for some people" (Cox 1996: 23; see also Panitch 1996: 83–4; Bierstecker 1992: 118–20). Stephen Gill (1996) argues that these usages of the term "globalization" are "ideological in the sense of a set of ideas that justify and legitimate forms of class domination (i.e., of capital)" (p. 211); James Mittelman (1996b) shows that the values of economic liberalism enshrine free markets as a "positive sum game" (p. 231).

Advocates of this "game" believe it is necessary to subordinate states and politics to the requirements of capital accumulation (Panitch 1996: 83–4). These advocates have included a progressively wider and more inclusive span of politicians around the globe, following the influential endorsements this ideology and its attendant programs received from Margaret Thatcher and Ronald Reagan in the early 1980s. At that point – and during the subsequent decade – a set of historical forces came together which influenced economic policies on the global level. Among these were persisting problems of structural unemployment and an aging population in the advanced countries, along with stagflation there, which prompted a questioning of the interventionist Keynsian model then in use. Particularly under attack were welfare state redistributionist policies and powerful labor unions, which were accused of limiting "the freedom" of capital and capitalists. These problems strained national budgets at the same time that stagnant growth failed to increase these states' revenues.

At the same time, the accelerating expansion of production facilities of multinational corporations to poorer countries, which became export platforms, encouraged calls for lower tariff barriers. Meanwhile, new financial instruments and technologies led to a new revolutionary explosion of finance capital seeking freedom to roam the globe through international agreements on property rights and stable currencies, both overseen by such multilateral agencies as the World Bank.

By the end of the 1980s, with the collapse of the Soviet Union and its satellite states, where command economies had emphasized heavy industry and military production, a disillusionment had set in. The low standards of living that had resulted from these political and economic policies, which their populations now hoped to redress, undercut the claims of socialism and, perhaps by implication, even social democracy. The upshot was that state economic management was discredited in both the west and the formerly "socialist" east.

In many less developed countries, especially throughout Latin America, unprecedented levels of inflation were provoked by problems with the import substitution industrialization (ISI) model, as populist redistributionist pressures joined with vast foreign debts often contracted by corrupt public, military, and civilian officials. Economic restructuring aimed at reducing government deficits was often undertaken by curtailing social expenditures, containing wages, and selling off state properties. Even leaders like erstwhile social theorist Fernando Henrique Cardoso and the head of the formerly pro-labor Argentine Peronist party, Carlos Menem, were prepared to follow Chile's free market example (Baer and Maloney 1997).

Though a few places did not follow suit (Cuba, North Korea, Southeast Asia, and parts of Africa, each for their own reasons), there was wide subscription to the policy package of neoliberalism championed by Thatcher and Reagan. Whether the reasons were world systemic factors (i.e. global economic conditions and "shocks," like the petroleum price increases of the 1970s or the world recession of the 1980s), changes in the power of domestic interests and the resulting coalitions in particular states (Frieden and Rogowski 1996), the growing clout of international institutions (such as the IMF and the World Bank), the contagion of ideas initiated in core states and emulated elsewhere, or from an amalgam of all these factors (Biersteker 1992), the broad content of the policies they dictated was startlingly similar around the globe as the 1990s unfolded.

These policies have both a domestic and an international component. Internally, they include disengagement of the government from the management of the domestic economy, deregulation, a privatization of state-owned enterprises, and cutbacks in social welfare programs. Internationally, they entail a reduction of tariff barriers, the opening of capital markets, and a liberalization of restrictions on foreign investment, combined with new incentives to attract it. Overall, they comprise a generalized enhanced reliance on market mechanisms and on the private sector as compared to the previous period, supposedly in the service of upgrading national competitiveness (Milner and Keohane 1996b: 24; Biersteker 1992: 106, 108; Cox 1996: 22; Gummett 1996: 15).

This discourse of neoliberal globalization extends far beyond politicians and policy-makers. Indeed, discussions about the current global economy, whether in the mass media or scholarly debate, often implicitly or explicitly accept these ideological assumptions. These notions, supported by a powerful array of material interests, promote the supposition that a number of trends are unfolding in an inexorable fashion, including the worldwide "decline of the state" and obeisance to the transformative power of markets.[1]

Thus, according to many observers, recent fundamental changes in the global economy make world markets and transnational corporate players more powerful than nation states (for a particularly clear academic explication of this view, see Strange 1996). They amount to a worldwide trend toward privatization and anti-statism (with the fall of the Berlin Wall and the collapse of communism and command economies cited as prominent evidence of the state's failure as an agent for prosperity). Instead, the international market for goods and capital (labor is still anchored in national territories) are seen as the purveyors of not only healthy economies, but good governance and satisfied citizenries. To be sure, various "dislocations" will occur and there will be clear "winners" and "losers" but, ultimately, in this vision, the neoliberal process will triumph (Strange 1996; Rodrik 1997). Although recently some of these commentators acknowledge that governments can play a constructive role in protecting workers via "social safety nets" (and may need to play that role again to preserve the legitimacy of the economic system) (Rodrik 1997; World Bank 1997), the general sense of this view is that states are inefficient, distort development, capture excessive rents through corruption, etc. They move by political imperatives, which are wasteful, rather than follow the laws of the self-regulating market.

According to the neoliberal world view, the state's main task should be to get out of the way so that the most efficient private entrepreneurs can maximize social welfare by investing resources to increase production. The invisible hand of the market will lead to the promised land. International mobility of the factors of production and technology mean that efficient late-comers can skip historical stages and jump to the head of the class. Economic development is often thought to necessarily bring with it social changes such as greater literacy and individualism, and the rise of new middle classes, which in turn lead to greater democracy. According to many students of "globalization," we are moving toward convergence of economic and political systems in which all will enjoy similar capitalist, *laissez faire* economies, western culture and values, and democratic political systems (for a recent scholarly exploration of this "convergence hypothesis" see Berger and Dore 1996).

This volume questions this view of globalization and the neoliberal paradigm sweeping the Western world and being exported to less developed countries. It brings together political scientists, sociologists, historians, and economists with expertise in Europe, the Americas, Asia, and Africa to examine ways in which states still matter. We attempt to test the putative generalizations noted above by comparing the experiences of particular states and regions across both time and space. Too often, students of world affairs surrender to their journalistic impulses to extract from today's and yesterday's events a trend line that can be extrapolated to tomorrow. Is neoliberalism's formula for the state's proper role really a one-size-fits-all solution that equally fits China, England, the United States,

Brazil and Rwanda? Don't geographic differences weigh in heavily, not just because of varying resource allocations, but because of different histories, cultures, and geopolitical circumstances? Can the changes of the last decade or two be extended into the distant future, that is, is history linear, or is it cyclical, instead? Is everyone wet by the same tide or are promontories less at risk than low-lying areas? Or, to change the metaphor, do some actors make the waves while others are hopelessly swamped by them? And, indeed, what is really so new about the pattern of globalization in the world today? A more patient perspective from the longer run helps remove some of the "noise" of the quotidian details given much weight by the journalists and think-tank pundits scurrying to meet their deadlines or to please their contributors and clients.

Certainly, international intercourse and economic liberalism have been long-standing and much of the current situation seems more like a return to pre-First World War days than a journey into a brave new world (Schwartz 1994; Mittelman 1996a; Rodrik 1997; see also this volume: Helleiner (Chapter 7) and Krasner (Chapter 2)). While we acknowledge that much has changed, change is a historic verity. What would be truly new is if nothing changed. Certainly the speed of many forms of international exchange has escalated. But the velocity, nature and extent of change varies depending on what factor one examines and in what part of the world.

Another of this volume's fundamental insights is that states not only still matter, but it makes no sense even to try to remove them, either physically or conceptually, from the economy. There is no inexorable logic of competition, capital accumulation, or technological imperatives driving neoliberal reforms. Rather, these policies reflect a political choice *made by state authorities*, chiefly in response to domestic and international political pressures as well as the peer pressure of global ideological conformity. Markets should not be essentialized, as natural things or arenas that assert the abstract laws of capitalist economics. Rather, they are social and political constructs; markets are embedded in political and social relations. Perhaps most importantly, the state is necessary to keep markets functioning and capitalism from destroying itself since capital is often short-sighted and markets irrational. (For instance, the market alone, shorn of political morality laws, tells us that drugs, guns, and prostitution are the most valuable commodities.) We see in the chapters that follow that globalization has not occurred *against* state sovereignty. Rather, to a considerable extent the leaders of states have not only chosen to be integrated into, but have shaped the direction of globalization (Panitch 1996: 84–5). Moreover, states have played a pivotal role in creating the financial and legal instruments necessary for increased global interactions (see Sassen, Chapter 8, this volume). While increased dependence on exterior markets, capital, and technology can undermine domestic sovereignty, under some circumstances, it can also bolster sovereignty under others (see in this volume: Krasner (Chapter 2), Lewis (Chapter 5), Schmidt (Chapter 9), Helleiner (Chapter 7), and Stubbs (Chapter 12)). Just as state policies are not uniform, neither are the consequences of greater international incorporation.

Indeed, the same state can lose authority in some domains while gaining it in others.

Since markets are political creations – and to some extent political actors – explaining the contributions of specific domestic regimes is important for grasping how different states will react, even in identical international contexts. Local cultural values and practices, class relations, political discourses, historical understandings, and expectations very much affect choices. National developments have a path dependency that cannot be erased by global pressures (Milner and Keohane 1996b: 253; Berger 1996: 1, 18–21).

States should not be reified. They are run by people using human logic and bias to make decisions. But they are more than just the tools of rulers. States themselves are embedded social relations, often with extensive capacity and their own rationales, channeled by entrenched interests and practices.

But at the same time, states must respond to the sometimes contradictory imperatives of promoting economic growth or "capital accumulation," while maintaining their political legitimacy in the eyes of those they rule (O'Connor 1973). States, as several of the following chapters show, play indispensable roles in maintaining economic dynamism: they preserve "order," enforce rules, cooperate and even collaborate with business, particularly by guaranteeing property rights. But governance always relies on some level of consent to legitimate authority (Weber 1947). Legitimization occurs when citizens (or subjects) accept state authority over them because they see their rulers as providers of physical security, dispensers of justice, overseers of economic growth, and providers and distributors of collective goods. However there is a tendency for an inherent tension to emerge between accumulation and legitimization, because the prerogatives of profit-making and the needs and demands of the masses often conflict. This stress is especially pronounced in democratic and democratizing countries (O'Donnell *et al.* 1986). Yet it is a dilemma that authoritarian rulers or ruling groups only ignore at their peril, as cases like the recent overthrow of kleptocratic Mobutu Seko in Zaire (and the troubles of his successor) drive home.

The contemporary discourse of neoliberal globalization, with its heavy emphasis on a nation's "economic efficiency" and "international competitiveness," seems designed to subvert the social welfare functions upon which many states' legitimacy are based. Gill (1996) suggests that, particularly in affluent democratic countries like the United States, the dominance of *laissez faire* ideology and the dismantling of the welfare state lead increasingly to feelings of personal insecurity, which, in turn, engender political apathy and indifference. People lose confidence in state authorities that can no longer "deliver." This indirect effect of economic globalization, reflected in the internal politics of nations, may have more impact on the decline of state sovereignty than more familiar direct effects (financial globalization, rising power of transnational corporations, rapid technological change, etc.) While their normative orientations are quite different, both Dani Rodrik (1997) and Immanuel Wallerstein (Chapter 1, this volume) see rising anti-statism, and the de-legitimization of the states and the existing political order, as a serious threat to the continued viability of contemporary global economy and the business interests that profit from it.

In sum, this volume argues that states still matter. How they matter is a complicated and variegated issue. The roles of states vary geographically, in part, because their places in the global system present different problems and challenges. Clearly, African states at the brink of civil war and famine with bare treasuries and rapacious bureaucrats face a different task than Eastern European states that managed great resources but lost popular legitimacy. The shift of the continental authoritarian Chinese communism into capitalist activities has to differ from Mexico, overshadowed by its large wealthy northern neighbor. And, of course, states in countries whose banks and multinational enterprises domi-nate the world market, and who have privileged control over international agencies, such as the World Bank, have much greater influence over global forces than those more peripheral to world events. The world economy is not a level playing field. History, resource bases, the nature of domestic class relations, geopolitics, and leadership's need for internal legitimacy all condition the state's role in the globalization process.

Organizational overview

This volume is divided into four sections: three overviews of the evolution of the global system, states, state sovereignty, and capital accumulation; three chapters on the relationships of states and the world economy since the eighteenth century; two studies of the nature and consequences of changes in global technology and financial practices; and six case studies of countries on four continents.

The ordering of the chapters enables us first to consider the broad long-term historical development of states in the world economy. Next, we look at three different forms of historical states: the large, economically and politically established states in China and Europe, the newly independent states of Latin America, and the colonized states of the Third World. Those three chapters illustrate some of the chief regionally specific issues of globalization in previous times, highlight issues that were relevant in the interaction of states with the global economy from the mid-eighteenth to the mid-twentieth centuries, and consider the forces these states help set into motion, forces that in time led to the creation of the modern world economy.

The two chapters on capital mobility and legal cultures and technologies that come next illuminate critical structural features that confront states in the world today and with which each of them must cope; these chapters also help the reader assess the extent to which such processes and constraints had precedents. But even these chapters expose the powerful forces confronting various states, and thereby create a framework for the historical and country/regional chapters that follow; at the same time both authors bring out the degree to which states matter more in the financial sphere than many other scholars imply, even if states matter in new and novel ways.

Finally, the case studies of six countries or regions on four continents provide empirical evidence of the variable coping strategies and disparate policy choices of national leaders in these places, as they struggle to accommodate the lure of the purported benefits of global economic involvement, yet maintain the consent and the favor of their domestic constituencies and citizenry. Here we see how the respective capacities of each of the depicted states – in terms of resources, leadership abilities, and historical constraints (including prior decision-making and the political and economic furrows of path dependence) – interact with pressures presented by the global economy. One lesson is clear: in more than one instance when leaders, by conscious choice and in response to specific, often domestically rooted incentives, become more deeply enmeshed in the world economy, they then found themselves swept into a dynamic process whose imperatives they would *not* have chosen willingly. By beginning with history and structure, we are better able to appreciate the situations and dilemmas of states in the world today, as well as the forces that have shaped them over time.

Review of chapters

The first three chapters all consider changes in the international arena over the broad sweep of the last four hundred years. We begin with Immanuel Wallerstein's chapter on the historic interrelationship of the state and capitalism. The state created the legal, social, and political conditions for capital accumulation and "the ever-increasing commodification of everything"(p. 20). It has done more than create a level playing field; it has directed accumulation by subsidizing certain participants, allowing legalized monopolies such as patents and property rights, and serving as very generous monopsonists. The "liberal" state also promoted an important ideology that legitimated itself and the capitalist *status quo*. This was the idea that it provided all citizens and their children the formal "opportunity" of upward mobility and success that made life palatable to the disadvantaged masses. Wallerstein believes that beginning in 1968, however, the very successful global liberalism "came unstuck" and this "opiate of hope" disappeared. As ever more people lost faith in their governments' ability to provide a better tomorrow, anti-government attitudes rose and state legitimacy waned. Increasingly, people "abandoned the state structures as vehicles of their collective betterment" and "return to the ancient solution of…providing their own security" (p. 31). Thus, "privatization" becomes the rage, and a general hostility to the state rises. Wallerstein argues that "for the first time in 500 years" states are "on a downward slide in terms of their sovereignty, inward and outward" (p. 32), not because of the strength of multinational corporations or multilateral agencies, but because of the declining legitimacy accorded to the states by their populations. Ironically, in a world where capitalists *need* governments, and conservative ideology has been preaching against "interventionist states," the de-legitimization of state authority raises the specter of a disastrous global business crisis. Wallerstein leaves us with a troubling vision of global capitalism in crisis, with the system offering no clear way out.

Stephen Krasner in Chapter 2 also takes a historical look at states, but at the concept of sovereignty rather than their relationship to capitalism. Krasner disagrees that globalization undermines sovereignty. First, historically states never enjoyed complete sovereignty and many enjoyed little at all. He shows how many powers of the state that today appear vulnerable were also open to challenge at various junctures in the past. Second, sovereignty is too awkward and amorphous a concept to analyze without first distinguishing the four different ways it is conceived: control or interdependence sovereignty, domestic sovereignty, Westphalian sovereignty, international law sovereignty. When discussing sovereignty's encounter with globalization, one must specify which definition is at play. For instance, Krasner notes a confusion between "control," some of which may be threatened by global forces, and the "authority" of states which is not. In light of these distinctions, there is little evidence that sovereignty *per se* is undermined. This becomes even more clear when one discards the "mythical past" posited by some scholars in which states actually did control their borders and internal populations and replaced it with a more realistic understanding of the limitations that all states at all times have faced.

In Chapter 3, which also considers the *longue durée*, Giovanni Arrighi points out that change in the world system is constant and cyclical. He notes that "key aspects of these [new] transformations are either not new at all or are new in degree but not in kind" (p. 53). Thus, the fact that the world is changing is to be expected. But, like Wallerstein, he believes that the world system is at a new juncture that will bring a tomorrow that looks quite different from today as it departs from the trajectory of the last five centuries. The rise of unipolar US dominance after 1989 is simply one step in the historic cycles of accumulation. What is different is the rise of East Asia. Arrighi argues that current US hegemony is more apparent than real. In fact, Asia is coming to dominate the world system. This, however, represents a qualitatively different step from the past. In the first centuries of the world capitalist system, power went to increasingly more powerful states: from the Italian city states to the Dutch Republic, to the British Empire, to the continental United States power. Military and economic power went hand in hand, since economic success stripped of force was unthinkable. But now we are embarking on a new stage because first, military power (still with the US) is separated from economic power (East Asia) and the economic powers are divided into a number of states. Since the new system is only being born, its specific shape is difficult to predict. Indeed, the recent linked crises in Thailand, Indonesia, South Korea, Japan, and Russia demonstrate the inchoate and shaky nature of this new system.

The second section in this volume also considers the sweep of history, but by concentrating on different forms of states and their relationships to the world economy. In Chapter 4, Kenneth Pomeranz focuses on the great established states and sketches the rise of western Europe since 1750 to argue that European domination of the capitalist world system did not come from the factors that are usually given to account for the West's earlier development: superior technology, indigenous capital formation, superior state formations that allowed civil society greater freedom, or better entrepreneurship and more faith in progress. Rather,

Pomeranz cites three crucial areas in which Europe differed from Asia: extra-territorial trade, colonial expansions, and military fiscalism. The West came to dominate the world economy because states, competing among themselves for power, used monopoly and coercion, particularly in creating overseas colonies in the Americas to accumulate capital and construct markets. State craft and markets were intimately involved. In China, where surprisingly, coercion and imperialism were less in evidence and the private sphere was freer to operate, industrial capitalism was slow to emerge, in large part because of a lack of foreign colonies. Involvement in the world economy strengthened the few European colonial states (at the expense of smaller, weaker European states) while either destroying the states of incorporated peoples as in the Americas, or subordinating the states of Asia.

In Chapter 5, Colin Lewis discusses a second form of state as he considers the first colonies to win their independence in Latin America. For the first century of statehood (roughly 1821–1930) Latin American leaders saw no conflict between state building and an intimate involvement in the world economy. Although they used foreign ideas and institutions, and for the most part the new states supported free trade and even espoused *laissez faire* liberalism, they in fact were enormously involved in creating and directing the economy: "if elsewhere states were 'made' by capitalists, in Latin America states created business"(p. 99). Interventionism was an enduring trait. Those states that were most successful in fashioning export economies, Argentina, Brazil, Chile and, after 1890, Mexico, were also those with the strongest sovereignty. States that had less economic success, such as in Central America and the Caribbean, were more likely to become weak "banana republics." After the Depression of the 1930s, autarchy came into fashion and remained so until the 1970s. Now states directed industrialization rather than export-led growth and were more sympathetic to the demands of urban masses. But the differences between the pre-1930 and post-1930 regimes has too often been exaggerated. The role of states shifted, but states always were central in the process of capital accumulation and market reinforcement. Lewis concludes, then, that there was no contradiction between growing involvement in the international market and state sovereignty: that markets were politically embedded. While one sees some forms of convergence in Latin America over time, clearly wide ranging differences remain.

In Chapter 6, William Gervase Clarence-Smith examines a third form of state, the colonial state in the nineteenth and twentieth centuries. Colonial regimes were the creation of European powers, but only in some cases were they much the objects of economic exploitation. "The wealthier the colonizing power was, the less it was interested in economic advantages," with the Germans acquiring some colonies as forms of "conspicuous consumption" (p. 122) Thus the political power of the colonizer did not necessarily integrate the colonial economies closely into the world economy. While some colonizers were guided by a mercantilist view of their relationship to their colonies, others, such as Great Britain and the United States tended to follow free-trade colonialism. Also, to a surprising degree, some colonial regimes enjoyed considerable domestic sovereignty, even while not being recognized in international law or Westphalian terms. In order to limit the cost of the colonial regime, colonial rulers had to strike up bargains with locals and attend to their needs. The policies of colonial regimes changed over time. As earlier efforts to integrate Africa into the world economy gave way to "game-park" visions of "traditional" life, Africa has escaped that fate of other regions that were inexorably sucked into the maelstrom of the world economy.

The third section of this book brings us to crucial structural features of the contemporary world economy as it covers the consequences of recent technological and institutional innovation, especially in the global financial sphere. Eric Helleiner in Chapter 7 outlines four variants of the claim that contemporary patterns of financial globalization challenge sovereign states. He finds three – which focus on changing information technology, pressures toward "competitive deregulation," and the decline of macroeconomic policy autonomy – less than fully persuasive. In his dismissal of the technologically based argument, he emphasizes the growing importance of key geographical nodes and points out that the states where these centers are located will have *increased* regulatory power, expressly because of the heightened clout they derive from their own superior technologically based surveillance systems. Similarly, pressure for competitive deregulation has had uneven effects, with some states (like the United States and those in East Asia) retaining considerable influence. He argues that while there has been some erosion of governments' macroeconomic policy autonomy linked to financial globalization, strategies to control exchange rates can mitigate the effect. Helleiner also points out that states did not even attempt to achieve macroeconomic control until recent decades, so the current diminution of these tools should not be seen as a critical change. Finally, he suggests that the most convincing argument that financial globalization really is undermining the state involves the "unraveling of territoriality" – a point also made by Sassen in Chapter 8 (see below). But, rather than interpret this as a basic decline in sovereignty, Helleiner suggests a more limited conclusion that "financial globalization erodes state authority claims based on territoriality" (p. 149).

Saskia Sassen's empirical focus is also on high finance, with special emphasis on how the currently evolving global institutions are being constructed in places like New York City. She begins by arguing that globalization, properly understood, is *not* just about cross-border flows like trade and investment, but sometimes involves profound changes with*in* particular countries, cities, and even neighborhoods and business districts. In this context, globalization involves the "de-nationalization of national territory" (cf. Helleiner, discussed above). Sassen's interest centers on the complex institutions that emerge to mediate and regulate transnational corporate transactions and international financial exchanges in these key global cities. She emphasizes that financial globalization is *not* simply the result of ineluctable market forces, techno-determinism, or diffuse global cultural/ideological pressures of neoliberalism. Rather, these "reforms" (and the new institutions they give rise to) are *socially constructed* – the result of the work of corporate specialists in law, accounting or finance, often with the assistance of states and state functionaries. The result is the development of an institutional nexus, a particular "business culture," and a peculiarly globalized regulatory climate in places like the City of London or the heart of Manhattan, where high-level international arbitrage operates in veritable "free trade zones" of international finance. How does this relate to state and sovereignty? Sassen explicitly rejects the argument that global economy and nation states are engaged in a grand zero-sum game, and that the shift to economic globalization requires diminished power or sovereignty for national states. Instead, global capital needs the state's assistance in the creation of the emerging command posts of corporate and finance capital and to legitimate the new legal regimes required to make them work. In fact, the move toward various types of global economic regulation, unequivocally *strengthens* some aspects of the sovereignty of a select group of core states. These states definitely still matter, a great deal! But she does allow that globalization may be leading to "substantive transformations" even in these cases.

In the final section of this volume, we bring analyses about the development of the world economy and its current structural constraints to bear on the situations of six cases. These chapters in some instances examine world regions, such as Southeast Asia, Eastern Europe, and Sub-Saharan Africa; in others they focus on just one country, as is the case for Mexico and China (though their authors compare them to other states within their regions); and in one chapter the three leading countries of the European Union, France, Germany, and Britain are discussed and compared to each other.

Our purpose in selecting these varying countries and world areas was explicitly to examine states at vastly different developmental levels, with widely varying power, sizes, and resources of all kinds – from those at the peak of economic development to those at the bottom; with grossly disparate political institutions and leadership styles – from former command economies-cum-authoritarian states to advanced capitalist democracies to post-colonial dictatorships; and with widely divergent historical traditions and cultures.

In each case, the author takes care to point to the historical antecedents that have deeply informed contemporary choices, thereby undercutting a view that a vacuum of pressures from global forces alone is simply, inexorably, and indiscriminately sucking in states of every sort, independent of domestic political dynamics. The set of chapters here illustrates forcefully variation among contemporary states in accord with their variable resources, institutions, class composition and historical trajectories.

In Chapter 9, Vivien Schmidt considers the three chief advanced industrial countries of the European Union. She notes that these nations are facing two different forces: globalization and Europeanization. The latter is often seen as a buffer for the former, even though it also means an international opening and integration. Within Europeanization are different trends. Schmidt underlines the importance of the varying historical roles of states in each of these economies, and analyzes the current role each is playing in both macro- and microeconomies. She also considers each state's relationship to business, labor, and welfare policy.

Finally, she shows the extent to which each has been able to develop a political discourse justifying its course to its citizenry. Britain led the way in embracing neoliberal policies, but is uncomfortable with many aspects of Europeanization even though, in large part because of its earlier start, it has had to make few recent adjustments in macroeconomic terms. France, with a greater *étatist* tradition and stronger social democratic ideology, faces greater transformations to become part of the EEC, it therefore has the most difficulty legitimating its stance to its own people. Germany, a leader of the Europeanization trend, must make the fewest changes to conform to the demands of the Maastricht Treaty. But is finding itself under stress because of international pressures of competition none the less.

Eastern Europe encounters a much more fundamental transformation. But, as Jóseph Böröcz explains in Chapter 10, change and dependency are centuries-old traditions in Eastern Europe. Anti-statist discourse has hit nowhere harder than in the former satellites of the Soviet Union. Although, in fact, there were decades of relative economic and social development, these have been forgotten in the wake of the fall of the Berlin Wall. So the leadership of what Böröcz calls "comprador states," which, in a twist, experienced capital accumulation prior to the establishment of private property, decided after their release from "actually existing socialism" that power lay in putting their countries under the hammer. These states have become "auctioneer states" in Böröcz's terms, which reward officially connected buyers of state properties. With the sudden displacement of the former regimes, social welfare has declined. Although these processes are new, emerging with the end of the Cold War, Böröcz seems to believe that the internal dynamics of Eastern European political economy, and a rereading of its immediate past in light of the current anti-statist ideology, rather than globalization *per se*, explain the plight of this part of the world.

Another dependent part of the world with a history of a strong state presence in the economy followed recently by privatization is Mexico. Manuel Pastor shows that although under the shadow of the US rather than the USSR, Mexico also has suffered as a result of following the neoliberal formula. But unlike Eastern Europe, which is privatizing in an effort to distance itself from Russia, Mexico's neoliberal program was partially driven in an effort to tighten ties with the US through NAFTA. To win political support in the US for NAFTA and in Mexico for the governing party, the PRI, Mexico allowed its peso to rise in value. This was not an economic decision as much as a political one. Yet, the market validated it, encouraging a huge influx of investment. Policy managers came to believe that the strong peso was evidence of the strength of the Mexican economy rather than just the temporary outcome of a chosen government policy. Indeed, the market was acting irrationally by validating a policy that economic conditions did not warrant. But capitalists try to win short-run profits, not to discipline economies for the economy's long-run benefit. Believing their own rhetoric, Mexicans followed a disastrous policy that could have been avoided if they had realized that they, in fact, had more space to maneuver than they came to believe.

Writing on Southeast Asia, Richard Stubbs in Chapter 12 claims that the four most economically successful states – Indonesia, Malaysia, Singapore, and Thailand – long realized that they have substantial freedom to maneuver. Ironically, these more sovereign states developed from weaker ones beset by external and internal enemies during the Cold War. The need to win internal legitimacy and external sovereignty prompted them to follow development policies that both required a strong state economic presence and popular social policies (though not equally so in all states). Stubbs underlines the importance of geopolitics: the role of the US in financing some state capacity during the Cold War, more recent Japanese investment, and the importance of an array of developmental influences, especially from other parts of Asia. These states also benefited from the creation of their own regional organization, ASEAN. In these countries globalization led to economic development and the bolstering of state sovereignty, without weakening the economic role of the state. Recent crises, that originated in Thailand have percolated to Indonesia, Malaysia and Singapore (and beyond to South Korea and Japan), and have revealed the unsteady foundations of the Southeast Asian "economic miracle." As a result the past year has seen the IMF and international investors sharply reduce the room for these states to maneuver. Still the impacts varied. The stronger the state and the more political sovereignty it has, the more it is able to transform its society so as to adapt to, and even at times take advantage of, the globalization process. Globalization has not led to increased democratization, however, as it has in Eastern Europe and Mexico. Political authoritarianism and economic growth complement each other well in Southeast Asia. This is particularly troubling in light of the recent developments.

China demonstrates yet another reaction to globalization. Edward Friedman in Chapter 13 describes a state that has lost neither sovereignty nor capacity, while vastly increasing its role in the international economy. A strong Communist Party and statist traditions ensure that the state continues to be central to growth. Friedman points out that it makes no sense conceptually to try to disentangle state and economy, just as the dichotomy socialism/capitalism is foolish (a point Sassen (Chapter 8) has also made). China demonstrates that a formal commitment to state "socialism," and an eager plunge into production for global capitalism can coexist with, and even nourish, each other. China, because of its size, traditions, and strongly consolidated state, has been able to enter the global arena on its own terms and indeed gain international sovereignty from this venture. None the less, Friedmann suggests that nationalist reactions to foreign influences may yet undermine these bold moves from within.

The final case we consider is perhaps the saddest: in Chapter 14, Julius Nyangoro examines Sub-Saharan Africa. These states have not lost sovereignty due to the new globalization because they had little to start with. Internal civil wars after independence, much as in Latin American 150 years earlier, undermined both state capacity and domestic sovereignty. States here cling to claims based on international law and some Westphalian sovereignty. But unable to take advantage of the growing international trade and capital flows that mark other regions, Africa is left to neglect and despair. It increasingly becomes a case for international relief agencies, rather than one for multinational investors. But lack of engagement with the international economy has not brought about either economic development or greater sovereignty. The historical legacy of western imperialism is real. Today's problems are political as well as economic: sharp internal divisions prevent economic development and state formation.

The fourteen chapters that make up this volume each, in its distinctive way, offers a sense in which states still matter. The first set does so with broad historical sweep, even as its authors point to ways in which the pressures and interactions of today's global economy present political leaders with new challenges. The second group does so by presenting its data in terms of choices and dilemmas that earlier leaders made and confronted as they unwittingly contributed to the design of the world economy of the present; this sets the stage for understanding the forces at work today and the moves taken by states now as, similarly, the outcome of an array of disparate but conscious choices. The second half of the book, which addresses the present, makes clear and explicit the nature of these choices – even as they are bounded in each case by resource endowment, leadership and institutional competence, economic imperatives, and history – even as those who take the choices must work to achieve domestic political consent. The authors show as well some of the most central parameters within which these choices are made.

The world is at a crucial crossroads. In the words of the old Chinese blessing and curse, we live in interesting times. We cannot be sure if we are on the cusp of a brave new world or are on an historical roller coaster ride. But too many political leaders, businessmen and scholars seem to be suffering from historical amnesia. In too many ways, today's policies, prognoses, and ideologies resemble those Karl Polanyi (1957) outlined in *The Great Transformation*. Blind faith in the unfettered market without concern for social consequences led to fascist and Stalinist states last time. Freedom must be more than the right to accumulate property; justice more than the protection of property rights. Let us hope that there truly is progress – and not only for the select few.

Note

1   Exceptions in the academic literature are carefully qualified treatments by Gummett 1996; Berger and Dore 1996; Jackson and James 1993; and Milner and Keohane 1996.

References

Baer, W. and Maloney, W. (1997) "Neoliberalism and income distribution in Latin America," *World Development* 25 (3): 311–27.

Berger, S. (1996) "Introduction," in S. Berger and R. Dore (eds) *National Diversity and Global Capitalism*. Ithaca, NY: Cornell University Press, pp. 1–25.

Berger, S. and Dore, R. (eds) (1996) *National Diversity and Global Capitalism*, Ithaca, NY: Cornell University Press.

Biersteker, T.J. (1992) "The 'triumph' of neoclassical economics in the developing world: policy convergence and the bases of governance in the international order," in J.N. Rosenau and E.-O. Czempiel (eds) *Governance without Government: Order and Change in World Politics*, Cambridge: Cambridge University Press, pp. 102–31.

Cox, R. W. (1996) "A perspective on globalization," in J. Mittelman (ed.) *Globalization: Critical Reflections*, Boulder, CO: Lynne Reinner Publishers, pp. 21–30.

Greider, W. (1997) *One World Ready Or Not: The Manic Logic of Global Capitalism*, New York: Simon & Schuster.

Feuntes, A. and Ehrenreich, B. (1984) *Women in the Global Factory*, Boston, MA: South End Press.

Friedan, J.A. and Rogowski, R. (1996) "The impact of the international economy on national policies: an analytical overview," in R. Keohane and H. Milner (eds) *Internationalization and Domestic Politics*, Cambridge, UK: Cambridge University Press, pp. 25–47

Frobel, F., Heinrichs, J., and Kreye, O (1981) *The New International Division of Labor*, New York: Cambridge University Press.

Giddens, A. (ed.) (1978) *Emile Durkheim*, New York: Penguin Books.

Giddens, A. (1981) *The Nation–State and Violence* (vol. 2 of *A Critique of Contemporary Historical Materialism*), Berkeley: University of California Press.

Gill, S. (1996) "Globalization, democratization, and the politics of indifference," in J. Mittelman (ed.) *Globalization: Critical Reflections*, Boulder, CO: Lynne Reinner Publishers, pp. 205–28.

Gummett, P. (ed.) (1996) *Globalization and Public Policy*, Cheltenham, UK: Edward Elgar.

Hall, S. (1984) "The state in question," in D. Held and S. Hall (eds) *The Idea of the Modern State*, Philadelphia, PA: Open University Press, pp. 1–28.

Jackson, R.H. and James, A. (1993) "The character of independent statehood," in R. Jackson and A. James (eds) *States in a Changing World: A Contemporary Analysis*, Oxford, UK: Clarendon Press, pp. 3–25.

Keohane, R.O. and Milner, H.V. (eds) (1996) *Internationalization and Domestic Politics*, Cambridge, UK: Cambridge University Press.

Krasner, S.D. (1984) "Approaches to the state: alternative conceptions and historical dynamics," *Comparative Politics* 16 (2): 223–46.

—— (1993) "Economic interdependence and independent statehood," in R. Jackson and A. James (eds) *States in a Changing World: A Contemporary Analysis*, Oxford, UK: Clarendon Press, pp. 301–21.

Marx, K. ([1872] 1972) "Manifesto of the Communist Party," in R. Tucker (ed.) *The Marx–Engels Reader*, New York: W.W. Norton, pp. 331–62.

Milner, H.V. and Keohane, R.O. (1996a) "Internationalization and domestic politics: an introduction," in R. Keohane and H. Milner (eds) *Internationalization and Domestic Politics*, Cambridge, UK: Cambridge University Press, pp. 3–24.

—— (1996b) "Internationalization and domestic politics: a conclusion," in R. Keohane and H. Milner (eds) *Internationalization and Domestic Politics*, Cambridge, UK: Cambridge University Press, pp. 243–58.

Mittelman, J.H. (ed.) (1996a) *Globalization: Critical Reflections*, Boulder, CO: Lynne Reinner Publishers.

—— (1996b) "How does globalization really work?" in J. Mittelman (ed.) *Globalization: Critical Reflections*, Boulder, CO: Lynne Reinner Publishers, pp. 229–41.

—— (1996c) "The dynamics of globalization," in J. Mittelman (ed.) *Globalization: Critical Reflections*, Boulder, CO: Lynne Reinner Publishers, pp. 1–19.

Nettl, J.P. (1968) "The state as a conceptual variable," *World Politics* 20: 559–92.

O'Connor, J. (1973) *The Fiscal Crisis of the State*, New York: St. Martin's Press.

O'Donnell, G., Schmitter, P. and Whitehead, L. (eds) (1986) *Transitions from Authoritarian Rule: Prospects for Democracy*, Baltimore, MD: Johns Hopkins University Press.

Panitch, L. (1996) "Rethinking the role of the state," in J. Mittelman (ed.) *Globalization: Critical Reflections*, Boulder, CO: Lynne Reinner Publishers, pp. 83–113.

Polanyi, K. (1957) *The Great Transformation*, Boston, MA: Beacon Press.

Rhodes, M. (1996) "Globalization, the state and the restructuring of regional economies," in P. Gummet (ed.) *Globalization and Public Policy*, Cheltenham, UK: Edward Elgar, pp. 161–80.

Rodrik, D. (1997) *Has Globalization Gone Too Far?* Washington, DC: Institute for International Economics.

Ruggie, J. (1983) "Continuity and transformation in the world polity: toward a neorealist synthesis," *World Politics* 35: 261–85.

Schwartz, H.M. (1994) *States Versus Markets: History, Geography, and the Development the International Political Economy*, New York: St. Martin's Press.

Skocpol, T. (1985) "Bringing the state back in: strategies of analysis in current research," in P. Evans, T. Skocpol, and D. Rueschemeyer (eds) *Bringing the State Back In*, New York: Cambridge University Press, pp. 3–37

Smith, D.A. and Böröcz, J. (eds) (1995) *A New World Order? Global Transformations in the Late Twentieth Century*, Westport, CT: Greenwood Press.

Strange, S. (1996) *The Retreat of the State: The Diffusion of Power in the World Economy*, New York: Cambridge University Press.

Thomson, J. (1995) "State sovereignty in international relations," *International Studies Quarterly* 39: 213–33.

Wade, R. (1996) "Globalization and its limits: reports of the death of the national economy are greatly exaggerated," in S. Berger and R. Dore (eds) *National Diversity and Global Capitalism*, Ithaca, NY: Cornell University Press, pp. 60–88.

Weber, M. (1947) *The Theory of Social and Economic Organization* (trans. A.M. Henderson and T. Parsons), New York: The Free Press.

—— (1978) "Political communities," in G. Roth and C. Wittich (eds) *Economy and Society: An Outline of Interpretive Sociology*, vol. 2, Berkeley: University of California Press.

World Bank (1997) *World Development Report 1997: The State in a Changing World*, New York: Oxford University Press.

1   States? Sovereignty?

The dilemmas of capitalists in an age of transition

Immanuel Wallerstein

There have long been debates, as we all know, about the relationship of the individual states to the capitalists. Views range from those who emphasize the degree to which states are manipulated by capitalists to serve their individual and collective interests to those who emphasize the degree to which states are autonomous actors who deal with capitalists as one interest group among several or many. There has also been debate about the degree to which capitalists could escape control by the state machineries, and there are many who are arguing that their ability to do this has increased considerably in recent decades, with the onset of the transnational corporation and so-called globalization.

In addition, there have long been debates about the relationship of so-called sovereign states to each other. Views range from those who emphasize the effective sovereignty of the various states to those who are cynical about the ability of so-called weak states to resist the pressures (and blandishments) of so-called strong states. This debate is often kept separate from the debate about the relationship of individual states to capitalists, as though we were dealing with two different questions. It seems to me difficult, however, to discuss these issues intelligently without looking at them in tandem, because of the peculiar structure of the modern world-system.

The modern world-system, in existence in at least part of the globe since the sixteenth century, is a capitalist world-economy. This means several things. A system is capitalist if the primary dynamic of social activity is the endless accumulation of capital. This is sometimes called the law of value. Not everyone, of course, is necessarily motivated to engage in such endless accumulation, and indeed only a few are able to do so successfully. But a system is capitalist if those who do engage in such activity tend to prevail in the middle run over those who follow other dynamics. The endless accumulation of capital requires in turn the ever-increasing commodification of everything, and a capitalist world-economy should show a continuous trend in this direction, which the modern world-system surely does.

This, then, leads to the second requirement, that the commodities be linked in so-called commodity chains, not only because such chains are "efficient" (meaning that they constitute a method that minimizes costs in terms of output), but also that they are opaque (to use Braudel's term). The opacity of the distribution of the surplus-value in a long commodity chain is the most effective way to minimize political opposition, because it obscures the reality and the causes of the acute polarization of distribution that is the consequence of the endless accumulation of capital, a polarization that is more acute than in any previous historical system.

The length of the commodity chains determines the boundaries of the division of labor of the world-economy. How long they are is a function of several factors: the kinds of raw materials that need to be included in the chain, the state of the technology of transport and communications, and perhaps most important the degree to which the dominant forces in the capitalist world-economy have the political strength to incorporate additional areas into their network. I have argued that the historical geography of our present structure can be seen to have three principal moments. The first was the period of original creation between 1450 and 1650, during which time the modern world-system came to include primarily most of Europe (but neither the Russian Empire nor the Ottoman Empire) plus certain parts of the Americas. The second moment was the great expansion from 1750 to 1850, when primarily the Russian Empire, the Ottoman Empire, southern and parts of Southeast Asia, large parts of West Africa, and the rest of the Americas were incorporated. The third and last expansion occurred in the period between 1850 and 1900, when primarily East Asia, but also various other zones in Africa, the rest of Southeast Asia, and Oceania were brought inside the division of labor. At that point, the capitalist world-economy had become truly global for the first time. It became the first historical system to include the entire globe within its geography.

Though it is fashionable to speak of globalization today as a phenomenon that began at the earliest in the 1970s, in fact transnational commodity chains were extensive from the very beginning of the system, and global since the second half of the nineteenth century. To be sure, the improvement in technology has made it possible to transport more and different kinds of items across great distances, but I contend that there has not been any fundamental change in the structuring and operations of these commodity chains in the twentieth century, and that none is likely to occur because of the so-called information revolution.

Still, the dynamic growth of the capitalist world-economy over 500 years has been extraordinary and very impressive, and of course we are dazzled by the ever more remarkable machines and other forms of applied scientific knowledge that have come into existence. The basic claim of neoclassical economics is that this economic growth and these technological accomplishments are the result of capitalist entrepreneurial activity, and that, now that the last remaining barriers to the endless accumulation of capital are being eliminated, the world shall go from glory to glory, wealth to wealth, and therefore satisfaction to satisfaction. Neoclassical economists, and their associates in other disciplines, paint a very rosy picture of the future, provided their formulae are accepted, and a quite dismal one if these formulae are rejected or even hampered.

But even neoclassical economists will admit that the last 500 years have not been in reality ones of unlimited "free flow of the factors of production." Indeed, that is what the talk about "globalization" tells us. Seemingly, it is only today, and not even yet, that we are seeing this truly free flow. If so, one has to wonder how the capitalist entrepreneurs have been able to do so well prior to the last few decades, since persons of virtually every intellectual and political persuasion seem to agree that capitalist entrepreneurs have indeed, as a group, done quite well over the past few centuries in terms of their ability to accumulate capital. To explain this seeming anomaly, we have to turn to that part of the story that the neoclassical economists since Alfred Marshall have been strenuously excluding from consideration, the political and social story. And here is where the states come in.

The modern state is a peculiar creature, since these states are so-called sovereign states within an interstate system. I contend that the political structures that existed in non-capitalist systems did not operate in the same way, and that they constituted qualitatively a different kind of institution. What, then, are the peculiarities of the modern state? First and foremost, that it claims sovereignty. "Sovereignty," as it has been defined since the sixteenth century, is a claim not about the state but about the interstate system. It is a double claim, looking both inward and outward. Sovereignty of the state, inward-looking, is the assertion that, within its boundaries (which therefore must necessarily be clearly defined and legitimated within the interstate system) the state may pursue whatever policies it deems wise, decree whatever laws it deems necessary, and that it may do this without any individual, group, or substate structure inside the state having the right to refuse to obey the laws. Sovereignty of the state, outward-looking, is the argument that no other state in the system has the right to exercise any authority, directly or indirectly, within the boundaries of the given state, since such an attempt would constitute a breach of the given state's sovereignty. No doubt, earlier state forms also claimed authority within their realms, but "sovereignty" involves in addition the mutual recognition of these claims of the states within an interstate system. That is, sovereignty in the modern world is a reciprocal concept.

However, as soon as we put these claims on paper, we see immediately how far they are from a description of how the modern world really works. No modern state has ever been truly inwardly sovereign de facto, since there has always been internal resistance to its authority. Indeed, in most states this resistance has led to institutionalizing legal limitations on internal sovereignty in the form, among others, of constitutional law. Nor has any state even been truly outwardly sovereign, since interference by one state in the affairs of another is common currency, and since the entire corpus of international law (admittedly a weak reed) represents a series of limitations on outward sovereignty. In any case, strong states notoriously do not reciprocate fully recognition of the sovereignty of weak states. So why is such an absurd idea put forth? And why do I say that this claim to sovereignty within an interstate system is the peculiar political characteristic of the modern world-system, in comparison to other kinds of world-system?

The concept of sovereignty was in fact formulated in western Europe at a time when state structures were, in reality, very weak. States had small and ineffective bureaucracies, armed forces they did not control very well, and all sorts of strong local authorities and overlapping jurisdictions with which to deal. It is only with the so-called new monarchies of the late fifteenth century that the balance begins – just begins – to be redressed. The doctrine of the absolute right of monarchs was a theoretical claim of weak rulers for a far-off utopia they hoped to establish. Their arbitrariness was the mirror of their relative impotence. Modern diplomacy, with its recognition of extra-territoriality and the safe passage of diplomats, was an invention of Renaissance Italy and spread Europe-wide only in the sixteenth century. The establishment of a minimally institutionalized interstate system took over a century to realize, with the Peace of Westphalia in 1648.

The story of the past 500 years has been the slow but steady linear increase, within the framework of the capitalist world-economy, of the internal power of the states and of the authority of the institutions of the interstate system. Still, we should not exaggerate. These structures went from a very low point on the scale to somewhere further up the scale, but at no point have they approached anything that might be called absolute power. Furthermore, at all points in time, some states (those we call strong) had greater internal and greater external power than most other states. We should of course be clear what we mean by power here. Power is not bombast and it is not a theoretically (that is, legally) unlimited authority. Power is measured by results; power is about getting one's way. The truly powerful can be (and usually are) soft-spoken, respectful, and quietly manipulative; the truly powerful succeed. The powerful are those who are heeded, even when their legitimacy is only partially accorded. Their threat of force most often obviates the need to use it. The truly powerful are Machiavellian. They know that their ability to use force in the future usually is diminished by the very process of actually using it in the present, and they are therefore quite sparing and prudent in such use.

This political system of sovereign states within an interstate system, of states and an interstate system both having an intermediate degree of power, suited perfectly the needs of capitalist entrepreneurs. For what do persons whose goal is the endless accumulation of capital need in order to realize their objectives? Or, another way of asking this is, why isn't the free market sufficient for their purposes? Could they really do better in a world in which no political authority existed at all? To ask the question is to see that no capitalist or capitalist apologist, not even Milton Friedman, not even Ayn Rand, has ever quite asked for this. They have insisted at the very least on having the so-called night-watchman state.

Now what does a night watchman do? He sits in relative darkness, twiddling his thumbs in boredom, occasionally twirling his baton or revolver when not asleep, and waiting. His function is to ward off intruders who intend to pilfer property. He does this primarily just by being there. So here we are at basics, the universally noted demand for securing property rights. There's no point in accumulating capital if you can't hold on to it.

There are three major ways in which entrepreneurs can lose accumulated capital outside market operations. Capital can be stolen; it can be confiscated; it can be taxed. Theft in one form or another is a persistent problem. Outside the modern world-system, the basic defense against serious theft had always been to invest in private security systems. This was even true of the capitalist world-economy in its early days. There exists however an alternative, which is to transfer the role of providing anti-theft security to the states; generically this is called the police function. The economic advantages of shifting the security role from private to public hands is admirably laid out in Frederic Lane's *Profits from Power* (1979),[1] in which he invents the term "protection rent" to describe the increased profits that result from this historic shift, a benefit from which some entrepreneurs (those in strong states) drew far greater advantage than others.

For the truly rich, however, theft has probably been a smaller problem, historically, than confiscation. Confiscation always was a major political and economic weapon in the hands of rulers, especially of powerful rulers in non-capitalist systems. Confiscation has undoubtedly been one of the major mechanisms whereby capitalists were prevented from making the priority of the endless accumulation of capital prevail. This is why institutionalizing the illegitimacy of confiscation via the establishment not only of property rights but of the "rule of law" has been a necessary condition of constructing a capitalist historical system. Confiscation remained widespread in the early days of the modern world-system, if not directly then indirectly via state bankruptcies (see the four successive ones of the Spanish Hapsburgs), and confiscation via socialization has been a phenomenon of the twentieth century. None the less, the remarkable thing is not how much but how little confiscation there has been. There has been no comparable level of security for capitalists in any other world-system, and this security against confiscation has actually grown with time. Even the socialization processes have been frequently effectuated "with compensation" and furthermore, as we know, they have often been reversed and therefore, from a systemic point of view, have been only temporary. In any case, the pervasiveness of the rule of law has tended to make future levels of income more predictable, which allows capitalists to make more rational investments and therefore ultimately more profit.

As for taxation, no one wants to be taxed of course, but capitalists as a class have never been opposed to what they think of as reasonable taxation. From their point of view, reasonable taxation is the purchase of services from the state. As with all other purchases, capitalists prefer to pay the lowest rates available, but they do not expect to get these services gratis. In addition, as we know, taxes on paper are not the same as taxes really paid. Still, it is fair to say that the rate of real taxation has grown over the centuries of the capitalist world-economy, but this is because the services have grown. It is not at all sure that it would be less costly for capitalists to assume the costs of these necessary services directly. Indeed, I would argue that relatively high rates of taxation are a plus for large capitalists, since much, even most, of the money is recycled to them in one way or another, which means that state taxation tends to be a way of shifting surplus-value from small enterprises and the working classes to the large capitalists.

What are the services that capitalists need of the state? The first and greatest service they require is protection against the free market. The free market is the mortal enemy of capital accumulation. The hypothetical free market, so dear to the elucubrations of economists, one with multiple buyers and sellers, all of whom share perfect information, would of course be a capitalist disaster. Who could make any money in it? The capitalist would be reduced to the income of the hypothetical proletarian of the nineteenth century, living off what might be called "the iron law of profits in a free market," just enough barely to survive. We know that this is not how it works, but that is because the real existing market is by no means free.

Obviously, any given producer will be able to increase his returns to the extent that he monopolizes the market. But the free market does tend to undermine monopolies, which is of course what the spokespersons of capitalists have always said. If an operation is profitable, and monopolized operations are by definition so, then other entrepreneurs will enter the market if they can, thereby reducing the price at which a given item is sold on the market. "If they can"! The market itself puts only very limited constraints on entry. These constraints are called efficiency. If an entrant can match the efficiency of existing producers, the market says welcome. The really significant constraints on entry are the doing of the state, or rather of the states.

The states have three major mechanisms that transform the economic transactions on the market. The most obvious one is legal constraint. The states can decree or forbid monopolies, or create quotas. The most utilized methods are import/export prohibitions and, even more important, patents. By re-labeling such monopolies "intellectual property," the hope is that no one will notice how incompatible this notion is with the concept of a free market, or perhaps it lets us see how incompatible the concept of property is with that of a free market. After all, the classic mugger's opening gambit, "your money or your life," offers a free market alternative. So does the classic terrorist menace, "do *x* or else."

Prohibitions are important for entrepreneurs but they do seem to violate grossly much of the rhetoric. So there exists a certain amount of political hesitation to use them too frequently. The state has other tools in the creation of monopolies that are somewhat less visible and hence probably more important. The state can distort the market very easily. Since the market presumably favors the most efficient, and efficiency is a question of reducing cost for comparable output, the state can quite simply assume part of the cost of the entrepreneur. They assume part of the costs whenever the state in any way subsidizes the entrepreneur. The state can do this directly for a given product. But more importantly, the state can do this on behalf of multiple entrepreneurs simultaneously in two ways. It can build so-called infrastructure, which of course means that given entrepreneurs do not have to assume those costs. This is usually justified on the grounds that the costs are too high for any single entrepreneur and that such state expenditure represents a collective sharing of the cost that benefits everyone. But this explanation assumes that all entrepreneurs benefit equally, which is seldom the case, certainly not transnationally and most often not even within the boundaries of the state. In any case, the costs of the infrastructure are not usually imposed on the collectivity of beneficiaries but on all taxpayers, and even disproportionately on non-users.

Nor is such direct assumption of costs via infrastructure the largest single assistance given by the states. The states offer the entrepreneurs the possibility of not paying the costs of repairing the damage they do to what is not their property. If an entrepreneur pollutes a stream and doesn't pay the costs either of avoiding the pollution or of restoring the stream to pristine state, de facto the state is permitting the transmission of the cost to society at large, a bill that is often not paid for generations thereafter, but which eventually must be paid by someone. In the meantime, the absence of constraint on the entrepreneur, his ability to "externalize" his costs, is a subsidy of considerable importance.

Nor does this end the process. There is a special advantage of being an entrepreneur in a strong state that entrepreneurs in other states do not enjoy to the same degree. And here we see the advantage of the location of states in an interstate system from the point of view of the entrepreneurs. Strong states can prevent other states from conferring monopolistic advantages against certain entrepreneurs, usually citizens of their own state.

The proposition is very simple. Real profit, the kind that permits a serious endless accumulation of capital, is only possible with relative monopolies, for however long they last. And such monopolies are not possible without the states. Furthermore, the system of multiple states within an interstate system offers the entrepreneurs great assistance in making sure that the states restrict themselves to helping them and do not overstep their bounds and hurt them. The curious interstate system permits entrepreneurs, particularly large ones, to circumvent states that get too big for their britches, by seeking the patronage of other states, or using one state mechanism to curb another state mechanism.

This brings us to the third way in which states can prevent the free market from functioning freely. The states are major purchasers in their national markets, and large states command an impressive proportion of purchases in the world market. They are frequently monopsonists, or near-monopsonists, for certain very expensive goods; for example, today, for armaments or super-conductors. They could of course use this power to lower prices for themselves as purchasers, but instead they seem for the most part to use this power to permit the producers to monopolize a roughly equal share of the market, and to raise their prices scandalously.

But, you will think, about what then was Adam Smith so agitated? Did he not inveigh against the state's role in creating monopolies? Did he not call for *laissez faire, laissez passer*? Yes, he did, up to a point. The reason why, however, is the crucial thing to see. Obviously, one man's monopoly is another man's poison. And entrepreneurs are always competing first of all with each other. So, natu-rally, those who are out are always screaming against state-induced monopolies. Adam Smith was the spokesman of these poor, benighted underdogs. To be sure, once the underdogs have undone the monopolies in which they did not partici-pate, they happily proceed to try to create new ones of their own, at which point they tend to cease citing Adam Smith and instead bankroll neoconservative foundations.

Of course, monopoly is not the only advantage capitalists obtain from the state. The other main advantage, regularly noted, is the maintenance of order. Order within the state means first of all order against insurgency by the working classes. This is more than the police function against theft; it is the state's role in reducing the efficacy of class struggle by workers. The way this is done is through a combination of force, deception, and concessions. What we mean by a liberal state is one in which the amount of force is reduced and the amount of deception and concessions increased. This works better, to be sure, but it is not always possible, especially in peripheral zones of the world-economy, where there is too little surplus available to permit the state to allocate much of it to concessions. Even in the most liberal state, however, there are serious legal constrictions on the modes of action by the working classes, and on the whole these constrictions are greater, usually far greater, than those reciprocally imposed on employers. No legal system is class-blind although, as a result of workers' political activity over the past two centuries, the situation did tend to get somewhat better after 1945 than it previously had been. It is this improvement in the position of the working classes that the resurgent conservative ideology around the world since the 1970s has been contesting.

What, however, about interstate order? Schumpeter, in one of his few naive moments, insisted that interstate disorder was a negative from the point of view of entrepreneurs and a social atavism. Perhaps it was not naivety on his part, but merely Schumpeter's desperate need not to accept the economic logic of Lenin's *Imperialism* that led him to insist on this. In any case, it seems to me quite clear that capitalists generally feel about war what they feel about taxation. Their attitude depends on the particular circumstances. War against Saddam Hussein may seem positive in terms of preserving certain possibilities of capital accumulation for certain capitalists. Even world wars are useful for particular capitalists, usually provided they are serving the winning side, and are located somewhat out of the direct line of fire, or if their production is particularly geared to wartime needs of either side.

Still, Schumpeter has a point in general, in that too much or too persistent interstate disorder makes it difficult to predict the market situation, and leads to capricious destruction of property. It also makes impossible, or at least very difficult, certain kinds of economic transactions, interfering with previous routes of commodity chains. In short, if the world-system were continuously in a state of "world war," capitalism probably wouldn't work very well. So the states are needed to prevent this. Or rather it is useful to have a hegemonic power that can institute a certain degree of regulation in the system, which increases predictability and minimizes capricious losses. But once again the order a hegemonic power imposes is always better for some capitalists than for others. Collective unity of the capitalist classes is not too strong in this domain. We could sum this up by saying that waging war is, at many points in time and for certain capitalists, a great service, even if this is not always true. I certainly do not wish to suggest that capitalists, singly or collectively, call wars on and off. Capitalists are powerful in a capitalist world-economy, but they do not control everything. Others get into the picture of deciding on wars.

It is at this point that we must discuss the so-called autonomy of the states. Capitalists seek to accumulate capital. Politicians, for the most part, primarily seek to obtain, and remain in, office. One might think of them as petty entrepreneurs who, however, exercise considerable power beyond their own capital. Remaining in office is a function of support – support of capitalist strata to be sure, but also support of voters/citizens/popular strata. This latter support is what makes possible the minimal legitimacy of a state structure. Without this minimal legitimacy, the cost of remaining in office is very high, and the long-run stability of the state structure is limited.

What legitimates a state within the capitalist world-economy? Surely it is not the fairness of the distribution of the surplus-value or even of the application of the laws. If one says it is the myths that every state uses about its history or origins or special virtues, one still needs to ask why people buy into these myths. It is not self-evident that they will. And in any case we know that popular insurrections occur repeatedly, some of which even involve cultural revolutionary processes that call into question these basic myths.

So, legitimacy needs explaining. The Weberian typology allows us to understand the different fashions in which people legitimate their states. What Weber calls rational–legal legitimization is of course the form that liberal ideology preaches. In much of the modern world, this form has come to prevail, if not all of the time, at least for a good deal of the time. But why does it prevail? I insist not only on the importance of this question but on the fact that an answer is far from self-evident. We live in a highly unequal world. We live in one in which polarization is constantly increasing, and in which even the middle strata are not keeping up proportionately with the upper strata, despite any and all improvements in their absolute situation. So why do so many persons tolerate this situation, even embrace it?

There are, it seems to me, two kinds of answers one might give. One is relative deprivation. *We* may be badly off, or at least not well enough off, but *they* are really badly off. So let us not rock the boat, and above all, let us prevent them from rocking the boat. That this kind of collective psychology plays a major role seems to me to be very widely accepted, whether one applauds it by talking of a sizable middle class as the basis of democratic stability or deplores it by talking of a labor aristocracy having false consciousness, and whether one thinks of it as operating primarily within states or within the world-system as a whole. This explanation is a structural one; that is to say, it is an argument that a certain collective psychology derives from the very structure of the capitalist world-economy. If this aspect of the structure remains intact, that is, if we continue to have a hierarchical structure that has many positions on the ladder, then the degree of legitimation resulting from this structure should remain constant. At the moment, the reality of a hierarchical ladder of positions does seem to have remained intact, and therefore the structural explanation cannot explain any variation in legitimation.

There does, however, seem to me a very important second factor that accounts for continuing legitimation of state structures. This factor is more conjunctural, and therefore can vary; and it has indeed varied. The degree of legitimation of the capitalist world-economy before the nineteenth century was undoubtedly quite low, and it has remained low in most of the peripheral zones right into the late twentieth century. The continuous commodification of productive transactions seemed to bring changes, many or even most of which were negative from the point of view of the direct producers. Still, after the French Revolution, the situation began to change. It is not that the impact of commodification became less negative, at least for the large majority. It is that their restiveness took the form of insisting that sovereignty could not be discussed merely as a definition of authority and lawful power. One had to ask the question: Who exercised this power? Who was the sovereign? If the answer were not to be the absolute monarch, what alternative was there? As we know, the new answer that began to be widely accepted was "the people."

To say that the people are sovereign is not to say anything very precise, since one then has to decide who are the people and by what means they can collectively exercise this authority. But just suggesting that there was such an entity as "the people" and that they might exercise sovereign power had very radical implications for those exercising de facto authority. The result has been the great politico-cultural turmoil of the nineteenth and twentieth centuries surrounding the question of how to interpret, and tame, the exercise by the people of its sovereignty.

The story of the taming of the exercise of popular sovereignty is the story of liberal ideology – its invention, its triumphal ascendancy in the nineteenth century as the geoculture of the capitalist world-economy, its ability to transform the two competitor ideologies (conservatism on the one hand and radicalism/socialism on the other) into avatars of liberalism.[2] Let me just resume here the essential.

Liberalism presented itself as a centrist doctrine. The liberals preached that progress was desirable and inevitable, and could best be achieved if a process of rational reform were instituted, one controlled by specialists, who could, on the basis of an informed analysis, implement the necessary reforms throughout the historical system, using the authority of the states as their basic political lever. Faced with the impetuous demands of the "dangerous classes" of the nineteenth century – the urban proletariat of western Europe and North America – the liberals offered a three-pronged program of reforms: the suffrage, the beginnings of a welfare state, and a politically integrating racist nationalism.

This three-pronged program worked exceptionally well and, by 1914, the original dangerous classes, the urban proletariat of western Europe and North America, were no longer dangerous. Just then, however, the liberals found themselves confronted with a new set of "dangerous classes" – the popular forces in the rest of the world. In the twentieth century, the liberals sought to apply a similar reform program at the interstate level. The self-determination of nations served as the functional equivalent of universal suffrage. The economic development of underdeveloped nations was offered as the equivalent of the national welfare state. The third prong, however, was unavailable since, once one was trying to include the entire world, there was no outside group against whom one could construct an integrating, racist nationalism.

None the less, the twentieth-century version of world-level liberalism seemed also to work up to a point, and for a while, especially in the "glorious" years after 1945. But the formula came unstuck as of 1968. To be sure, the self-determination of nations offered little problem. But world-level redistribution, even to a modest degree, threatened to put an enormous strain on the possibilities of endlessly accumulating capital. And the third prong was entirely absent. As of the 1970s, global liberalism no longer seemed to be viable.

To understand why this is so devastating to the system, we have to understand what it was that liberalism had offered and why therefore it had successfully stabilized the system politically for a long while. The three-pronged program that the liberals had used to tame the dangerous classes did not offer the dangerous classes what they wanted and had initially demanded – easily enough summarized in the classic slogan of the French Revolution: liberty, equality, fraternity. If these demands had been met, there would no longer have been a capitalist world-economy, since it would have been impossible to ensure the endless accumulation of capital. What the liberals offered therefore was half a pie, or more exactly about one-seventh of a pie: a reasonable standard of living for a minority of the world's population (those famed middle strata). Now this small pie was doubtless a lot more than this one-seventh had had before, but it was far less than an equal share of the pie, and it was almost nothing at all for the other six-sevenths.

Giving this much did not significantly diminish the possibilities of accumulating capital for the large capitalists, but it did accomplish the political objective of pulling the plug on revolutionary ferment over the middle run. The one-seventh who benefited materially were for the most part quite grateful, all the more so when they saw the conditions of those they left behind. (Remember Tawney's image of the talented "scrambl(ing) to shore, undeterred by the thought of drowning companions!"[3]) What is more interesting is the reaction of the drowning companions. They came to interpret the ability of the talented to swim to shore as evidence of hope for them. This was understandable psychologically if imprudent analytically.

Liberalism offered the opiate of hope, and it was swallowed whole. It was swallowed not least by the leaders of the world's antisystemic movements, who mobilized on the promise of hope. They claimed that they would achieve the good society by revolution, but of course they in fact meant by reform which they, as substitute specialists for those offered by the current authorities, would administer once they gained control of the levers of state power. I suppose that if you are drowning, and someone offers hope, it is not irrational to grab hold of whatever is extended as a life-saver. One cannot retrospectively reprimand the popular masses of the world for offering their support and their moral energy to the multiple antisystemic movements who voiced their grievances.

Those in authority, faced with voluble, vigorous, and denunciatory anti-systemic movements could react in one of two ways. If they were frightened, and they often were, they could try to cut off the heads of what they saw as vipers. But since the beasts were in fact hydra-headed, the more sophisticated defenders of the status quo realized that they needed more subtle responses. They came to see that the antisystemic movements actually served in a perverse way the interests of the system. Mobilizing the masses meant channeling the masses, and state power for the leaders had very conservatizing effects. Furthermore, once such movements were in power, they moved themselves against the impetuous demands of their followers, and tended to do so with as much, even more, severity than their predecessors. Furthermore, the sedative of hope was even more efficacious when the peddler was a certified revolutionary leader. If the future was theirs, the popular masses reasoned that they could afford to wait a while, especially if they had a "progressive" state. Their children, at least, would inherit the earth.

The shock of 1968 was more than momentary. The shock of 1968 was the realization that the whole geoculture of liberalism, and especially the construction of historical optimism by the antisystemic movements, was tainted, nay fraudulent, and that their children were not scheduled to inherit the earth; indeed, their children might be even worse off than they. And so these popular masses began to abandon the antisystemic movements, and beyond the movements all of liberal reformism, and therefore abandoned the state structures as vehicles of their collective betterment.

To abandon a well-worn path of hope is not done with lightness of heart. For it does not follow that the six-sevenths of humanity were ready to accept quietly their fate as oppressed and unfulfilled human beings. Quite the contrary. When one abandons the accepted promises of hope, one searches for other paths. The problem is that they are not so easy to find. But there is worse. The states may not have offered long-term betterment for the majority of the populations of the world, but they did offer a certain amount of short-term security against violence. If, however, the populations no longer legitimate the states, they tend neither to obey its policemen nor to pay its tax collectors. And thereupon the states are less able to offer short-term security against violence. In this case, individuals (and firms) have to return to the ancient solution, that of providing their own security.

As soon as private security becomes once again an important social ingredient, confidence in the rule of law tends to break down, and therefore so does civil (or civic) consciousness. Closed groups emerge (or reemerge) as the only safe haven, and closed groups tend to be intolerant, violent, and inclined toward zonal purifications. As intergroup violence rises, the leadership tends to become more and more "mafioso" in character – mafioso in the sense of combining muscular insistence on unquestioning intragroup obedience and venal profiteering. We see this all around us now, and we shall see much more of it in the decades to come.

Hostility to the state is fashionable now, and spreading. The anti-state themes common to conservatism, liberalism, and radicalism/socialism, which had been ignored in practice for over 150 years, are now finding deep resonance in political behavior in all camps. Should not the capitalist strata be happy? It seems doubtful that they are, for they need the state, the strong state, far more than their official rhetoric has ever admitted.

No doubt they don't want peripheral states to interfere with the transactions flows of the world-economy, and now that the antisystemic movements are in deep trouble, the big capitalists are currently able to use the IMF and other institutions to enforce this preference. It is, however, one thing for the Russian state no longer to keep out foreign investors; it is quite another thing for the Russian state to be unable to guarantee the personal safety of the entrepreneurs who visit Moscow.

The official line of neoliberalism is that the market is objective and therefore "disciplining." What it disciplines, of course, is everyone's perverse instincts to make social decisions on any basis other than the maximization of profits. When states make social decisions on such grounds, they are being "arbitrary."

But let the states try not to be "arbitrary" when important capitalist interests are at stake, and you will hear the shouting. When in 1990, major US financial institutions were in danger of bankruptcy, Henry Kaufman wrote an op-ed piece in the *New York Times* in which he said:

> Financial institutions are the holders, and therefore, the guardians of Americans' savings and temporary funds, a unique public responsibility. Truly letting the marketplace discipline the financial system would mean acquiescing in an avalanche of potential failures.[4]

So there we have it, clearly outlined. It is welcome for the market to discipline the states when they are arbitrary, but irresponsible if the states allow the same market to discipline the banks. Social decisions to retain social welfare are irresponsible, but a social decision to save banks is not.

We must always keep clearly in mind not only that one man's monopoly (or arbitrary decision) is another man's poison, but that capitalists depend on the intervention of the states in such a multitude of ways that any true weakening of state authority is disastrous. The case we have been arguing here is that globalization is not in fact significantly affecting the ability of the states to function, nor is it the intention of large capitalists that it do so. The states are, however, for the first time in 500 years, on a downward slide in terms of their sovereignty, inward and outward. This is not because of a transformation of the world-economic structures but because of a transformation of the geoculture, and first of all, because of the loss of hope by the popular masses in liberal reformism and its avatars on the left.

Of course, the change in the geoculture is the consequence of transformations in the world-economy, primarily the fact that many of the internal contradictions of the system have reached points where it is no longer possible to make adjustments that will resolve once again the issue such that one sees a cyclical renewal of the capitalist process. These critical dilemmas of the system include among others the de-ruralization of the world, the reaching of limits of ecological decay, and the fiscal crises of the states brought on by the democratization of the political arena and the consequent rise in the levels of minimum demand for education and health services.[5]

The sovereignty of the states – their inward and outward sovereignty within the framework of an interstate system – is a fundamental pillar of the capitalist world-economy. If it falls, or seriously declines, capitalism is untenable as a system. I agree that it is in decline today, for the first time in the history of the modern world-system. This is the primary sign of the acute crisis of capitalism as an historical system. The essential dilemma of capitalists, singly and as a class, is whether to take full short-run advantage of the weakening of the states, or to try short-run repair to restore the legitimacy of the state structures, or to spend their energy trying to construct an alternative system. Behind the rhetoric, intelligent defenders of the status quo are aware of this critical situation. While they are trying to get the rest of us to talk about the pseudo-issues of globalization, some of them at least are trying to figure out what a replacement system could be like, and how to move things in that direction. If we don't want to live in the future with the inegalitarian solution that they will promote, we should be asking the same question. The state still matters – to the entrepreneurs above all. And because of the declining strength of the states, the transnationals find themselves in acute difficulty, faced as they are with a long-term profits squeeze for the first time and with states that are no longer in a position to bail them out. We have entered a time of troubles. The outcome is uncertain. We cannot be sure what kind of historical system will replace the one in which we find ourselves. What we can know with certainty is that the very peculiar system in which we live, and in which the states have played a crucial role in supporting the processes of the endless accumulation of capital, can no longer continue to function.

Notes

1 Frederic Lane, *Profits from Power: Readings in Protection Rent and Violence-Controlling Enterprises* (Albany: State University of New Press, 1979).
2 How this was done I have discussed at length in my book, *After Liberalism* (New York: New Press, 1995).
3 R.H. Tawney, *Equality* (London: George Allen & Unwin, 4th edn, 1952), p. 109.
4 Henry Kaufman, "After Drexel, Wall Street is Headed for Darker Days," *International Herald Tribune*, February 24–5, 1990 (reprinted from *New York Times*).
5 See the detailed analysis of the crisis in the structures of the capitalist world-economy in T.K. Hopkins and I. Wallerstein (eds) *The Age of Transition: Trajectory of the World-System, 1945–2025* (London: Zed Press, 1996).

2 Globalization and sovereignty

Stephen D. Krasner

Introduction

Globalization and sovereignty are terms that entice many observers to wax eloquent about the transformation of the international system at the approach of the second millennium. Some analysts have argued that the world is entering into a new era, one in which the existing institutional structures, especially the sovereign state (by which they often mean several different things) is being undermined, weakened, marginalized, or transmuted, by globalization.

The basic argument of this chapter is that sovereignty is not being fundamentally transformed by globalization. Globalization has challenged the effectiveness of state control; although it is not evident that contemporary challenges are qualitatively different from those that existed in the past. Globalization has not, however, qualitatively altered state authority which has always been problematic and could never be taken for granted.

The claim that globalization is undermining sovereignty is exaggerated and historically myopic. Both the control and authority of states have been persistently challenged. These challenges are an inherent element of any international system, including the present structure which is based on territorial states. Challenges to both authority and control are endemic in an anarchical system for two reasons. First, there is no authority structure that can definitively choose among competing normative prescriptions, including the conflict between non-intervention and various justifications for intervention in the internal affairs of other states such as the protection of human and minority rights. Second, states, especially weaker states, have never been able to guarantee their control over activities within or across their borders. The interests of the strong will not necessarily coincide with accepted norms.

Globalization can mean some mix of developments that might include the legitimization of human rights, the digitalization of transactions, the speed of communication, the density of global non-governmental organization (NGO) networks, the transmission of diseases, the growth of international capital markets, the surge of manufacturing in geographically dispersed areas, the universal availability of MTV, the increase in illegal migration, legal migration, and the like. Most analyses that emphasize the growing importance of globalization point to the transformatory nature of modern technology. The costs of communication and transportation have plummeted. The telephone, fax, and now the Internet have made instantaneous and relatively inexpensive communication available for tens of millions of people. A banker in New York sitting at a computer terminal might transfer billions of Deutsche marks between Hong Kong and London.

The term sovereignty has been commonly used in at least four different ways:

1   *Interdependence sovereignty* has referred to the ability of a government to actually control activities within and across its borders (including the movement of goods, capital, ideas, and disease vectors).
2   *Domestic sovereignty* has referred to the organization of authority within a given polity. [*removed control part*]?
3   *Westphalian sovereignty* has referred to the exclusion of external authority; the right of a government to be independent of external authority structures.
4   *International legal sovereignty* has referred to the recognition of one state by another; some entities have been recognized by other states; others have not. Recognition has been associated with diplomatic immunity and the right to sign treaties and join international organizations.

These four understandings or definitions of sovereignty are distinct both logically and in practice. It is possible to have one without having others. A state, for instance, Taiwan, can have Westphalian sovereignty, but not enjoy international legal sovereignty. A state can be recognized by other states, but lack domestic and interdependence sovereignty, the ability to control activities within and across its borders, a situation that characterized several failed states in Africa in the 1990s. A state can enjoy international legal sovereignty, be recognized by others but not have Westphalian sovereignty. For instance, more than twenty European states have signed the 1953 European Convention on Human Rights and subsequent protocols that established the European Court of Human Rights, whose decisions are enforceable in national court systems, and which gives individual citizens the right to sue their own governments.

Regardless of how sovereignty is understood, it is difficult to make a case that contemporary developments, notably globalization, are transforming the nature of the system. There has never been a mythical past in which states were secure in the exercise of either their control or their authority. Weaker states in particular have always had to struggle not only to maintain effective control within and over their borders but also to exclude external authority. Globalization has raised some new and unique problems for sovereignty understood as control, but states have confronted comparable challenges in the past. Some aspects of globalization, especially the spread of ideas such as women's rights and democracy, have influenced the legitimacy of particular national institutional forms (an aspect of domestic sovereignty), but there have been similar challenges in the past – including minority rights and national self-determination after the First World War. The threat to state control (interdependence sovereignty), which some see being posed by higher levels of international transactions, ignores the fact that trade and capital markets were as highly integrated in the period before the First World War, and that labor migration was even more pronounced. Moreover, the increasing levels of integration that have occurred during the last five decades (following the decline between 1914 and 1950) has been accompanied by higher levels of state activity. Globalization has strengthened the importance of international legal sovereignty because one way in which states have dealt with challenges to their control has been to enter into international agreements that facilitate international regulation when unilateral policy is ineffective.

In sum, globalization is not transforming sovereignty. By creating an imaginary past, observers have exaggerated the significance of contemporary changes. By failing to distinguish between challenges to control and challenges to authority, they have failed to understand how weakening control can actually strengthen authority through international cooperation, which depends on the validation of sovereignty through international recognition.

Globalization, sovereignty, and control

Globalization, the increase in international flows of ideas, people, goods, and factors, is apparent. Costs of communication and transportation have plummeted. Very rapid interactions, at trivial variable costs are available to anyone with access to e-mail. Given a day, it is possible to move one's body from one commercial airport to any other almost any place in the world. A shoe might be made from leather from one country that is cut in another, assembled in a third, and sold in a fourth. All over the world CNN can show a missile making a right turn over Baghdad and slamming into a military target. Pretty dramatic! Cross-border transactions in bonds and equities increased from 10 per cent of the GDP of the G-7 in 1980 to more than 140 per cent in 1995. Capital flows to transitioning and developing countries increased from $57 billion in 1990 to more than $211 billion in 1995. Foreign exchange transactions reached a daily turnover of almost $1.2 trillion in 1995, twice as large as they had been in 1989 (Simmons 1996: 1).

Many observers have suggested that the increase in globalization is a threat to sovereignty. What they usually mean is that the state is losing control over certain activities but some observers have at least hinted that this could lead to changes in authority structures as well. In his classic study, *The Economics of Interdependence* (1968), Richard Cooper pointed out that capital mobility was undermining the ability of states to control their own domestic monetary policy. (Eric Helleiner emphasizes in Chapter 7, this volume, however, that this is only true under a fixed exchange rate system; with floating rates, states can control their monetary policy. What they cannot do is control monetary policy and exchange rates at the same time in an environment with open capital flows.) One observer of the global telecommunications situation avers that:

> In the long run telecommunications will transcend the territorial concept and the notion of each country having territorial control over electronic

communication will become archaic in the same sense that national control over the spoken (and later the written) word became outmoded.

(Noam 1987: 44)

James Rosenau asserts that new issues have emerged such as "atmospheric pollution, terrorism, the drug trade, currency crises, and AIDs" that are a product of interdependence or new technologies and are transnational rather than national. States cannot provide solutions to these and other issues (Rosenau 1990: 13).

The argument that globalization has meant the erosion of sovereignty suffers from two defects. First, it confounds one meaning of sovereignty – effective state control – with other meanings of sovereignty that are related to issues of authority and legitimacy. Second, globalization arguments are historically myopic, sometimes implicitly assuming some golden age in the past where states could exercise effective control, and ignoring the fact that many measures of international flows were as high at the end of the nineteenth century as they are now. It is not self-evident that the contemporary environment poses qualitatively different challenges to state control (Thomson and Krasner 1989).

The degree of change that has taken place in recent years can easily be exaggerated. States have always operated in an integrated international environment. Capital is one area where this trend has been frequently remarked upon. Even in the area of international capital flows, however, the degree of change from the past and the extent to which global capital markets have been fully integrated has often been overstated. International capital markets are hardly a new development. International banking began in Europe in the later middle ages. A market for securities developed first in Amsterdam in the seventeenth century (Landes 1979: 10–11). In the early part of the sixteenth century the major financial and trading groups had operations throughout the world, not just Europe. The Welsers of Augsburg operated in Europe and the Mediterranean and opened a branch in Venezuela in 1528. The Fuggers controlled mines in central Europe and the Alps, had correspondents in Venice, were the dominant firm in Antwerp, the most important financial center of the time, and had branches in Portugal, Spain, Chile, Fiume, and Dubrovnik. They had an agent in both India and China by the end of the sixteenth century. "In short, the empire of this huge firm was vaster than the mighty empire of Charles V and Philip II, on which as we know the sun never set" (Braudel 1982: 186–7, quote from p. 187).

In the early modern era, European rulers were highly dependent on international finance, much more dependent than would be the case for any more-or-less developed states in the contemporary era. Rulers could not secure the revenue that they needed to fight wars from domestic sources, and they were, therefore, compelled to borrow internationally, often at high interest rates that prompted periodic defaults. The rights of the king to levy taxes was not widely accepted until the seventeenth century and then, only after a series of revolts (de Jouvenel 1957: 186–8; Riley 1980: 1–3; Cohen 1986: 84–90). During the eighteenth century, the British government was able to secure about 10 per cent of national revenue in the form of taxes; France about 5 per cent (Brewer 1989: 91). This

inability to collect taxes made lending, including international lending a relatively more important source of resources for the state. In the eighteenth century,
the funding of the public debt accounted for more than 60 per cent of spending
by the British, French, and Dutch governments (Brewer 1989: 114, 131–3). It was
only in the nineteenth century that the major European states developed sophisticated national systems of finance, including revenue collection (Tilly 1990: 53).
From the time of their independence in the 1820s Latin American states have
experienced periodic booms followed by debt crisis as a result of their inability to
pay back international loans. There were major defaults in the 1820s, 1873,
1890, and 1921 (Marichal 1989: 4; Lindert and Morton 1989: 41–3). During the
interwar period, international bankers and governments were heavily involved in
international financial transactions that were linked to the German reparations
payments imposed after the First World War and their various revisions. When
American bankers engaged in the renegotiation of the German debt, one of the
things that they insisted on was that nothing like the Ruhr Occupation would be
repeated, for such actions would have made it impossible for Germany to repay
its loans (Craig and George 1990: 78–9).

Britain, the major source of international capital was much more dependent
on global transactions before the First World War than is the case for any
country at the end of the twentieth century. Before the First World War, 10 per
cent of British income and 6 per cent of French income were drawn from
foreign investments (Feis 1965: 14, 16, 48, 72). In 1914, nearly a quarter of
British wealth was invested overseas (Gilpin 1987: 308; Cohen 1986: 90). Barings
Brothers, the British financial institution that suffered a spectacular collapse in
1995 as a result of speculative dealings by a broker in Singapore, would have
ceased to exist in 1890 as a result of questionable loans that had been made to
Argentina had it not been for the intervention of the Bank of England, the Bank
of France, the British Treasury, and J.P. Morgan (Cohen 1986: 94–5).

Not only is international banking not new, nor the involvement of major
states in international finance, nor the dependence of smaller weaker states on
foreign capital, but the uniqueness of contemporary levels of international
capital market integration have been exaggerated, at least by political scientists.
Economists have recognized since the early 1980s that real interest rate differentials across countries have remained substantial. Returns to direct investments by
foreigners have been lower than the returns to nationals (Feldstein and Horioka
1980). In a fully integrated global capital market, such disparities would not
exist.

Moreover, by some measures the level of integration of international capital
markets is no higher now than it was in the nineteenth century. Using the ratio of
current account to national income as a measure of international capital flows,
Obstfeld and Taylor show that capital markets for some fifteen countries were
highly integrated in the nineteenth century with current account deficits (which
must be balanced by capital flows) reaching 5 per cent of national income in the
1880s. In the 1930s the ratio was 1.5 per cent, and in the 1950s and 1960s it was
as low as 1 per cent. In the period 1989–96, the average for 12 countries reached

2.3 per cent, still below the levels that prevailed from 1870 to 1914 (Obstfeld and Taylor 1997: 8 and Table 2.1).

International migration rates reached their highest levels in the nineteenth century. Without immigration after 1870, the US labor force might have been 24 per cent smaller in 1910 than it actually was; the Argentine 86 per cent smaller, the Australian 42 per cent, and the Canadian 44 per cent. In contrast the Irish, Italian, and the Norwegian labor forces would have been 45, 39 and 24 per cent larger, respectively. For Ireland and Sweden emigration rates reached almost 10 per cent of the population for some decades during the nineteenth century (Williamson 1996: 16, 18 and Table 2.1). These large migration flows coupled with international capital market integration contributed to a convergence of real income levels during the nineteenth century. Disparities increased during the first half of the twentieth century because factor movements became more constrained (Williamson 1996: 10–12, 20). Likewise international trade flows, measured as a ratio of trade to GNP, increased rapidly during the nineteenth century, fell from the period 1914 through the late 1940s and only reached their earlier levels for some countries in the 1980s (Thomson and Krasner 1989).

In arenas other than economics, the claim that the contemporary era represents a qualitative break with the past should be met with some skepticism. Some observers have pointed to AIDs as an example of the way in which the world has been more globalized. A disease that probably had its origin in non-human animals in Africa spread rapidly throughout the world during the 1980s causing the death of tens of millions of people. The black death, however, took the lives of 30–40 per cent of the population of Europe in the fourteenth century. It probably originated in the Gobi desert, an area that Europeans could not locate on a map if only because they did not have accurate maps. The black death fundamentally altered property rights in Europe as a result of the change in land labor ratios. Influenza epidemics have killed millions of people at various times during the twentieth century. AIDs is a great tragedy but its impact in terms of the proportion of the population affected and the effects on social, political, and economic institutions is far less than earlier pandemics.

The spread of ideas is not new. Christianity transformed the Roman Empire in the fourth century. The ideas of Mohammed led a group of tribes from the Arabian peninsula to conquer much of the Mediterranean world in the seventh and eighth centuries. The Reformation transformed the political map of Europe within a decade after Luther had posted his 95 Theses on the door of the Schlosskirche in Wittenberg. Indeed, religious ideas, tied to men's concern about their moral behavior on earth and their immortality someplace beyond, were more politically consequential than any of the leading ideas of the late twentieth century, which are so effectively communicated by phone, fax, and the Internet. Getting prices right is one thing; burning in hell for all eternity is quite another. Ultimately, the religious wars of the sixteenth and seventeenth centuries in Europe were so destructive (the Thirty Years War killed more than fifty per cent of the German population in some areas (Holsti 1991: 28–9)), that European rulers were compelled first to accept religious toleration and then later religious freedom. One of the central issues of political life in Europe, perhaps the central issue from the fourth to the seventeenth century, the relationship between the state, God, and the salvation of individuals, more or less disappeared from the political agenda.

I do not want to claim that globalization has had no impact on state control. This would be fatuous. But challenges to state control as a result of transnational flows are not new. The problems for states have become more acute in some areas, but less in others. There is no evidence that globalization has systematically undermined state control. Indeed, the clearest relationship between globalization and state activity is that they have increased hand in hand. The level of government spending for the major countries has, on average increased substantially since 1950 along with increased trade and capital flows. This ought to be no surprise: governments have intervened to provide social safety nets that make more open economic policies politically acceptable. There has been no empirical relationship between levels of government spending and capital flows; government policy has not been hamstrung by the openness of international capital markets. Levels of investment are not clearly related to corporate tax rates. Indeed, higher levels of government spending are essential for the creation of infrastructure – education, telecommunications, transportation – that are essential for modern firms (Garrett 1998).

In sum, global flows are not new. In some issue areas, such as migration, flows were higher in the nineteenth century than they are now. Government initiatives have not been crippled by globalization. Indeed, the provision of collective goods and social stability have created the conditions that have made higher levels of trade and capital flows tolerable in the postwar period.

Sovereignty and authority

Aside from the issues of sovereign control, which have been associated with arguments about globalization or interdependence sovereignty, sovereignty has also been understood in three other ways – all of which are related to authority: domestic sovereignty, Westphalian sovereignty, and international legal sovereignty. First, sovereignty has referred to the domestic constitutional order of the state; for instance whether it is a unitary or federal state, or a monarchy or democracy. Second, sovereignty has referred to autonomy, the extent to which central state authorities or rulers are independent of external authority. Third, sovereignty has referred to international recognition; whether or not a state is recognized as a sovereign entity by other states (see Thomson 1995: 214; Deudney 1995: 198. Thomson is particularly effective in emphasizing the distinction between control and authority.) There is no indication that domestic sovereignty, Westphalian sovereignty or international legal sovereignty are being challenged in historically unprecedented ways by the contemporary global environment.

Certain global developments might be influencing domestic authority structures, but even if this is the case, a much disputed point, such influence would not speak to the question of whether the nature of sovereignty as an institutional structure for organizing political life is changing. Some elements of globalization related to ideas about human rights have challenged sovereignty understood as the exclusion of external authority, but these challenges are not unique. Indeed, efforts by external actors to regulate relations between rulers and ruled have been an endemic characteristic of the international system. Globalization has enhanced the importance of sovereignty understood as mutual recognition, because one of the ways in which states have responded to increased flows that they cannot control unilaterally has been to enter into international agreements.

Domestic sovereignty: globalization and constitutional structures

The term sovereignty is most closely associated with the establishment of domestic political authority. The analyses of Bodin and Hobbes, the two most important early theorists of sovereignty, are both driven by a desire to establish the legitimacy of some one final source of authority within the state (Skinner 1978: 287). In his study of sovereignty, F.H. Hinsley writes:

> at the beginning, at any rate, the idea of sovereignty was the idea that there is a final and absolute political authority in the political community; and everything that needs to be added to complete the definition is added if this statement is continued in the following words: "and no final and absolute authority exists elsewhere."
>
> (Hinsley 1986: 25–6)

Later theorists from Locke, to Mill, to Marx, to Dahl have challenged the notion that there has to be some one final source of authority within a state.

Polities can be constitutionally structured in many different ways. Authority may be concentrated in the hands of one actor, as Bodin and Hobbes advocated, or divided among different institutional structures, as is the case in all modern democracies. There can be federal structures in which different issues are controlled by the central government as opposed to individual states, as is the case for the United States and Germany, or unitary structures where the central government has final authority over all issues, as is the case for France.

Some analysts have suggested that the organization of domestic political authority is being influenced by global trends. Francis Fukuyama's claims about the triumph of liberal ideas is one obvious example. Even if such developments are taking place, however, and Fukuyama has been challenged by a number of observers, notably Samuel Huntington, this does not imply that the nature of sovereignty is qualitatively changing (Fukuyama 1992; Huntington 1996). The domestic organization of state structures has always been influenced by international trends whether this involved the formation of Protestant polities in the sixteenth century, of absolute monarchies in the seventeenth century, of republics in the nineteenth century, or of fascist, communist, and now democratic states in the twentieth century. There is no compelling indication that the level of convergence is greater now than it has been in the past. Democracy has not swept the globe. Capitalism has many different forms. The liberal individualistic human rights emphasis of the west has been rejected by many Asian leaders. Religious fundamentalism has become more, not less, salient in recent years. Nationalist appeals have animated developments in far flung areas of the world.

There is absolutely nothing new in the fact that the global spread of certain ideas has influenced the organization of domestic political authority.

Westphalian sovereignty: globalization and the exclusion of external authority sovereignty

Sovereignty has been related not only with the organization of domestic authority but also with the exclusion of external authority, what is referred to here as Westphalian sovereignty. (In fact the Peace of Westphalia had almost nothing to do with what has come to be known as the Westphalian model. The notion that external authority should be excluded was only developed explicitly in the writings of Wolff and Vattel at the end of the eighteenth century. See Krasner 1993; Thomas and Thomas 1956: 4–6; Vincent 1974: 26–7; Vattel 1852: 155.) States exist in specific territories. Within these territories domestic political authorities are the only arbiters of legitimate behavior; whether or not there is one clear source of internal authority, as Bodin asserted there must be, or multiple sources, as modern democratic theory suggests, Westphalian sovereignty still implies the exclusion of any external authority.

In recent years a number of analysts have used Westphalian sovereignty as a bench mark to assert that the character of the international system is changing in some fundamental ways. Writing of the pre-1950s world James Rosenau contends that:

> In that system, legitimate authority was concentrated in the policy-making institutions of states, which interacted with each other on the basis of equality and accepted principles of diplomacy and international law. Their embassies remained inviolable and so did their domestic affairs. Intrusion into such matters were met with protests of violated sovereignty and, not infrequently, with preparations for war. For all practical purposes, the line between domestic and foreign affairs was preserved and clearly understood by all. The norms of the Western state system lodged control over external ties in the state and these were rarely defied and even more rarely revised.
>
> (Rosenau 1990: 109)

Philip Windsor states that:

> It is fashionable, at present, to suggest that the old Westphalian system of a world of non-interventionist states is on the decline, and that the dangers of growing intervention by different powers in the affairs of other states have

been on the increase. The Westphalian system represented some remarkable achievements: the absolute sovereignty of a state rested on a dual basis whereby internal authority was matched by freedom from external interference; and in this way the principle of *cuius regio eius religio*, codified in the Religious Peace of Augsburg, laid the foundation of the modern states system.

(Windsor 1984: 45)

The way in which some analysts have defined sovereignty in terms of the Westphalian model is brought out clearly by authors who have studied human rights, because claims about such rights are seen as a contradiction of sovereignty. David Forsythe suggests that:

The most fundamental point about human rights law is that it establishes a set of rules for all states and all people. It thus seeks to increase world unity and to counteract national separateness (but not necessarily national distinctions). In this sense, the international law of human rights is revolutionary because it contradicts the notion of national sovereignty – that is, that a state can do as it pleases in its own jurisdiction.

(Forsythe 1983: 4)

Writing in the 1990s about the status of minority groups Kay Hailbronner claims that "Modern public international law seems to have broken through the armour of sovereignty" (Hailbronner 1992: 117). Similarly Brian Hehir has asserted that "In the Westphalian order both state sovereignty and the rule of nonintervention are treated as absolute norms." He then goes on to suggest that this Westphalian system is under an unprecedented level of assault (Hehir 1995: 6).

The leitmotif of all of these arguments is that sovereignty, here understood as the exclusion of external authority, is being undermined by one specific aspect of globalization, the spread of human rights norms. States can no longer do what they please within their own borders because certain values about the relationship between rulers and ruled have become almost universally accepted.

The argument that concerns for human rights are undermining the sovereign states system is historically myopic. Relations between rulers and ruled have always been subject to external scrutiny. Weaker states especially have never been free of interference from their more powerful neighbors. What has shifted is the specific focus of concern. From the middle of the seventeenth century to the first part of the nineteenth century, rulers were concerned with religious toleration. Beginning with the Treaty of Vienna and much more forcefully in a series of agreements associated with the Balkans in the nineteenth century and with the Versailles peace after the First World War, the primary focus of international attention was with ethnic minorities. After the Second World War individual human rights received greater attention. Whether the issue was religious toleration, minority rights, or human rights sovereignty, understood as the exclusion of external authority, has constantly been challenged throughout the history of the modern state system.

Virtually every major peace settlement in Europe from the 1555 Peace of Augsburg to the 1815 Congress of Vienna contained provisions for the treatment of religious minorities, which were designed to prevent civil conflict that could disrupt both domestic and international peace. The leaders of Europe were not enthusiastic about religious toleration but the experience of the religious wars that wracked France, Britain, and Germany in the sixteenth and seventeenth centuries convinced them that they had no alternative. Internationally guaranteed provisions for religious toleration, provisions that violated the Westphalian model, were included in major peace settlements. The Peace of Augsburg of 1555 recognized both the Catholic and Lutheran faiths. At the same time, it endorsed the principle that the prince could set the religion of his territory (*cuius regio, eius religio*). *Cuius regio eius religio* was entirely consistent with the Westphalian model, but even the Augsburg settlement made some provision for religious toleration. Religious dissenters were to be allowed to emigrate rather than being killed. Offices in some German cities with mixed populations were to be shared between Protestants and Catholics. The rulers of ecclesiastical states could not change the religion of their domains (Scribner 1990: 195–7; Gagliardo 1991: 16–21; Little 1993: 324–5).

The Peace of Westphalia itself (which consisted of the separate Treaties of Osnabruck and Munster) had much more to say about religious toleration than about what later came to be seen as the modern state system. The right of the princes of the Holy Roman Empire to sign treaties, often seen as a major accomplishment of the Peace and a break with the medieval world, was noted in only one sentence, which concluded that the treaties should not be against the Emperor or the Empire (Treaty of Munster, XIV). The provisions for religious toleration in Germany were much more extensive. They included the right to private worship, to participation in merchant associations, to burial, to emigration, and to share offices in certain German cities with mixed populations. Perhaps most significantly Catholics and Lutherans were to be equally represented in imperial assemblies, and religious issues were to be decided by consensus; likewise any religious decisions emanating from the imperial courts required the approval of at least some judges from each religion (Treaty of Osnabruck, V 11–42, VII. (See Parry 1969; see also Krasner, 1993).

The Vienna settlement after the Napoleonic Wars provided that the rights of Catholics should be recognized in the Dutch constitution (Laponce 1960: 23–7; Macartney 1934: 158–9). The settlement also included, for the first time, provisions for an ethno-national minority. In the Congress of Vienna Final Act, Austria, Prussia, and Russia committed to provide Poles "a Representation and National Institutions...that each of the Governments to which they belong shall judge expedient and proper to grant them" (Article I).

Minority rights became an increasing focus of attention during the nineteenth century, especially with regard to the Balkans. At the close of the Napoleonic Wars virtually all of the Balkans was still part of the Ottoman Empire. By 1878 Romania, Serbia, Montenegro, Greece, and Bulgaria (although formally a tributary state until 1908) had become independent. As a condition of international recognition, all of these states had to agree to provide equal civil rights for religious and ethnic minorities. The major power of Europe made this acceptance of civic equality a condition of international recognition. France, Britain, Russia, Germany, and Austria imposed this requirement not so much because of any commitment to civil liberty (indeed such liberties were woefully lacking in Russia itself), but rather because they wanted to prevent ethnic conflict in the Balkans from spilling over and undermining European security. These fears about the consequences of ethnic strife in the Balkans for European stability proved all too tragically accurate in the summer of 1914.

Efforts to secure minority rights reached their apogee with the Versailles settlement at the conclusion of the First World War. All of the new polities as well as several established states whose boundaries were changed signed minority-rights treaties or made unilateral pledges regarding minority rights. Minority rights were established in treaties concluded by the Allied powers in 1919 with Poland, Austria, Czechoslovakia, Yugoslavia, Bulgaria, and Romania, in 1920 with Hungary, Turkey, and Greece, and again in 1923 with Turkey; in declarations made as a condition for admission to the League by Albania in 1921, Lithuania in 1922, Latvia and Estonia in 1923, and Iraq in 1932; and through League guarantees for the treatment of minorities in bilateral conventions concerning the Free City of Danzig and Upper Silesia (Poland/Germany, 1920 and 1922), the Aaland Islands (Sweden/Finland, 1921), and the Memel Convention (Lithuania/Germany, 1924) (Lerner 1993: 83; Claude 1955: 16; Jones 1991: 45; Bartsch 1995: 84–5).

The protections were detailed and elaborate. In the Polish minority treaty, the model (verbatim in most cases) for League minorities obligations, the Polish government undertook:

> to assure full and complete protection of life and liberty to all inhabitants of Poland without distinction of birth, nationality, language, race or religion.... Differences of religion, creed or confession shall not prejudice any Polish national in matters relating to the enjoyment of civil or political rights, as for instance admission to public employments, functions and honours, or the exercise of professions and industries.
>
> (Articles 1 and 7)

It granted citizenship rights to all individuals habitually resident or born within its territory of habitually resident parents even if not currently in Poland. Minority-language schooling would be provided in areas with a considerable number of non-Polish speakers, although the teaching of Polish could be obligatory (Article 8). Additionally, Jews could decline official duties which would violate the Sabbath and Polish leaders committed "to refrain from ordering or permitting elections, whether general or local, to be held on a Saturday" (Article 11, reprinted in Macartney 1934, 502–6; see also Sharp 1979: 174; Fouques-Duparc 1922: 112).

For the dominant figure at Versailles, Woodrow Wilson, the international protection of minority rights represented a key pillar of a peaceful postwar order in Europe. This order was to be based on collective security, the principle that peace-loving states would join together to resist depredations by any aggressor. Only liberal democratic states would make such commitments. Liberal democracy in turn was founded on self-determination, yet ethno-national populations were inextricably mingled in much of Europe. The treaties sought to resolve this problem by making minorities loyal citizens of the states in which they happened to reside. If minorities were ill-treated, they could cause disorder within their countries of residence and threaten international peace if a patron state came to their assistance (Macartney 1934: 275, 278, 297). In Wilson's words at the Paris Peace Conference:

> Nothing, I venture to say, is more likely, to disturb the peace of the world than the treatment which might in certain circumstances be meted out to minorities. And therefore, if the major powers are to guarantee the peace of the world in any sense, is it unjust that they should be satisfied that the proper and necessary guarantees have been given?
>
> (quoted in Sharp 1979: 175)

The Wilsonian vision of collective security trumped the Westphalian norm of non-intervention.

The major powers justified minority-rights guarantees in terms of established norms and diplomatic precedent. The defining justification of the League minorities system, the 1919 letter from French leader Georges Clemenceau accompanying the Polish minorities treaty, illustrates that the Westphalian norm of non-intervention was explicitly contradicted by other norms endorsed by the ascendent powers:

> This Treaty does not constitute any fresh departure. It has for long been the established procedure of the public law of Europe that when a State is created, or even when large accessions of territory are made to an established State, the joint and formal recognition of the Major powers should be accompanied by the requirement that such States should, in the form of a binding international Convention, undertake to comply with certain principles of Government....it is to the endeavours and sacrifices of the Powers in whose name I am addressing you that the Polish nation owes the recovery of its independence....There, rests, therefore, upon these Powers an obligation, which they cannot evade, to secure in the most permanent and solemn form guarantees for certain essential rights which will afford to the inhabitants the necessary protection, whatever changes may take place in the internal constitution of the Polish State.
>
> (quoted in Macartney 1934: 238)

After the Second World War minority rights were almost forgotten. The Versailles regime was regarded as a failure. The United States focused on individual rights after 1945. The Soviet Union with its diverse ethnic population had no interest in highlighting minority rights. The UN Charter did not mention the issue.

Instead, human rights became the focus of attention of issues related to relations between rulers and ruled. By the 1990s more than twenty United Nations human rights conventions had been signed. There were various regional accords as well. Human rights were included in the 1975 Helsinki accords, a decision that the leaders of the Soviet bloc came to regret, since this agreement helped to organize resistance groups in eastern Europe (Thomas 1991).

Some of these human rights agreements had little impact on the behavior of signatories. Others, however, were quite extensive. The European Human Rights convention not only established the European Court of Human Rights but also gave individuals, not just states, access to the Court.

The proliferation of human rights accords is a new development in the international system. These agreements have been almost entirely voluntary, although many lacked any kind of monitoring much less enforcement mechanism. The fact that the European Convention gives individuals standing, while not unique, is a clear challenge to Westphalian sovereignty and to international law or recognition sovereignty as well, which has viewed states as the only legitimate actors in the international system. Nevertheless, as the extensive and highly rationalized and legitimated history of international action to protect religious and minority rights indicates, there never was some golden period in the past when the Westphalian model was universally, or even mostly, honored. Globalization – manifested in the widespread, although not universally accepted, emphasis on individual human rights – is not an historically unique breach in the armor of sovereignty. Rather it is but the most recent manifestation of the fact that the norm of non-intervention or the exclusion of external authority has always been challenged by alternative principles that legitimated international constraints on the domestic practices that governed relations between rulers and ruled.

International law sovereignty: mutual recognition and contracting

The term sovereignty has been used to refer to international recognition, as opposed to state control, or domestic constitutional order, or the exclusion of external authority. This is the most common usage by international lawyers. States mutually recognize each other.

International recognition is almost universally desired by rulers. It provides a number of useful benefits. Because recognition is such a widely accepted institutional form it will enhance the support that a ruler might get from his subjects. Recognition is no guarantee of domestic support, as civil disorder in many states indicates, but better to be recognized than not.

More germane for the discussion here is the fact that recognition gives a state the presumptive right to join international organizations and to make agreements with other states. Again, this right has not simply been limited to states. Not only were the Dominions of the British Empire – Canada, South Africa, Australia, and

New Zealand, members of the League of Nations, but so was India as well, even though it was a colony. The Palestine Liberation Organization has had observer status at the United Nations. The Order of Malta has signed accords with a number of states even though it is itself not a state. Taiwan is only recognized by a small number of other states but it is a member of the Asian Development Bank, albeit under conditions that were negotiated with the involvement of the Republic of China. The Commissioner of the European Union meets with the heads of states of the G-7, the seven largest industrial countries.

Nevertheless, having international recognition makes things easier; a state that is not recognized will have more trouble contracting with other states. A political entity that is not recognized will have a harder time finding a seat at the table. National as well as international law is based on mutual recognition. Recognition provides an easily observed sign that an actor can enter into international accords.

If anything, globalization has made international legal sovereignty more important. The number of international agreements and organizations has proliferated in the last few decades. Many of these represent efforts to capture the benefits of globalization and compensate for the loss of national control by establishing new coordinating and regulatory mechanisms at the international level.

GATT and its successor, the World Trade Organization, can be seen in this light. Technology has opened new trade opportunities. These opportunities have, however, increased potential conflicts over issues such as market access, financial services, intellectual property rights, trade related investments, and dispute settlement. To avoid unilateral retaliation that could leave everyone worse off, states have entered into international agreements in which they constrain their own freedom of action in exchange for similar commitments being offered by others.

In response to the increasing mobility of capital and the growth of transnational banks, states have made agreements regarding bank capital requirements. No single state can unilaterally adopt measures that would assure bank security, but the failure of a small number of banks could have negative repercussions for the stability of the global financial system as a whole. Moreover, because banking systems vary, bank capital has been calculated differently in different countries. The Basle agreement of 1987, negotiated under the auspices of the Bank for International Settlements, specified different kinds of bank capital and their associated risks and set minimum requirements based on these stipulations. The guidelines agreed to at Basle have been voluntarily adopted by many states (Kapstein 1989; Simmons 1996).

States, international legal sovereigns, are the usual participants in agreements like the World Trade Organization and the Basle Accord and, of course many other international treaties and organizations. Mutual recognition makes it easier to reach such pacts because it provides a simple rule for who can be a player. It is states, not multinational corporations, or non-governmental organizations, or foundations that enter into international agreements. Globalization has enhanced the incentive to reach agreements in some areas because unilateral control is more difficult. Viewed from the perspective of international law, however, these agreements enhance rather than undermine sovereignty. Indeed, the agreements would be impossible in the first place if states did not mutually recognize their capacity to enter into them.

Conclusion

Only by creating a mythical past have contemporary observers been able to make facile comments about the impact of globalization on sovereignty. Sovereignty has been understood in a number of different ways. Some analysts have simply confounded sovereignty with control and argued that globalization is weakening control. State control, however, has never been a given either internally or externally. Technological change has complicated state control in some areas, but there is no evident secular trend. International capital markets were as integrated, perhaps more integrated, at the end of the nineteenth century than at the end of the twentieth century. Trade flows increased dramatically during the nineteenth century but then fell during the first half of the twentieth. Labor migration was higher in the nineteenth century than it is now. Moreover, one of the most common responses to the loss of unilateral control has been the conclusion of international agreements designed to re-establish the regulation of activities at the international rather than the national level. These agreements are based on another understanding of sovereignty – mutual recognition. Assertions that the acceptance of human rights principles have pierced the armor of sovereignty ignore the fact that relations between rulers and ruled have always been subject to external scrutiny and breaches of domestic autonomy. What has changed is not the extent of external authority but rather than specific focus of attention. Actors were concerned with religious toleration from the sixteenth into the nineteenth centuries, with minority rights in the nineteenth and first half of the twentieth centuries, and with human rights since the end of the Second World War.

Challenges to sovereignty however understood ought not to be surprising. The international system is weakly institutionalized. The mechanisms that can embed institutions and make behavior and institutional principles conform with each other, notably socialization and path dependence, are only weakly present in the international system. There are no mechanisms for deciding among mutually inconsistent norms such as non-intervention and human rights. Sovereignty is an institution characterized by organized hypocrisy (Brunsson 1989). Actors say different things, invoke different principles. The demands of legitimacy may be at odds with those of interest and efficiency. Rulers do one thing and say another. Globalization has highlighted some tensions between norms and behavior, but there is no evidence that this is leading to some transformation of the international system.

References

Bartsch, S. (1995) *Minderheitenschutz in der internationalen Politik: Volkerbund und KSZE/OSZE in neuer Perspektive, Oplanden*, Germany: Westdeutscher Verlag.

Braudel, F. (1982) *Civilization and Capitalism: 15th–18th Century, Vol. II, The Wheels of Commerce*, New York: Harper and Row.

Brewer, J. (1989) *The Sinews of Power: War, Money and the English State, 1688–1783*, New York: Knopf.

Brunsson, N. (1989) *The Organization of Hypocrisy: Talk, Decisions and Actions in Organizations*, Chichester, England: John Wiley and Sons.

Claude, I.L., Jr (1955) *National Minorities: An International Problem*, Cambridge: Harvard University Press.

Cohen, B.J. (1986) *In Whose Interest? International Banking and American Foreign Policy*, New Haven: Yale University Press.

Cooper, R. (1968) *The Economics of Interdependence: Economic Policy in the Atlantic Community*, New York: McGraw-Hill.

Craig, G.A. and George, A.L. (1990) *Force and Statecraft : Diplomatic Problems of our Time*, 2nd edn, New York: Oxford University Press.

De Jouvenel, B. (1957) *Sovereignty: An Inquiry into the Political Good*, Cambridge: Cambridge University Press.

Deudney, D.H. (1995) "The Philadelphian system: sovereignty, arms control, and balance of power in the American states–union *circa* 1787–1861," *International Organization* 49 (2): 191–228.

Feis, H. (1965) *Europe, the World's Banker, 1870–1914*, New York: Norton.

Feldstein, M.S. and Horioka, C. (1980) "Domestic savings and international capital flows," *Economic Journal* 90: 314–29.

Forsythe, D.P. (1983) *Human Rights and World Politics*, Lincoln: University of Nebraska Press.

Fouques-Duparc, J. (1922) *La Protection des Minorités de Race, de Langue, et de Religion: Etude de Droit des Gens*, Paris: Librairie Dalloz.

Fukuyama, F. (1992) *The End of History and the Last Man*, New York: Free Press.

Gagliardo, J. (1991) *Germany Under the Old Regime, 1600–1790*, London: Longman.

Garrett, G. (1998) "Global markets and national politics: collision course or virtuous circle?" *International Organization* 52: 787–824.

Gilpin, R. (1987) *The Political Economy of International Relations*, Princeton: Princeton University Press.

Hailbronner, K. (1992) "The legal status of population groups in a multinational state under public international law," in Y. Dinstein and M. Tabory (eds) *The Protection of Minorities and Human Rights*, Dordrecht: Martinus Nijhoff.

Hehir, J.B. (1995) "Intervention: from theories to cases," *Ethics and International Affairs* 9: 1–14.

Hinsley, F.H. (1986) *Sovereignty*, 2nd edn, Cambridge: Cambridge University Press.

Holsti, K.J. (1991) *Peace and War, Armed Conflicts and International Order, 1648–1989*, Cambridge: Cambridge University Press.

Huntington, S.P. (1996) *The Clash of Civilizations and the Remaking of World Order*, New York: Simon & Schuster.

Jones, D.V. (1991) *Code of Peace: Ethics and Security in the World of the Warlord States*, Chicago: University of Chicago Press.

Kapstein, E.B. (1989) "Resolving the regulator's dilemma: international coordination of banking regulations," *International Organization* 43 (2): 323–7.

Krasner, S.D. (1993) "Westphalia and all that," in J. Goldstein and R.O. Keohane (eds) *Ideas and Foreign Policy: Beliefs, Institutions, and Political Change*, Ithaca: Cornell University Press.

Landes, D.S. (1979) *Bankers and Pashas; International Finance and Economic Imperialism in Egypt*, Cambridge: Harvard University Press.

Laponce, J.A. (1960) *The Protection of Minorities*, Berkeley: University of California Press.

Lerner, N. (1993) "The evolution of minority rights in international law," in C. Brolmann, R. Lefeber, and M. Zieck (eds) *Peoples and Minorities in International Law*, Dordrecht: Martinus Nijhoff.

Lindert, P.H. and Morton, P.J. (1989) "How sovereign lending has worked," in J.D. Sachs (ed.) *Developing Country Debt and Economic Performance*, Chicago: University of Chicago Press.

Little, D. (1993) "Religion: catalyst or impediment to international law? The case of Hugo Grotius," *The American Society of International Law, Proceedings of the 87th Annual Meeting*, Washington, DC, pp. 322–7.

Macartney, C.A. (1934) *National States and National Minorities*, Oxford: Oxford University Press

Marichal, C. (1989) *A Century of Debt Crises in Latin America: From Independence to the Great Depression 1820–1930*, Princeton: Princeton University Press.

Noam, E.M. (1987) "The public telecommunications network: a concept in transition," *Journal of Communication* 37 (1): 30–48.

Obstfeld, M., and Taylor, A.M. (1997) *The Great Depression as a Watershed: International Capital Mobility Over the Long Run*, Cambridge, MA: National Bureau of Economic Research, Working Paper 5960.

Parry, C. (1969) (ed.) "Treaty of Osnabruck," in *The Consolidated Treaty Series, Vol. I 1648–1649*, Dobbs Ferry, NY: Oceana.

Riley, J.C. (1980) *International Government Finance and the Amsterdam Capital Market, 1740–1815*, Cambridge: Cambridge University Press.

Rosenau, J.N. (1990) *Turbulence in World Politics: A Theory of Change and Continuity*, Princeton: Princeton University Press.

Scribner, R.W. (1990) "Politics and the institutionalization of reform in Germany," in G.R. Elton (ed.) *The New Cambridge Modern History Vol. II, The Reformation 1520–1559*, 2nd edn, Cambridge: Cambridge University Press.

Sharp, A. (1979) "Britain and the protection of minorities at the Paris Peace Conference, 1919," in A.C. Hepburn (ed.) *Minorities in History*, New York: St. Martin's Press.

Simmons, B.A. (1996) "Divisibility, defection, and the emerging regulatory framework for international capital markets," paper presented at the American Political Science Association Annual Convention, San Francisco.

Skinner, Q. (1978) *The Foundations of Modern Political Thought: Vol II: The Age of Reformation*, Cambridge, Cambridge University Press.

Thomas A. and Thomas, A. (1956) *Non Intervention; The Law and Its Import in the Americas*, Dallas: Southern Methodist University Press.

Thomas, D. (1991) "Social movements and international institutions: a preliminary framework," paper presented at the American Political Science Association Annual Convention, Washington, DC.

Thomson, J.E. (1995) "State sovereignty in international relations: bridging the gap between theory and empirical research," *International Studies Quarterly* 39 (2): 213–34.

Thomson, J.E. and Krasner, S.D. (1989) "Global transactions and the consolidation of sovereignty," in E.O. Czempiel and J.N. Rosenau (eds) *Global Changes and Theoretical Challenges: Approaches to World Politics for the 1990s*, Lexington, MA: DC Heath.

Tilly, C. (1990) *Coercion, Capital, and European States, AD 990–1990*, Cambridge, MA: Basil Blackwell.

Vattel E. de (1852) *The Law of Nations; or, Principles of the Law of Nature, applied to the Conduct and Affairs of Nations and Sovereigns*, from the new edition (trans. Joseph Chitty), Philadelphia: T. & J.W. Johnson, Law Booksellers.

Vincent, R. (1974) *Nonintervention and International Order*, Princeton: Princeton University Press.

Williamson, J.G. (1997) "Globalization and the labor markets: using history to inform policy," lecture 1, in *Globalization Convergence and History*, Raffaele Mattioli Lectures, Milan: Banca Commerciale Italiana, Universita Commerciale Luigi Bocconi.

Windsor, P. (1984) "Superpower intervention," in H. Bull (ed.) *Intervention in World Politics*, Oxford: Clarendon Press.

3 Globalization, state sovereignty, and the "endless" accumulation of capital

Giovanni Arrighi

"Times of change," remarks John Ruggie, "are also times of confusion. Words lose their familiar meaning, and our footing becomes unsure on what was previously familiar terrain" (Ruggie 1994: 553). As we seek a firmer footing in seemingly well-established notions, as Stephen Krasner has done with "sovereignty" in Chapter 2, we discover that their past use is itself mired in hopeless confusion. And as we coin new terms, such as "globalization," to capture the novelty of emergent conditions, we compound the confusion by carelessly pouring old wine into new bottles. The purpose of this chapter is to show that in order to isolate what is truly new and anomalous in ongoing transformations of world capitalism and state sovereignty, we must preliminarily recognize that key aspects of these transformations are either not new at all or are new in degree but not in kind.

I shall begin by arguing that much of what goes under the catch-word "globalization" has in fact been a recurrent tendency of world capitalism since early-modern times. This recurrence makes the dynamics and likely outcome(s) of present transformations more predictable than they would be if globalization were as novel a phenomenon as many observers think. I shall then shift my focus on the evolutionary pattern that over the centuries has enabled world capitalism and the underlying system of sovereign states to become, as Immanuel Wallerstein puts it (Chapter 1, this volume): "the first historical system to include the entire globe within its geography." My contention here will be that the true novelty of the present wave of globalization is that this evolutionary pattern is now at an impasse. I shall conclude by speculating on possible ways out of this impasse and on the kinds of new world order that may emerge as a result of the re-centering on East Asia of world-scale processes of capital accumulation.

Section I

As critics of the notion of globalization have pointed out, many of the tendencies that go under that name are not new at all. The newness of the so-called "information revolution" is impressive, "but the newness of the railroad and the telegraph, the automobile, the radio, and the telephone in their day impressed equally" (Harvey 1995: 9). Even the so-called "virtualization of economic activity" is not as new as it may appear at first sight.

Submarine telegraph cables from the 1860s onwards connected intercontinental markets. They made possible day-to-day trading and price-making across thousands of miles, a far greater innovation than the advent of electronic trading today. Chicago and London, Melbourne and Manchester were linked in close to real time. Bond markets also became closely interconnected, and large-scale international lending – both portfolio and direct investment – grew rapidly during this period (Hirst 1996: 3).

Indeed, foreign direct investment (FDI) grew so rapidly that in 1913 it amounted to over 9 per cent of world output – a proportion still unsurpassed in the early 1990s (Bairoch and Kozul-Wright 1996: 10). Similarly, the openness to foreign trade – as measured by imports and exports combined as a proportion of GDP – was not markedly greater in 1993 than in 1913 for all major capitalist countries except the United States (Hirst 1996: 3–4).

To be sure, as Eric Helleiner and Saskia Sassen in Chapters 7 and 8, this volume, underscore from different perspectives, the most spectacular expansion of the last two decades, and the strongest piece of evidence in the armory of advocates of the globalization thesis, has not been in FDI or world trade but in world financial markets. "Since 1980" – notes Saskia Sassen – "the total value of financial assets has increased two and a half times faster than aggregate GDP of all rich industrial economies. And the volume of trading in currencies, bonds and equities has increased five times faster." The first to "globalize" and today "the biggest and in many ways the only true global market" is the foreign exchange market. "Foreign exchange transactions were ten times larger than world trade in 1983; only ten years later, in 1992, they were sixty times larger" (Sassen 1996: 40).

In the absence of this explosive growth in world financial markets, we would probably not be speaking of globalization, and certainly not as a *departure* from the ongoing process of world-market reconstruction launched under US hegemony in the wake of the Second World War. After all:

> Bretton Woods was a global system, so what really happened here was a shift from one global system (hierarchically organized and largely controlled politically by the United States) to another global system that was more decentralized and coordinated through the market, making the financial conditions of capitalism far more volatile and far more unstable. The rhetoric that accompanied this shift was deeply implicated in the promotion of the term "globalization" as a virtue. In my more cynical moments I find myself thinking that it was the financial press that conned us all (myself included) into believing in "globalization" as something new when it was nothing more than a promotional gimmick to make the best of a necessary adjustment in the system of international finance.
>
> (Harvey 1995: 8)

Gimmick or not, the idea of globalization was from the start intertwined with the idea of intense interstate competition for increasingly volatile capital and a consequent tighter subordination of most states to the dictates of capitalist agencies. Nevertheless, it is precisely in this respect that present tendencies are most reminiscent of the *belle epoque* of world capitalism of the late nineteenth and early twentieth centuries. As Sassen herself acknowledges,

> In many ways the international financial market from the late 1800s to the First World War was as massive as today's....The extent of the internationalization can be seen in the fact that in 1920, for example, Moody's rated bonds issued by about fifty governments to raise money in the U.S. capital markets. The Depression brought on a radical decline in this internationalization, and it was only very recently that Moody's once again rated the bonds of as many governments.
>
> (Sassen 1996: 42–3)

In short, careful advocates of the globalization thesis concur with critics in seeing present transformations as not novel except for their scale, scope and complexity. As I have argued and documented elsewhere (Arrighi 1994), however, the specificities of present transformations can be fully appreciated only by lengthening the time horizon of our investigations to encompass the entire lifetime of world capitalism. In this longer perspective, "financialization," heightened interstate competition for mobile capital, rapid technological and organizational change, state breakdowns and an unusual instability of the economic conditions under which states operate – taken individually or jointly as components of a particular temporal configuration, these are all recurrent aspects of what I have called "systemic cycles of accumulation."

In each of the four systemic cycles of accumulation that we can identify in the history of world capitalism from its earliest beginnings in late-medieval Europe to the present, periods characterized by a rapid and stable expansion of world trade and production invariably ended in a crisis of over-accumulation that ushered in a period of heightened competition, financial expansion, and eventual breakdown of the organizational structures on which the preceding expansion of trade and production had been based. To borrow an expression from Fernand Braudel (1984: 246) – the inspirer of the idea of systemic cycles of accumulation – these periods of intensifying competition, financial expansion, and structural instability are nothing but the "autumn" of a major capitalist development. It is the time when the leader of the preceding expansion of world trade reaps the fruits of its leadership by virtue of its commanding position over world-scale processes of capital accumulation. But it is also the time when that same leader is gradually displaced at the commanding heights of world capitalism by an emerging new leadership. This has been the experience of Britain in the late nineteenth and early twentieth centuries, of Holland in the eighteenth century, and of the Genoese capitalist diaspora in the second half of the sixteenth century. Could it also be the experience of the United States today?

At the moment the most prominent tendency is for the United States to reap the fruits of its leadership of world capitalism in the Cold War era. Indeed, various aspects of the seeming global triumph of Americanism that ensued from the demise of the USSR – most notably, the hegemony of US popular culture and the growing importance of agencies of world governance that are influenced disproportionately by the United States and its closest allies, such as the UN Security Council, NATO, the Group of Seven (G-7), the IMF, the IBRD and the WTO – are themselves widely held to be signs of globalization. The importance of these signs of a further Americanization of the world should not be belittled. But it should not be exaggerated either, particularly for what concerns US capabilities to continue to shape and manipulate to its own advantage the organizational structures of the world capitalist system. The chances are that the victory of the United States in what Fred Halliday (1983) has called the "Second Cold War" and the further Americanization of the world will appear in retrospect as closing moments of US world hegemony, just as Britain's victory in the First World War and the further expansion of its overseas empire were preludes to the final demise of British world hegemony in the 1930s and 1940s. As we shall see in section III of this chapter, there are good reasons for expecting the demise of US hegemony to follow a different trajectory than the demise of British hegemony. But there are equally good reasons for expecting the present, US-led phase of financial expansion to be a temporary phenomenon, like the analogous British-led phase of a century ago.

The most important reason is that the present *belle epoque* of financial capitalism, no less than all its historical precedents – from Renaissance Florence to Britain's Edwardian era, through the Age of the Genoese and the periwig period of Dutch history – is based on massive, system-wide redistributions of income and wealth from all kinds of communities to capitalist agencies. In the past, redistributions of this kind engendered considerable political, economic and social turbulence. At least initially, the organizing centers of the preceding expansion of world trade and production were best positioned to master, indeed, to benefit from the turbulence. Over time, however, the turbulence undermined the power of the old organizing centers, and prepared their displacement by new organizing centers endowed with the capacity to promote and sustain a new major expansion of world trade and production (Arrighi 1994).

Whether any such new organizing centers are today emerging under the glitter of the US-led financial expansion remains unclear, as we shall see. But the effects of the turbulence engendered by the present financial expansion have begun to worry even the promoters and boosters of economic globalization. David Harvey (1995: 8, 12) quotes several of them remarking that globalization is turning into "a brakeless train wreaking havoc," and worrying about a "mounting backlash" against the effects of such a destructive force, first and foremost "the rise of a new brand of populist politicians" fostered by the "mood…of helplessness and anxiety" that is taking hold even of wealthy countries. More recently, the Hungarian-born cosmopolitan financier George Soros has joined the chorus by arguing that the global spread of *laissez-faire* capitalism has replaced communism as the main threat to open democratic society.

> Too much competition and too little cooperation can cause intolerable
> inequities and instability....The doctrine of laissez-faire capitalism holds
> that the common good is best served by the uninhibited pursuit of self-
> interest. Unless it is tempered by the recognition of a common interest that
> ought to take precedence over particular interests, our present system...is
> liable to break down.
>
> (Soros 1997: 45, 48)

In reporting the proliferation of writings along Soros's lines, Thomas
Friedman – the early booster of the idea of globalization as virtue who later
invented the "brakeless train" metaphor – reiterates the view that "the integration of trade, finance and information that is creating a single global market and
culture" is inevitable and unstoppable. But while globalization cannot be stopped
– he hastens to add – "there are two things that can be done to it," presumably
for its own good: "We can go faster or slower....And we can do more or less to
cushion [its] negative effects" (Friedman (1997) "Roll Over Hawks and Doves,"
The New York Times, February 2, I: 15).

There is much *déja vu* in these diagnoses of the self-destructiveness of unregulated processes of world-market formation and related prognoses of what ought
to be done to remedy such self-destructiveness. Soros himself compares the
present age of triumphant *laissez-faire* capitalism with the similar age of a century
ago and suggests that the earlier age was, if anything, more stable than the
present (Soros 1997: 48).

> Our global open society lacks the institutions and mechanisms necessary for
> its preservation, but there is no political will to bring them into existence.
> I blame the prevailing attitude, which holds that the unhampered pursuit of
> self-interest will bring about an eventual international equilibrium....
> As things stand, it does not take very much imagination to realize that the
> global open society that prevails at present is likely to prove a temporary
> phenomenon.
>
> (ibid.: 53–4)

Soros makes no reference to his fellow countryman Karl Polanyi's now classic
account of the rise and demise of nineteenth-century *laissez-faire* capitalism.
Nevertheless, anyone familiar with that account cannot help but be struck by its
anticipation of present arguments about the contradictions of globalization
(on the continuing significance of Polanyi's analysis for an understanding of the
present wave of globalization, see among others, Mittelman 1996). Like Friedman,
Polanyi saw a slow-down in the *rate* of change as the best way of keeping change
going in a given *direction* without causing social disruptions that would result in
chaos rather than change. He also underscored that only a cushioning of the
disruptive effects of market regulation can prevent society from revolting in self-
defense against the market system (Polanyi 1957: 3–4, 36–8, 140–50). And like
Soros, Polanyi dismissed the idea of a self-adjusting (global) market as "a stark

utopia." He argued that no such institution can exist for any length of time "without annihilating the human and natural substance of [world] society." In his view, the only alternative to the disintegration of the world market system in the interwar years "was the establishment of an international order endowed with an organized power which would transcend national sovereignty" – a course, however, that "was entirely beyond the horizons of the time" (ibid.: 3–4, 20–2).

Neither Soros nor Polanyi provides an explanation of why the still dominant world power of their respective times – the United States today, Britain in the late nineteenth and early twentieth centuries – stubbornly stuck to and propagated the belief in a self-adjusting global market in spite of accumulating evidence that unregulated markets (unregulated financial markets in particular) do not produce "equilibria" but disorder and instability. Underlying such stubbornness we can none the less detect the predicament of a declining hegemonic agency that has become overly dependent, for profits as much as for power, on a process of widening and deepening integration of world trade and finance that the hegemonic agency at the height of its power promoted and organized, but the orderly development of which it can no longer ensure. It is as if the declining hegemonic power can neither afford to jump off the "brakeless train" of unregulated financial speculation, nor reroute the train into a less self-destructive groove.

Historically, the rerouting of world capitalism into a more creative than destructive groove has been premised upon the emergence, to borrow an expression from Michael Mann (1986: 28), of new "tracklaying vehicles." That is to say, the expansion of world capitalism to its present global dimensions has not proceeded along a single track laid once and for all some five hundred years ago. Rather, it has proceeded through several switches to new tracks that did not exist until specific complexes of governmental and business agencies developed the will and the capacity to lead the entire system in the direction of broader or deeper cooperation. The world hegemonies of the United Provinces in the seventeenth century, of the United Kingdom in the nineteenth century, and of the United States in the twentieth century have all been tracklaying vehicles of this kind (cf. Taylor 1994: 27). In leading the system in a new direction, they also transformed it. And it is on these successive transformations that we must focus in order to identify the true novelties of the present wave of financial expansion.

Section II

The formation of a capitalist world system, and its subsequent transformation from being a world among many worlds to becoming the historical social system of the entire world, have been based upon the construction of territorial organizations capable of regulating social and economic life and of monopolizing means of coercion and violence. These territorial organizations are the states whose sovereignty is said to be undermined by the present wave of financial expansion. In reality, most members of the interstate system never had the powers that states are said to be losing under the impact of the present wave of financial expansion; and even the states that had those powers at one time did not have them at another time.

In any event, waves of financial expansion are engendered by a double tendency. On the one hand, capitalist organizations respond to the overaccumulation of capital over and above what can be reinvested profitably in established channels of trade and production by holding in liquid form a growing proportion of their incoming cash flows. This tendency creates what we may call the "supply conditions" of financial expansions – an overabundant mass of liquidity that can be mobilized directly or through intermediaries in speculation, borrowing, and lending. On the other hand, territorial organizations respond to the tighter budget constraints that ensue from the slow-down in the expansion of trade and production by competing intensely with one another for the capital that accumulates in financial markets. This tendency creates what we may call the "demand conditions" of financial expansions. All financial expansions, past and present, are the outcome of the combined if uneven development of these two complementary tendencies (Arrighi 1997).

We are all very impressed, and rightly so, by the astronomical growth of capital that seeks valorization in world financial markets and by the intense competition that sets states against one another in an attempt to capture for their own pursuits a fraction of that capital. We should none the less be aware of the fact that at the roots of this astronomical growth there lies a basic scarcity of profitable outlets for the growing mass of profits that accumulates in the hands of capitalist agencies. This basic scarcity makes the pursuit of profit by capitalist agencies as dependent on the assistance of states as states are dependent in the pursuit of their own objectives on capitalist agencies. The dependence of capitalist agencies on states has been particularly evident in the recurrent crises that have punctuated the financial expansion, from the Latin American debt crisis of the early 1980s, through the collapse of "saving and loans" in the United States, right up to the recent East Asian financial crisis. On all these occasions, energetic state action rescued private capital from potentially catastrophic overexpansion. And on all occasions, it is hard to imagine who else, if not states, could have done so.

Be that as it may, all past financial expansions have been moments of disempowerment of some states – including, eventually, the states that had been the tracklaying vehicles of world capitalism in the epochs that were drawing to a close – and simultaneous empowerment of other states, including the states that in due course became the new tracklaying vehicles of world capitalism. Here lies the main significance of systemic cycles of accumulation. For these cycles are not mere cycles. They are also stages in the formation and gradual expansion to its present global dimensions of the world capitalist system.

This process of globalization has occurred through the emergence at each stage of organizing centers of greater scale, scope and complexity than the organizing centers of the preceding stage. In this sequence, city-states like Venice and transnational business diasporas like the Genoese were replaced at the commanding heights of the world capitalist system by a proto-nation-state like Holland and its chartered companies, which were then replaced by the British nation-state, formal empire and world-encompassing informal business networks, which were in their turn replaced by the continent-sized United States, its panoply of transnational corporations and its far flung networks of quasi-permanent overseas military bases. Each replacement was marked by a crisis of the territorial and non-territorial organizations that had led the expansion in the preceding stage. But it was marked also by the emergence of new organizations with even greater capabilities to lead world capitalism into renewed expansion than the displaced organizations (Arrighi 1994: 13–16, 74–84, 235–8, 330–1).

There has thus been a crisis of states in each financial expansion. As Robert Wade (1996) has noted, much of recent talk about globalization and the crisis of "nation-states" simply recycles arguments that were fashionable a hundred years ago (see also Lie 1996: 587). Each successive crisis, however, concerns a different kind of state. A hundred years ago the crisis of "nation-states" concerned the states of the old European core relative to the continent-sized states that were forming on the outer perimeter of the Eurocentric system, the United States in particular. The irresistible rise of US power and wealth, and of Soviet power, though not wealth, in the course of the two world wars and their aftermath, confirmed the validity of the widely held expectation that the states of the old European core were bound to live in the shadow of their two flanking giants, unless they could themselves attain continental dimension. The present crisis of "nation-states," in contrast, concerns the giant states themselves.

The sudden collapse of the USSR has both clarified and obscured this new dimension of the crisis. It has clarified the new dimension by showing how vulnerable even the largest, most self-sufficient, and second-greatest military power had become to the forces of global economic integration. But it has obscured the true nature of the crisis by provoking a general amnesia about the fact that the crisis of US world power preceded the breakdown of the USSR and, with ups and downs, has outlasted the end of the Cold War. In order to identify the true nature of the crisis of the giant states that have been dominant in the Cold War era, we must distinguish it from the long-term curtailment of national sovereignty that the globalization of the system of sovereign states has entailed for all but its most powerful members.

The principle that independent states, each recognizing the others' juridical autonomy and territorial integrity, should coexist in a single political system was established for the first time under Dutch hegemony by the treaties of Westphalia. The process of globalizing the territorial organization of the world according to this principle took several centuries and a good deal of violence to complete. More important, as often happens to political programs, Westphalian sovereignty became universal through endless violations of its formal prescriptions and major metamorphoses of its substantive meaning.

These violations and metamorphoses make eminently plausible Krasner's contention that, empirically, Westphalian sovereignty is a myth. To this we should none the less add that it has been no more a myth than the ideas of the rule of law, the social contract, democracy, whether liberal, social or whatever, and that, like all these other myths, it has been a key ingredient in the formation and eventual globalization of the modern system of rule. The really interesting question, therefore, is not whether and how the Westphalian principle of national sovereignty has been violated. Rather, it is whether and how the principle has guided and constrained state action and, over time, the outcome of this action has transformed the substantive meaning of national sovereignty.

When it was first established under Dutch hegemony, the principle of national sovereignty was meant to regulate relations among the states of Western Europe. It replaced the idea of an imperial–ecclesiastical authority and organization operating above factually sovereign states with the idea of juridically sovereign states that rely on international law and the balance of power in regulating their mutual relations – in Leo Gross' words, "a law operating between rather than above states and a power operating between rather than above states" (Gross 1968: 54–5). The idea applied only to Europe, which was thereby instituted as a zone of "amity" and "civilized" behavior even in times of war. The realm beyond Europe, in contrast, was turned into a residual zone of alternative behaviors, to which no standards of civilization applied and where rivals could simply be wiped out (Taylor 1991: 21–2).

For about 150 years after the Peace of Westphalia the system worked very well, both in ensuring that no single state would become so strong as to be able to dominate all the others and in enabling the ruling groups of each state to consolidate their domestic sovereignty. The balance of power, however, was reproduced through an endless series of increasingly capital-intensive wars and a broadening and deepening of European expansion in the non-European world. Over time, these two tendencies altered the balance of power both among states and between ruling groups and their respective subjects, eventually provoking a breakdown of the Westphalian system in the wake of the French Revolutionary and Napoleonic Wars (Arrighi 1994: 48–52).

When Westphalian principles were reaffirmed under British hegemony in the aftermath of the Napoleonic Wars, their geopolitical scope expanded to include the settler states of North and South America that had become independent on the eve or in the wake of the French Wars. But as the geopolitical scope of Westphalian principles expanded, their substantive meaning changed radically primarily because the balance of power came to operate *above* rather than *between* states. To be sure, the balance continued to operate between states in Continental Europe, where for most of the nineteenth century the Concert of Europe and the shifting of alliances among the Continental powers ensured that none of them would become so strong as to dominate all the others. Globally, however, privileged access to extra-European resources enabled Britain to act as the governor rather than a cog of the mechanisms of the balance of power. Moreover, massive tribute from its Indian Empire enabled Britain to adopt *unilaterally* a free-trade policy that, to varying degrees, "caged" all other members of the interstate system in a world-encompassing division of labor centered on Britain. Informally and temporarily but none the less effectively, the nineteenth-century system of juridically sovereign states was factually governed by Britain on the strength of its world-encompassing networks of power (Arrighi 1994: 52–5).

While the balance of power in the 150 years following the Peace of Westphalia was reproduced through an endless series of wars, Britain's governance of the balance of power after the Peace of Vienna produced, in Polanyi's words, "a phenomenon unheard of in the annals of Western civilization, namely, a hundred years' [European] peace – 1815–1914" (Polanyi 1957: 5). Peace, however, far from containing, gave a new great impulse to the interstate arma-ment race and to the broadening and deepening of European expansion in the non-European world. From the 1840s onwards, both tendencies accelerated rapidly into a self-reinforcing cycle whereby advances in military organization and technology sustained, and were sustained by economic and political expan-sion at the expense of the peoples and polities still excluded from the benefits of Westphalian sovereignty (McNeill 1982: 143).

The result of this self-reinforcing cycle was what William McNeill calls "the industrialization of war," a consequent new major jump in the human and financial costs of war-making, the emergence of competing imperialisms, and the eventual breakdown of Britain's nineteenth-century world order, along with widespread violations of Westphalian principles. When these principles were once again reaffirmed under US hegemony after the Second World War, their geopolitical scope became universal through the decolonization of Asia and Africa. But their substance was curtailed further.

The very idea of a balance of power that operates between rather than above states and ensures their factual sovereign equality – an idea that had already become a fiction under British hegemony – was discarded even as fiction. As Anthony Giddens (1987: 258) has noted, US influence upon shaping the new global order both under Wilson and under Roosevelt "represented an attempted incorporation of US constitutional prescriptions globally rather than a continua-tion of the balance of power doctrine." In an age of industrialized warfare and increasing centralization of politico-military capabilities in the hands of a small and dwindling number of states, that doctrine made little sense either as a description of actual relationships of power among the members of the globalizing inter-state system or as a prescription for how to guarantee the sovereignty of states. The "sovereign equality" upheld in the Charter of the United Nations for all its members was thus "specifically supposed to be legal rather than factual – the larger powers were to have special rights, as well as duties, commensurate with their superior capabilities" (Giddens 1987: 266).

The enshrining of these special rights in the charter of the United Nations institutionalized for the first time since Westphalia the idea of a suprastatal authority and organization that restricted juridically the sovereignty of all but the most powerful states. These juridical restrictions, however, paled in compar-ison with factual restrictions imposed by the two preeminent state powers – the United States and the USSR – on their respective and mutually recognized "spheres of influence." The restrictions imposed by the USSR relied primarily on military–political sources of power and were regional in scope, limited as they were to its Eastern European satellites. Those imposed by the United States, in contrast, were global in scope and relied on a far more complex armory of resources.

The far-flung network of quasi-permanent overseas bases maintained by the United States in the Cold War era was, in Krasner's words, "without historical precedent; no state had previously based its own troops on the sovereign territory of other states in such extensive numbers for so long a peacetime period" (Krasner 1988: 21). This US-centric, world-encompassing politico–military regime was supplemented and complemented by the US-centric world monetary system instituted at Bretton Woods. These two interlocking networks of power, one military and one financial, enabled the United States at the height of its hegemony to govern the globalized system of sovereign states to an extent that was entirely beyond the horizons, not just of the Dutch in the seventeenth century, but of Imperial Britain in the nineteenth century as well.

In short, the formation of ever more powerful governmental complexes capable of leading the modern system of sovereign states to its present global dimension has also transformed the very structure of the system by gradually destroying the balance of power on which the sovereign equality of the system's units originally rested. As juridical statehood became universal, most states were deprived either *de jure* or *de facto* of prerogatives historically associated with national sovereignty. Even powerful states like former West Germany and Japan have been described as "semisovereign" (Katzenstein 1987, Cumings 1997). And Robert Jackson (1990: 21) has coined the expression "quasi-states" to refer to ex-colonial states that have won juridical statehood but lack the capabilities needed to carry out the governmental functions traditionally associated with independent statehood. Semisovereignty and quasi-statehood are the outcome of long term trends of the modern world system and both materialized well before the global financial expansion of the 1970s and 1980s. What happened in the 1970s and 1980s is that the capacity of the two superpowers to govern interstate relations within and across their respective spheres of influence lessened in the face of forces that they had themselves called forth but could not control.

The most important among these forces originated in the new forms of world economic integration that grew under the carapace of US military and financial power. Unlike the nineteenth-century world economic integration instituted by and centered on Britain, the system of global economic integration instituted by and centered on the United States in the Cold War era did not rest on the unilateral free trade of the hegemonic power and on the extraction of tribute from an overseas territorial empire. Rather, it rested on a process of bilateral and multilateral trade liberalization closely monitored and administered by the United States, acting in concert with its most important political allies, and on a global transplant of the vertically integrated organizational structures of US corporations (Arrighi 1994: 69–72).

Administered trade liberalization and the global transplant of US corporations were meant to maintain and expand US world power, and to reorganize interstate relations so as to contain, not just the forces of Communist revolution, but also the forces of nationalism that had torn apart and eventually destroyed the nineteenth-century British system of global economic integration. In the attainment of these objectives, as Robert Gilpin (1975: 108) has underscored with reference to US policy in Europe, the overseas transplant of US corporations had priority over trade liberalization. In Gilpin's view, the relationship of these corporations to US world power was not unlike that of joint-stock chartered companies to British power in the seventeenth and eighteenth centuries: "The American multinational corporation, like its mercantile ancestor, has performed an important role in the maintenance and expansion of the power of the United States" (Gilpin 1975: 141–2).

This is true but only up to a point. The global transplant of US corporations did maintain and expand the world power of the United States by establishing claims on the incomes, and controls over the resources, of foreign countries. In the last resort, these claims and controls constituted the single most important difference between the world power of the United States and that of the USSR and, by implication, the single most important reason why the decline of US world power, unlike that of the USSR, has proceeded gradually rather than catastrophically (for an early statement of this difference, see Arrighi 1982: 95–7).

Nevertheless, the relationship between the transnational expansion of US corporations and the maintenance and expansion of the power of the US state has been just as much one of contradiction as of complementarity. For one thing, the claims on foreign incomes established by the subsidiaries of US corporations did not translate into a proportionate increase in the incomes of US residents and in the revenues of the US government. On the contrary, precisely when the fiscal crisis of the US "warfare–welfare state" became acute under the impact of the Vietnam War, a growing proportion of the incomes and liquidity of US corporations, instead of being repatriated, flew to offshore money markets. In the words of Eugene Birnbaum of Chase Manhattan Bank, the result was "the amassing of an immense volume of liquid funds and markets – the world of Eurodollar finance – outside the regulatory authority of *any* country or agency" (quoted in Frieden 1987: 85; emphasis in the original).

Interestingly enough, the organization of this world of Eurodollar finance – like the organizations of the sixteenth-century Genoese business diaspora and of the Chinese business diaspora from pre-modern to our own times – occupies places but is not defined by the places it occupies. The so-called Eurodollar market – as Roy Harrod (1969: 319) characterized it well before the arrival of the information super-highway – "has no headquarters or buildings of its own.... Physically it consists merely of a network of telephones and telex machines around the world, telephones which may be used for purposes other than Eurodollar deals." This "space-of-flows" falls under no state jurisdiction. And although the US state still has some privileged access to its services and resources, this privileged access has come at the cost of an increasing subordination of US policies to the dictates of non-territorial high finance.

Equally important, the transnational expansion of US corporations has called forth competitive responses in old and new centers of capital accumulation that weakened, and eventually reversed, US claims on foreign incomes and resources. In the 1970s, the accumulated value of non-US (mostly Western European) foreign direct investment grew one-and-half times faster than that of US foreign direct investment. By the 1980s, it was the turn of East Asian capital to outcompete both US and Western European capital through the formation of a new kind of transnational business organization – an organization that was deeply rooted in the region's gifts of history and geography, and that combined the advantages of vertical integration with the flexibility of informal business networks (Arrighi *et al.* 1993).

In 1980, it was estimated that there were over 10,000 transnational corporations of all national origins, and by the early 1990s more than three times as many (Stopford and Dunning 1983: 3; Ikeda 1996: 48). This explosive growth in the number of transnational corporations was accompanied by a drastic decrease in the importance of the United States as a source, and an increase in its importance as a recipient, of foreign direct investment. Moreover, no matter which particular fraction of capital won, the outcome of each round of the competitive struggle was a further increase in the volume and density of the web of exchanges that linked people and territory across political jurisdictions both regionally and globally.

This tendency has involved a fundamental contradiction for the global power of the United States – a contradiction that has been aggravated rather than mitigated by the collapse of Soviet power and the consequent end of the Cold War. On the one hand, the US government has become prisoner of its unprecedented and, with the collapse of the USSR, unparalleled global military capabilities. These capabilities remain essential, not just as a source of "protection" for US business abroad, but also as the main source of the lead of US business in high technology both at home and abroad. On the other hand, the disappearance of the communist "threat" has made it even more difficult than it already was for the US government to mobilize the human and financial resources needed to put to effective use or just maintain its military capabilities. Hence the divergent assessments of the actual extent of US global power in the post-Cold War era.

> "Now is the unipolar moment," a triumphalist commentator crows. "There is but one first-rate power and no prospect in the immediate future of any power to rival it." But a senior U.S. foreign policy official demurs: "We simply do not have the leverage, we don't have the influence, the inclination to use military force. We don't have the money to bring the kind of pressure that will produce positive results any time soon."
>
> (Ruggie 1994, 553)

Section III

The true peculiarity of the present phase of financial expansion of world capitalism lies in the difficulty of projecting past evolutionary patterns into the future. In all past financial expansions, the old organizing centers' declining power was matched by the rising power of new organizing centers capable of surpassing the power of their predecessors not just financially but militarily as well. This has been the case of the Dutch in relation to the Genoese, of the British in relation to the Dutch, and of the US in relation to the British. In the present financial expansion, in contrast, the declining power of the old organizing centers has been associated not with a fusion of a higher order but with a fission of military and financial power. While military power has become centralized further in the hands of the United States and its closest Western allies, financial power has become dispersed among a motley ensemble of territorial and non-territorial organizations which, *de facto* or *de jure*, cannot aspire to match the global military capabilities of the United States (Arrighi, Silver *et al.* 1999).

This anomaly signals a fundamental break with the evolutionary pattern that has characterized the expansion of world capitalism over the last 500 years. Expansion along the established path is at an impasse – an impasse which is reflected in the widespread feeling that modernity or even history is coming to an end, that we have entered a phase of turbulence and systemic chaos with no precedent in the modern era (Rosenau 1990: 10; Wallerstein 1995: 1, 268), or that a "global fog" has descended upon us as we blindly tap our way into the third millennium (Hobsbawm 1994: 558–9). While the impasse, the turbulence and the fog are all real, a closer look at the extraordinary economic expansion of the East Asian region over the last thirty years can give some insights into the truly new kind of world order that may be emerging at the edges of the impending systemic chaos.

In a recent comparative analysis of rates of economic growth since the 1870s, the Union Bank of Switzerland (UBS) finds "nothing comparable with the [East] Asian economic growth experience of the last three decades." Other regions grew as fast during wartime dislocations (e.g. North America during the Second World War) or following such dislocations (e.g. Western Europe after the Second World War). But "the eight-percent plus average annual income growth set by several [East] Asian economies since the late 1960s is unique in the 130 years of recorded economic history." This growth is all the more remarkable in having been recorded at a time of overall stagnation or near stagnation in the rest of the world, and in having "spread like a wave" from Japan to the Four Tigers (S. Korea, Taiwan, Singapore and Hong Kong), from there to Malaysia and Thailand, and then on to Indonesia, China and, more recently, to Vietnam (Union Bank of Switzerland 1996: 1).

Even more impressive is the advance of East Asia in global high finance. The Japanese share of the total assets of *Fortune*'s top fifty banks in the world increased from 18 per cent in 1970, to 27 per cent in 1980, to 48 per cent in 1990 (Ikeda 1996). As for foreign exchange reserves, the East Asian share of the top ten central banks' holdings increased from 10 per cent in 1980 to 50 per cent in 1994 (*Japan Almanac* 1993 and 1997).

An overabundance of capital, of course, brings problems of its own, as witnessed by the collapse of the Tokyo stock exchange in 1990–2 and the devastating financial crisis that swept Southeast and East Asia in 1997. For all their devastations, however, these crises (and the other crises that in all likelihood will hit the region in the years to come) in themselves are no more a sign of a roll-back of East Asian financial power vis-à-vis the United States than Black Thursday in Wall Street in 1929 (and the devastations of the US economy that ensued) were a sign of a roll-back of US financial power vis-à-vis Britain. As Braudel has pointed out in discussing the financial crisis of 1772–3 – which began in London but reflected an ongoing shift of world financial supremacy from Amsterdam to London – "any city which is becoming or has become the centre of the world-economy, is the first place in which the seismic movements of the system show themselves." As further and more compelling evidence in support of this hypothesis, he notes that the crisis of 1929–31 began in New York but reflected an ongoing shift of world financial supremacy from London to New York (Braudel 1984: 272).

Braudel does not explain why this should have been so. A good part of the explanation, however, can be inferred from Geoffrey Ingham's observation that in the 1920s the United States had not yet developed the capacity to replace Britain as the organizing center of the global economy, in spite of its spectacular advances in production and capital accumulation. At that time, the US financial system was in no position to produce the necessary international liquidity through a credit-providing network of banks and markets. "London had lost its gold, but its markets remained the most important single center for global commercial and financial intermediation" (Ingham 1994: 41–3).

Mutatis mutandis, similar considerations apply to London vis-à-vis Amsterdam in the 1770s, and to Tokyo and other East Asian financial centers vis-à-vis New York and Washington in the 1990s. The very speed, scale and scope of capital accumulation in the rising centers clashes with the latter's limited organizational capabilities to create the systemic conditions for the enlarged reproduction of their expansion. Under these circumstances, the most dynamic centers of world-scale processes of capital accumulation tend to become the epicenters of systemic instability. In the past, this instability was an integral aspect of the ongoing structural transformations of world capitalism that several decades later resulted in the establishment of a new hegemony. Whether the present instability centered on East Asia is the harbinger of a future East Asian world hegemony remains to be seen. But whether it is or it is not, for now it validates rather than invalidates the hypothesis of an ongoing shift of the epicenter of world-scale processes of capital accumulation from the United States to East Asia (Arrighi, Silver *et al.* 1999).

Ironically, this shift originated in major US encroachments on the sovereignty of East Asian states at the onset of the Cold War. The unilateral military occupation of Japan in 1945 and the division of the region in the aftermath of the Korean War into two antagonistic blocs created, in Bruce Cumings' words, a US "vertical regime solidified through bilateral defense treaties (with Japan, South Korea, Taiwan and the Philippines) and conducted by a State Department that towered over the foreign ministries of these four countries."

All became semisovereign states, deeply penetrated by U.S. military structures (operational control of the South Korean armed forces, Seventh Fleet patrolling of the Taiwan Straits, defense dependencies for all four countries, military bases on their territories) and incapable of independent foreign policy or defense initiatives....There were minor démarches through the military curtain beginning in the mid-1950s....But the dominant tendency until the 1970s was a unilateral U.S. regime heavily biased toward military forms of communication.

(Cumings 1997: 155)

Within this "unilateral US regime" the United States specialized in the provision of protection and the pursuit of political power regionally and globally, while its East Asian vassal states specialized in trade and the pursuit of profit. This division of labor has been particularly important in shaping US–Japanese relations throughout the Cold War era right up to the present. As Franz Schurmann wrote at a time when the spectacular economic ascent of Japan had just begun, "[f]reed from the burden of defense spending, Japanese governments have funneled all their resources and energies into an economic expansionism that has brought affluence to Japan and taken its business to the farthest reaches of the globe" (Schurmann 1974: 143). Japan's economic expansion, in turn, generated a "snowballing" process of concatenated, labor-seeking rounds of investment in the surrounding region, which gradually replaced US patronage as the main driving force of the East Asian economic expansion (Ozawa 1993: 130–1; Arrighi 1996: 14–16).

By the time this snowballing process took off, the militaristic US regime in East Asia had begun to unravel as the Vietnam War destroyed what the Korean War had created. The Korean War had instituted the US-centric East Asian regime by excluding Mainland China from normal commercial and diplomatic intercourse with the non-communist part of the region, through blockade and war threats backed by "an archipelago of American military installations" (Cumings 1997: 154–5). Defeat in the Vietnam War, in contrast, forced the United States to readmit Mainland China to normal commercial and diplomatic intercourse with the rest of East Asia, thereby broadening the scope of the region's economic integration and expansion (Arrighi 1996).

This outcome transformed without eliminating the previous imbalance of the distribution of power resources in the region. The rise of Japan to industrial and financial powerhouse of global significance transformed the previous relationship of Japanese political and economic vassalage vis-à-vis the United States into a relationship of mutual vassalage. Japan continued to depend on the United States for military protection. But the reproduction of the US protection–producing apparatus came to depend ever more critically on Japanese finance and industry. At the same time, the reincorporation of Mainland China in regional and global markets brought back into play a state whose demographic size, abundance of entrepreneurial and labor resources, and growth potential surpassed by a good margin that of all other states operating in the region, the United States included.

Within less than twenty years after Richard Nixon's mission to Beijing, and less than fifteen after the formal reestablishment of diplomatic relations between the United States and the People's Republic of China (PRC), this giant "container" of human resources already seemed poised to become again the powerful attractor of means of payments it had been before its subordinate incorporation in the European-centered world system.

If the main attraction of the PRC for foreign capital has been its huge and highly competitive reserves of labor, the "matchmaker" that has facilitated the encounter of foreign capital and Chinese labor is the Overseas Chinese capitalist diaspora.

> Drawn by China's capable pool of low-cost labor and its growing potential as a market that contains one-fifth of the world's population, foreign investors continue to pour money into the PRC. Some 80% of that capital comes from the Overseas Chinese, refugees from poverty, disorder, and communism, who in one of the era's most piquant ironies are now Beijing's favorite financiers and models for modernization. Even the Japanese often rely on the Overseas Chinese to grease their way into China.
>
> (Kraar 1994: 40)

In fact, Beijing's reliance on the Overseas Chinese to ease Mainland China's reincorporation in regional and world markets is not the true irony of the situation. As Alvin So and Stephen Chiu (1995: Chapter 11) have shown, the close political alliance that was established in the 1980s between the Chinese Communist Party and Overseas Chinese capitalists made perfect sense in terms of their respective pursuits. For the alliance provided the Overseas Chinese with extraordinary opportunities to profit from commercial and financial intermediation, while providing the Chinese Communist Party with a highly effective means of killing two birds with one stone: to upgrade the domestic economy of Mainland China and at the same time to promote national unification in accordance with the "One Nation, Two Systems" model.

The true irony of the situation is that one of the most conspicuous legacies of nineteenth-century Western encroachments on Chinese sovereignty is now emerging as a powerful instrument of Chinese and East Asian emancipation from Western dominance. An Overseas Chinese diaspora had long been an integral component of the indigenous East Asian tribute–trade system centered on imperial China. But the greatest opportunities for its expansion came with the subordinate incorporation of that system within the structures of the European-centered world system in the wake of the Opium Wars. Under the US Cold War regime, the diaspora's traditional role of commercial intermediation between Mainland China and the surrounding maritime regions was stifled as much by the US embargo on trade with the PRC as by the PRC's restrictions on domestic and foreign trade. Nevertheless, the expansion of US power networks and Japanese business networks in the maritime regions of East Asia, provided the diaspora with plenty of opportunities to exercise new forms of commercial intermediation between these networks and the local networks it controlled. And as restrictions on trade with and within China were relaxed, the diaspora quickly emerged as the single most powerful agency of the economic reunification of the East Asian regional economy (Hui 1995).

It is too early to tell what kind of political–economic formation will eventually emerge out of this reunification and how far the rapid economic expansion of the East Asian region can go. For what we know, the present rise of East Asia to most dynamic center of processes of capital accumulation on a world scale may well be the preamble to a re-centering of the regional and world economies on China as they were in pre-modern times. But whether or not that will actually happen, the main features of the ongoing East Asian economic renaissance are sufficiently clear to provide us with some insights into its likely future trajectory and implications for the global economy at large.

First, the renaissance is as much the product of the contradictions of US world hegemony as of East Asia's geo-historical heritage. The contradictions of US world hegemony concern primarily the dependence of US power and wealth on a path of development characterized by high protection and reproduction costs – that is, on the formation of a world-encompassing, capital-intensive military apparatus on the one side, and on the diffusion of wasteful and unsustainable patterns of mass consumption on the other. Nowhere have these contradictions been more evident than in East Asia. Not only did the Korean and Vietnam wars reveal the limits of the actual power wielded by the US warfare–welfare state. Equally important, as those limits tightened and expansion along the path of high protection and reproduction costs began to yield decreasing returns and to destablize US world power, East Asia's geo-historical heritage of comparatively low reproduction and protection costs gave the region's governmental and business agencies a decisive competitive advantage in a global economy more closely integrated than ever before. Whether this heritage will be preserved remains unclear. But for the time being the East Asian expansion has the potential of becoming the tracklaying vehicle of a developmental path more economical and sustainable than the US path.

Second, the renaissance has been associated with a structural differentiation of power in the region that has left the United States in control of most of the guns, Japan and the Overseas Chinese in control of most of the money, and the PRC in control of most of the labor. This structural differentiation – which has no precedent in previous hegemonic transitions – makes it extremely unlikely that any single state operating in the region, the United States included, will acquire the capabilities needed to become hegemonic regionally and globally. Only a plurality of states acting in concert with one another has any chance of bringing into existence an East Asian-based new world order. This plurality may well include the United States and, in any event, US policies towards the region will remain as important a factor as any other in determining whether, when and how such a regionally based new world order would actually emerge.

Finally, the process of economic expansion and integration of the East Asian region is a process structurally open to the rest of the global economy. In part, this openness is a heritage of the interstitial nature of the process vis-à-vis the networks of power of the United States. In part, it is due to the important role played by informal business networks with ramifications throughout the global economy in promoting the integration of the region. And in part, it is due to the continuing dependence of East Asia on other regions of the global economy for raw materials, high technology, and cultural products. The strong forward and backward linkages that connect the East Asian regional economy to the rest of the world augur well for the future of the global economy, assuming that the economic expansion of East Asia is not brought to a premature end by internal conflicts, mismanagement, or US resistance to the loss of power and prestige, though not necessarily of wealth and welfare, that the re-centering of the global economy on East Asia entails. Whether this is a realistic expectation is, of course, an altogether different matter.

References

Arrighi, G. (1982) "A crisis of hegemony," in S. Amin, G. Arrighi, A.G. Frank and I. Wallerstein (eds) *Dynamics of Global Crisis*, 55–108. New York: Monthly Review Press.

—— (1994) *The Long Twentieth Century. Money, Power and the Origins of Our Times*, London: Verso.

—— (1996) "The rise of East Asia. World-systemic and regional aspects," *International Journal of Sociology and Social Policy* 16 (7/8): 6– 44.

—— (1997) "Financial expansions in world historical perspective. A reply to Robert Pollin," *New Left Review* 224, 154–9.

Arrighi, G., Ikeda, S., and Irwan, A. (1993) "The rise of East Asia: one miracle or many?" In R.A. Palat (ed.) *Pacific-Asia and the Future of the World-System*, Westport, CT: Greenwood Press, pp. 41–65.

Arrighi, G., Silver, B.J. *et al.* (1999) *Chaos and Governance in the Modern World System*, Minneapolis, MN: University of Minnesota Press.

Bairoch, P. and Kozul-Wright, R. (1996) "Globalization myths: some historical reflections on integration, industrialization and growth in the world economy," UNCTAD discussion paper, no. 113.

Braudel, F. (1984) *The Perspective of the World*, New York: Harper and Row.

Cumings, B. (1997) "Japan and Northeast Asia into the 21st century," in P.J. Katzenstein and T. Shiraishi (eds) *Network Power. Japan and Asia*, Ithaca, NY: Cornell University Press, pp. 136–68.

Frieden, J.A. (1987) *Banking on the World. The Politics of American International Finance*, New York: Harper and Row.

Giddens, A. (1987) *The Nation State and Violence*, Berkeley, CA: California University Press.

Gilpin, R. (1975) *U.S. Power and the Multinational Corporation*, New York: Basic Books.

Gross, L. (1968) "The Peace of Westphalia, 1648–1948," in R.A. Falk and W.H. Hanrieder (eds) *International Law and Organization*, Philadelphia: Lippincott, pp. 45–67.

Halliday, F. (1983) *The Making of the Second Cold War*, London: Verso.

Harrod, R. (1969) *Money*, London: Macmillan.

Harvey, D. (1995) "Globalization in question," *Rethinking Marxism* 8 (4): 1–17.

Hirst, P. (1996) "Global market and the possibilities of governance," paper presented at the conference on Globalization and the New Inequality, University of Utrecht, November 20–22.

Hobsbawm, E. (1994) *The Age of Extremes: A History of the World, 1914–1991*, New York: Vintage.

Hui, P-k. (1995) "Overseas Chinese business networks: East Asian economic development in historical perspective," Ph D dissertation, Department of Sociology, State University of New York at Binghamton.

Ikeda, S. (1996) "World production," in I. Wallerstein *et al.* (eds) *The Age of Transition. Trajectory of the World-System 1945–2025*, London: Zed Books.

Japan Almanac (various years) Tokyo: Asahi Shimbum Publishing Co.

Ingham, G. (1994) "States and markets in the production of world money: sterling and the dollar," in S. Corbridge, R. Martin, and N. Thrift (eds) *Money, Power and Space*, Oxford: Blackwell.

Jackson, R. (1990) *Quasi-states: Sovereignty, International Relations and the Third World*, Cambridge: Cambridge University Press.

Katzenstein, P. (1987) *Policy and Politics in West Germany: The Growth of a Semisovereign State*, Philadelphia: Temple University Press.

Kraar, L. (1993) "The new power in Asia," *Fortune* October 31, pp. 38–44.

Krasner, S. (1988) "A trade strategy for the United States," *Ethics and International Affairs* 2: 17–35.

Lie, J. (1996) "Globalization and its discontents," *Contemporary Sociology* 25 (5): 585–7.

McNeill, W. (1982) *The Pursuit of Power: Technology, Armed Forces and Society since A.D. 1000*, Chicago: University of Chicago Press.

Mann, M. (1986) *The Sources of Social Power, Vol I. A History of Power from the Beginning to A.D. 1760*, Cambridge: Cambridge University Press.

Mittelman, J.H. (ed.) (1996) *Globalization: Critical Reflections*, Boulder, CO: Lynne Reinner Publications.

Ozawa, T. (1993) "Foreign direct investment and structural transformation: Japan as a recycler of market and industry," *Business & the Contemporary World* 5 (2): 129–50.

Polanyi, K. (1957) *The Great Transformation: The Political and Economic Origins of Our Time*, Boston, MA: Beacon Press.

Rosenau, J. (1990) *Turbulence in World Politics: A Theory of Change and Continuity*, Princeton, NJ: Princeton University Press.

Ruggie, J. (1994) "Third try at world order? America and multilateralism after the Cold War," *Political Science Quarterly* 109 (4): 553–70.

Sassen, S. (1996) *Losing Control? Sovereignty in an Age of Globalization*, New York: Columbia University Press.

Schurmann, F. (1974) *The Logic of World Power. An Inquiry into the Origins, Currents, and Contradictions of World Politics*, New York: Pantheon.

So, A.Y. and Chiu, S.W.K. (1995) *East Asia and the World-Economy*, Newbury Park, CA: Sage.

Soros, G. (1997) "The capitalist threat," *The Atlantic Monthly* 279 (2): 45–58.

Stopford J.M. and Dunning, J.H. (1983) *Multinationals: Company Performance and Global Trends*, London: Macmillan.

Taylor, P. (1991) "Territoriality and hegemony, spatiality and the modern world-system," Newcastle upon Tyne: Department of Geography, University of Newcastle upon Tyne.

—— (1994) "Ten years that shook the world? The United Provinces as first hegemonic state," *Sociological Perspectives* 37 (1): 25–46.

Union Bank of Switzerland (1996) "The Asian economic miracle," *UBS International Finance* (Zurich) 29: 1–8.

Wade, R. (1996) "Globalization and its limits: reports of the death of national economies are greatly exaggerated," in S. Berger and R. Dore (eds) *National Diversity and Global Capitalism*, Ithaca, NY: Cornell University Press.

Wallerstein, I. (1995) *After Liberalism*, New York: The New Press.

4 Two worlds of trade, two worlds of empire

European state-making and industrialization in a Chinese mirror

Kenneth Pomeranz

Introduction

What difference did the political environment of numerous armed, competing, and roughly comparable states in early modern Europe make to the emergence of industrial capitalism in Europe, and to a world economy centered there? This paper reexamines those questions in light of recent and forthcoming research showing that as late as 1750 Europe did not have unique advantages in physical productivity, human capital, or the capacity to accumulate financial capital; its economic supremacy and centrality are nineteenth-century phenomena. The comparisons here are largely limited to China which, since it was one empire rather than many states, provides a useful foil.

Consequently, this chapter is only indirectly related to most of the others in this volume, which ask how much autonomy states can have under contemporary conditions. But nobody would claim that, say, eighteenth-century China was much constrained by Britain, or vice versa, or that capital flight was as constant a worry for eighteenth-century policy-makers as some people argue it is today. Instead, I ask about the effects of state policies that we know varied enormously.

Still, the chapter does have some connections to these contemporary concerns. First, it suggests – as do many of the other chapters in this volume – that "globalization" is hardly new, and that it creates possibilities as well as limitations for states. For instance, we will see that the Spanish Empire in the New World, which may seem a quintessentially unilateral initiative, depended for its survival on simultaneous developments in East Asia (supposedly an "external area" to the Atlantic-centered world economy until the nineteenth century). Second, we will see that the direction of influence was not always from core to periphery: rather, we will see more or less autonomous developments in primary-product-exporting hinterlands powerfully shaping their associated cores. Third, we will examine what might at first seem an embryonic version of today's global political economy – early modern Europe – and see new relationships among economic development, state-formation, and interstate competition.

Interstate competition in early modern Europe was intense, and leaders understood that economic growth increased a state's fiscal base and thus its power. And the span of the European state system was small enough that capital, technology, and some skilled labor could cross political boundaries fairly easily. Thus, it has been argued, politico-military competition forced European states to create favorable climates for capital accumulation, technological innovation, and economic growth, creating the political matrix that produced a major economic breakthrough in the nineteenth century. The logic, if not the scale, of the argument is similar to those about the contemporary global political economy. But this chapter casts doubt on that logic.

First, policies which maximized *state* revenues, even over the long term, did not necessarily promote growth. Second, a part of the world with a very different political economy – China – kept pace economically with Europe until at least the late eighteenth century. Third, this chapter provides a new explanation of why Northwestern Europe did enjoy unique successes in the nineteenth century – one in which it is largely state activities *outside* Europe that matter. Instead of hitting upon a species of political economy (the British one) that favored growth at home and political success abroad through a sort of Darwinian selection, Western Europeans were lucky that some features of their state system which were *not* particularly salutary when applied within Europe did prove advantageous when they were projected abroad.

Finally, our arguments about multidirectional influences merge with the critique of the European state system as the crucible of uniquely adaptive institutions. Northwest Europe's emerging political economy did not succeed abroad because competition at home had made its armies, much less its firms, uniquely effective. A series of peculiar conjunctures made them successful: conjunctures that they did not create alone. Thus this chapter challenges both the standard histories of how the world economy emerged and a contemporary situation that these histories seem to represent in an early, microcosmic form: that winners in the global economy emerge through an internally driven process in which capital accumulators at the core relentlessly maximize their own interests.

European state-making and warfare were important, but not in the ways most often suggested. Many alleged advantages of state competition as a context for economic development – as a supposed spur to demand, to technological innovation, and (through concessions made by cash-hungry rulers) to the development of secure property and effective markets – evaporate upon a comparison with China. (For examples of many of these arguments, see Jones 1981: 67, 105–28.) So does the argument that the emerging division of labor between Eastern and Western Europe (which, Wallerstein argues, was only possible with multiple states) differed sufficiently from core–periphery relationships elsewhere in the Old World to explain Western Europe's unique development path (Wallerstein 1974: 45, 64–5, 71–85 is the most famous example; on war-making strategies and different systems of labor see for instance Tilly 1992). The role of force (and luck) outside Europe, especially in the New World – which did not just "open" areas for trade, but shaped them so that they complemented the existing core – was far more significant.

First, though, a word about units. China does not resemble single European countries, but the whole continent; we need to compare like regions within each area. (See Wong 1997, for a fuller discussion of strategies for comparison.) Thus, the Northwest European core (composed of Britain, the Low Countries, plus bits of France and Germany) can be compared to China's Lower Yangzi region, or perhaps its second most dynamic region, Lingnan (roughly contemporary Guangdong and Guangxi provinces). The grain- and timber-exporting Baltic would be roughly comparable to China's Upper Yangzi, or perhaps even the far southwest, and so on. And despite a very different political context, relationships between Eastern and Western Europe turn out to share certain important characteristics with those between Chinese core regions and their peripheries, both in and beyond China proper.

However, Northwest Europe's relationships with the New World and African slaving areas developed quite differently. These differences, which owe much to the different political contexts of China and Europe, go a long way toward explaining why proto-industrial and commercial growth could lead to massive industrialization in nineteenth-century Western Europe (though it did not have to), while China's proto-industrial groth slowed or even reversed.

In particular, the actions of European governments and government-sponsored agents overseas (e.g., the East and West India Companies) *perpetuated* and *expanded* a pattern in which the New World supplied land-intensive commodities in exchange for European manufactures: a pattern that was essential if Western Europe was to intensify its specialization in manufactures, and if its standard of living was to hold up (much less improve) during the enormous population boom that accompanied industrialization. And since, as we shall see, the usual pattern in the Old World was for any particular core–periphery trade to rather quickly encounter diminishing returns – whether it involved peripheries with more or less free labor (e.g., Manchuria and the Upper Yangzi) or those with bound labor (e.g., Eastern Europe or Southeast Asia) – the role of the state in making the New World a different kind of periphery must have involved more than enforcing a free-labor regime in the core and bound labor in the periphery.

But before we can analyze these relationships, it is necessary to justify two parts of my claim for broad comparability between Chinese and European cores; both may initially seem unlikely. The first holds that the processes of agricultural, commercial, and proto-industrial growth in Chinese and Western European cores were roughly comparable *circa* 1750, so that it makes sense to focus on political differences. I will then examine some arguments that hold that the basic difference between a single Chinese empire and a Europe of multiple states engaged in escalating military competition created a more favorable environment for industrial development in Europe than in China, and show that they are unconvincing. After that, I argue for a second counter-intuitive premise: that, at both ends of Eurasia, demographic and proto-industrial growth were leading to serious and similar shortages of certain land-intensive commodities, which could only be relieved through enduring relationships with areas that would supply these commodities and import manufactures. While sustaining such relationships was not a sufficient condition for industrialization, it was a necessary one, since industrialization meant both more people and much higher per capita resource use. After showing that cores at both ends of eighteenth-century Eurasia shared these obstacles to further growth, and could not escape them through consensual trade alone, we will then look at how Europe's New World empires *did* allow it to escape.

In other words, the argument to this point suggests that rather than emphasizing the effects of different regimes on capital accumulation – which many societies appear to have done enough of to finance early industrialization – we might better explore how different regimes affected the possibilities for escaping the ecological cul-de-sac threatening advanced proto-industrial economies. We will then see more clearly how Europe's interstate rivalries, when married to a peculiar global conjuncture (partly shaped, ironically, by Chinese demand for silver), helped the New World play a distinctive role in Europe's subsequent development; one that neither internal frontiers nor Southeast Asia could play for China's cores.

These assumptions are justified at much greater length in a forthcoming book, and are treated here in a fashion that may be too long for some readers but still too short to be convincing. Readers who prefer to grant these premises for the sake of argument are invited to skim the second, fourth and seventh sections of this chapter.

Core regions in Europe and China

Agricultural productivity was far higher in the paddy-rice regions of eighteenth-century East Asia than anywhere in Europe, allowing much denser populations to have similar nutritional standards. These nutritional standards are reflected in rural Chinese life expectancies, which, even at the end of the eighteenth century, were still comparable to those in England, and higher than those anywhere else in Europe (Lavely and Wong 1991; Li Zhongqing and Guo Songyi 1994: 7–10). Indeed, since Chinese birth rates (contrary to myth) were lower than those in Europe from 1550 to 1850, while its rate of population growth was about the same, its death rates must have been no higher than the average for Europe as a whole.

Institutionally, China was at least as much of a market economy as Europe. Virtually all land was freely alienable, and regularly leased and sub-leased by contract; except for a few economically trivial occupations (e.g., musicians) labor was free; and interregional migration and long-distance trade (including massive trading in grain and other bulky staples) were vastly larger than anything in pre-nineteenth century Europe (Wang 1992: 52; Marks 1991). At least in the more developed regions, the overwhelming majority of households were regular participants in the cash economy. Probably more of them confronted a real market (with plural and competing buyers and sellers) for their wares than in much of Western Europe, where the merchants who "forestalled" crops and "put out" manufactures often divided territories and used credit to limit many producers to one possible buyer (Braudel 1982: 41–7; Kriedte *et al.* 1981: 99, 102–5; Wallerstein 1974: 84–5).

Before the nineteenth century, major industries in Western Europe and East Asia were not radically different. Decentralized handicraft production predominated in both areas, with textiles, the largest sector in both places, largely produced in rural homes. In both places, proto-industrialization was accompanied by a population boom, with roughly similar dynamics.

These resource/ecological problems – and the need to devote resources to subsistence rather than accumulation – are linked to population growth, and it has often been held that China suffered more severely from this tendency than Europe. While this became true later, it was not at this point – if anything, eighteenth-century Chinese were probably more successful at limiting their fertility in response to economic incentives than were Europeans at the same time (Li Zhongqing and Guo Songyi 1994: 18–58; Li Bozhong 1994b: 38–63; Goldstone 1996: 4–6). Surplus above subsistence, which was potentially available for investment, was substantial in both cases (Hajnal 1965, 1982; Riskin 1975). Moreover, it seems increasingly likely that Chinese in the core regions were not only as long-lived as any Europeans, but enjoyed a comparable standard of living. For instance, the Chinese in 1750 probably consumed about as much cloth per capita as the French in 1789, and far more than the Germans even in 1830, who were certainly not the poorest of Europeans. (Pan-European estimates are lacking.) More important for our purposes, the Lower Yangzi appears to have *produced* roughly as much cotton cloth per capita in 1750 as the UK did cotton, wool, linen and silk cloth combined in 1800 – plus an enormous quantity of silk (see Pomeranz, forthcoming: Appendix F).

Comparative state-making and European development: a skeptical view

Thus, there may be no purely internal European advantage *circa* 1750 to explain based on warfare and interstate competition. However, scholars have argued for three possible benefits of pre-industrial war-making for European development: technological spill-over, stimulus from increased demand, and incentives for governments to adopt institutions that favored economic growth.

Since the reasons for technological change are not well understood, we cannot completely dismiss arguments that warfare spurred innovations. However, the number of pre-1800 military innovations with important civilian applications is surprisingly small. Moreover, pre-industrial warfare probably did not increase the total effort that went into seeking new technologies; it is more likely that it simply drew skilled people away from other more productive projects. It seems even less likely that warfare provided crucial stimulus by increasing demand. While contracts for munitions, uniforms and the like stimulated particular industries at particular times, such demand was ultimately financed through taxation, depressing private demand. At most, it moved demand from some sectors to other sectors: and not toward a particularly price or efficiency-conscious consumer.

Arguments that Europe's interstate competition generated institutional arrangements uniquely favorable to economic development are more varied and complex. In their most general form, these arguments hold that since monarchs often granted greater security of property – the *sine qua non* of a market-based economy – in return for revenue to meet military needs, the emergence of secure property was a product of military competition among relative equals. Here, we need to distinguish between the route by which property rights became more secure in Europe and an implicit claim that this is the *only* way that such rights could emerge. The latter claim relies on the notion that something like "oriental despotism" prevailed where states did not face as much pressure to engage in constant military expansion, or at least that (as Chaudhuri claims) merchants could only gain security where rising revenue needs forced states that despised commerce to recognize them anyway; the Chinese Empire is a common negative example (see for instance Braudel 1977: 68–71; Chaudhuri 1985: 210, 214).

Since markets in China often hewed closer to neoclassical principles than eighteenth-century European ones, this cannot be true for security of "property" in its modern sense: fee simple ownership of land, capital, and commercial assets. Interstate competition may have been vital to securing such rights in Europe, but societies elsewhere reached them by other means.

Moreover, we need to be careful about claims that the limits that the state placed on its own treatment of property had straightforward and necessary effects on development. In a study of English interest rates from 1540 to 1837, Gregory Clark finds that while the rates paid by the government itself were sensitive to regime changes that suggested greater security for property and freedom from taxation (e.g., the Glorious Revolution), these events had no discernible effect on the cost of capital in private transactions; the risk premium for private credit was unaffected even by the huge land confiscations and government bankruptcy of the mid-seventeenth century. While growth required some basic level of security for property and contract, the empirical record does not suggest that a gradual "perfection" of these rights was connected to an acceleration in economic growth (Clark 1996: 563–88; for the view being criticized see North and Weingast 1989: 803–32). The situation thus differed from contemporary scenarios, which assume that only states that continuously improve the climate for mobile capital can hope to remain economically viable. Indeed, the kind of property that ongoing warfare did most to secure was quite different and quite likely growth-retarding: property in privileges, from tax farms and venal office to state grants of monopolies, and confirmation of guild privileges in return for fiscal contributions.

This disaggregation of "property rights" also reminds us that we must *a fortiori* keep separate a number of changes within certain European societies – in property rights, the development of representative government (at least for the propertied) and the spread of certain civil liberties – which have often been treated as a single package of "modernization," "liberalization," or "rationalization," and then treated as the traits that made for survival in a Darwinian struggle among European states. Since many of these concessions by the state were granted in return for revenue to meet military needs, and all appear related to the licensing of some kind of internal competition (for power, in the market-place, or in the "marketplace of ideas") it has been easy to conclude that intense interstate competition favored societies that were most characterized by the "competitive spirit," and which were thus the best adapted for other pursuits as well as war: a logic that seems borne out by the (temporary) triumph of liberal Britain. But the evolutionary analogy will not survive much scrutiny.

First, such arguments apply only to states that followed what Charles Tilly calls the "capital intensive" or "coercion and capital intensive" paths to state-building, rather than his "coercion intensive" path. And while some of the biggest winners (notably England and France) came from the "coercion and capital intensive" group, not all did (Russia being the biggest counter-example); and the purely "capital intensive" group (such as the Dutch Republic) did not fare very well (Tilly 1992: 134–7, 150–1, 153).

Second, not all of these liberalizing changes had the same relationship either to warfare or to internal competition. Representative government and various sorts of property rights were often granted or confirmed in return for revenue needed for war; such liberties as freedom of speech were usually won through different paths that had little to do with military mobilizations. Moreover, not even the property rights involved had a consistent relationship to economic liberalism. Not only were many of the property rights that were granted anti-competitive privileges; even what are today considered less peculiar property rights often interfered with, rather than promoted, Smithing efficiency. In France, for instance, the state's revenue needs induced it to confirm rights for local property-holders, which preserved minority vetoes on the consolidation and enclosure of plots, and the conversion or parceling out of commons; this made much technically feasible swamp drainage and other improvements close to impossible legally until after the Revolution.[1]

Even if creating transferable privileges depressed output in the short to medium term, it could have encouraged capital accumulation, and thus increased output over the longer term. A narrow version of this argument would be that the guarantee and sale of all sorts of future income streams (from tax farms and so forth) helped develop instruments that allowed other sorts of future income streams to be securitized. Thus state finance paved the way for new private debt instruments, and for a new kind of ownership: the corporation.

Partnerships, of course, existed all over the world, but a business form with eternal life, a separate legal personality, and structures that particularly favor the long-term accumulation of capital within the firm is a Western creation. And as the case of the Dutch East India Co. (VOC) makes clear, what was really new about the early corporation was *not* primarily the capacity to collect investment from many partners. That had long been done, though somewhat more awkwardly, through older forms of partnerships that financed single ventures (relatively humble Venetians had taken shares in some voyages, as relatively humble Amsterdammers now could); and it was done by merchants outside Europe, too. What was truly new about the VOC was that even a large minority of shareholders who wished to wind up the partnership and distribute its assets could not force the directors to do so: instead the minority was allowed to sell its shares while the business continued. This novel privilege for the directors, which was accepted grudgingly, was, of course, *eventually* quite important to capital accumulation (Steensgaard 1982: 237–8, 245. For East Asian capital-raising partnerships see Ng 1983: 29–30, 155, 158; Zelin 1988: 87–109; Cushman 1975: 147).

However, corporations were not important for any activity within Europe until the railway era, which called for sums of patient capital too large to be assembled through the traditional (usually kin-based) networks that financed almost all other private endeavors, including the coal and textile sectors central to early industrialization (Griffin 1977: 63; Morris and Williams 1958: 137–48). Until then, corporations were mostly important in overseas colonization and armed trade, which were the activities that – thanks to the expenses of acting as a quasi-government, including making war – required the largest amounts of patient capital prior to 1830. In the interim, these new financing mechanisms were mostly important for the *overseas* build-up of special kinds of capital – ships, forts, land, and infrastructure. I shall return to the companies later.

A broader argument would be that the war-driven creation of privileges favored accumulation because it put wealth in the hands of people particularly likely to reinvest it for maximum gain: i.e., capitalists. But in this transformation, government offices, tax farms, and titles figure as obstacles, not as part of the solution; and in this sense the military competition that led almost every state in Europe to put more of these privileges on the market were most likely an impediment to the accumulation of wealth as capital in the modern sense. For instance, Geoffrey Parker has noted that even in entrepreneurial Holland, bondholders were often upset to see wars end, since this deprived them of a safe, lucrative, and prestigious place to put their money: productive investment was something that these people turned to *faute de mieux* (Parker 1988: 63–4). Under the circumstances, it is hard to see how military fiscalism can be said to have contributed much to economic development within Europe itself: and we have not even discussed the destruction caused by wars themselves.

Shared resource constraints

In the mid-eighteenth century, three places on the globe – China, Japan, and Western Europe – reached new population highs, and would henceforth always be above their earlier peaks. The result was intense pressure on the land, especially in the core areas of each region. In this period, Malthus's observation that producing any of four basic human necessities – food, fuel, fiber, and building materials – required hard-to-reduce quantities of land was still essentially true. And since industry did not yet make synthetic fertilizers, fibers or other substitutes for land, its presence in core areas only helped to the extent that it allowed them to trade manufactures with less densely populated regions and obtain land-intensive commodities in return.

None of these areas faced immediate food shortages, but other kinds of biological stress were evident. In China and Japan, output of both food and fiber crops at least kept up with population growth, but at the cost (by the nineteenth century) of serious deforestation, hillside erosion, and a concomitant increase in flood dangers; and without a breakthrough to a new kind of farming (one making heavy use of mined or synthetic fertilizer), it is hard to see how even this sort of ecologically costly expansion could have continued much longer. And the situation in Western Europe was no better.

On the one hand, much of Western Europe used its agricultural resources rather inefficiently (e.g., failing to adopt convertible husbandry). Consequently, there were some "slack" resources that could be tapped as institutional change and shifts in prices made it profitable to do so (e.g., Grantham 1989a: 11–18; Grantham 1989b 137–61). To that extent, the *in*efficiency of European farming left a potential cushion against Malthusian crisis that was less present in East Asia.

However, this "slack" could not be easily mobilized to meet the new population and other pressures of the nineteenth century. Grantham's data shows that the turn to more productive farming occurred very unevenly, even in relatively advanced Northern France. Meanwhile in England, where both industrialization and population growth were most rapid, there was probably very little of this slack left to exploit. English agricultural productivity made only very limited gains after 1750 (Clark 1991: 456–9; Thompson 1968: 189, 193), until it began importing (and later synthesizing) fertilizer to relieve its intensely worked land. And since overall European population roughly doubled between 1750 and 1850 (Grantham 1989a: 11–13), mobilizing slack capacity on the Continent still could not generate significant surpluses to sell to Britain, which would have to turn to the New World and Australia (Alfred Crosby's "Neo-Europes" – see Crosby 1986:2–3, 6–7, 299–308) to meet its soaring food deficit.

Moreover, the argument that growing markets stimulated large productivity gains is limited to food crops. Comparable gains were not possible with fiber crops, which require much more labor and greatly deplete the soil. And indeed, when cloth production skyrocketed in the late eighteenth and nineteenth centuries, Europe began to import vastly more of its fiber than China had to, or probably could have.

And if fiber supplies were less elastic than food supply, the supply of building materials and fuel – the last two of Malthus's four necessities – was even less so. None of the late eighteenth-century cores seemed able to increase their production of this vital commodity very much: instead all faced rising demand for wood, shrinking local forests, and stagnant timber yields. Here, then, was a severe ecological barrier to accelerating growth in both Western Europe and East Asia. (For the Chinese evidence, see Li Bozhong 1994a: 91–5.)

By contrast, though China had little agricultural slack, it had other sources of breathing room. Even in relatively backward, dry-farming North China, the balance between nutrient inputs and extraction in farming *circa* 1800 appears to have been more favorable than in England, where per crop yields and cropping frequencies were nearing the limits of what was sustainable without off-farm fertilizer (calculated in Pomeranz 1995: 8–9). And in the rice paddies, completely different ecological rules applied: this kind of farming was still capable of staggering increases in per acre yields even without modern technology, and could produce as many as twenty-four consecutive rice crops without crop rotation or soil degradation (Smil 1985: 140). Even in fuel supply, developed parts of China seem to have been no worse off than their European counterparts, despite greater population density: differences in cooking techniques and other advantages evened the balance, as a lengthy set of calculations I have done elsewhere shows (Pomeranz forthcoming: Chapter 5 and Appendix B). But these figures also show how quickly population growth could eat away at the supply of wood in a dynamic economy: even one that used resources quite efficiently. It would not take long for these forces to close the ecological window within which further growth could occur without a massive turn to fossil fuels *and* imported primary products. In both China and Europe, an ecological bottleneck was at hand. And as we shall see momentarily, trade provided only limited relief before the nineteenth century.

Trading with Old World peripheries: the limits of Smithian solutions to Malthusian problems

For Western Europe, this meant at first the Eastern European grain, timber, and cattle trades. For Lingnan, there were some imports from Southeast Asia and even India; the Lower Yangzi relied primarily on rice and timber from upstream, cotton from North China, sugar from the far South and Southeast Asia, and after 1680, on timber and soybeans from Manchuria. (Meanwhile, the Lower Yangzi's population had stopped growing by 1800; see Li Bozhong 1994b: 34–5; Skinner 1987: 72–6.) Northwestern Europe, the Lower Yangzi, and Lingnan all sold manufactured goods, mainly textiles, in order to buy frontier imports. But that pattern of exchange faced at least two possible limitations.

One was that raw materials exporters often began to manufacture locally what they had previously imported. (For a clear model of how diminishing returns in agriculture shift labor to proto-industry, see Mokyr 1976: 134–62.) Import substitution accelerated, thus reducing the export of raw materials from a particular periphery. Today, import substitution is often thought of as contrary to the "natural" tendencies of the market, using tariffs, subsidies and the like to "artificially" improve the competitive position of nascent industries. But 200-plus years ago, the technological gaps between cores and peripheries were smaller, and copying was easier; very few production processes required large investments of fixed capital; and relatively high transport costs provided some "natural" protection, at least for the bulky low-value items used by ordinary people. Thus, import substitution was not a "forced" process in the pre-1800 world: it seems to have occurred fairly routinely in peripheries where laborers were free to switch their efforts into new kinds of production and to decide which goods to produce at home and which to purchase.

Indeed, import substitution eventually spread through most of the parts of

China with which the Lower Yangzi and Lingnan traded. Thus, despite the remarkable efficiency of China's long-distance product markets, a division of labor based on the exchange of manufactured goods for raw materials was not indefinitely sustainable, much less expandable.

Western Europeans faced different constraints in dealing with Eastern Europe. Eastern European institutions (especially bound labor) tended to delay import substitution; the chance for Western Europe to perpetually sell manufactures and obtain primary products there was correspondingly enhanced.

But a "feudal" trading partner posed different problems. Institutional rigidities limited its capacity to increase exports: and it was not much of a market for the imports that would pay for exports in the first place. Thus, though serfdom and quasi-serfdom helped stop this trade from contracting, it also kept it from growing much. Despite the vast quantities of grain, wood, etc., that Eastern Europe was *ecologically* capable of exporting, its trade with the West peaked rather quickly, and at levels that are quite minor compared with the long-distance flows of grain, timber, and fertilizer in China.[2] Baltic forests, for instance, were comparatively lightly tapped compared to what was possible, to the Chinese interior, or to what was happening in trade-deficit areas such as Canada and New England (Lower 1973: 22, 31–2 on the late-eighteenth century Baltic, New England and Canada; also Tucker and Richards 1983: xii–xvii). Thus, though world-systems theorists often see a global division of labor unfolding more or less naturally from exchanges between "feudal" Eastern and "capitalist" Western Europe (Wallerstein 1974: 71–89), that trade had inherent limits, which also constrained Western Europe's ability to expand its supplies of primary products. Merely finding "less advanced" trading partners did not solve any core's problems for long. It took a certain kind of periphery to give Western Europe a trading partner that uniquely combined very rapid and sustained growth and a continued specialization in primary product exports – precisely what Europe needed if it was to undergo an unprecedented growth in its industrial production and primary product consumption.

The New World and expandable core–periphery relations

That periphery was created by colonialism and slavery in the New World. Much of the New World bonanza consisted of silver, which we will return to later. But first let us focus on more directly consumable New World goods.

Most New World farm exports were produced by slaves or indentured laborers. Moreover, the new plantations were almost all close to coastlines. Consequently, exports from the circum-Caribbean plantation zone did not plateau the way that exports from the Chinese interior did when free farmers and woodsmen ran into diminishing returns and devoted more time to handicrafts; nor were they beset by the soaring transport costs that affected Old World foresters once they moved away from the banks of rivers. And because New World plantation-owners (unlike the lords of Eastern European estates or

Southeast Asian pepper fields) *purchased* most of their laborers, and often curtailed their subsistence production, Western Europe's trade with this area escaped both the "small market problem" that had dogged its trade for Eastern European raw materials and the limits that import-substitution created on trade with freer peripheries. Exports had to be high enough to cover the costs of importing slaves, and a substantial portion of the costs of feeding and clothing them; slave purchases alone equaled over one-quarter of Caribbean and Brazilian sugar exports in the late eighteenth century (figures for 1821–6 from Ludwig 1985: 107, 314, using a rough price of 250,000 *reis* per slave (Miller 1986); Brazilian exports for 1806 and 1826 from Morineau 1985: 177–8).

Thus, the slave trade played a major role in making Euro-American trade fundamentally different and more expandable than the exchanges between Old World cores and peripheries. A free labor periphery like Southwest China would not have served Europe as well, even if it had been as ecologically bountiful as the New World; nor would a periphery like Eastern Europe (or later Java) in which participants in a still-functioning subsistence-oriented economy were mobilized part-time as servile producers of exports. The circum-Caribbean region exported so much sugar, tobacco, coffee, and later cotton not only because it was ecologically capable of doing so, but because it was sociologically and politically set up to "need" so much else.

In essence, because the circum-Caribbean region became such an *extremely* sparsely populated frontier in the wake of European-borne epidemics, it later became a perversely large market for imports. In fact, it became the first raw-materials-exporting region to assume a now familiar "Third World" profile: that of a massive importer of capital goods (in this case, walking, talking, kidnapped ones), exporting products that kept falling in price as production became more efficient, capital-intensive, and wide-spread. By contrast, the prices of most forms of energy produced in Europe, including food, rose throughout the eighteenth century, relative both to wages and to manufactured goods (see, for instance, the chart in Goldstone 1991: 186), and the price of the exports from most Old World peripheries, like timber, tended to rise sharply as the volumes shipped increased. Thus, the plantation areas of the New World were a new kind of periphery: one that would buy enough expensive "capital goods" and mass-market non-luxury consumer goods to make its trade with the core a fairly balanced one, and one whose imports and exports could be counted on to stimulate each other. More sugar exports consistently led to more slave imports (Richardson 1987: 745–6), more food and clothing imports and (often) more short-term plantation debt that had to be covered by selling more sugar next year, at whatever price.

Moreover, the near monocultures in most plantation areas greatly facilitated one of the most important achievements of Europe's trans-Atlantic traders: the roughly 50 per cent decline in trans-Atlantic shipping costs over the course of the eighteenth century, even without substantial technological change. One major factor in this decline was a sharp decrease in the amount of time spent acquiring cargo: this allowed a faster turnover of working capital, a more intensive use of ships, and very large savings in sailors' wages (Shepherd and Walton 1972: 81–4).

Thus, it took a demographic catastrophe, colonial legislation, and *particular* forms of bound labor to create a periphery so perfectly suited to be an ever-expanding source of raw materials in an era before most forms of production required expensive capital goods, and when most people still had some connection to subsistence production. The form of labor control on the periphery was indeed crucial, but not all forms of coerced cash-cropping (or mining) had the same potential. New World slavery, and New World colonialism, were different in very important ways.

Similarly, though the New World was a significant market for burgeoning British industry (Richardson 1987: 768), that was not its major significance. European markets were growing, too, and off a much larger base. Moreover the ability of demand *per se* to create major increases in production is dubious (Mokyr 1985). What is crucial here is that the New World was a particular *kind* of trading partner, which was crucial to maintaining increases in production. It offered what an expanding home market could not: ways in which manufactured goods created without much use of British land could be turned (either directly or indirectly) into ever-increasing amounts of land-intensive food and fiber that returned to England at falling prices.

Measuring ecological relief in industrializing Britain

The quantities involved were vast. As I have calculated elsewhere, replacing Britain's new World imports *circa* 1830 with home-grown products would have required at least 25 million acres (Pomeranz, forthcoming: Appendix D). This surpasses Britain's total crop and pasture land: it also surpasses Anthony Wrigley's estimate that by 1815 Great Britain's coal industry was substituting for the yield of 21 million acres of forest.[3]

Moreover, land-saving New World imports kept growing thereafter, helping to sustain an Industrial Revolution that could otherwise have choked on its own appetite for primary products: for decades these imports kept pace quite nicely with the progress of mineral-based energy, which in many ways defined the industrial transformation. Britain's coal output would increase 14 times from 1815–1900 (Mitchell 1988: 247), but its sugar imports increased 11-fold over the same period (calculated based on Mitchell 1988: 709–11), until they reached 14 per cent of all British calories (Mintz 1985: 133); and its cotton imports 20 times (Farnie 1979: 7 compared with Bruchey 1967: Table 2-A). And after mid-century, Britain also began to live off American grain, beef, and other primary products; lumber imports soared; and the New World, at last, also became a significant outlet – in fact a huge one – for surplus population from various parts of Europe.

These later imports, of course, came mostly from free labor zones, and even most slave areas ceased to *import* many slaves after 1807. But once industrialization and mass migration were underway, markets carried the ecologically crucial trades forward. New technology had made possible still more dramatic declines in trans-Atlantic shipping costs than had occurred in the eighteenth century, and other changes (particularly the railroad) were revolutionizing inland transport. Aided by cheap transport, mechanized production, and the tastes that migrants brought with them, Europe could now sell large amounts of consumer goods in the New World, too – without needing colonial restrictions on American manufacturing. Thus, yet another kind of trading partner – still sparsely populated and resource rich, but market- rather than subsistence-oriented, generally accessible, and now an outlet for large flows of people and equipment as well as of capital and labor embodied in manufactured consumer goods – was in place, and was perfectly suited to meet the needs of an increasingly densely populated and industrial Europe.

Finally, we must consider New World silver, which did more than just allow Western Europeans to buy additional goods in places like Eastern Europe or South and Southeast Asia. It also helped create European military commanders and paymasters who became ever-more influential partners (and in the nineteenth century, masters) of the elites who presided over the extraction of these goods. And consumption taxes on plantation-grown sugar and tobacco also played a non-trivial role in building these overseas military capabilities (Mintz 1985: 156–7, 163, 170; Morgan 1975: 198). All told, taxes on sugar, rum, tobacco, raw silk, and Indian cloth accounted for 22 per cent of all government revenue in Britain between 1788 and 1792 (see O'Brien 1988: 11). Thus, the exploitation of the New World, and of the Africans taken there to work, mattered in many ways above and beyond those reflected in our ghost acreage figures.

Comparative empires and comparative frontiers: the Sino-European comparison reconsidered

Having at last reframed the problem, let us return to how Europe's interstate competition and "military fiscalism" (Wolfe 1972; Tilly 1992; Parker 1988) shaped these relationships with distant peripheries, and compare this with how the Chinese Empire – which faced only occasionally serious military threats, and was preoccupied with reproducing internal stability – shaped the relationships of Chinese cores with peripheries both within and outside the empire.

Interstate competition, of course, drove much of European overseas expansion in the first place. Moreover, it created tools (including some of the fiscal and organizational forms discussed above) which shaped much of the New World into peculiarly useful kinds of peripheries. Thus, the projection overseas of the European state system not only "opened" new fields for capitalism, but, through various efforts interfered with markets, preserved these areas as ecologically critical *complements* to the core. By contrast, though the Qing did plenty of empire-building, they did not do so in ways that complemented developments in Jiangnan or Lingnan; instead their policies towards internal peripheries encouraged them to imitate existing cores as best they could.

To some extent, the conquests themselves were the result of military competition within Europe, which nurtured new military technologies and tactics that
were then used overseas, which often helped Europeans triumph overseas despite
the limited size of their forces there. But we should be wary of attributing too
much of Europe's overseas successes to the "military revolution." Many of the
Europeans' gains in Asia were at least as attributable to encountering foes who,
not used to fighting over land (as opposed to captives) abandoned territory to
them (as occurred in parts of Southeast Asia (Reid 1988: 122–3)), or whose own
problems of the moment created situations in which small-scale interventions
could make an unusually large difference (as in Bengal – see generally Bayly
1989 and specifically Marshall 1987: 39–40, 92–103, 196–216). And even so,
European gains in the Old World were quite limited (and in some places, temporary – Marshall 1980: 13, 15, 20, 22) until the nineteenth-century Industrial
Revolution was well under way. And in the New World, where European adven-
turism really paid off, diseases were probably more important than military
technology or organization (Crosby 1986: 39–40, 92–103, 96–216).

Equally important – though less often noted – is the role that licensed monopolies, tax farms, and other privileged entities created by revenue-hungry states
played in expanding and shaping Europe's New World presence. In doing so,
these institutions made European expansion in the New World far more consequential than, for instance, the penetration without state backing of Chinese
merchants into Southeast Asia, even though Southeast Asia was also quite
sparsely populated at the time, was capable of supplying vast quantities of land-
intensive resources, and featured Chinese communities comparable in size to
most European cities in the New World prior to 1800.

European colonization in the New World involved considerable costs for military protection (from unconquered Amerindians, other Europeans, and the
African slaves who outnumbered Whites in many areas) and for political organization. Such costs were most easily borne by a single party (whether state or
licensed monopolist) that could count on receiving a significant share of the
profits on all exports, and so avoid "free rider" problems. (Indeed, in the 1670s a
man working in Virginia's tobacco fields earned more for the crown than he did
for either himself or his master – Morgan 1975: 198.) And the large profits per
unit of export (both for merchants and the royal treasury) made possible by
monopoly agreements certainly made it more worthwhile for people in Europe
to finance further settlement by others than it would have been had New World
exports been sold in a more open market.

Though religion motivated some migrants, the new colonies could not have
grown much had the colonists not found goods to export. Many of the settlers
may have wanted a piece of land on which they could live relatively self-suffi-
ciently, rather than rely on a fluctuating market, but less than a third of white
settlers financed their own passage, and those who did finance colonization were
far more interested in profitable exports than in helping their poorer compatriots
live their dreams; we have already seen how the ability to export from further
inland was essential to populating North America (Galenson 1989: 56–64).

Moreover, the cost of emigration itself, already high relative to the savings of the poor, would have been far higher had American exports been lower; sugar and tobacco carriers, lacking sufficient return cargo, competed aggressively to carry emigrants (ibid.: 7). And above all, the flow of Africans to the circum-Caribbean region (including southern North America and Brazil) – which was until 1800 much larger than that of Whites – was quite clearly driven by the expansion of European luxury demand. (For a general treatment of the importance of European demand in driving the economic development even of colonial North America – the least export-dominated part of the New World – see McCusker and Menard (1985), especially the general statement of issues on pp. 17–34.)

This analysis may at first seem irrelevant to the Spanish parts of the New World. There, by far the most important product was silver, which was mined with indigenous labor. Moreover, the main demand for silver came from China, where the world's largest economy was gradually converting to a primarily silver-based system after unhappy experiences with paper and copper. Eventually, somewhere between one-third and two-thirds of all New World silver wound up in China. As Dennis Flynn and Arturo Giraldez (1985) have shown, it was this enormous Chinese demand that allowed Spain to levy heavy mining royalties without making New World silver production uneconomic: indeed the huge European inflation of the sixteenth and early seventeenth centuries suggests that even with China (and some other areas) drawing off so much New World silver (and supplying goods that the silver still in Europe could chase) its value was falling rapidly. Without Asian demand, the New World mines would soon have become unable to both make profits and pay the rents that sustained Spanish administration in the New World.

But for Asian silver demand to be effective demand, Asian silk, cotton cloth, porcelain, and spices had to flow to Europe and the Americas. The increased volume of these exports depended, not only on the remarkable productivity of Asian proto-industries (as emphasized by Andre Gunder Frank: see Frank 1998), but also on external demand for those goods, and thus on the chartered monopoly companies that encouraged and managed these imports. The circumstances of these licensed, profit-seeking quasi-states made them keenly aware that they needed high volumes, not just high mark-ups – and made them well-suited to pursue them (Steensgaard 1982: 245–6, 252).

Indeed, Niels Steensgaard has argued that it was precisely because of the huge fixed costs of maintaining armed trading settlements and private navies in Asia – costs that were paralleled by those of conquering, settling, and carrying out armed trade with New World colonies – that the Dutch East India Co. could not be run like earlier trading partnerships, which had been liquidated at pre-set dates, with both capital and profit returned to the partners. Instead it became necessary to imagine much of the company's capital as permanent, and to retain much of the profit as circulating capital, in order to reach a business volume over which to spread large fixed costs and from which to compensate the contributors of a capital that never would be liquidated. And because not all original investors were patient enough for this sort of enterprise, ownership and control of the firm had to be firmly separated, with a market in shares that allowed dissatisfied owners to exercise an "exit" option in place of the "voice" denied them by this new kind of firm (Steensgaard 1982: 235–58; on "exit" and "voice" see Hirschmann 1970).

Steensgaard's further claim that the corporation was more efficient *as a purely economic enterprise* than various Asian merchant organizations is dubious. It was, however, clearly well suited to armed trading and settlement in both the East and West Indies – and to recovering its protection costs by broadening markets for what had been luxuries.

Surprisingly, European states also often encouraged consumption of exotic goods. Though mercantilist politicians bemoaned the importation of luxuries – and joined some nobles in promoting ineffectual sumptuary laws – various European governments simultaneously encouraged the import of Asian and American goods for reexport to the rest of Europe (from which they profited in several ways). And here the plurality of European states did matter. With multiple companies seeking markets throughout Europe, smuggling was rife, and efforts to promote demand – which indirectly allowed Chinese silver buyers to support Spain's New World empire – were far more effective than efforts to limit it.

For other New World regions, the connections were more direct. European demand made it profitable to expand New World production; growing production and shipping volumes helped push down per unit transaction costs, and so made it worthwhile for private parties to settle further from the original ports, and for merchants to finance the importation of more people (slave, indentured, or free), the expansion of port facilities, and so on. Meanwhile, the duties on growing volumes of exports financed governments for growing settlements, and created the preconditions for a much more rapid expansion of settlement and exports in the nineteenth century. That later trade would include many staples, but the early stages were driven by demand for non-necessities like tobacco. And both the revenue hunger of European states and the needs of the companies they had chartered (and periodically milked) were central to the deliberate expansion (Mintz 1985: 163–4, 170) and fulfillment of this demand.

Clearly, the European state system alone does not explain why only Europe wound up with important overseas possessions. (Nor are overseas possessions the only important difference between Europe and East Asia.) Accidents of geography, epidemiology, and many other factors make it useless to insist on a single explanation. Still, it is worth considering what a different context for colonization was provided by European state-making than by Chinese political economy. Let us begin with Qing policy towards internal peripheries.

Thus far, I have emphasized the degree to which population growth, proto-industrialization, and import substitution were "normal" processes for peripheries with more or less free labor and no special restrictions (e.g., colonial monopolies). But it is also true that the Qing state, which favored these developments as a way to reproduce the material basis of the Confucian good life (and stable tax-paying households) on the widest possible basis, did not simply trust to market dynamics to make this happen. The state encouraged large-scale migration to less populated areas, providing information, infrastructure, and even loans to individual settlers. And Qing land tax policies – both the *de jure* assessment of heavy tribute quotas on Jiangnan and a few other rich areas and the *de facto* policy of often allowing newly settled or re-settled land to escape taxes altogether – certainly had the effect of favoring "peripheral" development, while possibly restraining that of the empire's foremost core. The state also made considerable if sporadic efforts to promote the spread of best practices in both agriculture and handicrafts: introducing new crop varieties and hiring Jiangnan weavers to come teach people in other areas, for instance (Mann 1992; Wong 1997). And in North and Northwest China, the Qing undertook major efforts to make subsistence more secure in areas that were ecologically marginal. The biggest such project, the Yellow River conservancy (which served other purposes as well) probably consumed over 10 per cent of total government spending in the early nineteenth century, when many other governments spent almost all of their budgets on wars, debt, and the royal court (Pomeranz 1993: 153–265).

We cannot, of course, measure the impact of such policies precisely. Japan shows a somewhat similar pattern of very limited core growth – in fact, population in the Kantō and Kinai *fell* after the mid-eighteenth century – accompanied by population and proto-industrial growth in peripheral areas (compare Saito 1985: 211 and Iwahashi 1981: 440; see also Roberts 1991: 87–91), despite very different rulers and policies. But surely Qing policies had some effect: one that worked with markets to promote growth and import substitution in what might otherwise be seen as Jiangnan's "Internal colonies." And when we turn to overseas expansion, we see equally fateful differences from European policies.

The Qing doubled the size of the empire between 1680 and 1760, but mostly in central Asia, which had little potential as a trading partner for China's cores. Meanwhile, large groups of Chinese merchants already dotted sparsely populated Southeast Asia: Chinese Manila in 1603 was larger than New York or Philadelphia would be in 1770 (Bernal 1966: 51). The region included both future sugar and tobacco plantations (potential "Caribbeans") and river deltas which would later become Southeast Asian "North Americas": i.e. enormous exporters of food and timber, and recipients of huge nineteenth-century migrations. Fujian and Guangdong – where the merchants came from – were exporting farmers to Taiwan and various internal frontiers; a few also joined relatively short-lived communities of Chinese miners and cash-crop growers in pre-1850 Southeast Asia (Heidhues 1996: 164–82) But massive agricultural colonization was not a serious possibility in the eighteenth century: not only because the Chinese state provided no military and political backing for its subjects' overseas forays, but also because no merchants (with one brief exception) could ever become the exclusive link between the huge Chinese market and overseas sources of imports, and thus recover the initial costs of empire-building.

The story of Chinese sugar production near Batavia is instructive here. The Chinese cleared and cultivated this land, and owned the vast majority of the mills; but these rural Chinese were administratively and economically separate from the wealthy and influential Chinese merchants within the city. The Dutch

East India Company bought the sugar at controlled prices for sale to Persia and Europe. Even when a market slump led to social disorder and an eventual Dutch-sponsored ethnic massacre, there is no sign that urban and rural Chinese had any significant contacts (Blussé 1981: 167, 169, 172–7; Blussé 1986: 94–7). And later, when the Qing debated possible retaliation, two premises seem to have been shared by all the officials. The first was that the interests of South Chinese engaged in overseas trade (including their safety when they went abroad) were important and *should* be protected; the Qing knew well that both their subjects and the imperial treasury gained from overseas commerce. But everyone also agreed that those who *settled* overseas were no longer subjects worthy of the emperor's solicitude (Cushman 1978: 137–56; Fu 1966: 173–4). It was not foreign trade that the state blocked, but colonization and armed trading.

There was one exception to the rule that overseas Chinese were never in a position to monopolize imports back to China. That one exception – the Zheng family's maritime empire – became remarkably rich in its heyday (1645–83), and its success in both commercial and naval battles with the Dutch (whom it drove off Taiwan, and out of various lucrative Southeast Asian markets) should undermine any claim that "the Chinese" could not carry off a European-style combination of armed trade and colonial/maritime expansion. Moreover the Zhengs did sponsor colonization on Taiwan and made threats to occupy Luzon (leading to another massacre of resident Chinese) (Wills 1994: 223–8; on Philippine events, see Guerrero 1966: 33–4). But the Zheng empire flourished only during a Chinese dynastic crisis, and never had a secure (much less privileged) base back home for procuring exports and marketing imports; the mainland ports it held were constantly besieged. Moreover, the Zhengs were primarily interested in mobilizing resources overseas to fund their hopeless campaign to retake China for the Ming, not in an overseas empire *per se*. They thus stand as a suggestive example of Chinese succeeding at activities that made a huge difference for Europe, but which were prohibited when the Chinese state was stable.

In the normal run of things, overseas Chinese traders lacked even the protection needed to encourage them to put money into land, much less the power to seize monopoly privileges. Moreover, none ever gained an import monopoly back home, and even a monopoly on say, sugar imports would have done little good in light of China's huge domestic production. Forced to remain within a competitive market, their ventures took different directions from those of the European Companies. Competitive trade with margins only slightly higher than in the rice trade may have made 1730s Taiwan alone a sugar exporter equal to about one-third of the entire New World in the 1750s (compare Shepherd 1993: 156–66 with Phillips 1990: 59, 61; Steensgaard 1990: 140; Deerr 1949–50: 193–203, 235–42), but it did not generate the *concentrations* of profit that would have made, say, an attempt to seize Northern Luzon worth considering – even though, given Spain's weak eighteenth-century grip on this area (see, for instance, deJesus 1982 on the flimsiness of Spanish control), its proximity to Taiwan, and the presence of an important Chinese merchant community in

Manila, this might have been a perfectly logical step for an imaginary group of Fujianese merchants who had the same relationship to their home government that their European counterparts had.

Moreover, the state itself lacked a revenue interest in the new "everyday luxuries." With 90 per cent of China's sugar, and all of its silk and tobacco, produced internally, Qing officials lacked the motives for promoting these trades that their Western counterparts had. Officials concerned that sugar shipments from Taiwan were too large were no more "anti-market" than were European mercantilists who opposed the export of silver to buy silk; after all, they wanted to keep Taiwan exporting rice to the commercial, handicraft, and cash-cropping parts of Fujian, not to make either place autarkic (Shepherd 1993: 162–8). But unlike European silver hawks, they were not confronted by treasury, military, and colonial officials with interests in these new trades.

This is not to say that only the relationship between extra-continental trade, colonial expansion and military fiscalism separated Europe from China. Even in a different political setting, it still seems unlikely that the Chinese would have made of Southeast Asia what Europeans (and African slaves) made of the New World: for one thing, the natives would not have died off as they did in the Americas. Nor would the New World bonanza have created an industrial Europe without independent technical developments (in coal mining, in particular). But had Europe not had a political economy of military fiscalism and state-licensed and privileged capitalism in addition to the market economy it shared with China, it probably would not have used the New World as it did, either; and if it had not done so, it would have lacked the ecological breathing room that was the necessary complement of early nineteenth-century technological changes. Here, then, European statecraft – in the context of lucky conjunctures – crucially affected Western Europe's capacity to escape the constraints it shared with other cores, and to enter a new world in which population and *per capita* resource use could both grow as never before.

Notes

1 See Brenner 1985: 284–323, on the connections between French state-building and obstacles to enclosure, consolidation, etc; and Rosenthal 1992: 43–50, 70–4, 87–94 on local adjudication and the barriers they posed to improvement. If Rosenthal and J.P. Cooper (1985: 186–91) are right that the hold-outs against improvements protected here were often the wealthy and privileged (rather than the smallholders, whose claims Brenner emphasizes), the point would be all the stronger.

2 Food imports from the Middle Yangzi fed perhaps as many as 5 million people per year in the Lower Yangzi, and the soybeans that the Lower Yangzi imported could have fed another 3 to 4 million people had most of them not been used as fertilizer. Even Shandong, a not particularly commercialized province with perhaps 23 million people in 1800 (Huang 1985: 322) imported enough food to feed 700,000 to 1 million people a year, and exported a like amount. By contrast, the Baltic grain trade fed about 600,000 people a year at its peak, and all of Europe's long-distance grain trade put together at most 2.5 million people at its pre-1800 peak. For numbers on the

grain trades, see DeVries 1976: 17, 56; Braudel 1981: 127; Adachi 1978; Wu 1985: 277; Xu 1995: 86; Marks 1991: 76–9; Wang 1989: 423–30; Lu 1992: 493.

3 See Wrigley 1988: 54–5. Wrigley actually makes "the death of George III (1820)" his cut-off date, but according to the coal-production statistics in Mitchell 1988: 247, it would be 1815 when production actually reached the requisite 15 million tons. More importantly, Wrigley uses a very generous estimate of per acre timber yields. Were he to use the contemporary global mean (see Smil 1983: 36) his estimate of the contribution of coal would rise to slightly over 21 million "ghost acres." For Britain's total arable and pasture, see Mitchell 1988: 186; the figure is actually for a later date (1867), but it is the earliest one available, and seems to have been fairly stable at that point.

References

Adachi, K. (1978) "Daizukasu ryūtsū to shindai no shōgyō teki nōgyō," *Tōyōshi Kenkyu* 37 (3): 360–89.

Bayly, C.A. (1989) *Imperial Meridian: The British Empire and the World, 1780–1830*, London: Longman.

Bernal, R. (1966) "The Chinese colony in Manila, 1570–1770," in A. Felix (ed) *The Chinese in the Philippines 1570–1770*, Manila: Solidaridad Publishing.

Blussé, L. (1981) "Batavia 1619–1740: the rise and fall of a Chinese colonial town," *Journal of Southeast Asian Studies* 12 (1): 159–78 (March).

—— (1986) *Strange Company: Chinese Settlers, Mestizo Women, and the Dutch in VOC Batavia*, Dordrecht, Holland: Foris Publications.

Braudel, F. (1977) *Afterthoughts on Material Civilization and Capitalism*, Baltimore: Johns Hopkins University Press.

—— (1981) *The Structures of Everyday Life* (trans. S. Reynolds), New York: Harper and Row.

—— (1982) *The Wheels of Commerce* (trans. S. Reynolds), New York: Harper and Row.

Brenner, R. (1985) "The agrarian roots of European capitalism," in T.H. Aston and C.H. Philpin (eds) *The Brenner Debate*, Cambridge: Cambridge University Press.

Bruchey, S. (1967) *Cotton and the Growth of the American Economy 1790–1860*, New York: Harcourt Brace.

Chaudhuri, K.N. (1985) *Trade and Civilization in the Indian Ocean*, Cambridge: Cambridge University Press.

Clark, G. (1991) "Yields per acre in English agriculture 1250–1860: evidence from labour inputs," *Economic History Review* 44 (3): 445–60.

—— (1996) "The political foundation of modern economic growth: England 1540–1800," *Journal of Inter-Disciplinary History* 26 (4): 563–88 (Spring).

Cooper, J.P. (1985) "In search of agrarian capitalism," in T.H. Aston and C.H. Philpin (eds) *The Brenner Debate*, Cambridge: Cambridge University Press.

Crosby, A. (1986) *Ecological Imperialism: the Biological Expansion of Europe, 900–1900*, Cambridge: Cambridge University Press.

Cushman, J. (1975) "Fields from the sea," PhD dissertation, Cornell University, Ithaca, New York.

—— (1978) "Duke Ch'ing-fu deliberates: a mid-eighteenth century reassessment of Sino-Nanyang commercial relations," Papers on Far Eastern History 17: 137–56 (March).

Deerr, N. (1949–50) *The History of Sugar*, vol 1 and 2, London: Chapman and Hall.

deJesus, E.C. (1982) "Control and compromise in the Cagayan Valley," in E.C. deJesus and A.W. McCoy (eds) *Philippine Social History: Global Trade and Local Transformation*, Manila: Ateneo de Manila University Press.

DeVries, J. (1976) *The Economy of Europe in an Age of Crisis, 1600–1750*, Cambridge: Cambridge University Press.

Farnie, D.A. (1979) *The English Cotton Industry and the World Market, 1815–1896*, Oxford: Oxford University Press.

Flynn, D. and Giraldez, A. (1995) "China and the Spanish Empire," paper presented at the annual meeting of the Economic History Association, Chicago, September.

Frank, A.G. (1998*) Re-Orient: The Silver Age in Asia and the World Economy*, Berkeley: The University of California Press.

Fu Lo-Shu (1966) *A Documentary Chronicle of Sino-western Relations 1644–1820*, Tucson: University of Arizona Press.

Galenson, D. (1989) (ed.) "Labor markets in colonial America," in *Markets in History*, Cambridge: Cambridge University Press.

Goldstone, J. (1991) *Revolution and Rebellion in the Early Modern World*, Berkeley: University of California Press.

Grantham, G. (1989a) "Agrarian organization in the century of industrialization: Europe, Russia, and North America," in G. Grantham and C. Leonard (eds) *Agrarian Organization in the Century of Industrialization: Europe, Russia and North America*, Greenwich, CT: JAI Press.

—— (1989b) "Capital and agrarian structure in early nineteenth century France," in G. Grantham and C. Leonard (eds) *Agrarian Organization in the Century of Industrialization: Europe, Russia and North America*, Greenwich, CT: JAI Press, pp. 137–61.

Griffin, A.R. (1977) *The British Coal Industry: Retrospect and Prospect*, Buxton (UK): Moorland Publishing.

Guerrero, M. (1966) "The Chinese in the Philippines, 1570–1770," in A. Felix (ed.) *The Chinese in the Philippines 1570–1770*, Manila: Solidaridad Publishing.

Hajnal, J. (1965) "European marriage patterns in perspective," in D.V. Glass and D.E.C. Eversley (eds) *Population in History*, London: E. Arnold.

—— (1982) "Two kinds of preindustrial household formation system," *Population and Development Review* 8 (3): 449–94 (September).

Heidhues, M.S. (1996) "Chinese settlements in rural Southeast Asia: unwritten histories," in A. Reid (ed) *Sojourners and Settlers: Histories of Southeast Asia and the Chinese in Honor of Jennifer Cushman*, St Leonards NSW: Asian Studies Association of Australia with Allen and Unwin.

Hirschmann, A. (1970) *Exit, Voice and Loyalty*, Cambridge, MA: Harvard University Press.

Huang, P. (1985) *The Peasant Economy and Social Change in North China*, Stanford: Stanford University Press.

Iwahashi, M. (1981) *Kinsei Nihon bukkashi no kenkyū*, Tokyo: Ohara Shinseisha.

Jones, E. (1981) *The European Miracle*, Cambridge: Cambridge University Press.

Kriedte, P., Medick, H., and Schlumbohm, J. (1981) *Industrialization Before Industrialization*, Cambridge: Cambridge University Press.

Lavely, W. and Wong, R.B. (1991) "Population and resources in modern China: a comparative approach," paper presented at the Annual Meeting of the Association for Asian Studies, New Orleans.

Li Bozhong (1994a) "Ming Qing shiqi Jiangnan de mucai wenti," *Zhongguo shehui jingji shi yanjiu* 1: 86–96.

—— (1994b) "Kongzhi zengchang yi bao fuyu – Qingdai qian, zhongqi Jiangnan de renkou xingwei," *Xin shixue* 5 (3): 25–71 (September).

Li Zhongqing and Guo Songyi (1994) *Qingdai huangzu renkou xingwei de shehui huanjing*, Beijing: Peking University Press.

Lower, A.R.M. (1973) *Great Britain's Woodyard: British America and the Timber Trade, 1763–1867*, Montreal: McGill University Press.

Lu Hanchao (1992) "Arrested development: cotton and cotton markets in Shanghai, 1350–1843," *Modern China* 18 (4): 468–99 (October).

Ludwig, A.K. (1985) *Brazil: A Handbook of Historical Statistics*, Boston: G.K. Hall and Co.

Mann, S. (1992) "Household handicrafts and state policy in Qing times," in J.K. Leonard and J. Watt (eds) *To Achieve Security and Wealth: the Qing Imperial State and the Economy 1644–1911*, Ithaca, NY: Cornell University Press.

Marks, R. (1991) "Rice prices, food supply, and market structure in 18th century China," *Late Imperial China* 12 (2): 64–116 (December).

Marshall, P.J. (1980) "Western arms in maritime Asia in the early phases of expansion," *Modern Asian Studies* 14 (1): 13–28.

—— (1987) *Bengal: The British Bridgehead. Eastern India 1740–1828*, Cambridge: Cambridge University Press.

McCusker, J. and Menard, R. (1985*) The Economy of British America, 1607–1789*, Charlotte: University of North Carolina Press.

Miller, J. (1986) "Slave prices in the Portuguese Southern Atlantic, 1600–1830," in P. Lovejoy (ed.) *Africans in Bondage*, Madison: University of Wisconsin Press.

Mintz, S. (1985) *Sweetness and Power: The Place of Sugar in Modern History*, New York: Penguin.

Mitchell, B.R. (1988) *British Historical Statistics*, Cambridge: Cambridge University Press.

Mokyr, J. (1976) *Industrialization in the Low Countries, 1795–1850*, New Haven: Yale University Press.

—— (1985) "Demand and supply in the Industrial Revolution," in J. Mokyr (ed.) *The Economics of the Industrial Revolution*, Totowa, New Jersey: Rownan and Allanheld, pp. 97–118.

—— (1990) *Lever of Riches*, Oxford: Oxford University Press.

Morgan, E.S. (1975) *American Slavery, American Freedom: The Ordeal of Colonial Virginia*, New York: W.W. Norton & Co.

Morineau, M. (1985) *Incroyables Gazettes et Fabuleux Metaux*, Cambridge: Cambridge University Press.

Morris, J.H. and Williams, L.J. (1958) *The South Wales Coal Industry, 1841–1875*, Cardiff: University of Wales Press.

Ng, C.-k (1983) *Trade and Society: The Amoy Network on the China Coast, 1683–1735*, Singapore: Singapore University Press.

North, D. and Weingast, B. (1989) "Constitutions and commitment: the evolution of institutions governing public choice in seventeenth century England," *Journal of Economic History 49*: 4

O'Brien, P. (1988) "The political economy of British taxation 1660–1815," *Economic History Review* 2nd series, 41: 1.

Parker, G. (1988) *The Military Revolution: Military Innovation and the Rise of the West, 1500–1800*, Cambridge: Cambridge University Press.

Phillips, C.R. (1990) "The growth and composition of trade in the Iberian empires, 1450–1750," in J. Tracy (ed.) *The Rise of Merchant Empires*, Cambridge: Cambridge University Press.

Pomeranz, K. (1993) *The Making of a Hinterland: State, Society and Economy in Inland North China 1853–1937*, Berkeley: University of California Press.

—— (1995) "How exhausted an Earth? Some thoughts on Qing (1644–1911) environmental history," *Chinese Environmental History Newsletter* 2 (2): 7–11 (November).

—— (forthcoming) *Economy, Ecology, Comparisons, and Connections: the Industrial Revolution in Global Perspective*, Princeton, NJ: Princeton University Press.

Reid, A. (1988) *Southeast Asia in the Age of Commerce: The Lands Below the Winds*, New Haven: Yale University Press.

Richardson, D. (1987) "The slave trade, sugar, and British economic growth, 1748–1776," *Journal of Interdisciplinary History* 17 (4): 739–69 (Spring).

Riskin, C. (1975) "Surplus and stagnation in modern China," in D. Perkins (ed.) *China's Modern Economy in Historical Perspective*, Stanford: Stanford University Press.

Roberts, L. (1991) "The merchant origins of national prosperity thought in 18th century Tosa," PhD dissertation, University of Princeton, Princeton, NJ.

Rosenthal, J.-L. (1992) *The Fruits of Revolution: Property Rights, Litigation, and French Agriculture, 1700–1860*, Cambridge: Cambridge University Press.

Saito O. (1985) *Puroto-Kogyō no jidai: Seiyō to Nihon no hikakushi*, Tokyo: Nihon Hyoronsha.

Shepherd, J.Z. (1993) *Statecraft and Political Economy on the Taiwan Frontier, 1600–1800*, Stanford: Stanford University Press.

Sheperd, J.F. and Walton, G.M. (1972) *Shipping, Maritime Trade, and the Economic Development of Colonial North America*, Cambridge: Cambridge University Press.

Skinner, G.W. (1987) "Sichuan's population in the 19th century: lessons from disaggregated data," *Late Imperial China* 8: 1 (June).

Smil, V. (1985) *Carbon, Nitrogen, Sulfur*, New York: Plenum.

Steensgaard, N. (1982) "The Dutch East India Co. as an institutional innovation," in M. Aymard (ed.) *Dutch Capitalism and World Capitalism*, Cambridge: Cambridge University Press.

—— (1990) "Trade of England and the Dutch before 1750," in J. Tracy (ed.) *The Rise of Merchant Empires*, Cambridge: Cambridge University Press.

Thompson, F.M.L. (1968) "The Second Agricultural Revolution, 1815–1880," *Economic History Review* 21 (1): 62–77.

Tilly, C. (1992) *Coercion, Capital and European States, AD 990–1992*, Oxford: Basil Blackwell.

Tucker, R.P. and Richards, J.F. (1983) *Global Deforestation and the Nineteenth Century World Economy*, Durham, NC: Duke University Press.

Wallerstein, I. (1974) *Capitalist Agriculture and the Origins of the European World Economy*, New York: Academic Press.

Wang Yeh-chien (1989) "Food supply and grain prices in the Yangtze Delta in the eighteenth century," in *The Second Conference on Modern Chinese History*, Taibei: Academia Sinica.

—— (1992) "Secular trends of rice prices in the Yangzi Delta, 1638–1935," in T. Rawski and L. Li (eds) *Chinese History in Economic Perspective*, Berkeley: University of California Press.

Wills, J.E. (1994) *Mountain of Fame*, Princeton: Princeton University Press.

Wolfe, M. (1972) *The Fiscal System of Renaissance France*, New Haven: Yale University Press.

Wong, R.B. (1997) *China Transformed: Historical Change and the Limits of European Experience*, Ithaca: Cornell University Press.

Wrigley, E.A. (1988) *Continuity, Chance, and Change: The Character of the Industrial Revolution in England*, Cambridge: Cambridge University Press.

Wu Chengming (1985) *Zhongguo zibenzhuyi yu guonei shichang*, Beijing: Zhongguo shehui kexue chubanshe.

Xu Tan (1995) "Ming Qing shiqi Shandong de liangshi liutong," *Lishi dangan* 81–8.

Zelin, M. (1988) "Capital accumulation and investment strategies in early modern China: the case of the Furong salt yards," *Late Imperial China* 9 (1): 79–122 (June).

5 The economics of the Latin American state

Ideology, policy and performance c. 1820–1945

Colin M. Lewis

Three hypotheses frame this chapter. First, that in the hundred years between the 1840s and the 1940s, many Latin American states achieved the substance of sovereignty: they obtained international recognition, defined, and came to control national frontiers and exercised authority within those boundaries. Second, that state formation was conditioned by ideas and agents imported from overseas and that Latin American "state-builders" of the period saw no conflict between this and constructing "national" sovereignty. Third, that if elsewhere states were "made" by capitalists, in Latin America states created business. For much of the period Latin American decision-takers regarded the continent as part of the Western, capitalist world. Furthermore, there was little echo of a desire for distance from Europe, a sentiment that shaped US views of international relations and played a powerful role in domestic politics. The promulgation of the Monroe Doctrine by the USA in the 1820s excited little attention. Bolivian attempts to foster *americanismo* either ignored or were designed to marginalize the USA while trying to engage British and French attention.

The struggles for independence at the beginning of the nineteenth century weakened (and in the case of Spanish America virtually destroyed) existing systems of governance. The immediate consequences of the end of empire was state shrinkage and administrative weakness. With only a few exceptions, economic dislocation, incipient social revolution and intra-elite rivalry coupled with a loss of bureaucratic competence seriously weakened – if it did not destroy – the capacity of emergent states to govern. The reach of independent states was constrained by a loss of the monopoly of violence, foreign intervention, and a retreat into subsistence. Almost everywhere sovereignty was shared or surrendered as regional strongmen (*caciques* or *caudillos*), who often emerged from the irregular military forces of the independence period, exempted themselves and their provinces from the writ of newly established "nation-states." As governments in Mexico City, Rio de Janeiro, Buenos Aires, Bogotá, Caracas, and Lima sought recognition in London, Paris, Madrid, and Washington, national sovereignty was challenged by up-country interests and neighboring regimes.

Yet by the middle of the twentieth century, the symbols of statehood and sovereignty appeared to be respected and effective. With very few exceptions, by the 1940s the central state (and the central bureaucracy) was much stronger than its regional counterparts. Economic and political decision-making had become centralized and national governments appeared secure from internal challenge. Arguably, some of the most novel – and most effective – features of state sovereignty were to be found in the economy and the field of economic policy-making. New banking institutions, commodity boards, and regulatory agencies seemed to be firmly under bureaucratic control, rather then in the hands of producers or financiers (the coffee growers association, FEDCAFE, in Colombia was a notable exception). Domestic and foreign business apparently acquiesced to a larger role of the state as manager and producer – and sometimes as a competitor. Even in the oil sector, the nation-state was successfully flexing its muscles having expropriated foreign-owned petroleum companies in Mexico, established a state monopoly of exploration and exploitation in the Argentine and attempted to promote a national oil company in Brazil (Wirth 1985). The 1930s and 1940s also witnessed a larger government role in the provision of energy and transport services and, in some countries, attempts to establish (or modernize) heavy industries. By the 1940s, foreign intervention also appeared to be a figment of the distant past, save for circum-Caribbean statelets.

This transformation was brought about by effective insertion into the international system and by conscious attempts to promote economic activity. From the late nineteenth century until the 1960s or 1970s, Latin American states attempted to "embed enterprise." In the latter part of the nineteenth and early twentieth centuries this was done through external economic opening and pragmatic intervention in domestic markets. After the 1930s, and more especially the 1940s, government intervention became more explicit and the state sector increased in size while the economy was progressively (but only partially) de-linked from the global system. Nevertheless, the quest to foster business was sustained throughout this period, even if the policy rhetoric became more nationalistic and more statist after the 1930s.

The contrasts between the welfarism and developmentalism of post-1930s populist regimes and their predecessors are obvious but may be exaggerated. Latin American states in the third quarter of the nineteenth century supported business. State consolidation through international insertion had generated opportunities for local agents. Indeed, the exports that yielded fiscal resources that underwrote institutional consolidation signaled the valorized local assets. Railway building and to a lesser extent the proliferation of banks sustained capitalists (local and immigrant), not least by providing low-priced services, the costs of which were often socialized. In addition, while pursuing classical liberal functions of removing mercantilist barriers to individual initiative by abolishing "colonial corporations" (*fueros*), the nineteenth-century state managed a massive transfer of factors to the private sector. The attack on corporate and collective landholding and military campaigns against nomadic Indians produced windfall gains of land and labor for private capitalists who now benefited from greater security. The "liberation" of domestic factors was complemented in some areas by subsidized imports of capital and labor. The main beneficiaries were sometimes local capitalists, on other occasions immigrants, and yet others foreign enterprises. Nevertheless, the objective was to create "business," the assumption being domestic (or settler) enterprise. Positivism, "order and progress," was designed to create an indigenous entrepreneuriat while not seeking to exclude foreign agents.

For Latin America, the struggles for independence had been only the first step toward sovereignty. The principal issue was how to make that sovereignty effective – how to establish distinct, national institutions and to construct new states from the chaos of the collapse of Iberian empire. Contemporaries sought the answer in the construction of institutions and organizations modeled on those of the North Atlantic world, secured on growth fostered by applying theories of economic internationalism. This chapter will assess the extent to which these objectives were realized. It will examine the political economy of state construction and the mechanisms of growth. The first section identifies the main events shaping institution formation in the immediate post-independence decades. This is followed by an examination of the economic programs of the oligarchic state and of the emergent populist state that displaced it: tensions generated by these processes will also be identified. The final section assesses the consequences for state structures of integration into the world economy and relates these to issues of globalization and sovereignty.

Imperial collapse and state-building

Several factors influenced state formation in Latin America during the half-century following independence from Spain and Portugal in the 1820s. One involved the creation of "national institutions," a process conditioned (especially in Spanish America) by the near total destruction of existing administrative arrangements. Arguably, the only "colonial" organizations to survive were the landed estate and the Roman Catholic Church, though in most regions the influence of the Church was weakened by the destruction of property, loss of personnel, and ultimately, by a rising tide of anti-clericalism. Across the continent, the destruction of imperial authority – viceregal government, intendancies, systems of justice, commercial organizations and loyalist armed forces – coupled with the expulsion of Spanish bureaucrats and merchants and the flight of capital – created a power vacuum that was only filled with difficulty. Brazil accomplished the transition from colony to independent empire (and, in 1889, republic) with less difficulty. A short, but far from bloodless, encounter between nationalist forces and residual Portuguese authority facilitated the continuity of "colonial" institutions – monarchy, plantation, and slavery – with little crisis of legitimacy. However, even in Brazil, the struggle for independence assumed elements of civil war rather than a clear-cut conflict between American patriots and metropolitan authority. The principal difference with Spanish America, besides the intensity of the revolutionary wars, was the duration of the conflict which, in some regions, lasted from the 1800s to the 1820s. Hence, in several Spanish American republics independence proved more economically damaging, provoked greater social conflict and made the task of institution-building more problematic. In another respect, independence for

Latin America carried a high price tag. Unlike the USA, which enjoyed substantial material and financial aid from Spain and France during the conflict with Great Britain, Latin America had to cover the costs of independence from domestic sources and foreign borrowing, a burden that destabilized state finances for several decades – and invited foreign intervention (Marichal 1989).

Ideologies imported from abroad were another factor influencing state-building. By the end of the eighteenth century, and despite concerted attempts to discourage the circulation of sedition, new political ideas associated with the Enlightenment, the War of American Independence, and the French Revolution were circulating in Latin America. The dissemination of these ideas was fostered by closer inter-American commercial relations when communications with Europe were disrupted by the French Revolutionary and Napoleonic wars and as ports were opened to friendly commerce, in contravention of colonial commercial restrictions, by loyalist and insurgent administrations strapped for cash (Liss 1983). Everywhere, commercial contacts multiplied in the 1810s and 1820s. Foreign, particularly British and US, merchants displaced their Spanish and Portuguese counterparts in the principal ports and were also, occasionally, to be found in up-country retailing. By the beginning of the nineteenth century the writings of Adam Smith, Jeremy Bentham, and Tom Paine had been translated into Spanish and Portuguese and were circulating amongst the creole elite.

Unsurprisingly, the political debate in Latin American was influenced by the "models" of an independent USA and republican France just as the economic debate was shaped by the flood of cheap, largely British, imports and news about US expansion. In the face of the weakness and intransigence of the government in Madrid, concepts of independence, constitutionalism, and republicanism rapidly gained ground in Spanish-speaking regions as groups committed to the imperial connection or the establishment of constitutional monarchy were outmaneuvered (or routed) by more radical nationalists. Gradually, free-trade ideals also came to the fore, even in those republics like Mexico, where there were entrenched vested interests favoring protection (Potash 1983; Thomson 1989). While, in theory, protectionist measures may have been in force from time to time, exemptions, the suspension of regulations prohibiting imports, as well as smuggling, ensured that much of coastal Latin America was in effect a "free-trade zone" integrated into the "global economy" of the period. And, almost everywhere, newly installed governments viewed taxing foreign trade as a convenient device to raise revenue. Consequently, by the middle of the nineteenth century most republics were open to the world economy.

For some, "free trade" was representative of a larger commitment to economic liberalism. This is an oversimplification. While concepts of economic liberalism may have become dominant by the 1880s, in several countries protectionist (or mercantilist) forces fought a determined – and often successful – rearguard action (Nicolau 1975; Ospina Vásquez 1955; Potash 1983; Thomson 1989). And, as will be indicated below, interventionism was an enduring tradition. Nevertheless, freer trade with the rest of the world was one of the most immediate features of the end of Iberian empire in Latin America. This was part pragmatic and part ideological. Some of the more radical proponents of independence asserted that policies of *laissez faire* and *laissez passer* were the way forward. As their twentieth-century counterparts would re-state, nineteenth-century liberal political economists argued that there was no alternative to international insertion. Others simply saw enlarged prospects for exports through direct trade with the world economy. For yet other dominant groups, economic liberalism justified the abandonment of mercantilist regulation and taxation.

The immediacy of trade expansion in the 1810s and, to a lesser extent in the 1820s, masked limits to Latin American commercial participation in the global economy. Windfall commercial and financial opportunities at this point and the euphoric rhetoric of independence also disguised difficulties of institution-building. The rapid creation of nation-states was confounded by several problems. As implied above, in large parts of Spanish America, the scale of insti-tutional collapse served not as a *tabula rasa* on which a new order could be readily inscribed but, given the violent and protracted nature of the revolutionary strug-gles, intensified barriers to establishing new legitimate institutions. In part this was also due to the internecine and inter-ethnic nature of the wars of indepen-dence. Perhaps, too, the problem was due to the incomplete nature of the "revolution."

By the 1850s, and notwithstanding frequent insurgent recourse to the language of the French Revolution, it was clear that independence had resulted in little more than the substitution of one segment of the dominant (White) elite by another. In those societies with large Indian and *mestizo* populations, intra-elite conflict during and after the independence period always carried with it the threat of ethnic revolution from below (Anna 1978; Bonilla 1991; Lynch 1986). Hence, to describe the immediate post-independence period as one of building new institutions may be to dignify crude attempts by an alarmed White elite to reestablish the late-colonial social pecking order beneath a veneer of progress through a cosmetic and selective absorption of individual Blacks, Indians, and *mestizos* who had played a prominent role in revolutionary wars and by the removal of petty legal discrimination based on race (Halperín Donghi 1973). Murilo de Carvalho (1974) argues that a shared educational experience (sons of upper sections of the Brazilian oligarchy were educated at the University of Coimbra, Portugal, and later at the law schools of Pernambuco and São Paulo) and service in the imperial administration forged cohesion and a sense of "national project." This experience and training also condition in the governing class a view of the primacy of the state and, possibly, of the central state standing above – and arbitrating between – sectional interests (Pang 1988; Uricoechea 1980). It is equally likely that the existence of slavery – coupled with the example of slave revolt in Haiti at the beginning of the century – proved an effective social cement, limiting intra-elite factionalism at least until the 1870s.

Geography and economic crisis also inhibited the process of reestablishing order and reforging elite unity in Spanish America. Hence, while the political integrity of Portuguese America held, all the large Spanish viceregal administrative units splintered into states based loosely on colonial sub-divisions. With the rejection of Spanish authority, the tyranny of distance (coupled with regional rivalry dating from the colonial period) in part explains the Balkanization of Spanish America. Reduced economic resources also limited the ability of administrations which aspired to sustain the integrity of larger colonial units to do so (Halperin Donghi 1973; Lynch 1981). Economic contraction – and the conflict over resources that this often occasioned – fostered political disintegration. This was particularly the case in those colonies where the production of precious metals had served as an engine of growth and/or generated subsidies to finance defense and administrative costs. As the case of Mexico and, to a lesser extent, Upper (Bolivia) and Lower Peru demonstrated during the independence and early national periods, the mining sector was particularly susceptible to political instability. The mines depended on effective administrations to guarantee a flow of essential inputs – capital, labor and supplies – in order to maintain the infrastructure of production. Given the prevailing technology, plundered or abandoned mines proved virtually impossible to bring back into production once flooded or when labor supplies could not be guaranteed (Rippy 1959; Fisher 1977). As economic resources dwindled, politics rapidly became a zero sum game (Anna 1978; Stevens 1991). The result was a dangerous cocktail of social demands from below and intra-elite rivalry. Agricultural activities, even plantation economies dependent on slavery, proved more resilient than mining. Here the problem of regeneration was associated with the operation of the world market – the buoyancy of international demand and the threat of foreign competition.

The history of state-formation in the half-century following independence demonstrates that institution building proved most problematic in those areas where the revolutionary wars lasted longest (for example, northern South America and the River Plate region), where there were large indigenous populations (such as the Andes and Mexico) and where silver mining had been an important element in the colonial economy. In Brazil, where the struggle for independence was short and occurred "late," and in Chile, where military conflict was particularly short-lived, national administrations were fairly rapidly and successfully established. National consolidation was also sustained by economic growth. Although the relatively smooth nature of the transition from colony to co-Kingdom, when Rio de Janeiro became the capital of the Portuguese world, and independent empire should not be exaggerated, the early development of coffee exports, which rapidly outperformed the "colonial" staple, sugar, generated new opportunities and resources. Chile benefited from its strategic location as a West Coast entrepôt, producing and shipping grain to neighboring republics (and, after the 1840s, to California) and copper to mainland Asia and Great Britain (Bauer 1975; Véliz 1961).

This raised the question of whether domestic institutional order conditioned the ability to seize economic opportunities resulting from international economic growth or whether external commercial openings – and the resulting increase in resources – fostered regime consolidation. Many of those who promoted independence assumed that it was the former. The reality, however, may have been different, namely that it was the growth of the international economy after the 1840s that ultimately fostered domestic institutional consolidation and state modernization. Those societies most able to realize a flow of exports – particularly "new" commodities such as wool, wheat, non-precious metals and coffee – were amongst the first to enjoy domestic sovereignty and, possibly, pre-empt or reverse the process of territorial disintegration.

The political economy of the oligarchic state

In an early work Frank (1967) argues that Latin America was thoroughly incorporated into the modern capitalist economy by the sixteenth century. Few would now accept that assertion (Abel and Lewis 1993; Bushnell and Macaulay 1994). Latin America's integration into the world system – essentially the North Atlantic economy – was regionally and commodity-specific until the late nineteenth century. Only after the 1870s were all Latin American countries thoroughly integrated into the global economy. At this point domestic linkage effects proliferated as the size of the foreign trade sector expanded in both absolute and relative terms. The outward movement of the frontier of export production pressed upon subsistence: national economies were slowly integrated and monetised.

Applying the modern usage of the term, it can be safely stated that, with few exceptions, nation-states hardly existed in Latin America in 1850. Boundaries were ill-defined, administrative units separated from each other by distance rather than precisely demarcated frontiers. Few in the continent would have understood the concept of nationality – political rights were narrowly circumscribed, slaves were not citizens and, in many regions, Indian communities still existed as societies apart, subject to distinct legal and fiscal arrangements. For most people living in Latin America at mid-century, the landed estate, rather than the nation-state, constituted the "political universe." Linguistic and ethnic divisions, as well as the form of economic activity, isolated groups from one and another. By 1900 this had changed. The incidence of domestic political instability declined during the third quarter of the nineteenth century and there was greater security of international frontiers. Everywhere symbols of national sovereignty proliferated. Constitutions were enacted, legal codes passed into law, national armies created (substituting for provincial militias or irregular forces commanded by rural strongmen), national postal and telegraphic services were set up and national currencies were issued. There were, too, attempts to inaugurate national systems of primary education and, in some capital cities, newspapers began to aspire to a national status if not a to national circulation.

It was at this point that the struggle to conform Latin American political and economic norms to perceived practice in the North Atlantic world began to bear fruit, in contrast to failed attempts at modernization in the River Plate (Bagu 1966; Burgin 1946; Bushnell 1983; Lynch 1981) and further north (Gootenberg 1989; Lofstrom 1972; Safford 1976; Stevens 1991) in the 1820s and 1840s. The emergence of greater opportunities for Latin America in the world economy was illustrated by the buoyancy of primary product prices throughout the middle third of the nineteenth century (Foreman-Peck 1995; W.A. Lewis 1978). Some countries, like the Argentine were even able to skew the terms of trade in their favor beyond the turn of the century by diversifying export schedules. Export growth valorized local assets and generated additional resources, notably for the central state or groups strategically placed to capture a disproportionate share of additional resource flows. Arguably the most critical economic organizations in late-nineteenth-century Latin America were railways and banks, sectors where the national state assumed an increasingly important role either as promoter or operator or both (Coatsworth 1981; Kirsch 1977; C.M. Lewis 1983; Tede and Marichal 1994; Topik 1987). This implied greater state access to resources.

The Argentine and Peru were among the first countries to experience an export boom between the 1840s and 1880s involving "new" commodities – wool and guano, respectively (Chiaramonte 1971; Hunt 1973; Mathew 1977). Notwithstanding the controversy surrounding the international economics and politics of the guano age, it is undeniable that income for guano (which was a state monopoly) underwrote the modernization of various aspects of Peruvian economy and society. The abolition of slavery (with compensation) and the final demise of Indian tribute, long-held aspirations, was made possible by this new-found source of government income (Blanchard 1991; Gootenberg 1989; Hunt 1973). Despite massive waste, some guano revenue also found its way into public works projects and indirectly financed the modernization of sugar production and possibly sections of manufacturing (Hunt 1973; Mathew 1977; Thorp and Bertram 1978). In the Argentine, wool production similarly triggered social change, drawing immigrants, changing patterns of land ownership (in the north and east of the province of Buenos Aires), and dramatically increasing the value and vitality of exports (Chiaramonte 1971; Sabato 1990). In Brazil, coffee first shifted the economic center of gravity of the country from the northeast to the center – Rio de Janeiro, and subsequently to the center-south – Sao Paulo (Furtado 1963; Suzigan 1986).

The production of new commodities and the diversification of export schedules either promoted regime consolidation or, by modifying existing regional power relations, regime change. Either way, the net result was regime modernization. Much, of course, depended on the sectors to whom these new resources accrued and how they were spent. Nevertheless, it is instructive that in cases as distinct as the Peruvian and the Argentinian ones, the export of new commodities generated a massive increase in state resources and investment in infrastructure. Taking British investment data as a proxy for larger changes, between 1865 and 1887 the nominal value of Peruvian bonds placed on the London money market increased nine-fold: the British holding of Argentinian public bond increased by a slightly smaller factor. During the same period direct British investment in railways in Peru increased more than twelve-fold and in the Argentine by a factor of 10 (Edelstein 1982; Rippy 1959). (It should be remembered that a proportion of portfolio debt was also applied to railway building.) As well as promoting domestic market integration and export production, improved internal communications strengthened the hand of central government (Abel and Lewis 1993; Coatsworth 1981). Along with the Remington rifle, the railway and the telegraph became symbols of "progress" and "order."

With export expansion came imports and the prospect of enhancing state revenue. The immediate post-independence period witnessed a narrowing of the fiscal base in most countries. This was partly due to nationalist and partly to ideological considerations. Proponents of independence had protested against the burden of colonial taxation and fiscal transfers to Iberia. Spanish imperial administration had been financed by a multiplicity of indirect taxes on consumption (the *alcabala*), licenses (*patentes*) required to practice a profession or trade, state monopolies (*estanco*) and the sale of offices, as well as direct taxes, principally on silver production and, less significantly, land dues and Indian tribute. Imports and exports were also taxed. Many consumption taxes were abandoned at the time of independence and the scaling down of direct imposts by newly politically empowered elites unwilling to tax themselves was justified by reference to the need for liberal reform. Namely that fiscal changes would promote activity as they would allow producers to retain – and invest – a larger share of income generated from market production. Imports, financed by export earnings, appeared to promise a secure source of revenue and one, moreover, that could be mortgaged to underwrite foreign borrowing. If the growth in the foreign trade sector did not broaden the fiscal base, at least it deepened the purse into which a government could dip.

Inflows of foreign funds reduced the cost of state borrowing and may have weaned some administrations away from dependence on inflation as a means of financing the state (Marichal 1989). External borrowing, however, was not cost-less. It carried implications for domestic monetary policy and the threat – and sometimes the reality – of supervision by foreign banks as regimes in Buenos Aires, Lima, Rio de Janeiro, and beyond discovered in the 1890s, and even earlier (Fritsch 1988; Franco 1983; Marichal 1989). By the end of the nineteenth century, most Latin American governments were as concerned about overseas credit rating as their late twentieth-century and business counterparts.

It is, therefore, no coincidence that around the third quarter of the nineteenth century there were further efforts at institutional reform in many parts of the continent. Perhaps the most notable were attempts to impose capitalist norms on land and labor "markets." Overtly driven by liberal precepts of property, mechanisms such as the *Lei da terra* (1850) in Brazil and the *Ley Lerdo* (1856) in Mexico, were designed respectively to promote freehold and prohibit corporate/collective land-holding. The result was a massive transfers of assets into private hands, usually existing *latifundistas*. In the Argentine and Chile, the so-called "desert campaign" against nomadic Indians had a similar effect. Despite the liberal rhetoric, land-holding became increasingly less "democratic" between the 1860s and 1880s as one-off disposals resulting from the alienation of formerly communally held and ecclesiastical property and the seizure of fertile frontier zones from nomadic populations were commandeered by agro-export elites through the application of market and non-market mechanisms. By the beginning of the twentieth century, patterns of land ownership were particularly inequitable in Mexico, Central America and the Andes.

Legislation relating to "labor" was more piecemeal, often subject to repeated revision, though no less controversial in its impact. In plantation economies such as Cuba and Brazil, the massive surge in export production undoubtedly strengthened archaic institutions such a slavery. Yet even in these cases there were subtle changes in labor relations. The trans-Atlantic slave trade came to an end in the 1850s – around the time that the institution effectively died elsewhere in Latin America – and from the 1860s to the late 1880s (when slavery was finally abolished), immigration, the freeing of different categories of slaves, the use of Asian contract labor (in Cuba) and the recruitment of domestic non-slave labor made for greater complexity in labor markets in the dynamic coffee economy of Sao Paulo and the sugar sector in Cuba (Lamounier 1993; Moreno Fraginals 1984). During the last decades before abolition, and despite the concentration of slaves on *paulista* coffee *fazendas* and Cuban sugar estates, the majority of rural workers were technically free. Arguably, planter attitudes to workers (whether slave or free) did not necessarily change as dramatically. Did the Slave Code gradually evolve into a "Labor Code"? Similar controversy surrounds other mechanisms – debt peonage, share-cropping, and contract labor (*enganche*). Were these devices the means of extending slavery or did they constitute a phased transition to a "free" labor market? Relatively new research tends to challenge earlier negative constructions placed on these mechanisms and depicts them as contributing to the emergence of wage-labor (Bauer 1975; Gonzalez 1985; Katz 1977).

Mass immigration effected a more obvious and a more thoroughgoing change in the labor market and in labor relations. Between the mid-nineteenth and the mid-twentieth centuries, the Argentine received over 7.4 million immigrants and Brazil something less than 5 million (Sánchez Albornoz 1974). They were, respectively, the second and third most favored destinations of European emigrants after the USA. Other countries, notably Uruguay and Cuba, also received substantial numbers of immigrants. European immigrants also settled temperate regions of Chile, Colombia, and, to a lesser degree, Mexico. Indeed, virtually every country attracted immigrants but mass intercontinental free migration flowed overwhelmingly to the grasslands of southern South America. Immigration of this order had a significant demographic, social, and political impact. Between 1869 and 1914, net immigration accounted for almost one half of total population growth in the Argentine. Yet, while almost 70 per cent of all immigrants entering Brazil remained there, only a little over 50 per cent did so in the Argentinian case. This was undoubtedly due to the nature of immigrants. For several decades Brazil offered assisted passages to immigrant families (Holloway 1980). Assisted places were only available to emigrants to the Argentine for a very limited period in the late 1880s and by this time the entry of single, seasonal male workers represented a large proportion of gross immigration to the River Plate. Again, controversy surrounds the long-term impact of mass immigration. Did subsidized and contract labor depress wages or did subsidies represent a "savings" advance to would-be settlers?

Perhaps monetary reform was the other area where institutional change was most obvious. The early monetary history of independent Latin American countries was one of inflation and turmoil. The cost and method of funding revolutionary and post-independence conflict, coupled with a decline in silver production, undermined the currency. Additional pressure was placed upon money supply and the exchange by the adverse balance of trade: bullion and coins drained abroad. Export earnings and foreign investment facilitated greater monetary stability towards the end of the century. National coinage was both a symbol of sovereignty and a devise to advertise the paramountcy of the national state. But the route to monetary order – particularly the Gold Standard – was painful, not least for those regimes incorrigibly wedded to the "developmentalism" of unbacked paper currencies or mining regions that favored silver as a "national" metal – and there were limits to the quest for virtue. The benefits had to be seen to outweigh the costs and critics of the Gold Standard sustained a vociferous opposition from the sidelines, always ready with an alternative project should the price of fiscal discipline provoke generalized discontent (Fritsch 1988; Goldsmith 1986; Kirsch 1977; Marichal 1989).

By this stage, effective international insertion was reflected in other explicit commitments to the ethos of liberalism (Bushnell 1983; Bushnell and Macaulay 1994; Cardoso and Helwege 1992). Oligarchic liberal constitutionalism – though hardly democracy – was formally practiced in many countries. Mercantilist, colonial institutions – slavery, commercial monopoly, corporate privilege, Indian communalism and ethnic apartness – had virtually disappeared. And everywhere the language of economic policy was the language of economic liberalism. Yet, as Topik (1987) has shown, there was equally some distance between theory and rhetoric, on the one hand, and practice on the other. Economic liberalism was tempered with pragmatism and subject to sectionalist special pleading. Was this economic realism, a mercantilist hangover or a response to Listian and Hamiltonian ideas? After the 1880s in Brazil, Chile, and Mexico, domestic industrialists could count on a significant degree of protection even if the tariff was still primarily regarded as a fiscal device (Haber 1989; Kirsch 1977; Suzigan 1986; Topik 1987). Duties were becoming increasingly discriminatory and manufacturers also benefited from movements in the exchange. Less consistent tariff protection was also available to manufacturers in Peru and Colombia (Ospina Vásquez 1955; Thorp and Bertram 1978). Unsurprisingly, the ability of industrialists to influence what might be described as macroeconomic policy depended on their connections with the dominant export oligarchy and a capacity to press conjunctural or strategic advantage – governments were invariably more responsive to the clamor for protection when short of cash. "Emergency" tariff hikes were rarely rescinded when fiscal crises passed but the incidence of protection could be eroded by currency depreciation or import price falls (Kirsch 1977; Haber 1989; Suzigan 1986). In addition, politically influential sectors, like hard-pressed Argentinian and Brazilian sugar producers, could always rely on special assistance.

Nevertheless, the most audacious and successful producer-support scheme launched in Latin America during the period of oligarchic liberalism was undoubtedly the project devised in Sao Paulo to reverse the decline in coffee prices in international markets (Fritsch 1988; Topik 1987). Coffee valorization nicely illustrates a number of points. First, it signals the willingness of governments to intervene in the market when vital sectional or important national interests were threatened – the attachment to economic liberalism was pragmatic rather than dogmatic (Love and Jacobson 1988). Second, it reveals the bureaucratic competence of the state – an administration that considered itself sufficiently empowered to act and was prepared to do so in the face of not inconsiderable external opposition (Fritsch 1988; Topik 1987). Third, it confirms an awareness of the possibility of structural change in world markets. Where *paulista fazendeiros* led, others wished to follow. By the 1920s Argentinian wheat producers were clamoring for – and obtained – *ad hoc* price support. During the 1930s systematic programs of producer aid would be put in place in most countries, covering commodities destined for domestic and world markets.

Between the oligarchic and the populist state

In a number of countries, the oligarchic state was under pressure by the early decades of the twentieth century. Were demands for change triggered by precisely the sort of societal modernization associated with the production of linkage-rich "democratic" commodities identified in the River Plate republics by Furtado (1977)? Or was the re-ordering of political institutions a reaction to those demands? Alternately, did increased external-sector volatility undermine political arrangements created or sustained for so long by resource flows resulting from an early insertion into the world economy? Undeniably, the international economy was changing. Commodity prices were softening, the rate of growth of the volume of exports was slowing and capital flows becoming more erratic (Albert 1989; Cardoso and Helwege 1992; Sheaham 1987).

Even without the First World War, price instability, changes in global polarity and new institutional and ideological developments within the continent would have led to demands for greater economic and political accommodation in societies that were quite different in size and complexity from those that had existed in the mid-nineteenth century or even 1900. If many Latin American countries might have been depicted as largely subsistence economies and as societies of castes in the 1840s, by the 1920s everywhere the money economy was paramount, economic opportunities were more diverse, and society was obviously structured along class lines. And, in the Southern Cone, approximately half the population lived in towns. The old order collapsed first, and most obviously, in Mexico in 1910–11. That said, nowhere else in Latin America was there a social upheaval of a similar magnitude. The overthrow of the Porfirian system has been variously explained by regime sclerosis, bureaucratic inertia and miscalculation in the face of mounting opposition, the consolidation of a counter-elite and multiclass nationalism. There was, too, peasant land hunger, social discontent, and poverty triggered by decades of increasing inequity compounded by the cost of adjustment policies associated with the move onto the Gold Standard (Knight 1986). Other regimes confronted similar difficulties but there were differences of degree and no other government encountered organized opposition in the countryside to the same extent as the *porfiriato* in the late 1900s.

Arguably, the most potent forces working for change in many countries were nationalism and demands emanating for the largely urban middle classes for greater access to power. The latter was especially pronounced in the Southern Cone and was most precisely epitomized by the administration of Batlle Ordóñez in Uruguay, the Radical ascendancy in the Argentine and the Alessandri presidencies in Chile (Finch 1981; Kirsch 1977; Mamalakis 1976; Rock 1989). Perhaps because they were articulated earlier, these demands seemed to have been most easily accommodated in Uruguay. In the Argentine and Chile, export sector crisis made for messier political adjustments. Taking participation in the electoral process as a proxy for an extension of political citizenship and political rights, there was in these countries a substantial increase in those voting in presidential elections. In Chile the numbers voting in presidential elections doubled during the interwar decades, a period of relatively modest population growth. In Mexico the numbers of voters increased exponentially: 20,000 voted in the 1910 presidential election, more than two and a quarter million in 1934.

Nationalism, though not necessarily xenophobia and autarchy, became an increasingly potent force throughout Latin America in the interwar decades, associated in some countries with *indigenismo* and *hispanidad*. Nationalism heightened concerns about sovereignty, yielding more nuanced attitudes to foreign interests (notably foreign banks, insurance firms, and utility companies) operating in Latin America and challenged previous concepts about the role of the state. Nationalism also served as a cement for proto-populist alliances in some countries and assumed a more overtly anti-liberal and anti-internationalist tone by the 1930s. This tendency was not peculiar to Latin America (Love and Jacobson 1988). Nationalist and developmentalist regimes of the 1930s were framed by economic dislocation provoked by the First World War and, more especially, by the interwar depression and were influenced by criticism of the economics and politics of export-led growth voiced earlier by commentators like Bunge and Encina and by radical thinkers such as Mariátegui and Prado (Abel and Lewis 1993). These ideas were seized upon by sectors such as the military, bureaucrats and industrialists as well as nationalists who argued for a more pro-active role by government to ensure greater local consumption of commodities for which overseas demand had contracted, domestic production of items that could no longer be imported, and possibly, the application of *ad hoc* welfare measures to preempt further social discontent. All of this involved a greater role for the state – in factor markets, as a producer and as a regulator. During the interwar period, central banks were created (or existing agencies transformed into central banks) in all the major and middle-sized economies. Other financial institutions – credit agencies, reinsurance corporations and commercial banks – also proliferated. In the 1930s exchange control became the norm, commodity boards multiplied, and overseas trade and financial transactions were highly regulated (Bulmer-Thomas 1994; Cardoso and Helwege 1992; Sheaham 1987; Thorp 1984).

Policy debates and institutional developments of this period had an influence on post-Second World War strategies of import-substituting industrialization. The relatively speedy recovery of most Latin American economies from the worst effects of the depression by the early-mid 1930s similarly influenced later thinking by creating the impression of bureaucratic competence and macroeconomic management efficiency. Yet it would be a mistake to project back into this period expectations and programs of the post-Second World War decades. During the 1930s economic policy was piecemeal and directed toward export substitution – "economic internalization" – rather than industrialization *per se*. Indeed, increased domestic industrial production was an important element in this process but it was a part rather than the whole. Moreover, particularly in the early 1930s, Latin American policy-makers were by no means convinced that overseas demand for exports would not recover nor foreign capital markets not re-open. Hence, the predominance of orthodoxy in many spheres of domestic economic policy, attempts to service the foreign debt, and efforts to protect exporters, especially during the early part of the decade. How could it be otherwise when export interests remained politically powerful and fiscal resources were overwhelmingly derived from taxing overseas trade and borrowing. Only after 1936 did economic policies become more adventurous and unorthodox – and displayed a willingness to take advantage of great power rivalry (Abel and Lewis 1993; Bulmer-Thomas 1994; Weaver 1980).

Many contemporaries viewed these developments as signaling a heightened degree of domestic sovereignty, particularly "economic" sovereignty, and greater state competence. If the oligarchic state had been exercised by internal challenges to sovereignty emanating from recalcitrant provinces, the populist state was more concerned about class relations. Hence, the emphasis upon diffusing social "representation" within the state (Malloy 1979; Sikkink 1991). Paradoxically, and running counter to contemporary assumption, increased internal sovereignty may have been countered by a decline in "external" sovereignty. Volatility in world commodity and financial markets and attempts by foreign business interests, aided by their governments, to defend assets in Latin America in the face of nationalist demands, economic contraction, and increased international rivalry posed problems for a number of regimes. Responses to these challenges varied across the continent. Three categories of states may be identified. First, those that adopted a Gerschenkronian stance, employing "ideology" or "national project" in order to upgrade state competence and in so doing came to project an image of efficacious management of domestic and external relations (Gerschenkron 1965). Second, regimes that, due to a perceived lack of need (or an inability to do more), instituted only limited modifications to the *status quo*. Finally, states that surrendered a substantial degree of sovereignty in order to survive in the colder climate of global recession and rising internal and international tensions.

Countries such as Brazil, Chile, and Mexico were representative of the first group. In Chile and Brazil, a national project based upon industrial growth and regional economic regeneration gave the central state enhanced domestic sovereignty and, apparently, greater competence in the management of relations with other states (Abel and Lewis 1993; Hilton 1975; Weaver 1980). In the Mexican case, these objectives were subsumed in the "ideology" – and the iconography – of the Revolution (Knight 1986). Internal economic regeneration from the destructive phase of the Revolution and the impact of the interwar Depression culminated in the radicalism of the Cardenas *sexénio* that witnessed massive state action in the rural and urban sectors. In all three countries – though to a much greater degree in Mexico – domestic sovereignty appeared to have slipped in the 1920s. National and regional politics had become more violent in Brazil and Chile during the decade as challenges to the central administration proliferated. This instability was not unconnected with weakness in key export sectors. Possibly this made the task of reestablishing central authority more urgent and, ultimately, more successful. It is instructive that, although starting from very different positions, the central state in Brazil, Chile, and Mexico became highly interventionist. Welfare programs – education reforms, an extension in social insurance provision and labor legislation – was stressed in all three. Mexico and Chile were the first in Latin America to establish official organizations that would become national development agencies, namely, Nacional Financiera (NAFINSA) and CORFO, respectively. There was, too, a proliferation of price support or state buying agencies for a range of domestic and export staples, all firmly under the control of the central government and, in Brazil and Mexico, exhibiting distinctly corporatist tendencies, often entailing the "representation" of workers and employers, producers and consumers, and the state. Government intervention in the commercialization of commodities displaced private, often foreign, agents. Greater state action in the banking sector also facilitated more adventurous monetary, exchange and external debt-management strategies. Hence, these governments were depicted a "recapturing" control over monetary policy and adopting a nationalist stance in negotiations with foreign financial interests. Did this projection of national objectives into the management of international economic relations signal an attempt to influence activities outside national territory?

The Argentine and Colombia best typify the second group of countries. Here, despite similar developments in the banking sector and commodity marketing, there was less "ideology" and less "project." In the 1930s, the commitment to economic liberalism and the prevailing pattern of economic activities was more entrenched or, possibly, less challenged. There may have been less pressure for a radical redefinition of the reach of the state. Perhaps domestic politics was too riven – or rival blocs too evenly balanced – to permit the emergence of an opening for change. This may be the lesson of the upsurge in political violence in Colombia in the 1940s and the rupture in Argentinian politics represented by Peronism in 1946 (Palacios 1980; Rock 1989). The third group of states is probably best represented by Nicaragua and Cuba. These states might have acquired international recognition by the twentieth century and a degree of domestic sovereignty but they had hardly secured the exclusion of external authority. Now, in the interwar period, elements of sovereignty were ceded (or re-ceded) to US pro-consular officials and/or business as overt external assistance was vital to sustain the state and reorganize authority within the national territory (Dominguez 1978; Dunkerley 1988; Perez 1988).

Conclusion

In the second half of the nineteenth century, Latin American regimes saw little conflict between the requirements of state-building and insertion into a rapidly expanding global economy. On the contrary, the latter objective was regarded as a means of securing the former. Neither process, however, was painless nor unchallenged though the critics of openness to the world economy tended to multiply when the international system was less dynamic and when the domestic political game itself became more complex.

Effective integration into the global system transformed Latin America, promoting institutional change on several fronts. Some of these were anticipated and welcomed or relatively easily accommodated, other were not. For example, foreign immigrants were embraced as workers, settlers, and as vectors of social and ethnic "modernization" but not when they introduced ideologies and practices that challenged existing organizations or when their consumption patterns and desire to remit funds threatened the external accounts (Solberg 1970). Similarly, foreign capital was much appreciated save when clustered in key sectors or when foreign bankers, bondholders, or investors voiced adverse opinions about host government policy or clamored for home government action (Platt 1977). However, the expropriation of foreign-owned oil companies in Mexico, debt repudiation elsewhere, and a general defense of national producer interests (as typified by coffee valorization) seemed to point to a degree of confidence in the exercise of sovereignty by the national state and its competence to influence, if not entirely shape, external economic and political relations.

Some countries proved better at coping with external instability in the 1930s than with international insertion, and the disruption that this inevitably triggered in the 1880s and 1900s. But, as Domínguez (1978) argues for Cuba, a sudden, sharp economic contraction following a sustained phase of economic growth that had been accompanied by social mobilization was bound to provoke regime change, particularly if there was a coincidence of demographic and economic conjunctures. "Globalization" in the late-nineteenth and early twentieth centuries offered opportunities and posed challenges for states in Latin America. The gains from international insertion were not, however, shared equitably by all sectors nor by all countries. Was this because some areas were but imperfectly integrated into the world economy, because international markets were inherently unstable and moving against Latin American producers or were the rules of the game rigged against Latin American players? There were certainly considerable differences in the export and general economic performance of the Latin American economies during the period of oligarchic liberalism.

On the assumption that international conditions were broadly similar for all countries, the difference in performance may be explained in a number of ways. A recent explanation advanced by Bulmer-Thomas (1994) attaches particular importance to the timing of a country's insertion into the world economy and to factor endowment, namely luck in the commodity lottery. Furtado develops a structuralist and institutionalist approach, which also attaches considerable importance to resource base and the commodity composition of exports. Cardoso and Faletto (1979) stress the importance of institutions, notably state competence and elite coherence. These accounts are not mutually exclusive. Some commodities were more "democratic" than others. The production of temperate "frontier" food-stuffs such as cereals and, in some circumstances, sub-tropical commodities like coffee required massive inputs of labor and sustained "lumpy" investment in social overhead capital. These generated substantial forward linkages, income expansion, national integration, and welfare gains. The proliferation of wage employment, opportunities for upward social mobility, urbanization, and demographic growth reshaped regime and state as politics became more pluralistic and economic activities more diversified. These processes may also have generated a greater control over national assets and required states to be seen to be capable of projecting sovereignty domestically and internationally. Other commodities, for example "colonial" plantation products like sugar and minerals had different production profiles and price evolutions. Dependence on imported technology and the monopolization of production led to resource alienation and the perpetuation of archaic social structures and coercive, less open politics yielding less dynamic, fragile states that needed to be strong at home but were weak abroad.

Some states, however, were better placed than others to seize opportunities provided by the emergence of a world economy after the mid-nineteenth century. States such as Chile and Brazil, which, less damaged by the dissolution of the Iberian connection, emerged as institutionally coherent early in the post-independence period. They were positioned to maximize – and possibly internalize – gains available from international insertion. Others, like the Argentine and Mexico only acquired institutional stability with globalization. These states, which already enjoyed international recognition, rapidly assumed domestic sovereignty and aspired to exclude unwelcome external influences within their boundaries. Yet other states were so weakened by independence and centrifugal forces triggered by it that globalization proved to be threat not an opportunity. In the nineteenth century, states sufficiently strong to capture a share of economic resources resulting from the growth of the international economy were able to foster a modern domestic capitalism: weak states were less able to assist local agents who were consequently overwhelmed – or absorbed – by external actors.

References

Abel, C. and Lewis, C.M. (eds) (1993) *Latin America: Economic Imperialism and the State*, London: Athlone.

Albert, B. (1989) *South America and the First World War: The Impact of the War on Brazil, Argentina, Peru and Chile*, Cambridge: CUP.

Anna, T.E. (1978) *The Fall of Royal Government in Mexico City*, Lincoln, Neb.: University of Nebraska Press.

Bagú, S. (1966) *El plan económico del grupo rivadaviano, 1821–27: su sentido y sus contradicciones, sus proyecciones sociales, sus enemigos*, Buenos Aires: Ed. Pampa y Cielo.

Batou, J. (1991) *Between Development and Underdevelopment: The Precocious Attempts at Industrialisation of the Periphery, 1800–1870*, Geneva: Libr. Droz.

Bauer, A.J. (1975) *Chilean Rural Society from the Spanish Conquest to 1930*, Cambridge: Cambridge University Press.

Bethell, L. (ed.) (1996) *Ideas and Ideologies in Twentieth Century Latin America*, Cambridge: Cambridge University Press.

Blanchard, P. (1991) *Slavery and Abolition in early Republican Peru*, Wilmington: SR Books.

Bonilla, H. (ed.) (1991) *La independencia en el Perú*, Lima: Instituto de Estudios Peruanos.

Bulmer-Thomas, V. (1994) *Economic History of Latin America since Independence*, Cambridge: Cambridge University Press.

Burgin, M. (1946) *Economic Aspects of Argentine Federalism, 1820–1852*, Cambridge, Mass.: Havard University Press.

Bushnell, D. (1983) *Reform and Reaction in the Platine Provinces, 1810–1852*, Gainesville: University Presses of Florida.

Bushnell, D. and Macaulay, N. (1994) *The Emergence of Latin America in the Nineteenth Century*, New York: Oxford University Press.

Cardoso, E. and Helwege, A. (1992) *Latin America's Economy: Diversity, Trends and Conflicts*, Cambridge, Mass.: MIT Press.

Cardoso, F.H. and Faletto, E. (1979) *Development and Dependency in Latin America*, Berkeley: University of California Press.

Chiaramonte, J.C. (1971) *Nacionalismo y liberalismo económicos en Argentina, 1860–1880*, Buenos Aires: Ed. Solar.

Coatsworth, J.H. (1981) *Growth against Development: The Economic Impact of Railways in Porfirian Mexico*, DeKalb: Northern Illinois University Press.

Díaz Alejandro, C.F. (1970) *Essays on the Economic History of the Argentine Republic*, New Haven: Yale Univeristy Press.

Domínguez, J.I. (1978) *Cuba: Order and Revolution*, Cambridge, Mass.: Harvard University Press.

Dunkerley, J. (1988) *Power in the Isthmus: A Political History of Modern Central America*, London: Verso.

Edelstein, M. (1982) *Overseas Investment in the Age of High Imperialism: the United Kingdom, 1850–1914*, London; Methuen.

Finch, M.H.J. (1981) *A Political Economy of Uruguay since 1870*, London: Macmillan.

Fisher, J.R. (1977) *Commercial Relations between Spain and Spanish America in the Era of Free Trade, 1778–1796*, Liverpool: Liverpool University Press.

Foreman-Peck, J. (1995) *A History of the World Economy: International Economic Relations since 1850*, London: Harvester.

Franco, G.H.B. (1983) *Reforma monetária e instabilidade durante a transição republicana*, Rio de Janeiro: Banco Nacional de Desênvolvimento Econômico e Sociál.

Frank, A.G. (1967) *Capitalism and Underdevelopment in Latin America: Historical Studies of Chile and Brazil*, New York: Monthly Review Press.

Fritsch, W. (1988) *External Constraints on Economic Policy in Brazil, 1889–1930*, London: Macmillan.

Furtado, C. (1963) *The Economic Growth of Brazil: A Survey from Colonial to Modern Times*, Berkeley: University of California Press.

Furtado, C. (1977) *Economic Development of Latin America: Historical Background and Contemporary Problems*, Cambridge: Cambridge University Press.

Gerschenkron, A. (1965) *Economic Backwardness in Historical Perspective*, New York: Praeger.

Goldsmith, R.W. (1986) *Brasil, 1850–1984: desênvolvimento financiero sob um sé culo de inflação*, São Paulo: Ed. Brasiliense.

Gonzalez, M.J. (1985) *Plantations, Agriculture and Social Control in Northern Peru, 1875–1930*, Austin: University of Texas Press.

Gootenberg, P. (1989) *Between Silver and Guano: Commercial Policy and State in Post-independence Peru*, Princeton: Princeton University Press.

Haber, S.H. (1989) *Industry and Underdevelopment: The Industrialization of Mexico, 1880–1940*, Stanford: Stanford University Press.

——(ed) (1997) *How Latin America Fell Behind: Essays on the Economic Histories of Brazil and Mexico, 1800–1914*, Stanford; Stanford University Press.

Halperín Donghi, T. (1973) *The Aftermath of Independence in Latin America*, New York: Paidos.

Hilton, S.E. (1975) *Brazil and the Great Powers, 1930–1939: The Politics of Trade Rivalry*, Austin: University of Texas Press.

Holloway, T.H. (1980) *Immigrants on the Land: Coffee and Society in Sao Paulo, 1886–1934*, Chapel Hill: University of North Carolina Press.

Hunt, S. (1973) *Guano and Growth in Nineteenth-century Peru*, mimeo, Princeton.

Katz, F. (1977) *La servidumbre agraria en México en la é poca porfiriana*, México: Fondo de Cultura Económica.

Kirsch, H.W. (1977) *Industrial Development in a Traditional Society: The Conflict of Entrepreneurship and Modernization in Chile*, Gainesville: University Presses of Florida.

Knight, A. (1986) *The Mexican Revolution*, Cambridge: Cambridge University Press.

Lamounier, M.L. (1993) *Between Slavery and Free Labour: Experiments with Free Labour and Patterns of Slave Emancipation in Brazil and Cuba, c.1830–1888*, mimeo, London.

Lewis, C.M. (1983) *British Railways in Argentina, 1857–1914: A Case-study of Foreign Investment*, London: Athlone Press.

Lewis, P.H. (199) *The Crisis of Argentine Capitalism*, Chapel Hill: North Carolina University Press.

Lewis, W.A. (1900) *Growth and Fluctuations, 1870–1913*, London: George Allen & Unwin.

Liss, P.K. (1983) *Atlantic Empires: The Network of Trade and Revolution, 1713–1826*, Baltimore: Johns Hopkins University Press.

Lofstrom, W.L. (1972) *The Promise and Problem of Reform: Attempted Social and Economic Reform in the First Years of Bolivian Independence*, Ithaca NY.

Love, J.L. and Jacobson, N. (eds) (1988) *Guiding the Invisible Hand: Economic Liberalism and the State in Latin American History*, New York: Praeger.

Lynch, J. (1981) *Argentine Dictator: Juan Manuel de Rosas, 1829–1852*, Oxford: Oxford University Press.

—— (1986) *The Spanish American Revolutions, 1808–1826*, New York: Norton.

Malloy, J.M. (1979) *The Politics of Social Security in Brazil*, Pittsburgh: Pittsburgh University Press.

Mamalakis, M.J. (1976) *The Growth and Structure of the Chilean Economy: From Independence to Allende*, New Haven: Yale Univeristy Press.

Marichal, C. (1989) *A Century of Debt Crisis in Latin America: From Independence to the Great Depression, 1820–1930*, Princeton: Princeton University Press.

Mathew, W.M. (1977) "Antony Gibbs & Sons, the Guano Trade and the Peruvian Government, 1842–1861" in D.C.M. Platt (ed.) *Business Imperialism, 1840–1930: An Inquiry based on British Experience in Latin America*, Oxford: Clarendon Press.

Maxwell, K. (1973) *Conflict and Conspiracies: Brazil and Portugal, 1750–1808*, Cambridge: Cambridge University Press.

Moreno Fraginals, M. (1984) *El ingenio: el ejemplo económico social cubano del azúar*, Havana: Ed. del Consejo Nacionla de la Universidades.

Murilo de Carvalho, J. (1974) *Elites and State Building in Imperial Brazil*, mimeo, Stanford.

Nicolau, J.C. (1975) *Industria argentina y aduana, 1835–1854*, Buenos Aires: Ed. Devenir.

Ospina Vásquez, L. (1955) *Industria y proteccion en Colombia, 1810–1930*, Medellin: FAES.

Palacios, M. (1980) *Coffee in Colombia, 1850–1970: An Economic, Social and Political History*, Cambridge: Cambridge University Press.

Panettieri, J. (1983) *Devaluaciones de la moneda argentina, 1822–1935*, Buenos Aires: Centro Editor de América Latina.

Pang, E-S. (1988) *In Pursuit of Honor and Power: Noblemen of the Southern Cross in Nineteenth-century Brazil*, Tuscaloosa: University of Alabama Press.

Pérez, L.A. (1988) *Cuba: Between Reform and Revolution*, New York: Oxford University Press.

Platt, D.C.M. (ed.) (1977) *Business Imperialism, 1860–1930: An Inquiry Based on British Experience in Latin America*, Oxford: Clarendon Press.

Potash, R.A. (1983) *Mexican Government and Industrial Development in the Early Republic: el Banco de Avio*, Amhurst: University of Massachusetts Press.

Rippy, J.F. (1959) *British Investment in Latin America, 1822–1949*, Minneapolis: University of Minnesota Press.

Rock, D. (1989) *Argentina, 1516–1982*, London: I.B. Tauris.

Sabato, H. (1990) *Agrarian Capitalism and the World Market: Buenos Aires in the Pastoral Age*, Albuquerque: University of New Mexico Press.

Sabato, J.F. (1979) *Notas sobre la formación de la clase dominante en la Argentina moderna*, mimeo, Buenos Aires.

Sánchez Albornoz, N. (1974) *The Population of Latin America: A History*, Berkeley: University of California Press.

Sheaham, J. (1987) *Patterns of Development in Latin America: Poverty, Repression and Economic Strategy*, Princeton: Princeton University Press.

Sikkink, K. (1991) *Ideas and Institutions: Developmentalism in Brazil and Argentina*, Ithaca: Cornell University Press.

Solberg, C. (1970) *Immigration and Nationalism: Argentina and Chile, 1890–1914*, Austin: University of Texas Press.

Stevens, D.F. (1991) *Origins of Instability in Early Republican Mexico*, Durham, NC: Duke University Press.

Stolcke, V. (1988) *Coffee Planters, Workers and Wives: Class Conflict and Gender Relations on Sao Paulo Plantations, 1850–1980*, London: St Antony's/Macmillan Series.

Suzigan, W. (1986) *Indústria brasileira: orígem e desênvolvimento*, São Paulo: Ed. Brasiliense.

Tede, P. and Marichal, C. (eds) *La formación de los bancos centrales en España y América Latina (siglos XIX y XX)*, Madrid: Banco de Espanã.

Thomsom, G.P.C. (1989) *Puebla de los Angeles: Industry and Society in a Mexican City*, Boulder: Westview.

Thorp, R. (ed.) (1984) *Latin America in the 1930s: The Role of the Periphery in World Crisis*, London: St Antony's/Macmillan Series.

Thorp, R. and Bertram, G. (1978) *Peru, 1890–1977: Growth and Policy in an Open Economy*, London: Macmillan.

Topik, S.C. 1987) *The Political Economy of the Brazilian State, 1889–1930*, Austin: University of Texas Press.

Uricoechea, F. (1980) *The Patrimonial Foundations of the Brazilian Bureaucratic State*, Berkeley: University of California Press.

Véliz, C. (1961) *Historia de la marina mercante de Chile*, Santiago de Chile: Ed. Universitaria.

Weaver, F.S. (1980) *Class, State and Industrial Structure: The Historical Process of South American Industrial Growth*, Westport: Greenwood.

Williams, J.H. (1979) *The Rise and Fall of the Paraguayan Republic, 1800–1870*, Austin: University of Texas Press.

Wirth, J.D. (ed.) (1985) *Latin American Oil Companies and the Politics of Energy*, Lincoln, Nebr.: University of Nebraska Press.

Zeitlin, M. (1984) *The Civil Wars in Chile (or the Bourgeois Revolutions that Never Were)*, Princeton: Princeton University Press.

6 The modern colonial state and global economic integration, 1815–1945

William G. Clarence-Smith

Several contributors to this volume argue that globalization is not a new phenomenon, but one that has waxed and waned over time. This survey of modern sea-borne empires reinforces their point. However, rather than market forces causing global diffusion, colonial states were responsible for the spread of European domination. But the sovereignty of administrators in the colonies was often strengthened. Initially hesitant to dismantle mercantilist colonial pacts at the end of the Napoleonic Wars, colonial rulers came to embrace an active role as agents of economic and cultural globalization by the 1850s, often permitting considerable local decision-making. Second thoughts became widespread between the 1880s and 1914, but it took the cataclysmic trauma of the First World War to provoke a blinkered retreat into imperial autarky.

Changes in colonialism were inextricably linked to the wider environment. Although extreme free traders such as Cobden opposed colonialism on principle, the "imperialists of free trade" simply gave a special twist to the ideology by insisting that certain "backward" regimes were incapable of achieving free trade on their own. Similarly, dreams of imperial autarky cannot be separated from the growth of nationalism and racism in economically advanced countries from the 1880s (Clarence-Smith 1994a).

Colonial states and societies played some part in this story. While colonies have often been portrayed as helpless victims of all powerful metropoles, in fact they did not completely lose sovereignty. Some colonial interest groups were able to achieve their ends by working through either the local or the metropolitan state. Thus, the British in India shifted their support back and forth between assorted Maharajas and the great commercial communities of the sub-continent (Charlesworth 1982).

Degrees of colonial sovereignty

It is often assumed that colonial regimes were the very antithesis of sovereign states, given that colonies lacked the attributes of Westphalian and international sovereignty. Metropolitan governments were certainly always able to overrule colonial authorities. None the less, varying degrees of international recognition and Westphalian sovereignty were achieved before formal independence. This was most obvious in the case of Britain's "White Dominions" – Australia, New Zealand, South Africa, and Canada. Their independence dates are hard to pin down, so gradual was the transfer of power from Whitehall. Southern Rhodesia (Zimbabwe) was not a dominion, but it enjoyed the status of a self-governing colony run by European settlers from 1923, and pursued a tariff policy of its own (Cole 1968).

Nor were settler colonies the only ones to have an ambiguous status. British India even became a member of the League of Nations in its own right. Rulers subject to a loose form of British protection enjoyed significant autonomy and international status. The Rao of Kutch maintained his own currency and stubbornly refused to join the Indian customs union throughout the British period (Rushbrook-Williams 1958: 11). The Sultan of Johor, Malaya, was received like an independent monarch by the Emperor Meiji of Japan in 1883 (Nakahara 1994). The Sultans of Oman, in southern Arabia, and of Zanzibar, in eastern Africa, were examples of a similar kind (Bhacker 1992). Important decisions ultimately lay with London (as they often did in the case of nominally independent countries as well), but these colonial states formulated many of their own policies and acted as distinct entities in the international realm.

Such examples were not confined to the British Empire. The United States, uneasy colonizers in view of their own past, almost immediately set up an elected legislature in the Philippines, and gave the islands Commonwealth status in 1935 (May 1984; Giesecke 1987). The Ottoman Empire appointed a consul in Dutch Indonesia in 1883 to further pan-Islamic solidarity (Freitag and Clarence-Smith 1997). In return, the Dutch colonial authorities had "quasi-diplomatic representation in Arabia" to regulate the annual pilgrimage (Cribb 1994: 4). French Morocco was acquired late, partitioned with Spain, subject to a battery of international controls enshrined in treaties, administered through the foreign ministry rather than the colonial ministry, and headed by a powerful Sultan (Bidwell 1973). Even Portugal under the authoritarian and centralizing rule of Salazar was obliged to grant considerable *de facto* political power to the European settlers of Angola and Mozambique (Clarence-Smith 1985: Chapter 6).

Defining sovereignty in domestic terms, some colonial regimes were more sovereign than either the polities that preceded them or the states that succeeded them. In Sub-Saharan Africa, many colonies federated large numbers of small units of uncertain political status, and were replaced by exceedingly weak independent states (Oliver and Atmore 1981). At minimum, colonial authorities exercised effective control over their territory and cross-border relations, the essential attributes of this kind of sovereignty (as Krasner points out in Chapter 2, this volume).

Colonial states were not strong, however, in comparison to many Western ones. It has often been noted with surprise how a thousand elite civil servants, not all of them European, ruled 300 million Indians on the eve of independence (Dewey 1993). The golden rule of modern colonialism was that the enterprise should not cost anything to the metropolitan tax payer. This entailed both a minimalist "night watchman" administration and a political *modus vivendi*. Outbreaks of violent resistance were carefully avoided, especially if they necessitated expensive and politically unpopular intervention from the metropolis (Fieldhouse 1982).

The colonial state is frequently described as lacking legitimacy because it was a form of foreign occupation, but officials depended upon local support. The British and the Dutch wavered between backing traditional monarchs and slowly expanding the franchise for legislative councils (Porter 1975; Cribb 1994). In contrast, the French and Portuguese Republicans opted for colonial representation in the metropolitan parliament, while downgrading the status of "native chiefs" (Thompson and Adloff 1969; Clarence-Smith 1985).

The economic impact of colonialism

The strains placed on these political arrangements varied according to what metropoles expected to get out of their colonies. Although all colonial masters shared the rhetoric of dragging their wards into the mainstream of human progress, what we might today call globalization, there were widely differing definitions of this goal and of the speed at which it was to be achieved. The minimum function of a colony was to be a quiescent political appendage boosting national pride, but some metropolitan interest groups wanted a real economic return. As a rule of thumb, the wealthier a colonizing power, the less it was interested in economic advantages. The German Reich can be seen as having acquired colonies as a form of conspicuous consumption (Schinzinger 1984). Conversely, Portugal, the poorest and most backward colonial power, put great hopes in economic prosperity flowing from the possession of colonies (Clarence-Smith 1985).

Foreign trade by itself can have the perverse effect of reducing the internal mobility of factors of production, as with the rise of the "second serfdom" in eastern Europe (Aston and Philpin 1987). But in a path-breaking economic history of West Africa, Tony Hopkins (1973) argued that colonial rulers "opened" the region to the global economy through commerce and investment. External and internal "opening" most often went hand in hand.

The most difficult task of integrating into the world economy was to build the institutions and develop the "mental models" necessary for markets to thrive (Harriss *et al.* 1995). Settlers frequently brought appropriate attitudes, skills, and institutions with them, but their alienation of the indigenous inhabitants was a barrier to further diffusion, as in Algeria (Ageron 1983). Even without the settler problem, colonialism came up against widespread and tenacious cultural resistance. Colonial regimes sometimes tried energetically to overcome such cultural patterns, and at other times sought to accommodate them.

The contribution of colonialism to globalization depended on how hard rulers pushed for the "open economy." It was Peter Bauer (1976: Chapter 3; 1981: Chapter 9) who first suggested that policies of "closure" became apparent from the 1930s, precursors of more extreme measures adopted after independence. Patrick O'Brien (1997) has recently moved the crucial watershed back to 1914, showing how colonialism became less of an agent of economic globalization, in part because of security preoccupations. This chapter aims to refine the periodization and include factors other than trade.

Frustrated free trade colonialism from 1815 to the 1840s

Free trade notions were far from being hegemonic from 1815 to the 1840s, even in Britain (O'Brien 1997: 77, 94). The British Navigation Acts were not abolished until 1849–50, although the 1820s saw the substitution of "protectionist" for "prohibitive" duties (Holland 1913). The foundation of Singapore as a free port in 1819 was a quixotic act by Thomas Stamford Raffles, disapproved of by his employer, the monopolistic chartered East India Company. It was only the spectacular success of Singapore as an entrepôt that nullified the East India Company's various attempts to abrogate its status as a free port (SarDesai 1977: Chapter 2).

The East India Company itself was progressively reformed by acts of parliament, but mercantilist habits died hard. The company lost its trading monopoly in India in 1813, and all commercial functions in 1833; it was not finally wound up by the government of India until 1858 (Charlesworth 1982). Indian slavery was not abolished till 1843, and differential duties favoring British goods remained in place till 1859 (Kumar 1993; Cain 1980, 25).

In Sub-Saharan Africa, the British campaign to abolish the slave trade complicated matters. This crusade superficially contradicted the principles of free trade, even though there were close ideological and personal links between abolitionists and free traders. The short-term effects may have been to slow export growth, despite a marked increase in "legitimate exports" (Eltis 1987: Chapter 13).

Tariffs remained extremely protective of British planters in the West Indies, who paid just over a third of the duty imposed on foreign sugar entering Britain until the reforms of 1846 began to phase out this form of protection (Holland 1913: Chapter 10). The spectacular events of the abolition of the British slave trade in 1808 and of slavery in British crown colonies in 1834 disguised the fact that the inefficient institution of the estate was preserved, notably through the provision of indentured Asian laborers to replace slaves (Ward 1985: Chapters 2–3).

Outside the British Empire, free trade and liberal institutions were rarely even on the agenda. In the aftermath of the Napoleonic Wars, continental European governments actively attempted to turn the clock back to the *ancien regime*. In 1816, France went so far as to prohibit imports of a whole range of manufactured goods (Smith 1980: 18). The French and Portuguese Empires were mere shadows of what they once had been, but Britain allowed the Netherlands and Spain to retain some of their overseas possessions, and to expand them. This was to strengthen these countries against the danger of a resurgent France in Europe. The same preoccupation accounted for British tolerance of *ancien regime* colonial protection in Dutch Indonesia and the Spanish Philippines, despite protests by British commercial interests (Tarling 1992: Chapter 1).

Territories subjected to this twilight of *ancien regime* colonialism fared poorly. Duties had to be extremely high to protect metropolitan goods that were costly and of poor quality. Contraband flourished, but this represented a substantial added cost. Slavery, serfdom, and other forms of coerced labor persisted, together with great rigidities in land and credit markets. Indeed, forced cultivation was brought to its zenith under the infamous Dutch Cultivation System in Indonesia, which simultaneously reserved the export trade for Dutch ships bound for the Netherlands. Elson (1994) has argued that the Cultivation System eventually raised incomes, but incomes would probably have risen more without the system's ecological mismanagement, price distortions, and channeling of profits to the coffers of the Dutch state in Europe (Clarence-Smith 1994b).

The high noon of free trade colonialism, 1850s–1870s

From the 1850s to the 1870s, free trade triumphed in Britain, with major consequences for the empire. Successive governments abolished differential tariffs and reduced duties to low levels. An optimistic belief in the power of formal education made the task of institution-building appear easy. Colonial land legislation was reformed, the last vestiges of unfree labor were swept away, and indentured labor became almost indistinguishable from free emigration (Cain 1980; Porter 1975; Northrup 1995). It was the increasingly autonomous White Dominions that were least prepared to play the free trade game, forcing Britain to accept a certain level of protectionism (Holland 1913).

It is doubtful whether Gallagher and Robinson (1970) are right to contend that this triumph of free trade was merely the British way of gaining empire on the cheap. Part of the problem lies in their use of examples prior to the 1850s, when Britain was not a free trading nation (Cain 1980: 17). They are more convincing in explaining why the formal British Empire expanded in the heyday of free trade. Only extreme free traders opposed colonialism *per se*. Moderate free traders believed that in some parts of the world the local institutional framework was not conducive to peaceful and open trade. In such regions, "civilized" powers could impose order and appropriate institutions. As Lord Palmerston put it in 1860, "It may be true in one sense that trade ought not to be enforced by cannon balls, but on the other hand trade cannot flourish without security, and that security may often be unattainable without the exhibition of physical force" (Porter 1975: 11). More doubtful is Gallagher and Robinson's assumption that free trade colonialism served exclusively British interests. Many free traders sincerely believed that modern colonialism would benefit all parties concerned (Arndt 1987: 24).

The 1870s marked the high point of this type of endeavor, in which a colonizing power drew little or no direct economic benefit from gaining sovereignty in a given territory. Indeed, the radical wing of the British free trade movement believed that colonies would rapidly gain their independence for this very reason, unless they accepted the unlikely alternative of democratic representation in the British parliament in Westminster (Hodgart 1977: 6–8).

Looking beyond Britain reinforces the sense that free trade was not cynically adopted by those who thought themselves to be in a superior economic position. The France of Napoleon III took up free trade enthusiastically, a revolution in

French policy that even extended to the "old colonies" by 1866 (Smith 1860: 28–34). The French conquest of Vietnam from 1858 took place under the banner of free trade (Brocheux and Hemery 1995: Chapter 1). France participated in the wider Opium War of 1858–62 partly to obtain the liberalization of Chinese export duties, as the Lyon silk industry, suffering from the ravages of silk worm disease in Europe, looked increasingly to the Far East for its raw materials (Laffey 1969). Expansion up the Senegal River in West Africa was justified by the need to sweep away tolls and other impediments to commerce (Barrows 1974). In the political field, Napoleon III's vision of a *royaume arabe* in Algeria fell short of independence, but it was the most anti-settler policy adopted in the unhappy colonial history of that territory (Ageron 1983: 30–6).

The fervor of the free trade gospel swept over other colonial metropoles, albeit more slowly and less completely. The achievement of political power by the Liberals in the Netherlands in the 1860s led to a sharp reduction in colonial tariffs, the abolition of slavery in the Dutch Caribbean and Indonesia, and the first steps to dismantle the Cultivation System (Kossmann 1978: 264–74). Portugal and Spain were even slower to act, but in the 1870s a distinct liberalization of colonial tariffs and labor policies became apparent (Clarence-Smith 1985: Chapter 3; 1991). In 1882, Spain finally abolished the tobacco monopoly in the Philippines, similar in nature to the Dutch Cultivation System (Jesus 1980).

The great entrepreneurial diasporas intensified their dispersion around the world in these conditions, spurred on by cheap transport and liberal immigration policies. Hokkien from southern China, Gujarati from north-western India, and Arabs from Lebanon and Hadhrmaut were among those who fueled the Third World economic boom with their expertise and dynamism (Dobbin 1996; Issawi 1982: Chapter 5). They were particularly important in facilitating rising exports of cash crops (Clarence-Smith 1996). Such diasporas created powerful global networks, uncontrolled by the nation-state. They supported European empires when it suited their purposes, but their fluid structures cut across empires (Freitag and Clarence-Smith 1997; Sheffer 1986).

From the point of view of the colonized, this was a period of rapid economic growth, as the terms of trade moved fairly consistently in their favor (O'Brien 1997: 93). The price of Western manufactures fell drastically, and the cost of transport sank with the spread of steamers (Foreman-Peck 1983: Chapter 2). At the same time, rapid industrial expansion led to bottlenecks in the supply of raw materials, so that prices for Third World exports soared, despite rapidly increasing output (Munro 1976: Chapter 2; Issawi 1982: 39). In a book purporting to cover the period 1850 to 1960, Havinden and Meredith (1993: 304) imply that terms of trade were continuously unfavorable to British colonies, but the figures that they refer to begin in 1913.

Colonial powers did not merely entrench a division of labor in which the West turned out manufactures, while the Third World produced primary commodities with little added value. This was the period in which the dramatic decline of Indian handicraft production of cotton textiles was succeeded by the rise of factory industry, partly owned and financed by Indians (Charlesworth

1982: 36–9). Manufacturing in Japan also began its rapid ascent (Macpherson 1987). If pockets of Asian industry remained restricted, it was because the comparative advantages of exporting raw materials were so overwhelming. The decline of an earlier burst of manufacturing in Egypt sprang from the defects of a monopolistic and state-run system, which left factories unable to compete in a falling market (Owen 1981: 69–76, 150–2; Batou 1990: Chapter 3).

Protectionist temptations, 1880s–1914

O'Brien (1997: 98) rightly notes that the "liberal interlude of 1846–79 had been brief." In its place came autarkic policies that disrupted not only the free flow of international trade between empires, but also trade within colonial systems. As production bottlenecks were overcome, the abnormally high prices of raw materials came tumbling down. The fall in prices of manufactures helped to set off the "Great Depression" of 1873–96. The United States returned to protection during the Civil War of the 1860s, and erected a veritable tariff wall in the 1890s. A wave of European protectionism followed the German tariff of 1879. In 1913, the average level of import tariffs in continental Europe ranged from around 10 per cent in Germany to about 40 per cent in Russia and Spain (Capie 1994: Chapter 4).

The aggressive protectionism of southern European states was one of the detonators of the "scramble for colonies" that exacerbated inter-colonial tensions and favored strategic military aims over economic ones (Clarence-Smith 1987). Colonial protection built up in France even before the Meline law of 1892, with tariff assimilation decreed for Algeria in 1884 and Indochina in 1887 (Smith 1980: 200–1). Spain was quick off the mark, with tariff reforms for the Caribbean colonies in 1882, which were extended to the Philippines in 1891 (Clarence-Smith 1991). Italy, newly emergent as a colonial power, was no less eager to go down the protectionist road (Miège 1968). Portugal followed the French lead, promulgating a highly protectionist colonial tariff in 1892 (Clarence-Smith 1985). The key measure was the imposition of differential import duties in the colonies, granting a major advantage to goods made in the metropolis and carried in metropolitan vessels. These measures were largely successful in reserving the colonial market for expensive but shoddy manufactures, especially cotton textiles (Clarence-Smith 1985: Chapter 4; Marseille 1984: Chapter 2).

At the same time, southern European powers frequently refused to grant tariff reciprocity on their home markets, a fate suffered by the "non-assimilated" French colonies after 1892 (Aldrich 1996: 169–70). Spanish beet producers obtained a tariff in 1892 that effectively prevented the entry of Cuban, Puerto Rican, and Filipino cane sugar into Spain, thus helping to provoke the uprisings that contributed to the ending of Spanish rule in 1898 (Clarence-Smith 1991: 79).

Tariffs designed to favor imports from the metropolis went hand in hand with land alienation and labor coercion, despite the formal legal abolition of slavery. One of the great colonial scandals of the epoch was the forced collection of wild rubber in the French Congo (Coquery-Vidrovitch 1972). Another was the

Portuguese quasi-slave trade from Angola to the cocoa plantations of Sao Tome and Principe (Clarence-Smith 1990; 1993a). More generally, the state favored estates against smallholders, confiscating land for plantation companies, and forcing indigenous peoples to work on them. Although this was justified by the alleged scientific superiority of modern estates, the reality was that smallholders produced better and more cheaply. This was not so much because of the cheapness of family labor, but rather because of flexible labor contracts, notably sharecropping, and a sparing use of both labor and capital (Clarence-Smith 1995; 1996).

The attempt by the weaker European powers to extend the territory within which they could impose protectionism provoked Britain to defend freedom of trade (Porter 1994: 44). While this sometimes involved putting forward a proxy like King Leopold of Belgium in the Congo, Britain also annexed large areas (Munro 1984: 19). Despite the rise of a powerful lobby for imperial preference, Britain remained committed to free trade, especially when the Liberal Party was in power (Cain 1980: 47–9, 52). India in 1914 had a policy "as close to free trade as any country is likely to have" (Charlesworth 1982: 63).

While Britain clung to commercial freedom, hesitations became apparent in attitudes to land and labor. In Trinidad, a strong mid-century commitment to allocating land for smallholder agriculture was replaced by discrimination in favor of large estates (Phillips Lewis 1996). In the 1890s, colonialists generally assumed that large plantations would prevail in West Africa. In the absence of a well-established settler lobby of the Trinidadian or Sri Lankan type, local authorities came to realize that this was an absurdity that threatened social order. They gave no support to concessionaires whose land titles were challenged in court, and refused to supply forced labor to estates. The famous West African smallholder policy was thus initiated by colonial officials, rather than coming from Westminster (Phillips 1989: Chapters 3–4).

The colonial powers of continental northwestern Europe were somewhat less liberal. Germany, a new colonizer, allied moderate protection at home with rigorous free trade in her overseas empire, to reconcile different interests in Germany while keeping Britain happy (Schinzinger 1984). The transfer of the Congo from King Leopold to Belgium in 1908 signaled a move from pretense at free trade to something more recognizable as such (Gann and Duignan 1979). The Netherlands consolidated their hold over the Indonesian archipelago under free trade terms, despite some retreat from the ideals of the 1860s (Lindblad 1989). These three countries favored estates on much the same lines as southern European powers, and their labor systems were quite illiberal. Many influential Germans changed their minds, however, and in the 1900s praised the virtues of British West African smallholders (Clarence-Smith 1993b).

American policies were in some respects similar to those of southern Europe, but the similarity was superficial. Formal colonies were placed within the United States tariff wall, but, unlike the Spaniards, the Americans granted full tariff reciprocity from 1913. The United States formed such a large and dynamic economy that the effects were not far removed from those of full free trade. Furthermore, the Americans in the Philippines abolished corvée labor, developed one of the most progressive educational systems in the colonial world, restricted land concessions to corporations, surveyed land holdings, and distributed the lands of the religious orders to their former tenants (Giesecke 1987).

Japan was strongly free trading in her debut as a colonial power. In part, this was because of external pressure, for unequal treaties in Japan lasted till 1911 (Macpherson 1987: 39). Japan also lacked any strong motivation for turning colonies into protected markets, given her success in exploiting the free trade created by Western powers in Asia (Sugihara 1990; Akita 1996). The Japanese thus annexed Korea in 1910 without imposing protective import duties (Duus 1984: 161–2).

There was a strong emphasis on institutional reform in Japanese colonies, possibly as part of a drive to outshine Western models. In Taiwan, annexed in 1895, the Japanese supplied a reformed police force, a cadastral land survey, agricultural research facilities, private property guarantees, a unified system of weights and measures, a central bank, and a gold-exchange currency. These institutional reforms were at least as important to the rapid economic growth of Taiwan as the more conventional list of physical and social infrastructures, comprising railways, roads, telegraph lines, harbors, public health facilities, and education (Chang and Myers 1963: 440–5).

The hesitant ideological retreat from free trade around the world thus had less impact before 1914 than might have been imagined. Even in continental Europe and the USA, effective levels of protection remained much lower than nominal rates (Capie 1994: Chapter 5). The growth of world trade continued to be rapid, in part because this was the heyday of the gold standard, facilitating trade payments and investment flows (Drummond 1987; Foreman-Peck 1983: Chapters 4–6). International migratory movements reached new heights, as neither laborers nor entrepreneurs faced significant impediments to entering new lands (Emmer and Mörner 1992; Northrup 1995).

Nor was the growth of colonial manufacturing industry inhibited, despite certain discriminatory measures. Pressures from Lancashire workers and indus-trialists led to the complete abolition of import tariffs on cotton textiles entering India in 1882, and to the imposition of a countervailing excise duty when the Government of India adopted a 5 per cent import tariff for fiscal reasons in 1894. Nevertheless, Indian factory production of cotton goods boomed, and Indian industrialists conquered export markets for cotton yarn from Africa to China, to the detriment of British and Japanese producers alike (Charlesworth 1982: 36, 64; Tomlinson 1993: 109–12).

Prosperity thus continued to spread to ever more remote areas of the Third World. Michael Adas (1974) has memorably chronicled this process for the rice-exporting Burma delta, where items such as grandfather clocks were much prized. The "trickle down" effect was clearly at work, and there may have been a narrowing of economic differentials between the West and the Third World.

Conditions for Africa and Asia none the less worsened in certain ways. Creeping protectionism appeared surreptitiously, notably in the field of transport. Colonial powers tolerated shipping "conferences," cartels that first emerged on the

Britain to Calcutta route in 1875. These cartels stalled the favorable evolution of transport costs for the Third World, and put up barriers to entry into steam navigation for Third World shippers, notably Indians and Chinese (Hyde 1973: 26–41; Sturmey 1962: 323). Similar problems resulted from the creation of the subsidized KPM company in 1888, with a quasi-monopoly of Indonesian coastal shipping and close connections with the Batavia "conference" from the turn of the century (Campo 1992).

Perhaps the most insidious danger for the colonies was the rapid spread of social Darwinism. These ideas hardened attitudes towards indigenous entrepreneurs, and blocked earlier stirrings towards granting political autonomy to "people of color." Institution building was slowed and distorted, as ideas of "indirect rule" led to the abandonment of earlier ideas of rapid acculturation and assimilation (Clarence-Smith 1994a; Aldrich 1994).

War, recession, and managed economies, 1914–45

The Great War of 1914–18 resolved the hesitation of previous decades in favor of protectionism. Managed trade and fixed exchange rates characterized the war years themselves, and proved difficult to dismantle afterwards. The sharp recession of 1920–1 ended efforts at post-war liberalization, with both Britain and the USA promulgating protectionist legislation of an emergency nature. Attempts to return to free trade and the gold standard later in the decade achieved little, and the Wall Street crash of 1929 brought protectionism flooding back. The American Smoot-Hawley tariff of 1930 was one of the most protectionist pieces of legislation ever enacted by a democracy in peace time, unleashing a wave of retaliatory tariffs and quotas around the world. Even Britain partially caved in to protectionist pressures in 1931–2 (Capie 1994: Chapter 6; Drummond 1987: Chapter 2). The Second World War, more of a total war than its predecessor, brought economic management by the state to a peak (Munro 1984: 19; Tomlinson 1993: Chapter 4).

Another consequence of the war was the emergence of fascist colonial regimes. Italy, Portugal, Spain, and Japan in turn rejected economic liberalism, and took to protectionism and the expansion of the state's economic role. Colonial pacts were imposed, together with forced labor and land expropriation for settlers. Fascist powers were prone to grandiose colonial development plans, including some industrialization, but the economic viability of these schemes was poor (Sbacchi 1980; Clarence-Smith 1985: Chapter 6; Clarence-Smith 1991; Ho 1984).

Democratic powers never went so far down this road, but the 1928 tariffs in France marked a milestone (Thompson and Adloff 1969: 440). Jacques Marseille (1984) argues that declining fractions of French capital, in alliance with organized labor at home and French planters in the colonies, obtained a sheltered market for their products, at the expense of taxpayers and consumers in France and in the empire. Dynamic companies contested this new colonial pact, as imperial markets counted little for them, and they feared tariff retaliation in Western markets. Some French capitalists even contemplated making Vietnam a "new Japan" in Asia, by developing export industries.

Although Britain succumbed to the sirens of colonial protection, tariffs generally remained lower than in other empires. In 1917, the Imperial War Cabinet committed a reluctant British government to introducing preferential tariffs. In 1919, London decreed a one-sixth reduction in import duties on some empire products entering Britain, with the greatest effects for Caribbean sugar. Reciprocal advantages were proposed for British goods in the Dominions, but the Government of India refused to make any concessions. The Empire Conference of 1932 in Ottawa agreed a more general imperial preference package, but this muddled affair failed to halt the decline in Britain's share of the imports of her empire (Drummond 1974).

Tariff protection forced up the cost of living and production costs in the colonies, worsening the terms of trade. Nowhere was this clearer than in South and Southeast Asia, where Japan was a providential supplier of cheap and high-quality goods. To drive the Japanese out of these markets, colonial rulers used every weapon in their armory, including physical quotas. Fortunately for the colonized peoples, the Japanese were able to retaliate to some degree by threatening to suspend purchases of raw materials such as Indian raw cotton and Javanese sugar (Sugiyama and Guerrero 1994).

Equally negative for the colonies was the tolerance by colonial authorities of ever more powerful shipping cartels. Shipping magnates justified cartels by arguing that high capital investments in ships required special protection, and that consumers benefited from reliable and stable liner services. It is more likely that world recovery from recession was slowed by substantially higher freight rates, tempered only by fierce competition from tramp shipping (Leubuscher 1962).

Parallel cartels developed in commerce. In West Africa, the United Africa Company, part of the Unilever Group, established a particularly strong position in the export trade in the 1920s and 1930s, in tandem with two French companies, SCOA and CFAO (Hopkins 1973; Assidon 1989). "Pooling" arrangements kept down the purchase price of agricultural commodities, leading to the cocoa "hold-ups" of the 1930s, when producers refused to sell their crop (Munro 1984: 27–8). The grip exercised on the lucrative import trade encouraged these cartels to discourage investment in local manufacturing (Clarence-Smith 1994a: 70–1). There is evidence of the cartelization of colonial import–export trade elsewhere, under the indifferent or even approving gaze of authorities, for example in Java (Clarence-Smith 1997).

Exchange control began to acquire a new importance in ensuring "imperial solidarity," as the gold standard proved to have been irretrievably shattered by the war (Drummond 1987). The Indochinese piastre, the last currency independent of the franc in the French Empire, was locked into a fixed exchange rate in 1930. This helped to channel trade preferentially to the metropolis, making France Indochina's main commercial partner for the first time (Brocheux and Hémery 1995: 133, Chapter 6). In 1931, Salazarist Portugal pioneered the system of obligatory exchange of hard currency for escudos, which had the incidental effect of benefiting metropolitan exporters (Clarence-Smith 1985, 147).

British currency policies gradually became more oppressive. The pegging of colonial currencies to sterling had already begun before the Great War, with the setting up of the West Africa Currency Board in 1912, and others followed (Munro 1984: 19–20). These boards acquired a new significance with the collapse of the world payments system. To bolster the faltering value of sterling, large colonial reserves were held in London, amounting to as much as 100 per cent of note issue, which might better have been spent to stimulate economic activity in the colonies (Drummond 1974: 444–5). When Britain left the gold standard for the second time in 1931, a *de facto* Sterling Bloc emerged, including both colonies and independent countries. It was not until September 1939, however, that the Sterling Bloc became a rigorous mechanism to pool foreign exchange in London in time of war (Cain and Hopkins 1993: Chapter 5; Davies 1996: 600–5; Drummond 1974: 444).

A related burden was the overvaluation of local currencies. In India, the British insisted on a high exchange rate for the rupee from the 1920s, fearing that depreciation would lead to inflation and riots. A highly valued rupee also protected the value of investments in India, most of which were of British origin. The policy was disastrous for Indian exports of cotton textiles, as China remained on a silver system and the Japanese ensured that the yen was competitively priced. Indeed, currency overvaluation may have been the main cause of India's spectacular loss of Asian markets for manufactures in the interwar years (Tomlinson 1979; Sugihara 1990).

The colonies of the Gold Bloc faced their greatest crisis during the 1930s slump. France, Belgium and the Netherlands clung to the gold standard until 1935–6, and tied colonial currencies to their metropolitan equivalents. In the face of mounting overvaluation, the authorities stemmed the influx of imports with a barrage of tariffs and quotas, but found no way to make colonial exports more competitive (Vandewalle 1966; Brocheux and Hémery: Chapter 6; Sugiyama and Guerrero 1994: Chapter 6).

Colonial industrialization offset the impact of tariff and currency policies to some extent, but with ambiguous effects in the longer term. The push for manufacturing was a reaction to shipping difficulties in wartime, and to a sharp fall in foreign exchange earnings and employment during recessions. Such industries were import substituting in nature, and were often seen as belonging to the handicraft sector (Ray 1979; Brown 1994: Chapter 12). Moreover, they enjoyed substantial tariff protection. By 1931, the general import duty in India was 31.25 per cent, with an astonishing 190 per cent placed on imported sugar. This not only forced up the cost of living, but also encouraged inefficiency, discouraged manufacturing exports, and generated a mentality of dependence on the state (Tomlinson 1993: 132–4). The closed Indian economy was born well before independence in 1947.

Industrialization programs of this type reflected the growing autonomy of the colonial state. London tended to disapprove of colonial industries, while not actively hindering them (Drummond 1974: 439–42). When the authorities intervened to limit competition within the jute industry in the 1930s, it was the elected provincial government of Bengal that took on the task (Tomlinson 1993:

122). Similarly, the accession of the Philippines to Commonwealth status in 1935 resulted in a surge of import-substitution industrialization measures (Brown 1989). The Portuguese "prohibition" of colonial industries in 1936 was in reality an unstable compromise with settler lobbies, who gained the right to set up certain types of manufacturing, and who forced new concessions from Salazar almost as soon as the ink was dry on his decree (Clarence-Smith 1985: 164).

Export-oriented industrialization, which benefited from comparative advantage and economies of scale, was frustrated by job creation schemes in colonial metropoles, in response to the demands of labor organizations (Clarence-Smith 1989). Thus, Tate and Lyle developed its sugar-refining capacities in the 1920s in Britain rather than in the Caribbean (Ward 1985: 51). Similarly, a new tin smelter opened in Arnhem in the Netherlands in 1933, taking work away from existing factories in Singapore and Penang (Allen and Donnithorne 1954: 170–1).

The inter-war years witnessed expanded support for large planters, on grounds that mixed blatant racism and a misguided belief in "science." For no crop was this so clear as for natural rubber. Two major international agreements propped up estates by restricting smallholder output and planting, simultaneously penalizing consumers in the West and slowing recovery from recession (Drabble 1991; Bauer 1948). The French went so far as to give cash grants to European rubber companies in Indochina, in part financed from taxes paid by hard-pressed Vietnamese rice farmers (Murray 1980: 193–4, 261). To protect settler investments, the British forbade Africans to grow Arabica coffee in Kenya (Munro 1984: 32–5, 51–61). One-sided support for European settlers was not only economically misguided in the short term, but it also stored up an explosive sociopolitical legacy for the future, most obviously in French Algeria (Ageron 1983).

Other reactionary policies restricted the mobility of factors of production and inhibited institutions and mentalities favorable to markets. These policies were justified by the need to protect the weak, leading some historians to view them as progressive. The poor remained poor, however, while the upward mobility of indigenous entrepreneurs was frustrated. Colonial governments fixed rents, and protected tenants from eviction, leading to the uneconomic use of land. Propagating family labor as the ideal, officials curbed labor migration for indigenous smallholders. Communal tenure of land was defended, re-imposed, or even invented, hampering economic specialization and diminishing flows of rural credit, which were further restricted by measures against "usury" (Phillips 1989; Munro 1984: Chapter 5; Crook 1986; Tomlinson 1993: 64–6, 73). Entrepreneurial diasporas were a major target of campaigns against "usurers," reducing their contribution to every branch of the economy (Dobbin 1996: Chapters 5–7; Austin and Sugihara 1993: Chapters 7–9; Adas 1974).

Discrimination against minorities and entrepreneurs was linked to "romantic anti-capitalism," on both the left and the right of the political spectrum. The senseless slaughter in the trenches, followed by swelling unemployment, gave rise to a deep Western pessimism about capitalism, even in countries that rejected the blandishments of fascism and communism. At the same time, there was a positive reevaluation of "pre-capitalist" societies, stoked by the rise of social anthropology. Progress for the colonized on capitalist lines gave way to a defense of their pristine primitiveness. The result was a kind of "game park" vision of the Third World, reflected in educational policies that attempted to direct colonized peoples away from the mainstream of Western schooling (Clarence-Smith 1994a: 57–8, 69). A French governor of Cochinchina summed it up in 1935, opining that "there are times in the history of a people when progress consists in going backwards" (Brocheux and Hémery 1995: 314–15).

Conclusion

This survey suggests that scholars studying the contribution of modern colonialism to globalization need to pay more attention to factors limiting or facilitating trade. The "four Cs" come top of the list: customs duties, commodity agreements, currencies, and cartels. The existing emphasis on public investment (Reynolds 1985; Havinden and Meredith 1993) is misleading. Colonialism was at its most progressive when it tore down trade barriers, not when it channeled taxpayers' funds into "white elephants." Even a preoccupation with private investment from the metropoles underestimates surprisingly strong capacities for local savings (Austin and Sugihara 1993).

More fundamentally, research is required into the part played by colonialism in the growth or frustration of social institutions and "mental models" favorable to globalization. There was a yawning chasm between the Victorian belief that a cultural revolution was a central task of beneficent colonial rulers, and the post-1918 emphasis on keeping the colonized walled up in their "primitive" cultures. Both sets of attitudes were equally paternalist, but the Victorians were more successful in unlocking the gates of economic development. Moreover the nineteenth-century Western vision of global culture was tempered by a real respect for the patrimony of the periphery, to a greater extent than Edward Said would have us believe (MacKenzie 1995). The extraordinary popularity of Edward Fitzgerald's free rendering of the bitter–sweet Persian quatrains of Omar Khayyam, first published in 1859, are but one testimony to this.

References

Adas, M. (1974) *The Burma Delta: Economic Development and Social Change on an Asian Rice Frontier, 1852–1940*, Madison: University of Wisconsin Press.

Ageron, C.-R. (1983) *Histoire de l'Algérie contemporaine*, 8th edn, Paris: Presses Universitaires de France.

Akita, Shigeru (1996) "'Gentlemanly capitalism', intra-Asian trade and Japanese industrialisation at the turn of the last century," *Japan Forum* 8 (1): 51–66.

Aldrich, R. (1996) *Greater France: A History of French Overseas Expansion*, London: Macmillan.

Allen, G.C. and Donnithorne, A.G. (1954) *Western Enterprise in Indonesia and Malaysia*, London: George Allen&Unwin.

Arndt, H.W. (1987) *Economic Development: The History of an Idea*, Chicago: University of Chicago Press.

Assidon, E. (1989) *Le commerce captif: les sociétés commerciales françaises d'Afrique Noire*, Paris: Harmattan.

Aston, T.H. and Philpin, C.H.E. (eds) (1987) *The Brenner Debate: Agrarian Class Structure and Economic Development in Pre-industrial Europe*, Cambridge: Cambridge University Press.

Austin, G. and Sugihara, K. (eds) (1993) *Local Suppliers of Credit in the Third World, 1750–1960*, London: Macmillan.

Barrows, L.C. (1974) "The merchants and General Faidherbe: aspects of French expansion in Senegal in the 1850s," *Revue Française d'Histoire d'Outremer* 41: 236–83.

Batou, J. (1990) *Cent ans de résistance au sous-développement, l'industrialisation de l'Amérique Latine et du Moyen-Orient face au défi européen*, Geneva: Droz.

Bauer, P.T. (1948) *The Rubber Industry: A Study in Competition and Monopoly*, London: Longmans Green & Co.

—— (1976) *Dissent on Development*, London: Weidenfeld and Nicolson.

—— (1981) *Equality: The Third World and Economic Delusion*, London: Weidenfeld and Nicolson.

Bhacker, M.R. (1992) *Trade and Empire in Muscat and Zanzibar: The Roots of British Domination*, London: Routledge.

Bidwell, Robin (1973) *Morocco Under Colonial Rule: French Administration of Tribal Areas, 1912–1956*, London: Frank Cass.

Brocheux, P. and Hémery, D. (1995) *Indochine, la colonisation ambigu, 1858–1954*, Paris: Editions la Découverte.

Brown, I. (1989) "Some comments on industrialisation in the Philippines during the 1930s," in I. Brown (ed.) *The Economies of Africa and Asia in the Inter-war Depression*, 203–220, London: Routledge.

Brown, R.A. (1994) *Capital and Entrepreneurship in South-East Asia*, London: Macmillan.

Cain, P.J. (1980) *Economic Foundations of British Overseas Expansion, 1815–1914*, London: Macmillan (*Studies in Economic and Social History*).

Cain, P.J. and Hopkins, A.G. (1993) *British Imperialism, Crisis and Deconstruction, 1914–1990*, London: Longman.

Campo, J.N.F.M. (1992) *Koninklijke Paketvaart Maatschappij; stoomvaart en staatsvorming in de Indonesische archipel, 1888–1914*, Hilversum: Verloren

Capie, F. (1994) *Tariffs and Growth: Some Insights from the World Economy 1850–1940*, Manchester: Manchester University Press.

Chang, H.-Y. and Myers, R.H. (1963) "Japanese colonial development policy in Taiwan, 1895–1906: a case of bureaucratic entrepreneurship," *Journal of Asian Studies* 22 (4): 433–49.

Charlesworth, N. (1982) *British Rule and the Indian Economy, 1800–1914*, London: Macmillan (*Studies in Economic and Social History*).

Clarence-Smith, [W.]G. (1985) *The Third Portuguese Empire, 1825–1975: A Study in Economic Imperialism*, Manchester: Manchester University Press.

—— (1987) "'The imperialism of beggars': the role of the less developed powers in the 19th century scramble for colonies," *The City and the Empire*, vol. 2, London: Institute of Commonwealth Studies.

—— (1989) "The effects of the Great Depression of the 1930s on industrialisation in Equatorial and Central Africa," in I. Brown, (ed.) *The Economies of Africa and Asia in the Inter-war Depression*, 170–202, London: Routledge.

—— (1990) "The hidden costs of labour on the cocoa plantations of São Tomée and Príncipe, 1875–1914," *Portuguese Studies* 6: 152–72.

—— (1991) "The economic dynamics of Spanish colonialism in the 19th and 20th centuries", *Itinerario* 15: 71–90.

—— (1993a) "Labour conditions in the plantations of São Tomé and Príncipe," *Slavery and Abolition* 14 (1): 149–67.

—— (1993b) "Plantation versus smallholder production of cocoa: the legacy of the German period in Cameroon," in P. Geschiere and P. Konings (eds) *Itinéraires d'accumulation au Cameroun*, Paris: Karthala, pp. 187–216.

—— (1994a) "The organization of 'consent' in British West Africa, 1820s to 1860s," in D. Engels and S. Marks (eds) *Contesting Colonial Hegemony: State and Society in Africa and India*, London: British Academic Press, pp. 55–78.

—— (1994b) "The impact of forced coffee cultivation on Java, 1805–1917," *Indonesia Circle* 64: 241–64.

—— (1995) "Cocoa plantations in the Third World, 1870s–1914: the political economy of inefficiency," in J. Harriss, J. Hunter, and C. Lewis (eds) *The New Institutional Economics and Third World Development*, London: Routledge, pp. 157–71.

—— (ed.) (1996) *Cocoa Pioneer Fronts since 1800, The Role of Smallholders, Planters and Merchants*, London: Macmillan.

—— (1997) "Hadhrami entrepreneurs in the Malay world, c. 1750–c. 1940," in U. Freitag and W.G. Clarence-Smith (eds) *Hadhrami Traders: Scholars and Statesmen in the Indian Ocean, 1750s to 1960s*, Leiden: E.J. Brill.

Cole, R.L. (1968) "The tariff policies of Rhodesia, 1899–1963," *Rhodesian Journal of Economics* 2 (2): 28–47.

Coquery-Vidrovitch, C. (1972) *Le Congo au temps des grandes compagnies concessionnaires, 1898–1930*, Paris and The Hague: Mouton.

Cribb, R. (ed.) (1994) *The Late Colonial State in Indonesia: Political and Economic Foundations of the Netherlands Indies, 1880–1942*, Leiden: KITLV Press.

Crook, R. (1986) "Decolonisation, the colonial state and chieftaincy in the Gold Coast," *African Affairs* 338: 75–105.

Davies, G. (1996) *A History of Money from Ancient Times to The Present Day*, 2nd edn, Cardiff: University of Wales Press.

Dewey, C. (1993) *Anglo-Indian Attitudes: The Mind of the Indian Civil Service*, London: Hambledon.

Dobbin, C. (1996) *Asian Entrepreneurial Minorities: Conjoint Communities in The Making of the World Economy, 1570–1940*, Richmond: Curzon Press.

Drabble, J.H. (1991) *Malayan Rubber: The Interwar Years*, London: Macmillan.

Drummond, I.M. (1974) *Imperial Economic Policy 1917–1939: Studies in Expansion and Protection*, London: George Allen & Unwin.

—— (1987) *The Gold Standard and The International Monetary System, 1900–1939*, London: Macmillan (*Studies in Economic and Social History*).

Duus, P. (1984) "Economic dimensions of Meiji imperialism, the case of Korea, 1895–1910," in R.H. Myers and M.R. Peattie (eds) *The Japanese Colonial Empire, 1895–1945*, Princeton: Princeton University Press, pp. 128–71.

Elson, R. (1994) *Village Java under The Cultivation System, 1830–1870*, Sydney: Allen & Unwin.

Eltis, D. (1987) *Economic Growth and The Ending of the Transatlantic Slave Trade*, Oxford: Oxford University Press.

Emmer, P.C. and Mörner, M. (eds) (1992) *European Expansion and Migration: Essays on The Intercontinental Migration from Africa, Asia and Europe*, Oxford: Berg.

Fieldhouse, D.K. (1982) *The Colonial Empires: A Comparative Survey from The Eighteenth Century*, 2nd edn, London: Macmillan.

Foreman-Peck, J. (1983) *A History of The World Economy: International Economic Relations since 1850*, Brighton: Wheatsheaf Books.

Freitag, U. and Clarence-Smith, W.G. (eds) (1997) *Hadhrami Traders, Scholars and Statesmen in The Indian Ocean, 1750s to 1960s*, Leiden: E.J. Brill.

Gallagher J. and Robinson, R. (1970) "The imperialism of free trade," in A.G.L. Shaw (ed.) *Great Britain and The Colonies 1815–1865*, London: Methuen, pp. 142–63.

Gann, L.H., and Duignan, P. (1979) *The Rulers of Belgian Africa, 1884–1914*, Princeton: Princeton University Press.

Giesecke, L.F. (1987) *History of American Economic Policy in The Philippines during the American Colonial Period, 1900–1935*, New York: Garland.

Harriss, J., Hunter, J., and Lewis, C. (eds) *The New Institutional Economics and Third World Development*, London: Routledge.

Havinden, M. and Meredith, D. (1993) *Colonialism and Development, Britain and Its Tropical Colonies, 1850–1960*, London: Routledge.

Ho, S.P.-S. (1984) "Colonialism and development: Korea, Taiwan and Kwangtung," in R.H. Myers and M.R. Peattie (eds) *The Japanese Colonial Empire, 1895–1945*, Princeton: Princeton University Press, pp. 347–98.

Hodgart, A. (1977) *The Economics of European Imperialism*, London: Edward Arnold.

Holland, B. (1913) *The Fall of Protection 1840–1850*, London: Edward Arnold.

Hopkins, A.G. (1973) *An Economic History of West Africa*, London: Longmans.

Hyde, F.E. (1973) *Far Eastern Trade, 1860–1914*, London: Adam & Charles Black.

Issawi, C. (1982) *An Economic History of The Middle East and North Africa*, London: Methuen.

Jesus, E.C. de (1980) *The Tobacco Monopoly in The Philippines: Bureaucratic Enterprise and Social Change, 1766–1880*, Quezon City: Ateneo de Manila University Press.

Kossmann, E.H. (1978) *The Low Countries, 1780–1940*, Oxford: Clarendon Press.

Kumar, D. (1993) "Colonialism, bondage and caste in British India," in M. Klein, (ed.) *Breaking the Chains, Slavery, Bondage and Emancipation in Modern Africa and Asia*, Madison: University of Wisconsin Press, pp. 112–30, .

Laffey, J. (1969) "Roots of French imperialism in the nineteenth century: the case of Lyon," *French Historical Studies* 6: 78–92.

Leubuscher, C. (1962) *The West African Shipping Trade, 1909–1959*, Leiden: A.W. Sythoff.

Lindblad, J.T. (1989) "Economic aspects of the Dutch expansion in Indonesia, 1870–1914," *Modern Asian Studies* 23 (1): 1–23.

MacKenzie J.M. (1995) *Orientalism: History, Theory and the Arts*, Manchester: Manchester University Press.

Macpherson, W.J. (1987) *The Economic Development of Japan, c. 1868–1941*, London: Macmillan (*Studies in Economic and Social History*).

Marseille, J. (1984) *Empire colonial et capitalisme français, histoire d'un divorce*, Paris: Albin Michel.

May, G.A. (1984) *Social Engineering in the Philippines: The Aims, Execution and Impact of American Colonial Policy, 1900–1913*, 2nd edn, Quezon City: New Day.

Miège, J.-L. (1968) *L'impérialisme colonial italien de 1870 à nos jours*, Paris: Société d'Edition d'Enseignement Supérieur.

Munro, J.F. (1976) *Africa and The International Economy, 1800–1960*, London: J.M. Dent & Sons.

—— (1984) *Britain in Tropical Africa, 1880–1960: Economic Relationships and Impact*, London: Macmillan (*Studies in Economic and Social History*).

Murray, M.J. (1980*) The Development of Capitalism in Colonial Indochina, 1870–1940*, Berkeley and Los Angeles: University of California Press.

Nakahara, M. (1994) "Modern Japan in Asia: Meiji Japan in the eyes of the Maharaja Abu Bakar," *Waseda Journal of Asian Studies*, 16: 15–30.

Northrup, D. (1995) *Indentured Labor in The Age of Imperialism, 1834–1922*, Cambridge: Cambridge University Press.

O'Brien, P. (1997) "Intercontinental trade and the development of the Third World since the industrial revolution," *Journal of World History* 8 (1): 75–133.

Oliver, R. and Atmore, A. (1981) *Africa since 1800*, 3rd edn, Cambridge: Cambridge University Press.

Owen, R. (1981) *The Middle East in The World Economy, 1800–1914*, London: Methuen.

Phillips, A. (1989) *The Enigma of Colonialism, British Policy in West Africa*, London: James Currey.

Phillips Lewis, K. (1996) "The Trinidad cocoa industry and the struggle for crown land during the nineteenth century," in W.G. Clarence-Smith (ed.) *Cocoa Pioneer Fronts since 1800: The Role of Smallholders, Planters and Merchants*, London: Macmillan.

Porter, B. (1975) *The Lion's Share: A Short History of British Imperialism, 1850–1970*, London: Longman.

Porter, A. (1994) *European Imperialism, 1860–1914*, London: Macmillan.

Ray, R.K. (1979) *Industrialisation in India: Growth and Conflict in the Private Corporate Sector, 1914–1947*, Delhi: Oxford University Press.

Reynolds. L.G. (1985) *Economic growth in the Third World, 1850–1980*, New Haven: Yale University Press.

Rushbrook-Williams, L.F. (1958) *The Black Hills: Kutch in History and Legend: A Study in Indian Local Loyalties*, London: Weidenfeld and Nicolson.

SarDesai, D.R. (1977) *British Trade and Expansion in Southeast Asia, 1830–1914*, Columbia, Missouri: South Asia Books.

Sbacchi, A. (1980) *Il colonialismo italiano in Etiopia, 1936–1940*, Milan: Mursia.

Schinzinger, F. (1984) *Die Kolonien und das Deutsche Reich; die wirtschaftliche Bedeutung der deutschen Besitzungen in Übersee*, Stuttgart: Franz Steiner Verlag

Sheffer, G. (ed.) (1986) *Modern Diasporas in International Politics*, London: Croom Helm.

Smith, M.S. (1980) *Tariff Reform in France, 1860–1900*, Ithaca: Cornell University Press.

Sturmey, S.G. (1962) *British Shipping and World Competition*, London: Athlone Press.

Sugihara, K. (1990) "Japan as an engine of the Asian international economy, c. 1880–1936," *Japan Forum* 2 (1): 127–45.

Sugiyama, S. and Guerrero, M.C. (1994) *International Commercial Rivalry in Southeast Asia in the Interwar period*, New Haven: Yale Southeast Asia Studies.

Tarling, N. (ed.) (1992) *The Cambridge History of Southeast Asia, Volume 2: The Nineteenth and Twentieth centuries*, Cambridge: Cambridge University Press.

Thompson, V. and Adloff, R. (1969) *French West Africa*, 2nd edn, New York: Greenwood Press.

Tomlinson, B.R. (1979) *The Political Economy of the Raj, 1914–1947: The Economics of Decolonisation in India*, London: Macmillan.

—— (1993) *The Economy of Modern India, 1860–1970*, Cambridge: Cambridge University Press.

Vandewalle, G. (1966) *De conjuncturele evolutie in Kongo en Ruanda-Urundi, van 1920 tot 1939, en van 1949 tot 1958*, Gent: Rijksuniversiteit te Gent.

Ward, J.R. (1985) *Poverty and Progress in the Caribbean, 1800–1960*, London: Macmillan (*Studies in Economic and Social History*).

7 Sovereignty, territoriality and the globalization of finance

Eric Helleiner[1]

Financial globalization is often said to be one of the most important develop-ments challenging the sovereign state in the contemporary era. It is cited prominently by those who argue that we are witnessing a profound transforma-tion of world order of a kind that has not been experienced since the birth of the sovereign state system in seventeenth-century Europe at the Peace of Westphalia (e.g., Rosenau 1989; Ruggie 1993; Cox 1992; Wriston 1992; Cerny 1995; Sassen 1996). The notion that we are witnessing such a momentous upheaval in world politics is an exciting one. This chapter, however, questions whether the implica-tions of financial globalization for the sovereign state are quite so clear cut.

I suggest that it is useful to recognize that there are four different variants of the argument that financial globalization poses a challenge to the sovereign state. The first three focus on the impact of financial globalization on the regulatory power and macroeconomic policy autonomy of the state. In Stephen Krasner's (1997) typology, they associate a challenge to the sovereign state as a threat to "control sovereignty"; that is, a threat to the state's ability to *control* activities within and across its border. These arguments are the most prominent in the literature, but I argue in the first three sections of the chapter that they are less than fully persuasive in linking financial globalization to the erosion of the sovereign state. Specifically, these arguments are seen to suffer from two weak-nesses: (1) they overstate the impact of financial globalization on state power; and (2) they lack a long historical perspective on the world-order transformations they are analyzing. If financial globalization is undermining the sovereign state, I suggest that a more promising case is a fourth argument – which is least devel-oped in the existing literature. This argument associates financial globalization with an unraveling of territoriality. In Krasner's terms, sovereignty is seen here in terms of "authority" rather than "control." In the fourth section of the chapter, I present several ways in which this argument might be developed further and refined.

Argument 1: information technology and the regulatory capacity of states

Let us begin by evaluating perhaps the most popular of the arguments tying financial globalization to a decline of sovereignty. This line of argument is one that suggests states have a declining capacity to regulate finance because of technological changes that have propelled the globalization trend. Walter Wriston (1986; 1988; 1992) has made this argument most effectively. He argues that financial globalization is being driven primarily by the information technology revolution. In addition to dramatically reducing the costs associated with moving money around the world, this technological revolution is said to be rendering state initiatives to control finance quite futile.[2] From Wriston's standpoint, once states have lost the ability to regulate finance, they have lost a central aspect of sovereignty: the ability to control the value of their currency.

Wriston gives two principal reasons why information technologies have undermined state regulatory capacity in finance. The first is that money increasingly takes the form of digital blips of information that can be easily and cheaply transmitted through a multitude of sophisticated worldwide telecommunications networks. In this new form, money has become much more mobile and thus difficult for regulatory authorities to control. State authorities also encounter particular difficulties distinguishing – and thus being able to regulate – the electronic blips that relate to money movements from those that relate to other kinds of information. Second, regulatory initiatives are further stymied by the fact that financial trading increasingly seems to take place in a kind of cyberspace that recognizes no borders. In Wriston's words:

> The new world financial market is not a geographical location to be found on a map but, rather, more than two hundred thousand electronic monitors in trading rooms all over the world that are linked together. With the new technology no one is in control.
>
> (1992: 61)

Popular as Wriston's views may be, they are not entirely convincing. To begin with, it is important not to overstate the degree to which sovereign states have ever been able to regulate international movements of money. Well before the current age of financial globalization, sovereign states also had enormous difficulties attempting to control cross-border flows of money. Throughout the age of "mercantilism," most European states sought to control the international movements of precious metals and these initiatives were rarely successful. Not until the 1930s, and then during and after the Second World War, did most sovereign states begin to experiment with capital controls that were comprehensive and enforced by the full power of the modern administrative state. And, once again, even these controls were usually not fully effective. Even the use of postal censorship and the threat of the death penalty did not stop people from finding ways to evade extremely tight exchange control regulations in that era. For this reason, the capacity to control financial movements is not a very useful indicator of the status of the "sovereign state."

Still, it is interesting to address the question of whether information technologies have made these inherent difficulties in regulating finance worse for states, as

Wriston suggests. This is a more difficult question to answer than Wriston implies because states have made little effort to use information technologies to control finance in the contemporary age. But in the few instances where they have, Wriston's argument seems to be turned on its head: information technology strengthens rather than weakens state regulatory capacity in the financial sector.

This is best demonstrated by a brief look at the anti-money-laundering regulations that the US and other leading powers have begun to implement since the late 1980s. Despite the general trend towards financial liberalization over the last decade, most countries have begun to introduce selective regulations aimed at curtailing money-laundering activities, which have grown in the new integrated global financial system. These regulatory initiatives have demonstrated that information technology can bolster state regulatory power in three ways.

First, electronic fund transfers leave an electronic trace that can be more easily monitored than transactions in hard cash. For this reason, many analysts and regulatory authorities argue that efforts to discover and control money laundering will be helped enormously by the declining use of cash (Possamai 1992: 46). Where governments in the interwar years were forced to open mail in their searches for illicit money movements, governments today need only monitor the limited number of electronic payments systems that increasingly dominate the financial services industry.

Second, in contrast to Wriston's view, the payments systems through which international movements of finance travel are quite distinct from those carrying other electronic information flows. They are also very concentrated. Roughly 95 per cent of all international dollar transfers are channeled through the CHIPS network based in the US. Equally important is SWIFT, which transmits the instructions to execute most of the electronic funds transfers that take place through CHIPS and a second US-based network, Fedwire, that handles almost all US domestic payments. Any initiative to monitor and regulate international financial transactions can accomplish an enormous amount simply by focusing on movements within these systems. As part of their efforts to encourage financial institutions to know the identity of their customers, for example, the leading economic powers pressed SWIFT to broadcast a message on July 30 1992 to all its users asking them to include full identifying information concerning ordering customers and beneficiaries (Helleiner 1998: 394).

Initiatives of this kind may signal the first step along a potential route of transforming CHIPS, Fedwire, and SWIFT into "closed-circuit systems" that can be used only by those willing to adopt certain responsibilities *vis-à-vis* the regulation of money laundering. Such a move would be quite effective in controlling money laundering around the world. In Stephen Zamora's (1992: 203–4) words: "If the world community adopts a closed-circuit system, it will be essential to enter that system in order to take part in the Western financial system." Some might argue that such a move will encourage diversion to other clearing systems, but there are not many trustworthy alternatives for market actors to turn to and regulatory initiatives can quickly be extended to them. For this reason, the new international electronic payments systems appear to have made the multilateral regulation of financial flows easier.

The potential effectiveness of this kind of initiative also highlights the fact that financial markets *do* still rely on specific geographical places for their functioning, in contrast to Wriston's view. As Saskia Sassen (1991) and Nigel Thrift (1994) point out, financial globalization seems, in fact, to have *increased* the importance of geographical places for financial markets. As capital has become more mobile, financial activity has come to be more concentrated than ever in a few leading financial centers: above all, London and New York. This geographical concentration is caused not just by the need for centralized payments and clearing networks. It is also a product of the fact that the markets rely on a range of services – informational, legal, cultural – that are best provided in concentrated geographical locations. The concentrated nature of financial activity in specific geographical centers ensures that regulatory initiatives implemented by the states housing these centers are likely to be quite effective.

Finally, technological developments have also increased the potential for individual states to monitor suspicious financial movements in and out of their territory. United States officials, for example, have greatly enhanced their capacity to identify cross-border suspicious money movements by introducing in 1993 an artificial intelligence (AI) system, which analyses each week 200,000 currency transactions reports that are filed by financial institutions. US policy-makers have also noted that their monitoring capacity is further aided by the fact that financial institutions themselves are increasingly using sophisticated computer programs capable of retrieving specific wire transfer records as a service to their customers. Australian officials also now use an AI system to analyze data concerning not only large cash transactions but also all wire transfers – approximately 20,000 daily – in and out of the country. This system, which was developed initially by a US defense contractor to track incoming missiles, receives financial data within 24 hours of the transactions having taken place, thus helping regulatory authorities to respond in a proactive manner to suspicious flows (Helleiner 1998: 395).

If information technology has strengthened state regulatory power in these ways, why, then, has financial globalization taken place? One can certainly not deny that technological and market developments have encouraged private actors to move increasingly large sums of money around the world in the last several decades, as Wriston suggests. But what his explanation misses out is the equally important role played by states. Private actors could not have acquired the kind of freedom to move assets around the world that they have today unless states had liberalized their capital controls beginning as far back as the 1960s. Also significant have been the decisions of states to construct supervisory and regulatory frameworks that minimize the risk of international financial crises that might erode confidence in cross-border financial movements. As I have explained elsewhere (Helleiner 1994), these liberalization and regulatory decisions were not forced by inexorable technological developments. Instead, they reflected specific interests who came to favor financial liberalism during this period.

It is thus by no means clear that financial globalization signals the decline of the regulatory power of states. The trend was, after all, supported by states, and they continue to have the capacity to withdraw their support for it. A withdrawal of support could take the form of decisions to abandon commitments to the supervisory and regulatory frameworks that have been established to prevent international financial crises. It could also take the form of a reintroduction of some kind of restrictions – perhaps in the limited form of a Tobin tax – on international financial flows (Helleiner 1996). As in the past, such restrictions would not succeed in stopping all the flows they attempted to control. But information technologies, far from undermining such regulatory initiatives, may make them more effective than they have been before.

Argument 2: competitive deregulation and state regulatory power

If information technologies have not undermined the power of states to regulate finance, this power may have been eroded in a second way by the financial globalization trend. According to some authors, the heightened mobility of financial capital has unleashed powerful competitive deregulation pressures that prevent states from even being able to consider regulations in the financial sector. Phil Cerny has made this case most effectively. In his words, a kind of "whipsaw" (Cerny 1995: 610) effect has been unleashed by financial globalization in which states are forced to lower regulations in order to ensure that mobile financial capital and business is attracted to and kept in their own markets. Unilateral reregulatory initiatives are thus inhibited by a fear that they will render the national financial system uncompetitive. Cooperative initiatives are also rendered very difficult because they are constantly scuttled by individual financial centers that attempt to attract financial business and capital to their markets by not participating.

Cerny (1994: 320) concludes that the regulatory capacity of the state in finance has thus been "gravely challenged." From his perspective, this challenge has ramifications well beyond the financial sector because of the centrality and "structural hegemony" of financial markets within the contemporary global political economy. If states are unable to regulate finance, Cerny argues that their capacity to perform a wide range of other economic and political services is also being compromised to such a degree that a fundamental transformation of the nature of world order is under way. Only a turn to "supranational" (ibid.: 339) reregulatory initiatives is likely to succeed in bringing finance back under some degree of control.

Cerny's argument is an important one. Competitive deregulation pressures have undoubtedly played an important role in scuttling cooperative regulatory initiatives and encouraging states to liberalize financial markets. Indeed, I have given them an important role in my own analysis of these developments (Helleiner 1994). I have, however, also become increasingly convinced that their influence should not be overstated.

To begin with, their role in encouraging states to liberalize finance can easily be exaggerated. As Andrew Sobel (1994) reminds us, liberalization measures are often justified by invoking external competitive pressures when the real motivation is quite a different one. Sobel argues that the primary motivation for the recent liberalization trend has, in fact, been a domestic one: financial actors across the OECD region demanded liberalization in order to cope with the unraveling of cartel-like domestic market structures caused by the growth of government bond markets, new inflationary conditions, and the rise of institutional investors. Other analysts have highlighted additional important motives for the financial liberalization trend such as the growing ascendancy of neoliberal thought and the desire of an increasingly internationalized business sector to be freed from cumbersome capital controls (Goodman and Pauly, 1993; Helleiner 1994).

The persistence of distinct national regulatory structures in an age of financial globalization also raises questions about the power of competitive deregulation pressures. If these pressures were so dominant, one would expect a convergence of national financial structures towards a deregulated and liberalized model during the last two decades. In fact, as Louis Pauly (1994) highlights, many distinct national financial regulatory traditions remain. States in East Asia, in particular, retain considerable regulations in their financial systems that continue to give their states extensive power to influence national economic and political life. Most states outside the OECD region also retain capital controls despite the alleged power of competitive deregulatory pressures.

Competitive deregulation pressures have not only failed to inhibit states from regulating finance unilaterally in these distinct ways. They also have not prevented states from asserting their regulatory power at the international level in a cooperative fashion. Two recent initiatives demonstrate how states have been able to overcome competitive pressures in finance to construct a cooperative international regulatory regime. The first initiative was the 1988 agreement among G-10 central banks – the Basel Accord – to enforce a common set of standards for the capital adequacy of international banks as a means of reducing the risk of financial crises.[3] A second initiative was the creation of an international regime to curtail money-laundering beginning in the late 1980s. These illegal earnings were seen to be undermining not only domestic law-enforcement initiatives but also the stability of individual financial institutions and the financial system as a whole.

Both of these international initiatives suggest that the sovereign state's regulatory power in international finance is far from diminishing. Indeed, Kapstein (1994) points out that the Basel Accord represents an initiative by which the regulatory power of states is very much being *enhanced* through cooperative action. The construction of the anti-money-laundering regime represents perhaps an even more dramatic example of this phenomenon. Since the late 1980s, states have agreed to increase their surveillance and regulation of domestic financial systems to a degree that is quite unprecedented, especially with respect to the overriding of bank secrecy laws. Moreover, through technical and legal assistance programs, both regimes have helped to build up the regulatory power of

foreign governments who have little capacity or experience with financial regulation of this kind (Helleiner 1999).

Financial globalization, in other words, has not led to an overall decline in
state regulatory power over finance. Rather, it appears to have encouraged states
to enhance this power in new ways that are more domestically intrusive and
which are introduced in an internationally coordinated fashion. The objective in
both instances, after all, has been to defend the stability and integrity of the new
globalized financial order. It is also worth highlighting that the two regulatory
initiatives have been implemented and enforced through cooperation between
sovereign states rather than through the construction of powerful supranational
bodies. The international institutions at the center of both regimes – the Bank
for International Settlements in the case of the Basel Accord and the Financial
Action Task Force (FATF) in the case of money laundering – have few powers
over member states (and the FAFT is not even intended to be a permanent
body). All of the efforts to promote international cooperation with respect to
regulatory, information sharing and legal assistance are also designed to *bolster*,
rather than undermine, the power of the state to regulate its own markets and
financial institutions, albeit in an internationally harmonized way. Sovereignty –
if measured by the indicator of regulatory power – is being validated and rein-
forced from the outside through these initiatives.[4]

How were states able to overcome competitive deregulation pressures to
construct these two regulatory regimes? In both cases, the US played a key role,
pressuring states to cooperate by threatening to cut off access to its financial
markets, and even its clearing systems, unless other states complied with the new
standards. Because of the centrality of US financial markets and clearing
systems in the global financial system, these threats were very effective in encouraging foreign governments to comply (Kapstein 1994; Helleiner 1999).

Regulatory cooperation in both instances was also fostered by the fact that each
regulatory initiative was seen as necessary for the preservation of the new liberal
international financial order to which most leading powers had become committed
by the late 1980s. The debt crisis highlighted the risks of instability in the international banking system and encouraged central bankers to move towards the
Basel Accord. Several highly public scandals and crises associated with international money-laundering activity also helped to prompt state policy-makers to
recognize the dangers of this activity for the integrity of the international financial
system. The commitment of elite policy-makers to liberal norms and the defense
of the new global financial order, thus, appears to have been a more important
influence on state behavior than competitive deregulation concerns in these
instances.

Perhaps most interestingly, competitive pressures within financial markets
themselves have also encouraged these two reregulatory initiatives. In the case of
the Basel Accord, financial institutions and financial centers that have not abided
by the new capital standards have been perceived within the markets to be less
stable and secure than those that have adopted the standards. This, in turn, has
encouraged the exact opposite of the competitive deregulation dynamic: finan-

cial institutions and governments have been keen to adopt the new regulations in order to maintain their reputation within the financial markets. This "competitive *re*-regulation" dynamic has also encouraged financial institutions and governments to comply with the new anti-money-laundering regulations. A growing number of financial scandals and crises involving money laundering have drawn the attention of "clean" market actors to the risks of doing business with financial institutions and jurisdictions that have not complied fully with the standards and regulations outlined in the new anti-money-laundering regime. Once again, what Kapstein (1994: 190, fn. 40) calls "reputational effects" have driven a kind of upward harmonization process that has encouraged money-laundering regulations.

Argument 3: the decline of macroeconomic policy autonomy

Having critiqued arguments linking financial globalization and the decline of sovereign state to the diminishing regulatory power of the state, I now turn to a third set of arguments, which concentrate on a different issue: the impact of financial globalization on the macroeconomic policy autonomy of the sovereign state.[5] A number of different dimensions of the ability of sovereign states to conduct an independent macroeconomic policy are said to have been undermined by the increased mobility of financial capital. Independent tax policies are seen to be more difficult as individuals and corporations evade domestic taxation by moving assets abroad. Enormous movements of speculative capital also seem to inhibit autonomous monetary policies as governments find it hard to set independent interest rates or control their country's exchange rate. In particular, it is frequently said that expansionary Keynesian-style macroeconomic policies have been rendered obsolete in the new globalized financial context. One reason is the risk of capital flight as investors fear the low interest rates, devaluation, or inflation that may accompany such policies. A second is that governments running Keynesian-style deficits are likely to be charged a "risk premium" on loans by the international markets. The dramatic "U-Turn" of the Mitterrand government in 1983 is usually cited to support this argument about the collapse of national Keynesianism.

The problems that capital flight can pose for the loss of macroeconomic autonomy are said to be even more severe for non-OECD countries. Through the 1970s and 1980s, massive sums of flight capital moved from non-OECD countries to OECD countries. This capital flight was a major contributor to the debt crisis that erupted after 1982 and the consequent loss of policy autonomy which accompanied it. More recently, the power of the international financial markets to undermine the policy autonomy of Southern governments is said to have been even more dramatically demonstrated by the 1994 Mexican peso crisis. In this instance, an entire country's economic prospects appeared to have been devastated overnight by a sudden loss of confidence in the international financial markets.

As states lose macroeconomic autonomy, some authors are also keen to high-light the emergence of non-state bodies in the financial markets who are seen to be supplanting states as key authorities in world politics. Tim Sinclair (1994), for example, has called attention to the power of bond rating agencies in determining macroeconomic outcomes. He argues that these agencies signal the growing influence of "sovereignty-free actors" in world politics and the erosion of the Westphalian world order.[6] Thomas Friedman made a similar argument after Moody's Investors Services appeared to have triggered the Mexican peso crisis with a downgrade of Mexican bonds: "you could almost say that we live again in a two-superpower world. There is the US and there is Moody's. The US can destroy a country by leveling it with bombs. Moody's can destroy a country by downgrading its bonds" (quoted in Cohen 1996: 282).

These arguments present a more persuasive case than the first two arguments about some of the implications of financial globalization. But once again, they often overstate their case that financial globalization is undermining the sovereign state in several ways. To begin with, the declining macroeconomic power of the state is sometimes exaggerated. In the realm of monetary policy, the Mundell–Fleming model points out that states can retain a high degree of monetary policy autonomy in an atmosphere of capital mobility if they are willing to allow the exchange rate to fluctuate. Indeed, according to the model, monetary policy becomes even *more* effective in conditions of capital mobility. An expansionary monetary policy, for example, will trigger an outflow of capital that, in turn, will cause the exchange rate to depreciate, thus reinforcing the expansionary effect of the initial policy (Andrews 1994; Cohen 1996).

The importance of this insight can be seen in the case of Mitterrand's "U-Turn" in 1983. From a Mundell–Fleming standpoint, the constraint facing the Mitterrand government was not just capital mobility but also its membership in the European Monetary System (EMS), which prevented France from devaluing its currency once its unilateral expansion was underway. As Ton Notermans (1995) has highlighted, European governments such as Sweden and Norway that stayed out of the EMS – and maintained a floating exchange rate – succeeded in retaining an ability to pursue expansionary monetary policy throughout the 1970s and 1980s. From Notermans' perspective, these governments eventually abandoned expansionary macroeconomic policies *not* because of the external constraint of financial globalization but because of a growing inability to contain inflation domestically as tripartite collective-bargaining structures unraveled and domestic financial innovation undermined traditional monetary tools.

Indeed, Michael Loriaux's (1991) analysis of the Mitterrand U-Turn suggests that the French experience can be interpreted in a similar way. In the new atmo-sphere of floating exchange rates after 1973, he shows how the French government was increasingly unable to pursue expansionary policies because the inflationary consequences of a devaluation could not be easily contained. This inability to contain inflation was, in turn, related to domestic factors: the existence of an "overdraft economy" which resulted from the structure of the French domestic financial system. From this perspective, the French state lost control over its macroeconomic policy *not* because of financial globalization but because its domestic financial system was ill-suited to the macroeconomic imperatives of the new world of floating exchange rates.[7] Ironically, as Loriaux points out, the financial deregulation and liberalization program launched by the Mitterrand government after 1983 had the effect of *increasing* the ability of the state to control monetary policy rather than decreasing it. It enabled the state to regain control over monetary policy by eliminating the overdraft economy which had been fostered by the old financial system. Contrasting his view with that of Cerny noted in the previous section, Loriaux (1991: 89–90) concludes: "The logic of liberalization should therefore not be misconstrued: state strength and national power, not abdication to the marketplace, was the goal that liberalizing financial reform pursued."

The importance of exchange rate policy in providing a degree of macroeconomic autonomy can also be highlighted in the case of capital flight from Latin American countries. Jonathan Crystal (1994) argues that much of the capital flight experienced by Latin American countries in the 1970s and 1980s could have been avoided through the use of different exchange rate policies. As he demonstrates, countries maintaining overvalued exchange rates have suffered much more serious capital flight than those that did not. This point is also well demonstrated by the 1994 peso crisis, which was triggered by capital flight responding in part to the decision of the Mexican government to maintain an overvalued exchange rate policy. As Manuel Pastor argues in his contribution to this volume (Chapter 11), if the Mexican government had initiated a slow and controlled devaluation after 1992, the discipline of the international financial markets might not have been felt so severely. To be sure, that the government chose not to do so was partly a product of fears of the reaction of global investors (as well as of US Congress, which was debating NAFTA at this time). But this decision also reflected domestic constraints such as the erosion of tripartite pacts that restrained wage and prices as well as the fragility of the banking system, both of which encouraged the government to look to the exchange rate as a policy tool for containing inflation.[8] As in the French and Scandinavian cases, the Mexican government thus lost control over macroeconomic policy in this period not just because of international financial constraints but also because of domestic developments.

The new external constraints on fiscal policy also should not be overstated. As Garrett (1995) points out, many governments in the OECD region have used borrowing in international capital markets in the last two decades to finance their expanding government spending and fiscal deficits. In the 1970s and again since the early 1990s, developing countries in Latin America and East Asia have also found that global financial markets offer funds that *enhance* policy autonomy in the short-term. These borrowing experiences need not necessarily end up in debt crises that undermine policy autonomy over the medium term. That they often have done so has been a product of a number of factors, many quite unrelated to financial globalization such as unexpected sudden shocks to the world economy and particular patterns in the use of the borrowed funds.

These various points highlight the need to be cautious in linking financial globalization to a collapse of macroeconomic policy autonomy. This is not to deny that some erosion has taken place. The ability of governments to tax, for example, has certainly been undermined. The use of a flexible exchange rate to maintain an independent monetary policy also may not be an option open to all countries and it contains considerable risks given that foreign exchange markets are prone to overshooting behavior that is not acknowledged by the Mundell–Fleming model. The kind of discipline that the markets can impose on left-of-center governments – either via speculative capital flight of a kind not incorporated into the Mundell–Fleming model or via risk premiums – also cannot be ignored. Much capital flight from developing countries also clearly takes place for reasons unrelated to overvalued exchange rates. My point here is simply that the constraints imposed by financial globalization are sometimes overstated in current writings.

Regardless of the degree to which macroeconomic policy autonomy has been undermined, a more important objection to this third argument must be raised. Like the ability to control cross-border financial movements, declining macroeconomic policy autonomy is not a very good indicator of the erosion of the deep historical structure of the sovereign state. The notion of activist national macroeconomic planning is, after all, a relatively recent creation. In the several decades before 1914, financial capital was also highly mobile – indeed, more mobile than today according to some indicators (Wade 1996: 73–6) – and yet far fewer objections were raised about the challenge this situation posed to the sovereign state. The reason was simple: national macroeconomic planning was an idea foreign to that era. Many countries did not even have central banks at that time and the central banks that did exist were mostly private institutions whose principal macroeconomic goal was simply to maintain the convertibility of the national currency into gold. The notion that fiscal policy might be used to promote a macroeconomic objective such as the rate of employment was also absent, as indeed was the idea that a macroeconomic problem called "unemployment" existed. Even in the tax field, few states attempted to levy forms of taxes – such as income taxes – that could be easily evaded through international financial movements (Eichengreen 1992).

In that pre-1914 era, the only way in which global financial markets were seen to challenge the "macroeconomic policy autonomy" of sovereign states was in terms of the constraints they imposed on government spending. And the debates on this topic were little different from those today. On the one hand, international financiers seemed at times to challenge sovereignty when they dictated spending and tax policies to debtors who held outstanding loans. On the other hand, international financiers also enhanced the power of sovereign states at other times by offering them an easy way to raise funds for government spending. In an era when states often lacked the ability to collect domestic taxes in an efficient and comprehensive manner, loans from international financiers were in fact a central way in which states mobilized money to consolidate their sovereign power and authority (e.g. Riley 1980).

It was not until the interwar period, and especially after the early 1930s, that most states began to consider implementing the kinds of tax regimes and national macroeconomic planning policies that are today said to be threatened by capital mobility. Not coincidentally, this was also the period when states began to consider imposing comprehensive controls on cross-border financial flows for the first time. Some of the tensions between global finance and macroeconomic policy autonomy that are noted today would be very familiar to political economists of that earlier era. So, too, would the power of private financial actors over macroeconomic policy of states. Indeed, the power of J.P. Morgan's firm over many states' policy autonomy in the 1920s was undoubtedly much greater than the power of Moody's in the contemporary age.

If financial globalization challenges macroeconomic policy autonomy today, then, this challenge is less revolutionary in long historical terms than it is sometimes portrayed. It may pose a challenge to what Robert Cox (1987) has called the "welfare–nationalist" state, an historical form of state that reached its zenith of power in the middle decades of this century. But it is difficult to see how an erosion of macroeconomic policy autonomy challenges the deeper historical structure of the "sovereign state." For the same reason, it is hard to agree with those who argue that the powerful non-state authorities witnessed today in global financial markets signal the emergence of "post-Westphalian" world order. These private authorities have many parallels in the past including not just Morgan's firm in the 1920s but also others before it such as the Rothchilds, Barings, and Hope & Company. Indeed, these financiers were often involved in the broader arena of international politics to a degree that is unparalleled today.

Argument 4: the unraveling of territoriality

If the previous three arguments are less than persuasive in linking financial globalization to the decline of the sovereign state, does this mean that no convincing link can be drawn? If such a link is to be effectively made, I argue in this final section that attention needs to be given to a different understanding of sovereignty. A central weakness of the previous arguments is that they measure the status of the sovereign state according to the state's ability to *control* activities within and across its borders. Like Janice Thomson (1995), I have found this approach problematic. Not only is it unclear whether financial globalization has eroded this control significantly, but indicators such as regulatory power and macroeconomic autonomy are ahistorical. They refer to state functions that were either never fully performed by sovereign states or only assumed very recently by such states. As Thomson argues, a more fruitful approach would be to study the changing *authority* of the state.

Specifically, in the context of financial issues, attention should be focused on a fourth set of arguments that have linked financial globalization to an erosion of state authority based on the principle of territoriality. This fourth line of argument is a promising one since the principle of territoriality is one that Thomson and others argue has been at the core of the sovereign state's authority. Despite this promise, arguments linking financial globalization to an unraveling of territoriality have been much less prominent and well-developed in the literature. In this final section, I want to show three ways in which financial globalization can be seen to be eroding state authority claims based on the principle of territoriality.

John Ruggie (1993) has recently highlighted the unraveling of territoriality as the key indicator of the erosion of the Westphalian sovereign state system. His analysis helps us to identify a first way in which financial globalization may be linked to what Thomson (1995) calls a "deterritorialization of state authority claims." As evidence of his broader argument, Ruggie briefly cites the emergence of the "offshore" financial activity in eurocurrency centers. The significance of these centers, he argues, is that they represent a new kind of economic "region" that does not conform to the homogeneous and exclusive sense of territorial space that characterized the age of the sovereign state. Financial activities in eurocurrency markets, he notes, are housed within national territories but "are considered to exist in an extranational realm" (Ruggie 1993: 141). While Ruggie's analysis is very brief, Saskia Sassen (1996) develops this point in more detail. She argues that the euromarkets challenge the sovereign state by acting as locations within national territories that are created deliberately beyond its regulatory umbrella to service the global economy. In her words, the spread of this "offshore" financial activity represents an important example of a broader "denationalization of national territory" (Sassen 1996: xii).

This kind of argument is sometimes misunderstood by critics. Ethan Kapstein (1994), for example, critiques Ruggie's case by highlighting the continuing centrality of state regulatory power in the eurocurrency markets as evidenced by the Basel Accord. In his words, "to the extent that extranational banking activities do occur, they are at the discretion of national authorities" (p. 502). This critique misses the target. Ruggie's intention is not to question this regulatory power; that is, he is not making the kind of argument described in the first and second sections of this chapter. Instead, he is pointing to an unraveling of the link between territory and state authority.

Ironically, Kapstein's own work on the Basel Accord provides a second piece of evidence to support Ruggie's argument. As Kapstein (1994) shows, the Accord requires central banks to apply their domestic regulatory and supervisory practices to the global operations of their national banks. In his words, states have chosen to cope with the globalization of financial markets through this regulatory formula of "international cooperation based on home country control." This cooperative extraterritorial application of domestic rules provides an interesting example of the kind of phenomenon that Ruggie is pointing to: a deterritorialization of state authority claims. Krasner's (1997) typology of definitions of sovereignty is useful in clarifying this distinction between Ruggie's and Kapstein's arguments. As Kapstein points out, the Basel Accord demonstrates the continuing salience of "control sovereignty."[9] At the same time, however, the Basel Accord also represents a challenge to "Westphalian sovereignty" because of the way external authorities are no longer excluded from exerting regulatory influence within a state's territory.

The emergence of "offshore" financial activity and extraterritorial regulatory practices are not the only examples of how the globalization of financial markets is encouraging an unraveling of territoriality. A third example comes from the monetary sphere. Early theorists of sovereignty, such as Jean Bodin, argued that a sovereign state should maintain a homogeneous and exclusive currency circulating within the territory it governed. Financial globalization, however, is encouraging several monetary transformations that challenge this kind of "territorial currency" (Cohen 1998; Helleiner 1997). One such transformation has already been discussed in a slightly different context: the emergence of eurocurrency activity. The significance of eurocurrency markets is not only that they challenge territoriality by acting as a "regulation-free" offshore economic region in the way that Ruggie and Sassen highlight. They are also significant in challenging monetary territoriality by acting as places where foreign currencies can be used alongside the national currency within the territory of the state.

The link between financial globalization and the erosion of monetary territoriality can also be seen in several other contexts. In Latin America and elsewhere outside of the OECD region, foreign currencies have also begun to be used in a more widespread fashion as financial markets have become more liberalized and globally integrated, a phenomenon known as "currency substitution" or "dollarization." The need to establish "credible" policies in the eyes of global financial market operators is also encouraging some developing countries – such as Argentina – to introduce currency board arrangements that often formalize this arrangement. In Western Europe, heightened capital mobility has also played a significant role in encouraging states to consider the creation of a supranational currency. Also interesting has been the proliferation of sub-national "local currencies" in the last two decades, a phenomenon which has also been seen as a reaction to the globalization of financial markets (e.g. Rotstein and Duncan, 1991).

I have been suggesting, then, that the study of the unraveling of territoriality in these various ways – "offshore" financial activity, extraterritorial regulatory practices, deterritorialized currency structures – is the most promising way to link financial globalization to the decline of the sovereign state. But two important cautionary notes must immediately be registered concerning this line of argument. First, if the unraveling of territoriality in these ways signals an erosion of the sovereign state, this does not necessarily imply support for the thesis that a "post-Westphalian" world order is emerging. The reason is an historical one: the principle of territoriality was not a product of the Westphalian era in all sectors of political–economic life. Although scholars such as Ruggie associate the origins of territoriality in seventeenth-century Europe, this association is less clear in the sectors we have just been examining.

In the monetary sphere, for example, the principle that a state should maintain a territorially homogenous and exclusive currency was not widely endorsed until the nineteenth century, despite its advocacy by Bodin in the earlier Westphalian era. In the seventeenth and eighteenth centuries, European states frequently gave legal tender status to foreign currencies circulating within their territories and assigned them a formal value *vis-à-vis* the domestic currency they issued. Similarly, the circulation of sub-national "local currencies" was widely accepted in that era by state authorities. The principle of "sovereignty/territoriality" in the monetary sphere, thus, came to be accepted only quite late in historical terms. As I have argued elsewhere (Helleiner 1997), it is better seen as having accompanied the emergence of the "nation-state" in the nineteenth century than the developments surrounding the Peace of Westphalia in seventeenth-century Europe.

A similar point can be made about the growth of both extraterritorial regulatory practices and "offshore" financial activity. In terms of the former, Krasner (1997: 13) reminds us that the notion that external authorities should be excluded from domestic affairs was not developed explicitly until writings at the end of the eighteenth century. Likewise, while "offshore" financial centers may appear novel to contemporary observers, much of world trade and finance took place within similar loosely regulated locations, such as city-states, throughout the seventeenth and eighteenth centuries (Arrighi, 1994). Only with the emergence of the nation-state in the nineteenth century did territoriality become a central organizing principle for economic life in the leading states of the world and did "national economies" become the foundation of the world economy.

Consequently, while the unraveling of the principle of territoriality is certainly a better indicator of a decline of the sovereign state than the erosion of macroeconomic policy autonomy or regulatory control over finance, we need to be cautious in interpreting the historical significance of this development. Instead of overturning patterns of state authority first established around 1648 in Europe, these contemporary challenges to territoriality are calling into question authority claims that emerged only within the last two centuries.[10] The origins of sovereignty, in other words, are less deeply rooted in these economic spheres than Ruggie and other supporters of the "Westphalian hypothesis" imply. Instead, what Jens Bartelson (1995) calls the "modernity hypothesis" – which links the emergence of sovereignty to the rise of the nation-state – is more persuasive.

The second reason to be cautious in embracing the argument that financial globalization is eroding the sovereign state through challenges to territoriality is that these challenges result not just from the globalization trend. This can be most clearly seen in the case of the monetary transformations discussed above. The move toward monetary union in the EU, for example, is a product of many factors unrelated to capital mobility, a point highlighted by the fact that high levels of capital mobility between the US and Canada since the 1950s have done little to encourage interest in a currency union between the two countries. The growth of "local currencies" also has many causes unrelated to financial globalization, perhaps most importantly the rise of the green political movement. Similarly, the dollarization trend in Latin America is primarily a reaction to domestic inflationary policies and, as just noted, it has many historical precedents that predate the age of financial globalization.

A quick glance backwards in history also confirms that financial globalization need not necessarily pose a challenge to territorial currencies. The era in which many territorial currencies were first constructed was an era when financial capital was highly mobile: the period between 1870–1931. Indeed, it was often international financiers who were most keen on promoting this monetary reform in that era. For an integrated global financial order to operate smoothly and efficiently, the financiers saw the need for states to consolidate their chaotic domestic monetary systems on a more orderly territorial basis. For this reason, they encouraged such reforms as the establishment of central banks which would have a monopoly of the note issue and full control over a homogeneous and integrated monetary system (Helleiner 1997).

If a tension seems to exist today between global financial markets and territorial currencies, it is primarily because these monetary structures came to be used for more activist purposes than the financiers had originally intended. The financiers envisioned such currencies being managed in a very limited way; that is, according to the "rules of the game" of the gold standard. After the gold standard collapsed in the early 1930s and for the next several decades, however, territorial currencies began to be managed in quite different ways to serve more interventionist macroeconomic planning objectives and fiscal needs of the state. These forms of management are now more difficult to pursue because of the reemergence of global financial markets, as policy-makers are discovering. It is partly for this reason that alternatives to territorial currencies are being considered in the contemporary context, rather than because of any inherent incompatibility between global finance and territorial currencies.

In sum, the argument that financial globalization is associated with an unraveling of the territoriality of sovereign states is an important one. As I have shown, this association can be seen well through a number of developments, including the growth of offshore financial activity, the Basel Accord, and the erosion of territorial currencies. At the same time, the long historical significance of these challenges to territoriality also should not be exaggerated. The historical roots of state authority claims based on territoriality in these areas are more recent than is sometimes implied. Rather than signaling a dramatic erosion of the three-hundred-year-old "Westphalian" state system, these developments overturn structures of state authority that date back only into the last century. Moreover, the significance of financial globalization in encouraging these developments should not be overstated.

Conclusion

Is financial globalization undermining the sovereign state? This chapter has suggested that this question is more difficult to answer than much of the existing literature implies. I have argued that it is important to identify four different ways in which financial globalization has been linked to the emergence of a post-Westphalian world order in existing literature. Of these four arguments, the first three – which focus on the state's regulatory power and macroeconomic policy autonomy – have been found to be less than fully persuasive. Only the fourth argument concerning territoriality presents a more convincing case, even if this argument is rather underdeveloped in existing literature.

Two kinds of weaknesses have been identified in the first three arguments.

First, they often overstate the extent to which financial globalization has actually eroded state power either in the macroeconomic realm or the regulatory sphere. Moreover, even if financial globalization was undermining state power in the ways the first three arguments suggest, this would not necessarily indicate support for their case that the sovereign state was eroding. This is because of a second weakness in these arguments: they lack a long historical perspective on the world-order transformations they are analyzing. This weakness is especially evident when these arguments employ indicators such as "declining regulatory power" and "eroding macroeconomic policy autonomy" to measure the decline of the sovereign state. Like Thomson (1995: 216), I find these kinds of indicators to be quite ahistorical; these state functions were either never fully performed by sovereign states or only performed very recently by them.

A longer historical perspective also provides a reminder that today's globally integrated financial markets are less novel than they may initially appear. As Giovanni Arrighi (1994) reminds us, financial markets have also been highly "globalized" in several previous historical epochs, most notably in the several decades before 1931. This point is not always adequately acknowledged by supporters of the first three arguments. If they are to assert that financial globalization is eroding the sovereign state, they must do more to explain why sovereign states were able to easily coexist with – and indeed were often strengthened by – global financial markets in those earlier periods but are apparently being undermined by them today.

If the first three arguments are less than fully persuasive, the link drawn between financial globalization and the unraveling of the territoriality of the sovereign state is more convincing. The indicator used to measure the decline of sovereignty – territoriality – is one more widely accepted by historians of the sovereign state. Three important developments also seem to confirm the argument that territoriality is being challenged by financial globalization: the growth of offshore financial activity, changing regulatory practices, and the deterritorialization of currency structures. One must still be cautious, however, before concluding decisively that these two developments confirm the thesis that financial globalization is challenging the sovereign state. The relative importance of financial globalization in encouraging both developments is open to question. The late historical construction of territoriality in the monetary and financial sphere also suggests that its erosion may not provide the best evidence for the argument that a "post-Westphalian" world order is emerging.

In sum, the implications of financial globalization for the structure of world order are more complicated than they are often portrayed. Clearly, the process *is* associated with an important restructuring of the state. But much of this restructuring does not signal a decline of the sovereign state. Instead, it represents a set of more cyclical changes in which the state is being restructured in ways that are similar to earlier eras when "haute finance" was a dominant force in world politics, most notably the pre-1931 era. The "welfare–nationalist" form of state that triumphed in many parts of the world in the post-1931 era is being replaced by a "neo-liberal" form of state similar in some respects to that which existed before

1931. Regulatory instruments such as exchange controls, which became so common in the post-1931 era, are being dismantled, while international forms of regulatory cooperation to prevent financial crises and track illegal flows of money are being strengthened just as they were before the 1930s. Private forms of financial power and regulatory activities are also resurfacing in similar forms as existed in that earlier era. Each of these processes of restructuring involves important transformations in state–society relations, intrastate bureaucratic structures and even patterns of interstate interactions. But not all of this should be interpreted as a decline in the sovereign state. This more deeply rooted historical form of state is challenged only to the extent that financial globalization erodes state authority claims based on territoriality.

Notes

1 I am grateful to the Social Sciences and Humanities Research Council of Canada for helping finance some of the research underlying this chapter. For their comments on an earlier draft, I thank the editors as well as the other participants at the conference.
2 This parallels Rosenau's (1989) broader argument about the role of information technology in undermining the Westphalian state system. Indeed, Rosenau draws on Wriston's argument in developing his larger thesis. Kobrin (1997) also argues that the information technology revolution is about to erode state sovereignty further by enabling the rise of "e-money" which not only challenges state control over financial flows but also undermines the state's control over domestic monetary policy. I have critiqued this argument elsewhere (Helleiner 1998) and will not address it here because of space constraints.
3 Cerny (1994; 1993: 175–7) has recognized the Basel Accord as a counter-case to his thesis, but he suggests that it was an aberration that relied on quite special circumstances that are unlikely to be repeated.
4 If sovereignty is measured by the indicator of "territoriality," however, it is less clear that these regulatory initiatives are bolstering it, as is noted in the fourth section of this Chapter.
5 This argument was a key theme in many of the early writings on the impact of interdependence on the sovereign state: see Thomson's (1995) discussion. It is also taken up as an argument in many of the recent writings on the decline of the sovereign state: e.g., Rosenau (1989), Cox (1992), Wriston (1992), Cerny (1995), Sassen (1996).
6 Sassen (1996) also develops this theme, drawing on Sinclair's work.
7 This interpretation contrasts with Vivien Schmidt's interpretation of the U-Turn in Chapter 9, this volume.
8 Crystal also highlights how government decisions to maintain overvalued exchange rates reflected *domestic* political and economic constraints rather than the influence of global financial markets.
9 In Chapter 2, this volume, Krasner also highlights how it demonstrates the enduring importance of "international law sovereignty."
10 Moreover, leaving aside the common currency project in the EU, the "deterritorialization" of money is often furthest developed today in countries of the world that never were successful in fully consolidating territorial currencies historically. The "dollarization" trend in many Latin American countries today, for example, simply revives a practice that has been periodically common throughout the twentieth century.

References

Andrews, D. (1994) "Capital mobility and state autonomy," *International Studies Quarterly* 38: 193–218.

Arrighi, G. (1994) *The Long Twentieth Century*, London: Verso.

Bartelson, Js. (1995) *The Genealogy of Sovereignty*, Cambridge: Cambridge University Press.

Cerny, P. (1994) "The dynamics of financial globalization," *Policy Sciences* 27: 319–42.

—— (1995) "Globalization and the changing logic of collective action," *International Organization* 49: 595–625.

Cohen, B. (1996). "Phoenix arisen: the resurrection of global finance," *World Politics* 48: 268–96.

—— (1998) *The Geography of Money*, Ithaca: Cornell University Press.

Cox, R. (1987) *Power, Production and World Order*, New York: Columbia University Press.

—— (1992) "Global perestroika," in R. Miliband and L. Panitch (eds) *New World Order?* London: Merlin.

Crystal, J. (1994) "The politics of capital flight," *Review of International Studies* 20: 131–47.

Eichengreen, B. (1992) *Golden Fetters*, Oxford: Oxford University Press.

Garrett, G. (1995) "Capital mobility, trade and the domestic politics of economic policy," *International Organization*, pp. 657–88.

Goodman, J. and Pauly, L. (1993) "The obsolescence of capital controls?" *World Politics* 46: 50–82

Helleiner, E. (1994) *States and the Reemergence of Global Finance*, Ithaca: Cornell University Press.

—— (1996) "Post-globalization: is the financial liberalization trend likely to be reversed?" in R. Boyer and D. Drache (eds) *States Against Markets*, London: Routledge.

——(1997) *One Nation, One Money: Territorial Currencies and the Nation-State*, ARENA working paper, no.17, Oslo: University of Oslo.

—— (1998) "Electronic money: a challenge to the sovereign state?" *Journal of International Affairs* 51: 387–410.

—— (1999) "State power and the regulation of illicit activity in global finance," in R. Friman and P. Andreas (eds) *The Illicit Global Economy and State Power*, Lanham, Maryland: Rowman and Littlefield.

Kapstein, E. (1994) *Governing the Global Economy*, Cambridge: Harvard University Press.

Kobrin, S. (1997) "Electronic cash and the end of national markets" *Foreign Policy* 107: 65–77.

Krasner, S. (1997) "Globalization and sovereignty," paper prepared for the conference on States and Sovereignty in the World Economy, February, University of California, Irvine.

Loriaux, M. (1991) *France After Hegemony*, Ithaca: Cornell University Press.

Notermans, T. (1995) *Social Democracy and External Constraints*, ARENA working paper, Oslo: University of Oslo.

Pauly, L. (1994) "National financial structures, capital mobility and international economic rules," *Policy Sciences* 27: 343–63.

Possamai, M. (1992) *Money on the Run*, Toronto: Viking.

Riley, J. (1980) *International Government Finance and the Amsterdam Capital Market 1740–1815*, Cambridge: Cambridge University Press.

Rosenau, J. (1989) *Turbulence in World Politics*, Princeton: Princeton University Press.

Rotstein, A. and Duncan, C. (1991) "For a second economy," in D. Drache and M. Gertler (eds) *The New Era of Global Competition*, Montreal: McGill-Queen's.

Ruggie, J. (1993) "Territoriality and beyond: problematizing modernity in international relations," *International Organization* 47:139–74.

Sassen, S. (1991) *The Global City*, Princeton: Princeton University Press.

—— (1996) *Losing Control? Sovereignty in an Age of Globalization* New York: Columbia University Press.

Sinclair, T. (1994) "Between state and market: hegemony and institutions of collective action under conditions of international capital mobility," *Policy Sciences* 27: 447–66.

Sobel, A. (1994) *Domestic Choices, International Markets: Dismantling National Barriers and Liberalizing Securities Markets*, Ann Arbor: University of Michigan.

Thomson, J. (1995) "State sovereignty in international relations," *International Studies Quarterly* 39: 213–33.

Thrift, N. (1994) "On the social and cultural determinants of international financial centres," in S. Corbridge, N. Thrift, and R. Martin (eds) *Money, Power and Space*, Oxford: Basil Blackwell.

Wade, R. (1996) "Globalization and its limits," in S. Berger and R. Dore (eds) *National Diversity and Global Capitalism*, Ithaca: Cornell University Press.

Wriston, W. (1986) *Risk and Other Four-Letter Words*, New York: Harper and Row.

—— (1988) "Technology and sovereignty," *Foreign Affairs* 67: 63–75

—— (1992) *The Twilight of Sovereignty*, New York: MacMillan.

Zamora, S. (1992) "Remarks," *Proceedings of the 86th Annual Meeting of the American Society of International Law*, Washington: American Society of International Law.

8 Embedding the global in the national

Implications for the role of the state[1]

Saskia Sassen

Two notions underlie much of the current discussion about globalization. One is the zero-sum game: whatever the global economy gains, the national state loses, and vice versa. The other is that if an event takes place in a national territory, it is a national event, whether a business transaction or a judiciary decision. These assumptions about zero-sums and geography influence experts on the global economy as well as the general public. For experts it has meant that they have typically confined the concept of the global economy to cross-border processes, notably international trade and investment; and to a debate between those that think that globalization is destroying the national state and those that think that state sovereignty remains unchanged. This has produced a rather empirically and theoretically thin account about the features of economic globalization.

One of the roles of the state *vis-à-vis* today's global economy, unlike earlier phases of the world economy, has been to negotiate the intersection of national law and foreign actors – whether firms, markets, or supranational organizations. This condition makes the current phase distinctive. We have, on the one hand, the existence of an enormously elaborate body of law that secures the exclusive territoriality of national states to an extent not seen in earlier centuries, and on the other, the considerable institutionalizing of the "rights" of non-national firms, cross-border transactions, and supranational organizations. This sets up the conditions for a necessary engagement by national states in the process of globalization.

We generally use terms such as "deregulation," "financial and trade liberalization," and "privatization," to describe the outcome of this negotiation. The problem with such terms is that they only capture the withdrawal of the state from regulating its economy. They do not register all the ways in which the state participates in setting up the new frameworks through which globalization is furthered; nor do they capture the associated transformations inside the state.

There is scholarship that treats the relation between national states and the world economy in a way that goes beyond the zero-sum and geography assumptions referred to above. The world-system literature has made major contributions towards the development of analytic categories that allow us to understand the operation of international dynamics inside national territories (Wallerstein 1988; Arrighi 1994; Frank 1964, to cite just a few). And now an emerging body of scholarship shows that, to a large extent, global processes materialize in national territories (e.g., Mittelman 1996; Knox and Taylor 1995; Drache and Gertler 1991; Sassen 1991). I have long argued that many transactions that are a key part of the global economy do not cross borders, or do not do so in the ways that investment and trade do, but are located inside national economies. Further, I have tried to show how even the most digitized global financial market is grounded in a set of very material resources and spaces largely embedded in national territories.

Less attention, and the concern here, has gone to the formation of an emerging institutional framework to govern the global economy and the inevitable implications this has for the exclusive authority of the modern national state over its territory, that is, its exclusive territoriality. There is a new set of intermediary strategic agents that contribute to the management and coordination of the global economy. They are largely, though not exclusively, private. And they have absorbed some of the international functions carried out by states in the recent past, as was the case, for instance, with the predominantly protectionist regimes of the post-Second World War decades through which governments governed international trade. The role of these strategic agents is dramatically illustrated by a recent case involving China. When the Chinese government in 1996 issued a 100-year bond to be sold, not in Shanghai but mostly in New York, it did not have to deal with Washington, it dealt with J.P. Morgan. This example can be repeated over and over for a broad range of countries (see Sassen, in progress).

Private firms in international finance, accounting, and law, the new private standards for international accounting and financial reporting, and supranational organizations such as the WTO, all play strategic non-government centered governance functions. They do so, however, largely inside the territory of national-states. This signals the possibility of a whole series of engagements with various aspects of national states and a diversity of outcomes depending on the specifics of each national state.

I argue that precisely because to a large extent global processes materialize in national territories, a large number of national states have had to become deeply involved in the implementation of the global economic system and have, in this process, experienced transformations of various aspects of their institutional structure. In this process some components of national states may well gain power, e.g., ministries of finance and central banks, even as many others lose power. My working hypothesis is that while globalization leaves national territory basically unaltered, it is having pronounced effects on the exclusive territoriality of the national state – that is, its effects are not on territory as such but on the institutional encasements of that geographic condition.

Globalization, in this conception, does not only have to do with crossing geographic borders, as is captured in measures of international investment and trade. It also has to do with the relocation of national public governance functions to transnational private arenas and with the development inside national states – through legislative acts, court rulings, executive orders – of the mechanisms necessary to accommodate the rights of global capital in what are still national territories under the exclusive control of their states. One overall effect is what I am calling an "incipient denationalizing" of several highly specialized national institutional orders – the partial replacement of national legal and regulatory frameworks with "denationalized" ones (Sassen 1996: Chapter 1). One concrete version of this may well be the shift away from what are ultimately still Keynsian state agendas toward the needs of global capital to ensure its "rights" inside national territories. This is one way in which the state matters under conditions of globalization – that is, in its capacity as an administrative and technical apparatus that can be used to govern the operations of national as well as of non-national economic actors and institutions. If it is the case that some of the instruments necessary to accommodate a global economic system are implemented inside the national state through a denationalizing of select institutional realms, one could argue that the two types of sovereignty – Westphalian and international legal – privileged by Krasner in his analysis (see Chapter 2, this volume) may well be undergoing substantive transformations even though formally or *de jure* they may appear unchanged and unchallenged by globalization.

Territory and territoriality in the global economy

Economic globalization represents a major transformation in the territorial organization of key economic sectors. To what extent it also represents a possible transformation in the structures of politico-economic power is a difficult and controversial question. In my reading, the major dynamics at work in the global economy contain the capacity to undo the particular form of the intersection of sovereignty and territory embedded in the modern state and the modern state system. But this may not necessarily mean that sovereignty is less of a feature of the international system. Rather, it may signal the relocation of some components of national state sovereignty onto supranational authorities or privatized corporate systems. At the limit I would posit a partial denationalizing of state sovereignty. Similarly in the case of the state's exclusive control over its territory: economic globalization does not eliminate this feature of the interstate system but it does alter the particular type of institutional encasing of national territory we have seen develop since the First World War and especially after the Second World War.[2]

We can begin to address these questions by examining major aspects of economic globalization that contribute to what I think of as a new geography of power. Three components in this new geography of power are of interest here. One of these concerns the actual territories where much of globalization materializes in specific institutions and processes. A second component concerns the ascendance of a new legal regime to govern cross-border economic transactions, a trend not sufficiently recognized in the social science literature. There has been a massive amount of legal innovation around the growth of globalization. The third component of the new geography of power is the fact that a growing number of economic activities are taking place in digital space. The growing digitalization of economic activity, particularly in the leading information industries such as finance and specialized corporate services, may be contributing to a crisis in control that transcends the capacities of both the state and the institutional apparatus of the economy. Adding these three components of the new geography of power to the global "footlooseness" of corporate capital reveals aspects of the relation between global economy and national state that are not adequately, or usefully, captured in the prevalent notion of a duality global–national, conceived as two mutually exclusive realms.

For me, these processes raise a question about the kind of territoriality that they entail. One answer is that they point to the partial relocating of a growing number of activities under largely newly produced institutional umbrellas that are increasingly not governmental but private. However, in so far as these new institutional umbrellas govern processes that take place, at least partly, in national territories, they contain explicitly or implicitly a participation of select components of national states. Let me briefly elaborate on a few aspects. I will begin with the question of the spaces of the global economy, or the strategic geography of globalization, or more conceptually, the particular form of territoriality we see taking shape in the global economy today.[3]

The worldwide geographic dispersal of factories and service outlets is actually part of what are highly integrated corporate structures with strong tendencies towards concentration in control and profit appropriation. While conceivably this geographic dispersal of factories and offices could have gone along with a dispersal in control and profits, a democratizing if you will of the corporate structure, that has not happened. Indeed, many of these operations appear as "overseas sales" for large corporations. It is well known that a very high share (estimates range from 40 per cent to 70 per cent) of international trade is actually intrafirm trade (see United Nations Centre on Transnational Corporations (UNCTAD), various years).

There are two major implications here for the question of territoriality and sovereignty in the context of a global economy. First, when there is geographic dispersal of factories, offices and service outlets in an integrated corporate system, particularly one with centralized top-level control, there is also a growth in central functions. One way of saying it is that the more globalized firms become, the more their central functions grow – in importance, in complexity, in number of transactions.[4] Of importance to the analysis here is the dynamic that connects the dispersal of economic activities with the ongoing weight and often growth of central functions. In terms of territoriality and globalization this means that an interpretation of the impact of globalization as creating a space economy that extends beyond the regulatory capacity of a single state, is only half the story; the other half is that these central functions are disproportionately concentrated in the national territories of the highly developed countries.

I should perhaps clarify that by central functions I do not only mean top-level headquarters. I am also referring to all the top-level financial, legal, accounting, managerial, executive, planning functions necessary to run a corporate organization operating in more than one country, and increasingly in several countries. These central functions are partly embedded in headquarters, but also in good part in what has been called the corporate services complex, that is, the network of financial, legal, accounting, advertising, and other corporate services firms that handle the complexities of operating in more than one national legal system, national accounting system, advertising culture, etc. and do so under conditions of rapid innovations in all these fields (see Sassen 1991; Knox and Taylor 1995). Such services have become so specialized and complex, that headquarters increasingly buy them from specialized firms rather than producing them in-house. These agglomerations of firms producing central functions for the management and coordination of global economic systems, are disproportionately concentrated in the highly developed countries – particularly, though not exclusively, in the kinds of cities I call global cities. This concentration of functions represents a strategic factor in the organization of the global economy, and they are situated in, for example, New York, Paris, Amsterdam.

One argument I am making here is that it is important to unbundle analytically the fact of strategic functions for the global economy or for global operation, and the overall corporate economy of a country.[5] They are not completely overlapping worlds. Indeed, many components of a country's corporate economy have little to do with globalization and, conversely, many "national" corporate sectors have become deeply globalized in their orientation and have little resemblance to their erstwhile national-market orientation. For the purposes of some kinds of inquiry this distinction may not matter. However, for the purposes of understanding the global economy, it does.

Another instance today of this negotiation between a transnational process or dynamic and a national territory is that of the global financial markets. The orders of magnitude in these transactions have risen sharply, as illustrated by the 75 trillion US dollar turnover (as estimated by *The Economist*) in the global capital market, a major component of the global economy. These transactions are partly embedded in telecommunications systems that make possible the instantaneous transmission of money / information around the globe. Much attention has gone to this feature. But the other half of the story is the extent to which the global financial markets are located in particular cities in the highly developed countries. Indeed, the degrees of concentration are unexpectedly high. The topography of activities in many of the glo bal digitalized industries such as finance actually weaves in and out of digital space; and when it moves out of digital space and hits the ground it does so in massive concentrations of very material resources, from infrastructure to buildings (Sassen 1998: Chapters 9 and 10).

Operating a worldwide network of factories, offices, and service outlets, and implementing global financial markets, required major and minor legal innovations in national legal systems and the creation of whole new frameworks outside national systems. This is, in my reading, a second component of the new geography of power confronting national states. Here, I will confine myself to a few of the particular forms of legal innovation that have been produced and within which much of globalization is framed. These innovations entail specific forms of interaction with the state, or more specifically, with the sovereignty of the state. These legal innovations and changes are often summarized under the notion of "deregulation" and taken as somewhat of a given. In much social science, deregulation is another name for the declining significance of the state. There is, it seems to me, a more specific process contained in these legal changes, one that along with the reconfiguration of space discussed above may signal a more fundamental transformation in the matter of sovereignty, pointing to new contents and new locations for that particular systemic property we call sovereignty.

For instance, over the past 20 years, international commercial arbitration has been transformed and institutionalized as the leading contractual method for the resolution of transnational commercial disputes.[6] According to Dezalay and Garth (1995) it is a delocalized and decentralized market for the administration of international commercial disputes, connected by more or less powerful institutions and individuals who are both competitive and complementary (see also Salacuse 1991). A second instance of a private regulatory system is represented by debt security or bond rating agencies, which have come to play an increasingly important role in the global economy.[7] Ten years ago Moody's and Standard and Poor had no analysts outside the US. By 1993 they each had about 100 in Europe, Japan, and Australia (Sinclair 1994).

These and other such transnational institutions and regimes do raise questions about the relation between state sovereignty and the governance of global economic processes. International commercial arbitration is basically a private justice system and credit rating agencies are private gate-keeping systems. Along with other such institutions they have emerged as important governance mechanisms whose authority is not centered in the state. They contribute to maintain order at the top. Of particular concern here will be how the newly formed World Trade Organization negotiates the growth of these private regimes and the attempt to form supranational regimes still centered on states and the inter-state system. As Rosenau (1992) has noted, precisely because so many processes are transnational, governments increasingly are not competent to address some of the major issues confronting our societies; this is not the end of sovereignty, but rather an alteration in the "exclusivity and scope" of the competence of governments.[8]

New norms: convergence and formation of standards

Many of these rather abstract issues are well illustrated by the work being done to create new private international standards for accounting and financial reporting. The International Accounting Standards Committee (IASC) is an independent private sector body that has been working intensely to create uniform standards for use by business and government. It wants to bring these standards on line by 1999. In 1995 the International Organization of Securities Commission agreed to endorse the IASCs standards and set March 1998 as the target date for completion of a body of international accounting standards. It is worth noting that as of March 1997, IASC standards were accepted by all stock exchanges except Japan, Canada, and the US, though these were expected to join as I write. One of the issues for the US has been that it considers its own standards more stringent than the new standards being proposed. It is also the case that Anglo-American standards have emerged as *de facto* international standards over the last few years, producing an enormous amount of business for US and UK firms.

This evolution was not without incidents that made it clear to what extent national governments and firms resisted or had difficulty accepting the concept of other countries' standards, let alone uniform international standards as pursued by the IASC. Japan resisted moving away from its national accounting system, one lacking the criteria for transparency that have become the norm in international transactions. It was indeed Japan's reluctance to implement such standards of transparency in a wide range of business activities in conjunction with its resistance to continue deregulating its financial sector that aborted Tokyo's rise as a major international financial center. Tokyo remained too Japanese.

The sudden turnabout by German companies, including even Deutsche Bank, and their decision to adopt international accounting standards came as a shock to Japan's Ministry of Finance and many top businessmen. Indeed, that ministry announced recently that it would gradually implement a whole set of measures aimed at deregulation and transparency. But the sharpest pressure for change is coming from Japan's increasing dependence on international markets. Many Japanese companies have shifted production abroad; their major shareholders include US and European firms, and raising capital abroad has become increasingly attractive. So by the time the Ministry of Finance decided to change policy, some Japanese companies had already begun to implement accounting standards that are closer to Anglo-American standards, the norm for most international transactions.

Japanese firms interested in operating outside Japan recognize that not adhering to Anglo-American accounting standards will crowd them out of the global market. It has become necessary for firms from any country who want to work internationally to adjust to the most widely accepted standards in the world or not be a player in the world financial market. For example, lenders on the interbank market charge Japanese banks higher interest rates due to opaque accounting and insufficient disclosure of bad debts. Daiwa Bank was expelled from the US for hiding losses for 11 years. Indeed, the only Japanese financial institution listed on the New York Stock Exchange, The Bank of Tokyo-Mitsubishi Bank, conforms to US accounting standards, which are the world's most stringent, and in 1996 raised 2 billion US dollars with an international convertible bond issue.

The case of Japan is interesting because it is one of the most powerful countries in the world. It has resisted but finally had to accept the new norms under pressure of its own firms. The US stock exchange, another powerful actor, in turn resisted the implementation of the IASC standards and insisted on having its own standards (or something approaching them) be the international norm, but may well have to accept the IAS.

While this is a world of private actors and private standards, national states matter for the implementation and partial policing of corporate conduct.

Notes towards mapping a role for the state

The new geography of global economic processes – the strategic territories for economic globalization – had to be produced, both through the practices of corporate actors, the requisite infrastructure (i.e. global cities), and the work of producing new legal regimes. In so far as all of these take place, at least partially, in national territories under the exclusive control of national states, the latter must have been engaged. Mapping this engagement, with all the specifics of different national states, is a central part of my current research project (Sassen, in progress).

At this point, it is clear to me that there are multiple localizations to this engagement – court rulings, legislative acts, executive orders, private corporate decisions. I think of these engagements as representing a frontier zone, with many skirmishes between different vested interests and with many different outcomes across institutional worlds and across national states. There is also the work of legitimating the changes – for instance, a government endorsing the privatization of public sector firms and the deregulation of financial markets, both of which *de facto* entail today the opening of a country's economy to foreign investment. With these minor and major legal innovations has come what we could think of as a new normativity, one deeply embedded in the new logic of the global capital markets (Sassen 1996: Chapter 2). For this logic to become normative it required national states to endorse it and implement it as the "proper" way for governing a national economy. In this regard, the role of central banks has emerged as critical: although they have lost some of their macroeconomic authority, they have now become intermediary institutions through which the new international rules of the game are implemented in national economies. This leads to the new importance attached to the autonomy of central banks from the executive, which has become one of the components of IMF conditionality.

It is in this sense that I argue that representations that characterize the national state as simply losing significance are inadequate. They fail to capture this very important dimension, and reduce what is happening to a function of the global–national duality – what one wins, the other loses. I view deregulation not simply as a loss of control by the state but as a crucial mechanism to nego-tiate the juxtaposition of the interstate consensus to pursue globalization and the fact that national legal systems remain as the major, or crucial instantiation through which guarantees of contract and property rights are enforced.

Emphasizing the fact that much of the global economy materializes in national territories and that in doing so it requires changes in national institu-tional frameworks, suggests a possible interpretation in terms of the doctrine of extraterritoriality. We could ask whether the impact of economic globalization on national territory and state sovereignty is yet another form of extraterritori-ality, only one centered in economic rather than the more traditional political factors. If this is a form of extraterritoriality it would leave the sovereignty of the state fundamentally unaltered. My interpretation (Sassen 1996: Chapter 1) is that it is a development of a different sort, one wherein the sovereignty of the state is altered, one where both categories – exclusive territoriality and sovereignty – are partially transformed.

At this time, we can identify at least the following in an effort to map the role of the state in these processes.

First, the emergent, often imposed, consensus in the community of states to further globalization has created a set of specific obligations on participating states. The state remains as the ultimate guarantor of the "rights" of global capital, i.e. the protection of contracts and property rights. Thus, the state has incorporated the global project of its own shrinking role in regulating economic transactions (Cox 1987; Panitch 1996). Firms operating transnationally want to ensure the functions traditionally exercised by the state in the national realm of the economy, notably guaranteeing property rights and contracts. The state here can be conceived of as representing a technical administrative capacity that cannot be replicated at this time by any other institutional arrangement. Furthermore, this is a capacity backed by military power, with global power in the case of some states.

This guarantee of the rights of capital is embedded in a certain type of state, a certain conception of the rights of capital, and a certain type of international legal regime: it is largely embedded in the state of the most developed and most powerful countries in the world, in western notions of contract and property rights, and in a new legal regime aimed at furthering economic globalization (e.g., Trubek *et al.* 1993; Coombe 1993).[9] The state continues to play a crucial, though no longer exclusive, role in the production of legality around new forms of economic activity (Sassen 1996).

Second, while central, the role of the state in producing the legal encasements for economic operations is no longer what it was in earlier periods. Economic globalization has been accompanied by the creation of new legal regimes and legal practices and the expansion and renovation of some older forms that bypass national legal systems. This is evident in the rising importance of international commercial arbitration and the variety of institutions that fulfill rating and advisory functions that have become essential for the operation of the global economy (Dezalay and Garth 1995; Salacuse 1991; Sinclair 1994).

Third, what is generally called deregulation actually refers to an extremely complex set of intersections and negotiations which, while preserving the integrity of national territory as a geographic condition, do transform exclusive territoriality, i.e. the national and international frameworks through which national territory has assumed an institutional form. The discussion in the preceding sections brings to the fore the distinction between national territory and national territoriality. Territory and territoriality have corresponded tightly for much of the recent history since the Second World War, especially in the case of highly developed countries. Today, globalization and deregulation may be contributing to an incipient slippage in that correspondence. Much deregulation has had the effect of promoting that slippage and giving it a legitimate form in national legal frameworks.

Fourth, in the case of the global capital market, we can see that beyond the fact of its raw economic power, the logic of this market has assumed normative weight in the making of national economic policy.[10] We see this in countries as diverse as the US and Mexico and, most recently in countries such as France and Germany, that have long resisted this influence.[11]

Much of the above is concerned with a particular type of issue: the formation of new legal regimes that negotiate between national sovereignty and the cross-border operations of corporate economic actors. But there is a second, distinct issue: the particular content of this new regime. It contributes to strengthen the advantages of certain types of economic actors and to weaken those of others. Regarding broader questions of governance, central to my research project, these two aspects translate into two different agendas. One is centered on the effort to create viable systems of coordination/order among the powerful economic actors now operating globally. International commercial arbitration, credit rating agencies, and the new international standards for accounting and financial reporting can be seen as mechanisms for creating this type of order.

The second is not so much focused on how to create order at the top but on equity and distributive questions in the context of a globally integrated economic system with immense inequalities in the profit-making capacities of firms and in the earnings capacities of households. There is a larger theoretico/politico question here that has to do with which actors gain the legitimacy for governance of the global economy and the legitimacy to take over rules and authorities hitherto encased in the national state. [12]

Conclusion

The strategic spaces where global processes are embedded are often national; the mechanisms through which new legal forms, necessary for globalization, are implemented are often part of national state institutions; the infrastructure that makes possible the hypermobility of financial capital at the global scale is embedded in various national territories. This partial embedding of global dynamics in national territories in a context of exclusive territorial authority by the national state signals a necessary engagement with the national state. The national state could not be a mere bystander or passive victim. It had to participate through one or another of its instantiations in setting up the new legal frameworks and in legitimating the new norms. In this process it weakened many of its authorities, especially those linked to the social fund, but it also gained new powers, the latter a subject that needs more research. Thinking about globalization and the national state along these lines resists the simple duality of the national and the global and the notion that economic globalization is basically a set of macro-level cross-border processes.

One way of conceptualizing the multiple negotiations between the national state and the implementation of a global economic system is as a process of incipient denationalizing of select specialized national institutional orders. This process of denationalization cannot be reduced to a geographic conception as was the notion in the heads of the generals who fought the wars for nationalizing territory in earlier centuries. This is a denationalizing of specific institutional arenas: Manhattan and the City of London are the equivalent of free trade zones when it comes to finance. But it is not Manhattan as a geographic entity, with all its layers of activity, and functions and regulations, that is a free-trade zone. It is a highly specialized functional or institutional realm, with strong tendencies towards locational concentration in places such as Manhattan and London's City, that becomes denationalized. Some of what we code as national because it takes place in national territory has become the global. And some of what we code as global is contingent on the national state as an administrative capacity and as a source of legitimacy.

Notes

1   This chapter is part of a larger five-year project on governance and accountability in the global economy. The first phase of the larger project was partly published as the 1995 Leonard Hastings Schoff Memorial Lectures (*Losing Control? Sovereignty in an Age of Globalization*, Columbia University Press 1996). I want to thank the Schoff Memorial Fund for their support and Columbia University Press for allowing me to use portions of the published lectures.

2   For an explication of these issues see Sassen 1996: Chapter 1. Much of what follows in this section is derived from that source.

3   One starting point is to ask what are the spatial configuration and the legal/regulatory regimes that specify the practices that we see as constitutive of the global economy: global financial markets; ascendance of Anglo-American law firms in international business transactions; the Uruguay round of GATT and the formation of the WTO (World Trade Organization); the role of credit rating agencies and other such delightful entities in international capital markets; the provisions in GATS and NAFTA for the circulation of service workers as part of the international trade and investment in services; and immigration, particularly the circulation of low-wage workers (see Sassen 1996).

4   I have elaborated these issues in Sassen 1991. This process of corporate integration should not be confused with vertical integration as conventionally defined. See Gereffi (1995) on commodity chains and Porter's (1990) value-added chains, two constructs that also illustrate the difference between corporate integration at a world scale and vertical integration as conventionally defined.

5   These global control and command functions are partly embedded in national corporate structures but also constitute a distinct corporate subsector. This subsector can be conceived of as part of a network that connects global cities across the globe. In this sense, global cities are different from the old capitals of erstwhile empires, in that they are a function of cross-border networks rather than simply the most powerful city of an empire. There is, in my conceptualization, no such entity as a single global city as there could be a single capital of an empire; the category "global city" only makes sense as a component of a global network of strategic sites (see Sassen 1991).

6   Today international business contracts in a broad range of activities typically call for arbitration in the event of a dispute arising from the contractual arrangement (Dezalay and Garth 1995). The main reason given today for this choice is that it allows each party to avoid being forced to submit to the courts of the other. Also important is the secrecy of the process. Such arbitration can be "institutional" and follow the rules of institutions such as the International Chamber of Commerce in Paris, the American Arbitration Association, the London Court of International

Commercial Arbitration, or many others. Or it can be *ad hoc*, often following the rules of the UN Commission on International Trade Law (UNCITRAL). The arbitrators are private individuals selected by the parties. Usually there are three arbitrators who act as private judges, holding hearings and issuing judgments.

7 There are two agencies that dominate the market in ratings, with listings of over 3 trillion US dollars each. They are Moody's Investors Service, usually referred to as Moody's, and Standard & Poor's Ratings Group, usually referred to as Standard & Poor.

8 There is a wider systemic process here that needs to be distinguished from the effects of globalization: the worldwide and apparently growing distrust of governments and bureaucracies. Shapiro (1995) finds that this has contributed to the emergence of certain commonalities in law, notably the growing importance of constitutional individual rights that protect the individual from the state and other organizations. The particular hallmark of American constitutionalism is constitutional judicial review, which now has also emerged endogenously in Germany and Italy, and to some extent even in France (where there now is an active constitutional court and a constitutional bill of rights). The Court of Justice of the EU has evolved into a constitutional court with human rights jurisdiction (which entailed that constitutions and rights had to come about in Europe).

9 This dominance assumes many forms and does not only affect poorer and weaker countries. France, for instance, ranks among the top providers of information services and industrial engineering services in Europe and has a strong though not outstanding position in financial and insurance services. But it has found itself at an increasing disadvantage in legal and accounting services because Anglo-Saxon law dominates in international transactions. Foreign firms with offices in Paris dominate the servicing of the legal needs of firms, whether French or foreign, operating out of France (Carrez, 1991). Similarly, Anglo-American law is increasingly dominant in international commercial arbitration, an institution grounded in continental traditions of jurisprudence, particularly French and Swiss. (Dezalay and Garth 1995).

10 There is a whole other realm through which the question of sovereignty and territoriality is engaged, and which is part of my larger research project. Though in a manner very different from that of the global capital market, the emergent international human rights regime also engages the exclusive territoriality and sovereignty of national states. It posits rights not dependent on nationality and on their being granted by a state (Jacobson 1996; Reisman 1990). A key issue for me is the fact that this international regime largely becomes operative in national courts. It is then, yet another manner in which the state participates in transnational projects and is, at least in principle, transformed by this participation. These developments can then be seen as a move away from "statism" but not necessarily from the state as a key institution (see Franck 1992).

11 We are seeing the formation of an economic complex with a valorization dynamic that has properties clearly distinguishing it from other economic complexes whose valorization dynamic is far more articulated with the public economic functions of the state, the quintessential example being Fordist manufacturing. Fordist manufacturing needed the state in a much more direct way than do today's global markets in finance and advanced services. Keynesian state policies were a key "partner" in the setting up of the Fordist manufacturing complex.

12 It also raises a question about the condition of international public law. Do the new systems for governance that are emerging and the confinement of the role of national states in the global economy to the furthering of deregulation, markets, and privatization, indicate a decline of international public law? (See generally, Sassen, in progress).

References

Arrighi, G. (1994) *The Long Twentieth Century. Money, Power, and the Origins of Our Times*, London: Verso.

Carrez, Jean-François (1991) *Le développement des fonctions tertiaires internationales à Paris et dans les métropoles régionales*, Rapport au Premier Ministre, Paris: La Documentation Française.

Coombe, R.J. (1993) "The properties of culture and the politics of possessing identity: native claims in the cultural appropriation controversy," *The Canadian Journal of Law and Jurisprudence* VI (2): 249–85, July.

Cox, R. (1987) *Production, Power, and World Order: Social Forces in the Making of History*, New York: Columbia University Press.

Dezalay, Y. and Garth, B. (1995) "Merchants of law as moral entrepreneurs: constructing international justice from the competition for transnational business disputes," *Law and Society Review* 29 (1): 27–64.

Drache, D. and Gertler, M. (eds) *The New Era of Global Competition: State Policy and Market Power*, Montreal: McGill-Queen's University Press, 1991.

Franck, T.M. (1992) "The emerging right to democratic governance," *American Journal of International Law* 86 (1): 46–91.

Frank, A.G. (1964) *The Development of Underdevelopment*, New York: Monthly Review Press.

Gereffi, G. (1995) "Global production systems and Third World development," in B. Stallings (ed.) *Global Change, Regional Response: The New International Context of Development*, New York: Cambridge University Press, pp. 100–42.

Jacobson, D. (1996) *Rights Across Borders: Immigration and the Decline of Citizenship*, Baltimore: Johns Hopkins Press.

Knox, P.L. and Taylor, P.J. (eds) (1995) *World Cities in a World-System*, Cambridge, UK: Cambridge University Press.

Mazlish, B. and Buultjens, R. (eds) (1993) *Conceptualizing Global History*, Boulder: Westview Press.

Mittelman, J. (ed.) (1996) *Globalization: Critical Reflections. Yearbook of International Political Economy*, vol. 9, Boulder, CO: Lynne Riener Publishers.

Panitch, L. (1996) "Rethinking the role of the state in an era of globalization," in J. Mittelman (ed.) *Globalization: Critical Reflections. Yearbook of International Political Economy*, vol. 9, Boulder, CO: Lynne Riener Publishers.

Porter, M. (1990) *The Competitive Advantages of Nations*, New York: Free Press.

Reisman, W. M. (1990) "Sovereignty and human rights in contemporary international law," *American Journal of International Law* 84 (4): 866–76 (October).

Rosenau, J.N. (1992) "Governance, order, and change in world politics," in J.N. Rosenau and E.O. Czempiel (eds) *Governance without Government: Order and Change in World Politics*, Cambridge: Cambridge University Press, pp. 1–29.

Ruggie, J.G. (1993) "Territoriality and beyond: problematizing modernity in international relations," *International Organization* 47 (1): 139–74, Winter.

Salacuse, J. (1991) *Making Global Deals: Negotiating in the International Marketplace*, Boston: Houghton Mifflin.

Sassen, S. (1991) *The Global City: New York, London, Tokyo*, Princeton University Press.

—— (1996) *Losing Control? Sovereignty in an Age of Globalization*, The 1995 Columbia University Leonard Hastings Schoff Memorial Lectures, New York: Columbia University Press.

—— (1998) *Globalization and Its Discontents. Selected Essays*, New York: New Press.

—— (in progress) *Governance and Accountability in the Global Economy*, Chicago: University of Chicago, Department of Sociology.

Shapiro, M. (1993) "The globalization of law," *Indiana Journal of Global Legal Studies*, 1: 37–64, Fall.

Sinclair, T.J. (1994) "Passing judgement: credit rating processes as regulatory mechanisms of governance in the emerging world order," *Review of International Political Economy* 1 (1): 133–59, Spring.

Taylor, P.J. (1995) "World cities and territorial states: the rise and fall of their mutuality," in P.L. Knox and P.J. Taylor (eds) *World Cities in a World-System*, Cambridge, UK: Cambridge University Press, pp. 48–62.

Trubek, D.M., Dezalay, Y., Buchanan, R., and Davis, J.R. (1993) "Global restructuring and the law: the internationalization of legal fields and creation of transnational arenas," working paper series on "The Political Economy of Legal Change", N. 1, Madison, Wisconsin: Global Studies Research Program, University of Wisconsin.

United Nations (1992) *World Investment Report 1992: Transnational Corporations as Engines of Growth*, New York: United Nations.

—— (1993) Conference on Trade and Development, Programme on Transnational Corporations, *World Investment Report 1993: Transnational Corporations and Integrated International Production*, New York: United Nations.

Wallerstein, I. (1988) *The Modern-World System III. The Second Era of Great Expansion of the Capitalist World-Economy, 1730–1840s*, New York: Academic Press.

9 Convergent pressures, divergent responses

France, Great Britain, and Germany between globalization and Europeanization

Vivien A. Schmidt

For all advanced industrialized societies, the forces of globalization have imposed similar economic imperatives. The rise of international financial markets, global business competition, and supranational economic governance institutions and actors have ensured that governments everywhere, whether of the left or the right, now seek to downsize, deregulate, and privatize while businesses seek to rationalize and internationalize. Moreover, while the state has been getting smaller, business has been growing bigger in size and more global in scope, and consequently less in need of the compromises of the past with labor or of the traditionally close ties with national governments – even if it has not therefore become entirely "stateless."

For member states of the European Union, the forces of European integration have added another set of regional pressures. Europeanization has acted both as a conduit for global forces and as a shield against them, opening member states up to international markets and competition at the same time that they protect them through monetary integration and the single market. While European monetary integration has reduced the macroeconomic autonomy of member states as they instituted tight monetary policies and austerity budgets, maintained low inflation rates, and liberalized financial markets, the single market has diminished microeconomic control of these states, as they deregulated the rules governing business, privatized nationalized industries, and harmonized standards. But although these changes have on the whole produced healthier economies and more competitive businesses, they have also led to a concomitant loss of capacity in the socioeconomic sphere, as most member states find themselves unable to stop rising unemployment while they are forced to decrease social spending and cap benefits.

Globalization and Europeanization have served to transform European economies not only through the force of markets but also through the force of ideas. In all European member states, the concepts of globalization and Europeanization have become part of a political discourse that combines a set of liberal capitalist economic ideas with the European political economic policy program. This discourse is designed to justify the changes engendered by global and European forces as it promotes them.

But although globalization and Europeanization have led to a certain convergence in policies and ideas, great divergence nevertheless persists. European member states differ in their degree of vulnerability to external economic pressures, in their implementation of integrationary and deregulatory policies, and in their justificatory discourse. What is more, some member states have undergone much more profound change than others as a result of their particular economic and institutional configurations, and some have maintained a much more coherent political discourse in justification of such change than others.

Among the three major European powers, France has changed the most in the face of the pressures of globalization and Europeanization, whereas Great Britain and Germany both have changed comparatively little. Great Britain anticipated many of the changes required by Europeanization, especially with regard to deregulation and privatization, while it successfully resisted others, in particular in the areas of social policy and monetary integration, and it has always been most open to the forces of globalization. Germany has until recently been able to avoid change as a consequence of its economic strength and its institutional organization, having imposed its own macroeconomic patterns on the rest of Europe and having delayed microeconomic adjustment, negotiating deregulation and privatization very slowly and with little disruptive impact on traditional relations between business, government, and labor. France, by contrast with both, has been transformed, having given up the *dirigisme* of a largely state-directed economy and state-dominated industry in favor of a more market-oriented approach to government management of the economy, with deregulation and privatization having loosened the traditionally close ties between business and government.

For France, the transformation of the economy has brought with it a loss in socioeconomic capacity that has in turn precipitated a crisis in the polity, mainly because French governments have been unable to come up with a coherent political discourse that goes beyond a simple pro-European and anti-global rhetoric to create a vision of France in Europe and the world. This is in contrast to Great Britain, where the loss of socioeconomic capacity is less severe as well as less significant, mainly because the pro-global and anti-European rhetoric of British governments has been successfully embedded since Thatcher in a neoliberal discourse. It is also in contrast to Germany, where the loss of socioeconomic capacity has become serious only lately, and where the pro-global and pro-European rhetoric of German governments has, until recently, been successfully reconciled with their postwar, liberal social democratic discourse.

Between globalization and Europeanization

As a term, globalization refers first and foremost to the economic pressures that undermine national economic autonomy and control, whether they come from the international financial markets that push governments to balance national budgets, diminish social spending, rationalize public services, reduce public deficits, and guard against inflation or from the international competition that pushes governments to deregulate and privatize and businesses to consolidate, concentrate, and internationalize through mergers and acquisitions (Boyer and Drache 1996; Helleiner, Chapter 7, this volume; Cerny 1994). Second, globalization indicates the institutional pressures from the supranational economic governance organizations that, at the same time that they serve to moderate the loss of national economic autonomy and control from global economic forces through supranational regulatory arrangements, increasingly undermine national institutional autonomy as they gain in supranational authority (Kapstein 1994; Moran 1991; Coleman 1996); and from the supranational networks or associational linkages that, at the same time they take place within national territories, increasingly defy national institutional control (see Sassen, Chapter 8, this volume). Finally, globalization also encompasses the ideational pressures from the set of liberal capitalist ideas, not to say ideology, which in the postwar period have gone from the push for freer trade to the liberalization of markets and capital mobility and serve as the underlying rationale for political discourses that national governments have used with greater or lesser success to legitimate policies that have often produced radical changes in government management of the economy, in government relations with business and labor, and in government support of the social welfare system (see Sobel 1994; Helleiner 1994).

Globalization is not the only supranational force affecting nation-states. Regionalization – whether highly institutionalized as in the case of the European Union, much less institutionally developed as in the case of NAFTA, or much more informal as in the case of the Asia–Pacific Economic Cooperation (Katzenstein 1996) – is an equally potent force that serves at one and the same time to enhance global penetration and to protect against it.

For most European countries, the changes related to globalization cannot be considered apart from those related to the regionalization represented by European integration. But Europeanization is not just a complement to globalization. It is also a force in its own right, able to counter some of the effects of globalization.

To begin with, Europeanization does not simply add its own economic pressures to the global, undermining national economic autonomy and control with its own layer of Europe-specific financial market pressures on national economies, a set of Europe-generated competitive challenges for national business, and a Europe-induced squeeze on national social policy. Moreover, its specific policies involving monetary integration, market liberalization, and product harmonization do not solely act as a conduit for global forces by opening up the economies of member states to international financial markets and member states' businesses to international competition. They also serve as a shield against those forces, by containing them through the discipline imposed by monetary integration, the protection afforded by the single market, and the economies of scale promoted by product standardization as well as by business consolidation, concentration, and European expansion.

Similarly, Europeanization does not just add its own institutional pressures to the global pressures, with European institutions that serve to moderate global and European economic forces through European regulatory arrangements at the same time that they further undermine national institutional autonomy; and with European networks and associational linkages that further diminish national institutional control. For these institutional pressures differ not only in degree from other regional and international trade organizations, by providing much greater gains in supranational authority to offset the much greater loss of national economic autonomy and control, but also in kind. This is because European member states also give up constitutive autonomy and control over their institutions, as European institutional structures increasingly take precedence over national ones, diminishing executive policy-making autonomy, reducing parliamentary policy-making powers, and subordinating national judiciaries; and as European policy-making processes increasingly impinge on national ones, by decreasing governmental autonomy in policy formulation and flexibility in policy implementation (Schmidt 1997a). This is another issue, however, which is not the focus of this chapter.

Finally, even European ideational pressures are not simply complementary to global pressures – although they were indeed an outgrowth of the early postwar global set of liberal capitalist ideas tied to trade liberalization (Garrett and Weingast 1993). Since then the concept of Europeanization has expanded rapidly to include along with European market liberalization and capital mobility an increasingly ambitious political and economic program for European integration that goes way beyond any such program linked to globalization (Tsoukalis 1993). This European program, moreover, and in particular its economic and institutional effects, has made the legitimation task for European governments much more difficult than for non-European governments that have to deal with the impact of globalization alone, since in their political discourse they have to justify not only the greater economic changes but also the greater institutional changes that are also constitutive. Such a discourse is also more complicated to construct, because it uses globalization to reinforce its justification for changes in polity and economy in both positive ways, depicting it as complementary to Europeanization, and in negative ways, as a threat to be countered by Europeanization.

The convergent pressures related to Europeanization, in short, go way beyond those related to globalization. But for all this, neither the pressures from Europeanization nor those from globalization are in any way monolithic. Much the contrary, since European member states differ not just in *when* they responded to the forces of globalization and Europeanization, but also in *how* they responded, adjusting their economies to make up for their own particular economic vulnerabilities, adapting their institutions to fit with their own particular politico-economic structures and processes, and refashioning their political discourses to respond to their own national values and aspirations. Thus, although one could talk of convergence with regard to the general outlines of the macroeconomic, microeconomic, and socioeconomic policies governments adopted in response to global and European pressures, great divergence remains in the ways in which these policies are translated into national contexts and in the degree of change they provoke (see Berger and Dore 1996). Because of this, one cannot make any blanket statements about the impact of globalization or Europeanization on state sovereignty, whether understood as the state's ability to control activities within and across its borders or as the organization of domestic authority within a given polity (Krasner, Chapter 2, this volume). For some states have given up more internal control over economic activities than others in exchange for greater European control or global responsiveness, and some states have reorganized domestic economic authority more than others to meet the challenges of globalization and/or Europeanization.

Of the major countries in the European Union, France has undergone the greatest amount of change, generally using Europeanization as its protection against the forces of globalization and as its justification for the transformation of its economy. Great Britain, by comparison, has experienced less change, having preferred globalization over Europeanization for protection and for justification. Germany has so far changed the least, having been able to embrace both globalization and Europeanization without the same needs for protection or justification, because neither set of forces represented much threat to its economy until very recently.

The supranational pressures for convergence and the continuing divergence in national economies

The responses of European member states to the twin pressures of globalization and Europeanization have ensured a significant amount of convergence in the macroeconomic, microeconomic, and socioeconomic spheres, as well as in business and its relations with government and labor. Despite such convergence, however, there are tremendous divergences that have to do with the economic profiles of individual countries and institutional set-ups, and that force more change on some countries than others.

In the macroeconomic sphere, concerns about global financial markets have pushed all member states to sacrifice macroeconomic autonomy by committing themselves to European monetary integration and to focusing on taming inflation, diminishing government debt, and reducing public deficits. But although monetary integration has ensured a certain loss of autonomy for all member states, as they follow the lead of the German Bundesbank and seek to meet the Maastricht criteria, some member states have had to revise radically their approach to macroeconomic policy-making while others have been able to maintain theirs virtually unchanged. In the microeconomic sphere, similarly, although concerns about global and European business competition have encouraged all member states to relinquish a large measure of microeconomic control, and to deregulate and privatize national business, they have accomplished these at different rates in different ways with differing effects (Calleo and Morgenstern 1990).

Business, in turn, has consolidated, concentrated, and internationalized in response to the competitive challenges of globalization and the encouragement of the new regulatory environment promoted by national governments and the

EU (Bairoch 1996). Here, too, however, although a certain convergence has undoubtedly occurred – as big business grows bigger in size, more focused on core activities, more dispersed in operations, more European if not international in scope, and more interconnected through global alliances and networks – business has not therefore become entirely "stateless," nor has business organization or practice converged on a single model.

Most importantly, the main political linkages, cultural traits, and economic base of big business remain nationally focused. All multinational enterprises: retain national cultures and identity, if only in terms of leadership and control; remain tied to national economic governance contexts through ongoing relationships with labor and politicians; and maintain national policy linkages, if only to gain government favors, whether in the form of subsidies, export support, or international leverage (Schmidt 1995; Wright 1995; Hu 1992). Moreover, most economies remain more national than international, most multinational businesses still have most of their employees, assets, and shareholdings in their country of origin, and most "best practices" of business tend to discourage rather than encourage multinational business mobility, given just-in-time production techniques and flexible specialization that benefit from close proximity to suppliers and final markets (Wade 1996: 78–81).

What is more, not all major companies converge on a single "best practice," despite often general agreement on what that might constitute, because of country-specific institutional, organizational, and cultural realities (Streeck 1996). National or even regional economic governance contexts continue to inform firm practice and affect their competitiveness, although some sectors of industry have tended to converge more than others, and the structure of industry generally has changed more in some countries than others (Hollingsworth *et al.* 1994; Hayward 1995).

But although business remains nationally tied, it nevertheless finds itself increasingly emancipated from national government control as a result of government economic policies: that, in liberalizing financial markets, diminished business need for government funds; that, in deregulating the rules governing business, decreased state micromanagement of business activities; and that, in privatizing state-owned enterprise, increased the size of the private sector along with its autonomy. Enhancing this growing freedom from national government interference has been the rising importance not only of international markets and competition – which force business to look outside its country of origin when considering company financing and strategy and compel government to accept the potential resulting disloyalty – but also of supranational institutions. The European Union in particular has afforded European business unprecedented supranational policy-making access and influence at the same time that it has reduced national government policy-making autonomy. Decisions that governments formulated unilaterally in the past are now made through a system of multilevel governance at the EU level in consultation with member states, business, and other interests (Mazey and Richardson 1993; Marks *et al.* 1996).

Finally, at the same time that the supranational has been supplanting the national as a focal point for business attention, the subnational has also been coming into its own. Changes in management practice that favor closer linkages between firms and local suppliers, clients, governmental institutions, and associations, together with national governmental reforms that have devolved greater powers to local governments in most European states, have been making local economic governance contexts more and more central to firm activities while the national context, for the reasons outlined above, has been growing more peripheral. To put it another way, these changes have made multilevel governance a reality at the regional as much as at the supranational level, leaving national government one of many players – albeit still the most privileged (Smith 1996).

The increasing independence of business, in short, has unbalanced the traditional relationship between business and government and generally loosened the ties that have traditionally bound business more or less closely to government. But this is not all, for the new business independence has also undermined the traditional business relationship with labor. As business has grown more powerful and more mobile, it has had less need of the postwar compromises brokered with governments and/or labor that aimed at maintaining national economic growth and political stability through jobs and incomes policies, even though some countries saw an earlier and more emphatic end to the old compromises while others have occasionally constructed new compromises (Dore *et al.* 1994).

Labor today is much less mobile or powerful than business. Despite the Single Market Act that established the free movement not only of capital, goods, and services but also of people, capital mobility has far outstripped that of people. Language, culture, and family ties weigh heavily against movement, especially in the richer member states. Labor has also lost bargaining power, with unions on the decline and workers generally much less militant than in the past, unwilling to risk their jobs at a time of continuing high unemployment (although they can be mobilized effectively in response to the threat of job cuts). Business mobility, moreover, has also contributed to labor's loss of clout, since workers are now much more vulnerable to company pressures to moderate their wage demands in the face of threats to move abroad (Marginson and Sisson 1994).

Most importantly of all, however, labor for the most part can no longer count on government as a protector, partner, or arbitrator in its relations with business. As governments have liberalized, they have often cut off the umbilical cord with labor – although some, such as the Thatcher government in Great Britain with the miners' strike, have done so more brutally than others. In most member states, labor has seen the end of centralized wage bargaining and increasing wage differentials resulting from company-level negotiations. But even in countries where sector-wide wage negotiations continue, the contracts are much more flexible and often focused at the regional level, with plant-level agreements gaining greater currency.

These changes in business and its relationship to government and labor, together with the macroeconomic and microeconomic changes, have generated a loss of socioeconomic capacity. Member states, finding themselves without the wherewithal to maintain the welfare state as in the past, everywhere seek to limit

pension payments, cap unemployment compensation, reduce medical reimburse-
ments, and generally cut social spending (Mishra 1996; Leibfried and Pierson
1995). But although the loss of capacity has produced a certain convergence in
cost-cutting policies of member states, as the welfare state increasingly takes a
back seat to the competitive state, tremendous differences nevertheless remain.
Social protection systems continue to be highly differentiated as member states
conceptualize and prioritize the issues differently and employ different policy
instruments and funding mechanisms. And some systems have experienced more
disruption and loss of capacity than others as a result of the pressures to decrease
social spending (Hantrais 1995a).

In short, whatever the convergent pressures from Europeanization and globalization, and whatever the convergent policies adopted by member states,
individual countries nevertheless continue to exhibit very different patterns of
adaptation. Long-established institutions and processes are not so easy to change,
whatever the seeming rationality of the policies and however powerful the actors
pushing reform. This is amply illustrated in the cases of France, Great Britain,
and Germany.

France

Compared to Great Britain and Germany, France has had to change the most in
the face of global and European pressures (Boltho 1996). In the macroeconomic
sphere, France entirely replaced its post-war *dirigiste* system of state-guaranteed
finance and inflation-spurred growth with tight monetary policies, austerity
budgets, and a policy of "competitive disinflation" to damp inflation and maintain the franc *fort* (keeping the value of the franc high). In the microeconomic
sphere, France, having imposed deregulation out of necessity and privatization
out of ideology, dramatically reduced state ownership and control of business.
Moreover, the changes in business and its relations with government have been
most pronounced, given the exponential growth in business size and scope, and
the fact that state interventionism, where it remains, has become much more
circumscribed and market-oriented. In the socioeconomic sphere, finally, the loss
of capacity has been most dramatic, given that France through the 1980s had
increased its social spending and through the 1990s has experienced increasingly
high levels of unemployment. The problem for France today, in fact, is that while
the economy has been turned around and the business–government relationship
transformed, unemployment has grown, wages have stagnated, and social benefits have decreased.

In the macroeconomic sphere, until the collapse of the Bretton Woods
system, French governments were able to profit from their autonomy by using
the central bank in a zig-zag course against the fixed, dollar exchange rate
through inflation and devaluation in order to promote economic growth (Loriaux
1991). After the collapse of Bretton Woods, however, France's macroeconomic
autonomy was of little effect against global financial markets. Because France
has been highly vulnerable to global market forces and strongly buffeted by the

challenges of international competition, Europeanization through monetary integration became, in the view of French governments, the only effective shield against globalization and the only way to stabilize the economy and promote economic growth (Schmidt 1997b; Dillingham 1996). In 1983, with the "great U-turn" in macroeconomic policy-making, France abandoned not only its macro-economic autonomy but also its traditional *dirigiste* approach to policy-making in order to stay in the European Monetary System (EMS) (see Hall 1986; Schmidt 1996a).

Such macroeconomic change, moreover, ensured major microeconomic change, since the *dirigisme* of the indicative plans, national industrial policies, and *grands projets* could no longer work in a more open economy where the government no longer had the resources, given budgetary austerity, the freedom, given European competition policy and GATT agreements, or the will, given changes in elite and public opinion, to intervene as it had in the past (Schmidt 1997c). Deregulation and privatization naturally followed.

Deregulation, begun by the Socialists out of necessity as early as 1982, altered the regulatory environment of business. It diminished direct government control over business by lifting most price controls; easing workplace laws governing hiring, firing, and work hours; creating semi-independent agencies to supervise the stock market and the radio and television industries; and liberalizing the financial markets, thereby creating new, non-governmental sources of funding for business at a time when there were to be fewer government subsidies and low-cost loans (Schmidt 1996a).

Privatization, begun by the neoliberal right out of ideology as of 1986, also reduced French government control of business along with government owner-ship. Focused primarily on public enterprises in the competitive sector, it was highly *dirigiste* in approach, despite its anti-*dirigiste* effect, since the government reserved a 15–20 per cent share for a hard core of investors and limited foreign share acquisition. The resulting structure of business ownership and control, in which successive policies of the right and left involved full and partial privatiza-tions as well as the trading of shares among nationalized companies and the acquisition of shares in privatized enterprises by nationalized ones, has led to a mixed economy in which public and private financial and industrial concerns own and control one another in a manner somewhat resembling the German business-banking partnership (although without the strength of the German banks) (Schmidt 1996a).

Business has changed dramatically in direct consequence of these reforms as well as in response to the changing global and European environments. To begin with, it has become bigger, less nationally focused, and more internationally competitive. Beginning in the early to mid-1980s, French industrial enterprises underwent major restructuring and rationalization as they shed workers, stream-lined operations, closed antiquated plants and reengineered others, ameliorated their traditional relations with labor, returned to core business, and generally prepared themselves for European and global competition. Starting in the mid- to late 1980s, French industry turned outward, beginning a process of internationalization through mergers and acquisitions that saw foreign direct investment abroad by French companies jump from next to nothing to close to $30 billion in 1990 (Schmidt 1996a: 359–363).

These changes in business size and scope, together with government reforms, have also brought change in the traditional business–government relationship. Business has become more independent from the state and more interdependent, as businesses now look more to one another for guidance and to the markets for support than to the state. By the 1990s, in fact, the "heroic" policies formulated by governments without business input and then adapted to their needs in the implementation had been for the most part superseded by more "everyday" policies in which consultation occurs at the outset and government actions are often in response to business initiatives (Schmidt 1996c). Business now leads more and government directs less.

But these changes have not entirely stopped French governmental elites from seeking to influence business. Although they have abandoned the excesses of traditional *dirigisme*, they have nevertheless continued to intervene in a more circumscribed market-oriented way focused primarily on public firms in strategic areas (e.g., the privatization of Thomson and the merger of Aerospatiale and Dassault) or in trouble, especially in the public sector (Schmidt 1997c). The problem for the government in the still-nationalized, highly regulated sectors such as transport and telecommunications is that the public sector unions, despite their overall weakness, have managed to scuttle rationalization and privatization plans through strikes that have galvanized public support as symbolic protests over larger socioeconomic issues related to rising unemployment, increasing job insecurity, and declining social benefits.

France's socioeconomic difficulties are in fact particularly acute, given the need to trim public deficits and control public spending in the run-up to European monetary union. This is mainly because while most EU member states were successful at containing welfare costs in the 1980s, France's spending on social protection increased by more than 30 per cent between 1980 and 1989, reaching 30 per cent of GDP by the early 1990s. This rise in costs is particularly problematic for France, given its insurance-based social protection system, which is largely funded through employer and employee contributions at a much higher rate and with less state support than the insurance-based system of Germany, let alone the taxation-based system of the United Kingdom (Hantrais 1995b). This puts France at a competitive disadvantage and in danger from "social dumping" by corporations in search of lower wage costs and unwilling to pay France's 40 per cent payroll tax. Moreover, this competitive disadvantage exists despite the fact that the French managed to hold down wages from the mid-1980s on. This means that French labor, having seen its salaries stagnate over the course of the 1980s and into the 1990s, now finds its benefits also in jeopardy. Add to this high unemployment (at 12.8 per cent in 1997), and one can understand why the late 1995 strikes gained such public sympathy.

Great Britain

By comparison with France, Great Britain has experienced comparatively little change in response to Europeanization – globalization, by contrast, has been a major impetus to change. In the macroeconomic sphere, Britain has retained its traditionally liberal and international approach to macroeconomic policy-making and limited its commitment to European monetary integration, having found it anything but a shield against global forces. In the microeconomic sphere, Britain deregulated and privatized ahead of European pressures, having been ideologically committed to dismantling state control of an economy that was in any event less state dominated than that of France. The traditionally distant relationship between business and government, moreover, has only become more distant, as government has left British industry without the level of government support as in France. Finally, in the socioeconomic sphere, the loss of capacity has not been as significant as it has been for France, mainly because Great Britain has consistently had a lower rate of spending and today has much lower unemployment.

Unlike France, which has led European monetary integration along with Germany, Great Britain has taken steps to ensure that it would be minimally affected by European monetary integration. Most significantly, although it has been a member of the European Monetary System since 1979, it declined to join the key component of the EMS, the ERM, at the outset; joined only in 1990; bailed out in 1992; negotiated an opt-out from the EMU in the Maastricht Treaty; and only with the Blair government in 1997 did it declare its intention to join some time in the not-too-distant future.

The British decision to limit its commitment to monetary integration stems not simply from British concerns about the loss of national sovereignty or from doubts about whether it could work effectively. Britain's limited commitment is also related to the fact that the country has not needed monetary integration as much as has France, primarily because of its very different macroeconomic environment. Because Great Britain has traditionally had a more "liberal" and international approach to economic policy than most of its European neighbors, because it has traditionally been more free-trade oriented and had lower tariffs, and because it has had much larger financial markets (Shonfield 1958; Strange 1971; Blank 1978: 107–8), it has for a long time been much more responsive and therefore less vulnerable to the liberalization of global markets and trade than France, which lacked both Great Britain's economic openness and financial market strength. Moreover, its brief experience with the ERM convinced it that European monetary integration was no shield for it against global forces (Artis 1992), unlike for France. And this seemed confirmed by that fact that while France subsequently continued to struggle under the burden of comparatively high interest rates and slow growth, the British economy took off.

In the microeconomic sphere as in the macroeconomic sphere, Great Britain has changed little in response to Europe-related pressures, mainly because it anticipated much of Europe-instigated deregulation and privatization while it resisted Europe-mandated social policy reforms, gaining opt-outs here too (although Blair has now opted back in). In Great Britain, deregulation and privatization came early, ahead of European pressures, and were part of Prime Minister Thatcher's ideological commitment to rid the country of "socialism" and "corporatism." Thatcher's government anticipated many of the deregulatory initiatives of the European Community, going farther faster than any other European member state in dismantling state control of an economy that has in any case been less state regulated than those on the continent. In keeping with Thatcherite ideology, privatization – focused primarily on monopolistic public enterprise such as gas, telephone, water, and air transport – was highly *laissez faire*, with companies' shares freely floated on the stockmarket. In fact, the British "spectator state" – which has always intervened much less in business for reasons of lack of capacity (given in particular the reliance of business on the stock market rather than government for funds) as well as culture – has become even more of a spectator (Grant 1995), as it has exposed business to greater international competition and the vagaries of the markets without the level of government support or protection as in France. In Great Britain, unlike in France where the state led business transformation and cushioned its effects, the *laissez-faire* nature of reform made certain that privatized business would be more vulnerable to foreign acquisition; that the deregulated stockmarket would lead the moves toward industry concentration and consolidation; and that foreign acquirers would more often than not impose modernization and internationalization from the outside.

Having been left to sink or swim on its own, British industry has sunk more often than not. And yet, foreign-owned industry in Britain has done reasonably well, as have some large British companies such as ICI and British Airways. This is due not only to the welcoming investment environment but also to the low wage costs, high labor flexibility, and comparatively low labor militancy. This seeming transformation in British labor rates, rules, and relations results from a combination of harsh Tory policies toward labor that virtually crushed the unions in the early 1980s and of the amelioration in management practices with regard to labor, led in large measure by foreign manufacturing firms, in particular the Japanese. And it means that Britain, having been disdained for years for its failing industries and low productivity, has now become a preferred host for foreign direct investment (FDI) and its industries worthy global competitors, even if many are foreign owned.

These changes in Britain's economic profile have ensured that its socioeconomic problems are not as great as those of France. Britain does not have the same unemployment problems as its continental neighbors because it has much greater labor market flexibility. Like the US, what workers lack in job security they have gained in job availability, even if the jobs may be lower paying and part-time. Moreover, the major battles with regard to public spending in the social welfare and health systems were fought in the 1980s. But even here, although the social welfare and health systems were cut, it was much less than the rhetoric suggested, public outcry having kept Thatcher from carrying out much of the radical reform she had planned.

Germany

Germany, which has always been more internationally oriented and globally competitive, has so far had to change little by comparison with both Great Britain and France in response to the pressures of globalization or Europeanization. In the macroeconomic sphere, Germany maintained its traditionally conservative approach to macroeconomic policy-making through the largely independent Bundesbank. In the microeconomic sphere, Germany has been slowest to deregulate or privatize, having initially felt little need or ideological impetus to do so. Moreover, only now is the traditionally close business–government–labor relationship beginning to fray at the edges, as unemployment rises to unacceptable levels and social benefits begin to be capped.

As the lead European economy with the lead European currency, Germany has been the leader of European monetary policy through the Bundesbank's *de facto* control over European monetary affairs. As such, Europeanization in the macroeconomic sphere has been little more than an extension to the rest of Europe of Germany's own traditional macroeconomic patterns and prejudices (in particular, its emphasis on the importance of a strong currency, of price stability, and of the dangers of inflation) (see McNamara 1995). In addition, Europeanization has represented more a reinforcement through European enlargement of Germany's traditional, macroeconomic hedge against global forces than a new protection against them (although it did serve to protect its microeconomic competitiveness by ensuring that German exports would remain competitive in European markets). In short, neither the forces of globalization nor of Europeanization have had much impact on Germany's approach to macroeconomic policy-making or on its policy-making institutions – even if they have recently been taking their toll on the economy. This is also true for the microeconomic sphere.

Germany has been relatively non-ideological with regard to deregulation and privatization, and has been exceedingly slow at both as well. Only when pushed by Europe did it slowly negotiate change with the "social partners," business and labor, and with the Länder, the federal states, and in such a way that it has had little disruptive impact (Esser 1995). Germany has in fact felt less need to deregulate or privatize than either France or Great Britain because of the power of its economy and the solidity of its economic governance structures, as reflected in its continued "hidden flexibility within stable institutions," which has ensured that any change has involved a subtle process of shifting power and responsibilities without altering existing structures (Katzenstein 1989).

Germany's particular business structure, where its big businesses have long been export oriented and highly competitive, and have traditionally had a close partnership with the banks that provides long-term, low-cost financing at the same time that it protects it from takeovers, together with industry's near symbiotic relationship with subcontractors, suppliers, and customers, has made German business less vulnerable to outside pressures and more resilient. Moreover, Germany's cooperative industrial relations system has made possible innovations in production systems, and in particular the move from Fordism to flexible specialization (Piore and Sabel 1984), that spared it the radical restructuring and strikes that businesses of other nations went through from the late 1970s onward.

In the past couple of years or so, however, the German formula for economic success has come into question. As the costs of unification have mounted and the pressures of global competition have accelerated, Germany has increasingly suffered from expensive products, high labor costs, a high unemployment rate, a decline in in-country investment (foreign and domestic), a slowdown in productivity, and a drop in innovation. Moreover, its traditional business structures and economic governance system have also begun to erode as government negotiated coordination of capital and labor markets are increasingly difficult to maintain in the face of growing labor as well as capital mobility (Streeck 1997). The close business–banking partnership is becoming more distant as the banks internationalize and businesses increasingly rely on self-financing for cash and have been reducing their level of bank debt (Esser 1995). And the traditionally consensual, tripartite business–labor–government relationship is already beginning to fray at the edges, as German firms have begun the rationalizing of operations, the shedding of workers, and the export of core activities in the face of the pressures to internationalize production locations and market strategies that most French and British firms began much earlier.

Although corporatist bargaining has continued, employers have increasingly questioned whether it should continue – as with the reaction to the generous 1995 wage agreement negotiated by I.G. Metall – while the bargaining itself has increasingly involved give-backs by employees. Although the proposed reduction in sick-pay benefits from 100 per cent to 80 per cent of Fall 1996, was ultimately not adopted by large-scale employers in wage negotiations, the recalculation of sick pay to reflect only base pay without overtime has in fact meant that most workers now received 80 per cent of what they had before. Moreover, even if the give-backs in terms of social benefits are so far quite minor compared with Great Britain or France, as with the three-week stay in a spa every three years, which is no longer automatic and now comes for shorter periods and/or at longer intervals, they nevertheless signal a loss in socioeconomic capacity that threatens Germany's traditionally generous welfare state.

Political discourse and democratic legitimacy

In response to the pressures of Europeanization as well as globalization, in short, all three countries have sacrificed much socioeconomic capacity along with macroeconomic and microeconomic policy autonomy. This sacrifice has been felt more acutely by France, however, than Germany or Great Britain. What is more, France has found it harder to gain public acceptance of the necessary economic adjustments, mainly because it lacks a coherent political discourse that could serve to justify the sacrifice in terms of long-term goals. Great Britain, by contrast, has managed to construct a more-or-less coherent discourse since the advent of Thatcher while Germany's postwar discourse only began to show cracks in the mid-1990s (Schmidt 1997d).

The importance of developing a political discourse capable of justifying the changes in macroeconomic and microeconomic policy, let alone in socioeconomic policy, cannot be overestimated. Without a discourse that serves to set globalization and Europeanization coherently into national context, with a credible vision of how the country fits into an integrating Europe and a globalizing world, discussions of global and European imperatives tend to be heard more as rhetorical exhortations, with no greater rationale than as excuses for government policy, and with little lasting message other than that outside incursions are causing change within. At the best, in times of prosperity and complacency, the public will accept the rhetoric and the rationale with little question, and will respond to the message as a challenge; at worst, in times of recession and malaise, the public will reject the rhetoric and the rationale, finding itself left only with the message, to which it is most likely to respond as a threat, thereby increasing its vulnerability to political opportunism and demagoguery (see Schmidt 1997c).

French governments have been markedly unsuccessful in coming up with a coherent political discourse to justify their vision of an economically liberal but still socially solid France in an integrated Europe that protects it against the pressures of globalization. Ever since the Socialists abandoned their socialist discourse in the early 1980s once they converted to liberal economic policies (Schmidt 1996a: 96–106) and the right failed to sustain their neoliberal discourse of the mid-1980s in the face of electoral defeat (Godin 1996), French governmental elites have used their pro-European and anti-global rhetoric as a substitute for any well-developed political discourse capable of justifying the major changes in French economics, politics, and society since the early 1980s. European integration, in other words, acted as much as a political shield as an economic one. But although it worked for much of the 1980s, by the early to mid-1990s, its ability to protect the political class diminished with its decreasing ability to shield France in the face of economic recession and the increasing incursions on social policy.

The problem for French governmental elites of the left and the right is that they have yet to find a discourse that would serve to reconcile their expressed commitment to "social solidarity" with the effects of economic liberalization. And as French citizens see taxes and unemployment continue to rise while their social benefits and services are cut, they have been losing patience – not only with the policies that seem not to have succeeded in bringing prosperity and jobs to France but also with the processes that continually leave them out of the decision-making loop (Schmidt 1997b). The late 1995 strikes are testimony to this loss of patience (see "The 1995 Strikes," 1996). But whether the French government can live up to President Chirac's pledge in response to the strikes to engage in more dialogue and cooperative industrial relations remains to be seen, given that it has rarely achieved much dialogue or cooperation in the social arena with French citizens, and has generally sought more to impose or to pacify (in the face of protest) than to listen (although the Jospin government seems to have been more successful than the preceding Juppé government with regard to dialogue, if not always to cooperative industrial relations). But even if the government were truly eager to listen, the intermediary bodies necessary to cooperative industrial relations are either weak or missing, by contrast with Germany, and Parliament has never acted as an effective voice for the concerns of citizens, by contrast with Great Britain. What is more, the other main avenues for expression of citizen concerns – the press and the courts – have been viewed with growing suspicion by governmental elites as corruption scandals increasingly come to light (Schmidt 1997b).

The success of any such dialogue and cooperative industrial relations, moreover, depends upon the ability of French governmental elites to fashion a coherent political discourse to justify the conversion to a more liberal and open macroeconomy, to a more market-oriented microeconomy, and to a more restricted socioeconomy. Without such a justificatory discourse, the loss of socioeconomic capacity in the face of European and global forces is likely to raise politically opportunistic or demagogic questions instead about the vision of France in an integrated Europe, and to leave French citizens feeling increasingly under siege, threatened by the forces of European integration as well as globalization, thereby putting French democratic legitimacy at risk. It is a risk, moreover, that Great Britain and Germany run less, albeit for very different reasons given their very different political discourses.

Compared to France, British governments since Thatcher have been most successful in creating an overall vision that situates globalization and Europeanization within a coherent political discourse. Their pro-global rhetoric, which has roots in the country's more open economic history, in conjunction with their moderately anti-European rhetoric, which has enabled them to gain opt-outs from the social chapter of the Maastricht Treaty and from monetary union, fit in well with their neoliberal discourse, which propounds the roll-back of the state in all spheres – socioeconomic as much as macroeconomic and microeconomic. In fact, Britain's loss of socioeconomic capacity finds as much justification in the discourse, which ever since Thatcher has preached the need to dismantle the welfare state (even though the intended radical reforms were never instituted), as does the resistance to changes in macroeconomic policy related to membership in the EMS and EMU or to social policy, where the recent opt-in does not in any way reverse the British preference for flexibility in employment.

Moreover, none of the economic changes have had the same political ramifications as in France not only because of the discourse but also because British citizens have benefited from more dialogue – although not necessarily consultation – on all aspects of European integration as well as globalization. Citizens' concerns have at least been given more voice through a Parliament that, although almost as weak as the French when it comes to influencing policy, has always acted as a forum for the vigorous debate of ideas. The dialogue has been such, in fact, that the neoliberal discourse that had appeared so radical when first introduced by Thatcher now seems to have gained widespread acceptance countrywide, so much so that even the new Labor government has all but adopted it, even if it has not been given to the anti-European rhetoric of the previous government.

The problem for Great Britain in the last couple of years of Tory government was that the anti-European rhetoric risked becoming reality, as the Major government found it increasingly convenient to point out the dangers of Europeanization without mentioning its merits, whether in playing to the Euroskeptics in Parliament in order to retain their allegiance or to the Eurocrats in Brussels to broker the best deal. The danger for Britain has been that as the rhetoric escalated, the rational discourse that since Thatcher has consistently put European integration squarely within the neoliberal vision of Britain's future, as part of a larger, neoliberal Europe and world, may have been forgotten – not so much by the elite, and in particular the business elite, which is well aware of the necessity of continued integration for the country's global competitiveness – as by the population, making it more open to demagogic manipulation. The new Labor government that came to power after the elections in the Spring of 1997, therefore, is certain not only to have to reconstruct the political discourse to reflect its own particular brand of liberalism but also to recreate a vision of how Britain in Europe and the world is or ought to be that will also help it make the case for entry, or not, into the EMU.

Compared to both Great Britain and France, German governments have possibly been the most successful at creating an overall vision that situates globalization and Europeanization within a coherent political discourse. Not only has its postwar, liberal, social democratic discourse been the longest lasting, it has also managed to reconcile both pro-European and pro-global rhetorics within its vision of a peaceful Germany tied politically and economically to a wider Europe and world. The problem for Germany today, however, is that that vision has remained within the confines of a discourse that in the 1990s has been fraying at the edges as a result of the political changes resulting from the fall of the Berlin wall and the economic problems related to unification, integration, and globalization.

As long as the economy flourished and Germany managed to dominate European macroeconomic policy and delay adjusting national microeconomic policy, German governments found it relatively easy to reconcile their pro-global and pro-European stances with a social democratic discourse infused with liberal market notions that served to justify the "social market" economy. But now that they are beginning to face the loss of capacity in the socioeconomic realm, increasing deregulation in the microeconomic arena, and their own possible inability to meet the strict Maastricht criteria they themselves insisted on, they are finding the social democratic elements of their discourse increasingly at odds with the neoliberal policies promoted by Europeanization and globalization.

For the moment at least, German citizens, unlike the French, have kept their patience in the face of rising taxes and unemployment and decreasing social benefits and services – largely because dialogue and cooperative industrial relations continue with the intermediary bodies, despite sporadic strikes and increasing confrontation between business and unions. The federal structure of government is an added advantage by comparison with both France and Great Britain, as the Länder convey citizen concerns to the federal government at the same time that they respond to those within their own jurisdiction. Moreover, because both the "social partners" in the tripartite relationship and the "governmental partners" in the federal system are brought into European policy-making by the national government as a matter of course, German citizens have more access to EU policy formulation than either the French or British, and therefore require less flexibility in the implementation. Whether all of this together will ensure the survival of the postwar German corporatist system in the face of the changing economic realities remains to be seen, however. And it is therefore too soon to tell whether German governmental elites will be able to adapt the discourse to the new realities, or will have to invent another.

Conclusion

France, in sum, has experienced much greater institutional changes in response to the pressures of Europeanization and globalization than either Great Britain or Germany. With 1983 as the watershed year, France reluctantly began the transition from an economy that was quite closed to the outside, highly regulated on the inside, but nevertheless very vulnerable to the new competitive environment and global markets, to one less closed, less regulated, and more market oriented. France has abandoned its traditional interventionism characterized by a state-sanctioned cycle of inflation and devaluation and state-dominated industry in favor of a more German-style macroeconomic liberalism focused on taming inflation and maintaining a strong currency and a more British-style microeconomic liberalism focused on reducing state ownership and control of business through deregulation and privatization. Although all of this has been generally salutary for the French economy, it has been less so for French democracy. French governments have as yet to elaborate a sufficiently legitimating discourse for these changes or for their loss of capacity in the socioeconomic arena.

Although Britain has also changed tremendously, this change has come less from the pressures of Europeanization than from those of globalization, given an economy that has on the whole been more open to the outside with larger financial markets than France and which anticipated the neoliberal thrust of the European economic agenda in terms of deregulation while retaining more room for maneuver through macroeconomic and social policy opt-outs. And because as of 1979 it gained a government even more ideologically committed to freeing up the inside than any other European country, including France between 1986 and 1988, and more successful at it, it was able to create a neoliberal political discourse that served to legitimate all of the changes related to globalization, if not always Europeanization.

Germany, by comparison with both France and Great Britain, has changed little, despite the pressures of Europeanization or globalization, although unification has taken its toll and the signs of strain are mounting. Because of Germany's lead, macroeconomic role and its long-term economic success, its opening to the outside has had comparatively little impact up until very recently. Because Germany has benefited from more economically successful models of business structure and business–government–labor relationship, it has not only managed to adapt to the new competitive environment without the kind of foreign penetration experienced by Great Britain but it has also been able to deregulate where mandated by European integration without the kind of disruption to traditional patterns of interaction experienced by France. But although all of this had enabled Germany to feel less need to free itself up on the inside or to question its traditional liberal social democratic discourse, this is no longer the case. The strains of unification, human and financial, together with the costs of the social market and the strength of the mark that have made its products less competitive worldwide, have generated an economic crisis that threatens Germany's traditional business–government–labor relationship and, with it, Germany's democratic legitimacy for the first time in a very long time.

In other words, Germany may soon, like France, be seeking a new political discourse. But it cannot be a British discourse. Any political discourse must be able to take account of the impact of Europeanization and globalization within the context of the country's own historical, institutional, and cultural specificities. Moreover, if European integration is to survive, Germany as much as France must construct a discourse that is compatible with the further deepening as well as widening of the European Union. Europe can afford only one Britain.

References

Artis, M. (1992) "Monetary policy," in S. Bulmer, S. George, and A. Scott (eds) *The United Kingdom and EC Membership Evaluated*, London: Pinter.

Bairoch, P. (1996) "Globalization myths and realities: one century of external trade and foreign investment," in R. Boyer and D. Drache (eds) *States against Markets: The Limits of Globalization*, London and New York: Routledge.

Berger S. and Dore, R. (eds) (1996) *National Diversity and Global Capitalism*, Ithaca: Cornell University Press.

Blank, S. (1978) "Britain: the politics of foreign economic policy, the domestic economy, and the problem of pluralistic stagnation," in P. Katzenstein (ed.) *Between Power and Plenty*, Madison, WI: University of Wisconsin Press.

Boltho, A. (1996) "Has France converged on Germany? Policies and institutions since 1958," in S. Berger and R. Dore (eds) *National Diversity and Global Capitalism*, Ithaca: Cornell University Press.

Boyer, R. and Drache, D. (1996) *States against Markets: The Limits of Globalization*, London and New York: Routledge.

Calleo, D. and Morgenstern, P. (1990) *Recasting Europe's Economies: National Strategies in the 1980s*, Lanham, Maryland: Washington Foundation for European Studies and University Press of America.

Cerny, P. (1994) "The dynamics of financial globalization," *Policy Sciences* 27: 319–42.

Coleman, W. (1996) *Financial Services, Globalization, and Domestic Policy Change: A Comparison of North America and the European Union*, London: Macmillan.

Dillingham, A.J. (1996) "The costs of convergence: the case of France," *ECSA Review* IX, 2 (Spring/Summer).

Dore, R., Boyer, R., and Mars, Z. (1994) *The Return to Incomes Policy*, London: Pinter.

Esser, J. (1995) "Germany: the old policy style," in J. Hayward (ed.) *Industrial Enterprise and European Integration: From National to International Champions in Western Europe*, Oxford: Oxford University Press.

Garret, G. and Weingast, B. (1993) "Ideas, interests, and institutions: constructing the european community's internal market," in J. Goldstein and R.O. Keohane (eds) *Ideas and Foreign Policy: Beliefs, Institutions, and Political Change*, Ithaca: Cornell University Press.

Godin, E. (1996) "Le Néo-Libéralisme à la Française: Une exception?" *Modern and Contemporary France* NS4 (1).

Grant, W. (1995) "Great Britain: The spectator state," in J. Hayward (ed.) *Industrial Enterprise and European Integration: From National to International Champions in Western Europe*, Oxford: Oxford University Press.

Hall, P. (1986) *Governing the Economy: The Politics of State Intervention in Britain and France*, New York: Oxford University Press.

Hantrais, L. (1995a) *Social Policy in the European Union*, London: Macmillan.

—— (1995b) "French social policy in the European context," *Modern and Contemporary France* NS3 (4).

Hayward, J. (ed.) (1995) *Industrial Enterprise and European Integration: From National to International Champions in Western Europe*, Oxford: Oxford University Press.

Helleiner, E. (1994) *States and the Reemergence of Global Finance*, Ithaca: Cornell University Press.

Hollingsworth, R., Schmitter, P., and Streeck, W. (eds) (1994) *Governing Capitalist Economies*, Oxford: Oxford University Press.

Hu, Y. (1992) "Global corporations are national firms with international operations," *California Management Review* 34 (2): 107–26.

Kapstein, E. (1994) *Governing the Global Economy*, Cambridge: Harvard University Press.

Katzenstein, P.J. (1989) "Industry in a changing West Germany," in P.J. Katzenstein (ed.) *Industry and Politics in West Germany: Toward the Third Republic*, Ithaca: Cornell University Press.

——(1996) "Regionalism in comparative perspective," *Cooperation and Conflict* 31 (2).

Leibfried, S. and Pierson, P. (1995) "Semisovereign welfare states: social policy in a multi-tiered Europe," in S. Leibfried and P. Pierson (eds) *European Social Policy: Between Fragmentation and Integration*, Washington, DC: Brookings Institution.

Loriaux, M. (1991) *France after Hegemony: International Change and Financial Reform*, Ithaca: Cornell University Press.

Marginson, P. and Sisson, K. (1994) "The structure of transnational capital in Europe: The emerging Euro-Company and its implications for industrial relations," in R. Hyman and A. Ferner (eds) *Frontiers in European Industrial Relations*, Oxford: Basil Blackwell.

Marks, G., Hooghe, L., and Blank, K. (1996) "European integration since the 1980s: state-centric versus multi-level governance," *Journal of Common Market Studies* 34 (3): 341–78.

Mazey, S. and Richardson, J. (eds) (1993) *Lobbying in the European Community*, Oxford: Oxford University Press.

McNamara, K.R. (1995) "Consensus and constraint: the politics of monetary cooperation in Europe," PhD. dissertation, Columbia University.

Mishra, R. (1996) "The welfare of nations," in R. Boyer and D. Drache (eds) *States against Markets: The Limits of Globalization*, London and New York: Routledge.

Moran, M. (1991) *The Politics of the Financial Services Revolution: The USA, UK, and Japan*, New York: St. Martin's.

Piore, M. and Sabel, C. (1984) *The Second Industrial Divide: Possibilities for Prosperity*, New York: Basic Books.

Schmidt, V.A. (1995) "The New World Order, Incorporated: The rise of business and the decline of the nation-state," *Daedalus* 124 (2): 75–106.

—— (1996a) *From State to Market? The Transformation of French Business and Government*, Cambridge and New York: Cambridge University Press.

—— (1996c) "The decline of traditional state *dirigisme* in France: the transformation of political economic policies and policymaking processes," *Governance* 9 (4): 375–405.

—— (1997a) "European integration and democracy: the differences among member-states," *Journal of European Public Policy*, 4 (1): 128–45.

—— (1997b) "Economic policy, political discourse, and democracy in France," *French Politics and Society* 15 (2): Spring.

—— (1997c) "Running on empty: the end of *dirigisme* in French economic leadership," *Modern and Contemporary France* (forthcoming).

—— (1997d) "Discourse and (dis)integration in Europe," *Daedalus* 126 (3): 167–98 (Summer).

Shonfield, A. (1958) *British Economic Policy since the War*, London: Penguin

Smith, A. (1996) "Putting the governance back into multi-level governance: examples from French translations of the structural funds," paper prepared for presentation at the European Consortium for Political Research meetings, Oslo, March 30–April 3.

Sobel, A. (1994) *Domestic Choices, International Markets; Dismantling National Barriers and Liberalizing Securities Markets*, Ann Arbor: University of Michigan Press.

Strange, S. (1971) *Sterling and British Policy*, London: Oxford University Press

Streeck, W. (1996) "Lean production in the German automobile industry: a test case for convergence theory," in S. Berger and R. Dore (eds) *National Diversity and Global Capitalism*, Ithaca: Cornell University Press.

—— (1997) "German capitalism: Does it exist? Can it survive?" in C. Crouch and W. Streeck (eds) *Modern Capitalism or Modern Capitalisms?* London: Frances Pinter.

—— (1996) "The 1995 Strikes – Something New or Déjà Vu?" *French Politics and Society* 14 (1): Winter.

Tsoukalis, L. (1993) *The New European Economy: The Politics and Economics of Integration*, 2nd revised edn, Oxford: Oxford University Press.

Wade, R. (1996) "Globalization and its limits: reports of the death of the national economy are greatly exaggerated," in S. Berger and R. Dore (eds) *National Diversity and Global Capitalism*, Ithaca: Cornell University Press.

Wright, V. (1995) "Conclusion," in J. Hayward (ed.) *Industrial Enterprise and European Integration: From National to International Champions in Western Europe*, Oxford: Oxford University Press.

10 From comprador state to auctioneer state

Property change, realignment, and peripheralization in post-state-socialist central and eastern Europe[1]

József Böröcz

This chapter develops a conceptual overview of the recent transformations of the formerly socialist states of central and eastern Europe by examining the changing structures of their dependency, state sovereignty, and legitimacy.[2]

Socialism by empire

The transformation of the societies of central and eastern Europe *into* Stalinist state socialism after the Second World War was made possible by the Soviet conquest of the Nazi puppet states of central and eastern Europe in the context of the Allied Powers' military cooperation. The remolding into a Soviet-style state socialism and the imperial subordination of these societies to their Moscow center was hammered together by the joint forces of the great powers – through military alliance during the war and a grudging, but self-disciplined, global "Realpolitik." The structural insertion of the socialist states of central and eastern Europe into the world economy and the interstate system was, thus, marked by the feature that their legitimacy was, initially, completely external. It resided in the *status quo* of the great-power politics of the cold war: issues of their internal legitimacy were, at first, quite unimportant. The state developed as a local tool of this arrangement can be summed up as a "comprador state."[3] Its relation to its imperial center was analogous to the servitude that links the *comprador* bourgeoisies of the peripheries of the capitalist world economy to their respective centers of metropolitan capital. The central and east European socialist states were a structure of public authority severely deprived of their sovereignty by the imperial arrangement to which they were subjected.

Thus, any attempt at reforming the formal political structures of the state socialist societies toward a more harmonious relationship between state and society was doomed to failure as it ran into, and got stuck upon, the knot tied between socialism and the "geopolitical reality" of the great-power arrangement. Formal structures of representative democracy – an important possible source of internal legitimacy for the state – could not be introduced because of the possibility, indeed likelihood, that such democratic structures would assert sovereignty by abjuring the great-power arrangement. Formal political reform would, it was feared, dissolve the comprador state.

Imperial subordination was of course not new to this region. Much of these societies' modern history had been about the suppression of internal legitimacy due to repeated submission to the dynamics of the Czarist Russian, Prussian, Habsburg, and Ottoman imperial structures. Nazi German advances in their territories before and during the Second World War were "just" the last pre-state-socialist form of imperialism they experienced. The state-socialist imperial attempt was novel, however, in being established with the ambition of creating a world empire that would pose a substantive alternative to the capitalist logic of the world economy. This led, in effect, to the redoubling of global imperial structures: one capitalist, the other state-socialist, tied together by the logic of antagonistic cooperation and facing each other directly in what was emerging as the "Third World" as alternative models of modernization linked to alternative imperial centers.[4] This arrangement provided the underlying structural logic of military strategy and international relations. The two-actor game of negative cooperation to which it simplified was seen as a major source of global stability. Economic change under Stalinism was thus largely focused, after postwar reconstruction, on the needs of the imperial state concerning its bipolar global strategy. This resulted in the early socialist states' preoccupation with heavy industrial growth and the gross neglect of all other branches of their economies, including direct consumption and especially the services, broadly conceived.

The anti-Stalinist revolts in the GDR (1953), Poland, and Hungary (in 1956) all aimed at the abolition of comprador statehood and the easing of dependence of the local states on the USSR without explicitly demanding an end to socialism. The period that followed saw the state-to-state differentiation of the Soviet bloc. The uprisings were read in the imperial center as signals of tension in the imperial structure and appropriate arrangements were made for readjustment. A general sense of "softening the grip" of the imperial structures followed: The comprador state had to undergo partial reconstitution – without restoring its sovereignty.

Most important, concerning the state–society relationship in central and eastern Europe, the Moscow center undertook some significant, if limited, concessions to cater to the comprador states' needs for internal legitimacy. This did not alter the fact that the main locus of the legitimacy of these states was in the external realm; these new, internal forms of legitimacy added only secondary layers. Nevertheless they did complicate the initially simple – squarely Moscow-centered – arrangement. These additional layers of internal legitimacy-seeking measures took extremely varied forms.

In the early sixties all comprador states became "Yugoslavianized": They developed a set of new nation-specific policies presented to their populations as evidence of relative independence from Moscow. This was despite continued evidence to the contrary regarding the virtual absence of their sovereignty in the military, diplomatic, trade, economic-structural, personnel-policy, ideological, and even daily political realms. These measures were expected to increase the

internal legitimacy of the socialist states and to simplify the task of the administration of the empire. The core of the policies pursued as part of this project were
modernizationist strategies of "catching up" with the western half of the continent. They were seen as rapidly developing new provisions for publicly
subsidized basic consumption commonly known as the welfare state. Following
the austere restrictions on consumption under Stalinism, this appeared to be a
radical break away from the socialist state's previous behavior.

This presents us with an astounding resemblance between the early 1960s'
state-socialist policies and the policy suggestions of conventional modernization
theories for the Third World made, in the "West," at about the same time. These
ambitious, large-scale projects aimed at producing "spurt"-like outbursts of
economic development. In essence, they were adaptations to the state-socialist
context – characterized by the extreme concentration of the means of production, and many other societal resources, in the hands of the state – of the
institutional "special road" strategies described by Alexander Gerschenkron
under the notion of the "latecomer's advantage" (Gerschenkron, 1959). Advances
in industrial, transportation, urban housing,[5] public works, and communication
infrastructure were coupled, for the first time in these states' state-socialist
history, with serious investments into the health, public health care, social welfare,
educational, cultural, art, and research infrastructures.[6] These modernizationist
successes were of course readily interpreted in official discourse as accomplishments of socialism and so were seen as furnishing evidence for the idea, crucial to the
post-Stalinist comprador state, that socialism offered a real, seriously comparable
alternative to capitalism.

Political concessions were rarely formalized. The two main techniques used in
allowing concessions while avoiding any formally ratified, transparent, and norma-
tively enforceable democratization of socialism can be termed "informalization"
and "metaphorization." Informalization was achieved where the development of
"gelatinous," murky, and personal, informal solutions was encouraged around the
edges of rigid, transparent, and impersonal, formal institutions. Metaphorization,
on the other hand, marked the process in which essentially Stalinist political practices were reasserted in highly ceremonial ways – but, very importantly, this time
with a paternalistic "wink," suggesting that their enforcement can, and should,
be expected to be less than strict. Both techniques resulted in the redoubling of
social experience, especially with respect to the behavior of the state and to the state–
society relationship. Kádár – Hungary's state-socialist Perón – and his political
machine became a brilliant master of both techniques by the late 1960s and used
them with considerable success throughout the 1970s. The important advantage
of those practices was that they allowed a bifurcated political representation of
reality along the internal/external divide: Formal and post-Stalinist political
practices could be presented to the Moscow center as evidence of the eminently
socialist character of Hungarian society, state, economy, culture, etc., while references to informal alternatives and the metaphorized nature of the Stalinist
practices could serve as basis on which claims for a certain degree of internal
legitimacy could be made by the, by now quite sophisticated, comprador state.

Other leaderships either imitated parts of the Hungarian example with more or less success, or sought to gain increased internal legitimacy through different means. The latter involved, instead of informalizing or bracketing the state-socialist institutions of society – which was the essence of the Hungarian pattern – transgressing another tenet of the official "line" of the Moscow-affiliated communist parties of the region, the principle of discursive internationalism. This transgression involved the promotion of a nationalist, even racist discourse – manifested most clearly in Romania under Ceauşescu, but also in different ways and in such, otherwise so different contexts as Enver Hodzha's Albania and Ulbricht's GDR. Tito's Yugoslavia represented an interesting additional case as the official nationalism promoted there – advancing the idea of a Yugoslav nationhood – was of a supra-ethnic kind, akin to the notion of the supranational "Soviet nation" although the USSR was widely understood to be the most important external entity against which Yugoslav national unity was interpreted.

Socialism by dual dependency

Concessions to internal legitimacy carried economic imperatives. Efforts at "catching up" with the welfare states required large-scale investments in public consumption. By the 1960s, confiscation of the private means of production, simple extraction of natural resources, and skimming of the agricultural sector – the three main established methods of resource concentration by the socialist state – had been exhausted so much that they could not possibly provide suffi-cient funds for financing the socialist state's modernizationist project. Profitability and market access problems precluded large-scale reliance on revenues from the enterprises owned by the state itself. Technological backward-ness, the need to enter capitalist markets, and increasing demands for consumer goods from the populations – which, for their part, duly heeded their states' message that consumption was not only compatible with, but in some ways highly desirable under,[7] "the advanced stage of socialism" – all pointed in the direction of widening and strengthening ties linking the socialist states into the world economy.

In Hungary, Poland, and Bulgaria, and in its own technocratic way, also in the GDR, the state's concessions to internal legitimacy included serious measures aimed at reducing the firmness of the state's bureaucratic–proprietorial grasp. The resulting economic reform policies transferred crucial decision-making responsibilities from the owner (the socialist state) to the managerial elites. This transfer of control from the ministries and other state organs to management involved two important analytical elements. One of those – macro-organizational "decentralization" – is often noted: decision-making regarding the socialist economy was now, indeed, dispersed from a single command center to a previ-ously unseen multiplicity of relatively independent posts.

What is less often appreciated conceptually is that this in effect involved the transfer of an important ownership right – the right to exercise control over assets – to actors outside the realm of the state bureaucracy. This created the basic structures of a "managerial socialism" under continued state ownership. Under such conditions rights to deriving profits from, and alienating legal title to, property continued to rest with the owner (the socialist state, which continued to exercise those rights through a Weberian bureaucracy), but effective control over property was transferred from state bureaucrats to management. This introduced an entire new layer of interests in the running of the socialist state's assets. The resulting industrial organization was remarkably similar to the managerial capitalism emerging two to three generations earlier in the capitalist economies – except that this time around it occurred under the ultimate, more- or-less absentee ownership of the socialist state.

This combination of decentralization and de-bureaucratization increased pressures for investment and subsidy funds exerted by the managerial elites on the state. The central-state administrative and banking organs had little by way of institutional protection to resist such a barrage of requests for extra funding. Because the requested subsidies would flow into property legally owned by the same state from which the subsidies were "pumped," this reveals an important structural contradiction among the socialist state's multiple roles. Its interests as the largest property owner (a state-socialist specificity) clash here with its duties as the large-scale regulator of the accumulation process (a generic feature of modern states – capitalist and socialist alike). The confusion of these roles was most easily resolved by extreme permissiveness on part of the gatekeepers of state subsidies for unprofitable enterprises.[8]

Unable to adjust to the early 1970s oil crisis and the requirements of the world economy's move toward flexible accumulation, the resource shortages faced by all socialist states became particularly urgent. Meanwhile, because of the crisis of the imperial arrangement in Czechoslovakia, the comprador states' needs for additional internal legitimacy increased tremendously. This was particularly true for those states – Poland, the GDR, Hungary, and Bulgaria – that did participate alongside the USSR in the military invasion of Czechoslovakia. All those states faced a straightforward policy choice, and the pressures for change along one or another of those alternatives were mounting, particularly for those that had just abandoned their fellow-reformist Czechoslovak leadership. This put the Hungarian and Polish states (the two most reform–socialist comprador states involved in the Czechoslovak military action) in a particularly precarious political position.

One "solution" was curbing radically the costly aspects of their modernizationist projects. This would involve unraveling their welfare arrangements, halting the ambitious investment projects aimed at increasing productivity through the importation of recent technology, and extinguishing the consumer aspirations of the population. In sum, the essence of the first solution was disentanglement from the modernizationist project of "catching up" with western Europe. An easy-to-predict effect would be a new deficit of internal legitimacy to be compensated from another source. Romania and Albania were the two socialist countries of Europe that ended up in this predicament, and their "textbook" versions of state-supported official nationalism served as the main source from which enough internal legitimacy could be extracted to assure the survival of their comprador state.

The other alternative involved bringing in resources from the outside and using them to subsidize investment in both public and private consumption. As the USSR was unable or unwilling to provide such funds, this could be done either (1) by securing a stable flow of annual subsidies and a guaranteed "back-door" access to the European Community market – an opportunity open only for the GDR through its "inner-German" links to the Federal Republic of Germany – or, in absence of such a "special relationship," (2) by drawing on for-profit financing from the world market.

This was a policy of spectacular initial success. Investment and trade credits channeling private and state funds from the capitalist world economy to the socialist states provided a simple and straightforward opportunity to continue offering the popular (but costly) elements of the "reform path" of state socialism.[9] The willingness of the world's leading lenders to provide funds could be inter-preted as affirmation of the genuineness of the alternative to capitalism purportedly represented by the socialist states. With the new loans, some of the most devastating effects of "structural adjustment" could be averted – as can be seen in retrospect – for another generation.

The linkages of technological, trade and financial dependency that emerged from these subsidy-, backdoor-trade- and borrowing-based solutions produced the phenomenon described elsewhere (Böröcz 1992a and 1992b) as "dual depen-dency." This was marked by the geopolitical splitting of the comprador state's external linkage hierarchies: political–military controls kept the comprador states squarely in the Soviet orbit while new, ever more gripping structures of economic (technological, financial, and trade) dependency tied them to the most powerful core actors of the capitalist world economy. Those core actors included private transnational corporations and major governments as controllers of flows of technology, credits, as well as investment and consumer goods. The emergence of dual dependency was paralleled by the rapid dissimilation of the comprador states as for the degree of their internal legitimacy, the harshness of their polit-ical oppression and the particular ideological and cultural taboos they enforced, the living standards they provided, and the proliferation of informal economic, political, and cultural institutions they allowed. Other than their geographical proximity and their comprador nature under dual dependency, there was little by way of descriptive characteristics that warranted the treatment of the societies of central and eastern Europe as a "bloc" by the time of the collapse of state socialism.

Capitalism by state a(u)ction

The collapse of the Soviet side of the "two-actor game" of the Cold War caused the breakdown of the great-power balance of forces. The Soviet Union with-drew both its troops and most of its other, rather elaborate imperial structures from the region, causing the termination of the comprador states with astonishing speed and self-discipline. As for the center, the abolition of the state-socialist empire was managed with remarkable professionalism. The ensuing transformation of the comprador states, however, was much more disorderly, complex, contradictory, and crisis-ridden.

The specific events in the rapid large-scale process of institutional transformation – the demolition of the comprador state – produced an extremely wide range of patterns. These included:

- a settlement among various political and intellectual elites around a negotiating table with two (as in Poland) or three sides (as in Hungary), in essence transferring political power to alternative groups through completely peaceful means;
- repeated political demonstrations and police violence on demonstrators, followed by the precipitous collapse of the power apparatus once lack of Soviet support became evident (as in Czechoslovakia and Bulgaria);
- demonstrations and repressive violence coupled with an extended period of official paralysis and confusion ending in the breakdown of the command structure and a breakthrough involving the "flooding" of the gates (literally, of the GDR, metaphorically, of the central European state socialist project);[10] and
- generalized physical violence organized along ethnic (Yugoslavia) and elite factional (Romania) lines, the latter also involving tyrannicide as its focal element.

This variety in modalities of political breakthroughs relates to the diversity of the late state-socialist states as for their institutional patterns and the policy measures developed as part of their struggles for internal legitimacy and strategies of state-socialist modernization.[11] Meanwhile, the deeper, and slower-paced, transformations of the central and east European societies can be captured in simpler, more encompassing formulas by focusing on their similarities.

This is possible for two reasons. First, because the comprador states' collapse took place in the context of the capitalist world economy, which leaves much less room for "surprises" (Bodnár 1996) in the social-structural realm than the late state-socialist comprador state and its institutional complexities. This was so because, second, as the comprador state represented the structural point where the single "economic development" hierarchy of the core–periphery system clashed with the bipolar logic of the Cold War, the first and most important thing to be destroyed once the imperial arrangement was weakened substantially, was the anomaly of the comprador state. The triple crisis of state formation, nation formation, and class formation to which the comprador state's destruction has led has been addressed elsewhere (Böröcz and Smith 1995; Böröcz 1994).

As both nation formation and class formation are intimately connected with the abrupt transformation of the economic, political, and cultural structures known previously as the comprador state, here I will focus on the crisis of state formation and the emerging patterns of the insertion of these populations into the world economy. The current crisis of central European state formation can be comprehended in three realms:

- the institutional mechanisms of ownership regarding assets owned formerly by the comprador state are rearranged;
- the central and east European states' external political and military linkage matrices are in a flux; and, in connection to both of the above,
- the world-system position of the region's societies is eroding.

An anti-state ideological backlash has constituted an intrinsic element of the post-state-socialist *status quo*. In a perfect negative mirror image of the drives in the 1960s for "catching up" with the welfare states of western Europe, today's intense ideological fervor is directed against the very idea that the state should partake in alleviating the suffering of members of society. In the current slow but resolute destruction of the health care, public health, educational, retirement, cultural, and public consumption infrastructure of post-state-socialist societies, the requirements for the IMF-dictated "structural adjustment" policies find natural allies in the post-state-socialist ideological hegemony of a whole variety of anti-state rhetorics. These rhetorics range from a strikingly naive form of anti-state anarchism   through the utopian–ideological practice of reform– transform–Pangloss economics,[12] to socioconservative ideas advocating the family as the only functional vessel of social aid (in essence designating the female body as a "natural" replacement for the state in taking care of the needy). This anti-state ideological hegemony is, no doubt, fueled by the collective experience of practical disillusionment regarding the state's ability to deliver on its promises. This conclusion derives from a careless observation of the lapses in the late socialist state's performance in delivering many of those services during much of the recent period without taking into account the fiscal crisis of the socialist state (Campbell 1996) as an explanation.

Add to the anti-state backlash and the IMF pressures the power of potential investors from the centers of the world economy, promising technological modernization, world-market access and jobs to the debt-burdened post-state-socialist states struggling with ever-intense problems of technological obsolescence, and you are likely to have one of the largest-scale and most rapid institutional transformations of property ownership in the history of humankind, comparable in its scope only to the confiscation drives by the socialist states at the time of the establishment of state socialism. Because of the condition that the socialist states were the largest property owners in their respective economies – state-owned property exceeded two-thirds of all assets in each case at the time of the collapse of comprador statehood – the resulting reorganization of the institutional system of property relations involves the mobilization of an extremely concentrated form of assets.

This process could be described, from an arms-length perspective, as a new transition to capitalism through a "second" original accumulation of capital. However, a number of important differences do set the current transformation apart from the "classical" pattern, eroding the accuracy of that conceptual analogy.

- The ongoing sellout – to the extent that private property is indeed created on a massive scale in the process – is likely to be unique in the sense that never before has the institutional framework of ownership been transformed with respect to such a large and highly concentrated batch of assets in such a brief time. In other words, the sheer scale and speed of the transformation is unprecedented. To put it differently, in the post-state-socialist "second original accumulation of capital," the concentration of property preceded the establishment of private ownership.

- A large part of the emerging property arrangements is not straightforward "private property": often extremely complex institutional hybrids are created mixing various, elaborate schemes of private and public ownership.[13]

- Due to the lack of mobilizeable private savings in domestic hands to finance buyouts of state stakes, the private component in the emerging new property institutions tends to be (1) the result of the conversion of domestic managerial position, placing an enormous prize on managerial position before and during the collapse;[14] or (2) coming from abroad in the form of direct foreign investment.

- This liquidation of the property of the formerly socialist states is performed by the post-state-socialist successor states – to be termed, hence, "auctioneer states." The resulting institutional forms are thus likely to bear the imprinting of the institutional conditions of the post-socialist states and their peculiarities for a long time. The most important descriptive feature of that imprinting is the conflict between the role of the (post)-socialist state as the predominant property owner on the one hand (a socialist specificity) and as the regulator of the accumulation process (a generic feature of modern states). Because the feverish rearrangement of the property institutions is partly the acting-out of this role conflict of the state, virtually *any* transformation of the property structure is considered acceptable (as long as it represents a move away from the bureaucratic ownership patterns of the Stalinist past).[15] Although colonizing and colonial states have always been important vehicles of the original accumulation of capital, arguably never before have the national states played such a crucial role in original accumulation as in the post-state-socialist instance. To the extent that the current transformation does produce predominantly private capital (typically the case in foreign buyouts), the states act on perceived joint pressures from their populations, foreign investors, and lenders. By urging their states due to a post-state-socialist ideological *ressentiment* to plunder the institutional potential contained in the large bundle of economic assets available for collective control, post-state-socialist societies are eliminating a very important tool by which their world-system position could be potentially improved. Concentration of economic power in the state has been indeed the only instrument that has been used historically for that purpose in this region with any success (Gerschenkron 1959).

- Because of the radical unevenness of the interest of core capital in this region's economies, the differences in the economic profiles and potential world-market niches of the societies of the former socialist "bloc," and in the degree of the managerialization of the late state-socialist economies, the process of property transformation has produced radically different institutional outcomes *among* the societies in question. Hungary and the former GDR have emerged as the two most overrepresented economies in terms of foreign direct investment. This happened in very distinct ways and for different reasons in the two societies. The GDR state was "unwound" by way of a systematic privatization (and political cleansing) process providing extreme advantages for West German capital so that today, after the conclusion of the privatization process of the former GDR state assets and the dissolution of the *Treuhandanstalt*, the state property agency set up to run the privatization process, expert estimates suggest that over 85 per cent of the assets are held by former West German corporations and individuals. Eastern Germans, in contrast, own a mere 5 per cent of the assets of their former state. It is thus clear that the privatization strategy of the *Treuhandanstalt* was combining privatization with drawing on West German capital and assuring that the property of the former GDR state will remain in (West) German hands. As for Hungary – by far the most "marketized" society of all of the former eastern bloc by the time of the collapse of the imperial structure of state socialism – the legal, financial, and other institutional conditions for foreign direct investment were found unanimously attractive for foreign capital early on. This was boosted by such economic–geographical and historical exigencies as the country's key position as a transportation and communication crossroads in central Europe, its relative peace and social quietude (in contrast to the war-torn states of former Yugoslavia) and the pre-existing, historical linkages tying Hungary to its neighbors. All those suggested that Hungary could be a suitable launching pad for further forays into the former eastern bloc, in some ways playing a role vaguely reminiscent of Austria's niche during the preceding decades.

- *Within* those societies, especially those most exposed to capital inflows, inequities in the territorial and social distribution of foreign direct investment have also been tremendous.[16]

With the end of the overdetermined *status quo* of the Soviet military occupation, the strategic stability of all of the states of the region was shaken. Many underwent profound transformations in the most fundamental parameters, violating their territorial integrity: old borders have been moved, new borders have been erected, previously constituent parts have ceded from the body of their previous state, and state legitimacy has been widely questioned on ethno-national grounds. The former GDR was incorporated into the federal structure of the West German state. All three of the explicitly multiethnic states of the region – Czechoslovakia, Yugoslavia and the USSR – entered a path of multiplication by division.[17] The rush to small-nation sovereignty after the collapse of the state-socialist imperial reality can only be understood – from the perspective of the geographically more Western and economically more well-off entities that insisted on the breakup of their multiethnic states – in the context of the gradual and apparently unstoppable emergence and enlargement of the European Union literally on their borders. If small-state sovereignty can be achieved early enough, it may be possible to win earlier inclusion – and to negotiate more advantageous terms for the inclusion – than in the framework of the economically much more "backward" multiethnic states. The independent states of the Czech Republic, Slovenia, Croatia, Estonia, Lithuania, and Latvia were all imagined as offering a vastly better chance of achieving earlier, smoother and more accommodating admittance than the larger and clumsier states of Czechoslovakia, Yugoslavia, or the Commonwealth of Independent States. This calculation was meaningful under the assumption that a speedy "small-state" enlargement of the European Union in the eastern direction is a realistic prospect. So far (i.e., during the seven years since the collapse of the Soviet empire), however, nothing of the sort has come about: The European Union is giving Byzantine signals to the small, ready-and-eager states of the region regarding their chances for admittance.

Meanwhile, the fragmentation of the state structures of central and eastern Europe is a biting everyday reality. With the addition of new borders and the fragmentation of the structure of multiethnic states, the sheer number of the states of the region has increased *from nine to twenty* only in the European territory of the former CMEA, despite the fact that one of the former Soviet bloc states – the GDR – has been "unwound" without an independent successor. All other things equal, any rise in the number of actors is bound to increase the possibility of conflict and makes reconciling contending interests exponentially more difficult. Coalition formation, isolation, and the threat or actual exercise of various cross-border pressures and coercion emerge as possible tools of change in the international realm.

The fragmentation of some states also increases the perceived relative power of those states that do remain territorially intact. Small-scale "great-power" aspirations are now emerging, revealed most obviously in rump Yugoslavia (which used much of the Yugoslav military machine it had retained to wage a war largely against the civilian populations of its former federal partner states), Russia (which has done the same against some of its own internal minorities aspiring for small-state sovereignty), as well as, in much more subtle and modest forms, in the regional policies of Romania, Hungary, Albania, and Poland with respect to their neighbors. This is fanned by the new, small-state machineries' insistence on the development of new nation-state rhetoric threatening the collective interests of their internal ethnic minorities – some of which do have receptive cross-border nationalist ears in the neighboring states.

The main response to the increased international volatility of the region has been a rush to NATO, seen as the only serious external potential provider of security in local conflicts. As a result, the main point of contention in the realm of international relations between the states of central Europe and Russia has been the issue of their NATO membership. Increased military spending, partial relinquishment of new-found sovereignty in the military realm, and the possibility of being drawn into international conflicts that would otherwise not concern the area are seen by the new political elites as small prices to pay for the possibility of an umbrella of protection against your neighbors, promised by NATO.

The economic and social costs of these transformations have been tremendous. They involved the radical rearrangement of the external linkage structures. The wars have caused the suffering of millions of citizens of the states involved, making serious repercussions region-wide by forcing the war-torn nations' neighbors and conventional partners to come up with makeshift adjustments in order to compensate for their losses in export and import markets, as well as the blockage of their conventional transport and communication routes. Foreign buyouts have produced such textbook outcomes as market penetration from the outside, forced concessions in tax relief to foreign investors, and closure of companies by foreigners in order to eliminate strategic competitors. The large-scale transformation of the organization of ownership and control has resulted in massive displacements of labor and the production process, introducing the phenomenon of massive unemployment – an experience utterly unknown for the working classes of the state-socialist period. Unmitigated exposure to world-market competition has reduced labor remuneration rates, created hyper-inflation, and drops in national economic performance. This resulted in precipitous declines in the quality of human services, reflected in turn in stagnating and even decreasing figures of life expectancy at birth.[18] As Table 10.1 suggests, country rankings along the perhaps disputably named but substantively rather indicative Human Development Index (HDI) – a combination of country-specific life expectancy, adult literacy, and mean-years-of-schooling data presented by the United Nations Development Program – shows sudden declines for all countries leaving state socialism behind (except Slovenia).

Table 10.1 Changes in country-by-country ranking along the Human Development Index, 1990–1994

Country	HDI rank in 1990	HDI rank in 1994
Albania	49	102
Bulgaria	33	69
Croatia / Yugoslavia	34	77
Czech Republic / Czechoslovakia	27	39
Hungary	30	48
Macedonia / Yugoslavia	34	80
Poland	41	58
Romania	58	79
Slovakia / Czechoslovakia	27	42
Slovenia / Yugoslavia	34	35

Source: UNDP 1991 and 1997. Data for Serbia are missing.

The mean slide of the ten countries in Table 10.1 is 26.2 countries in four years. A mean drop of 26 countries in four years suggests very sudden peripheralization – especially astounding given that the successor countries of the former USSR are not included in these figures.

Conclusion

The end of state socialism in central and eastern Europe has involved the collapse of the largest imperial structure of the twentieth century. It removed the military and political bases of the comprador states, which has set off a number of unexpected transformations. This process affected the very base of the existence of these states – their territorial integrity and their multiple roles as owners and regulators of the accumulation process. As a result of these transformations of institutional structures, the process of peripheralization – which had begun in most cases before the collapse of the comprador states – has accelerated, revealed clearly in the significant reductions in quality of life measures for most populations. Property change, realignment of international relations, and peripheralization are all corollaries of the collapse of the comprador state, redefining itself in the transformation process as an auctioneer, liquidating its collective assets in the interest of hyper-adjustment to the perceived requirements of the world economy.

It is fairly clear that the socialist states of the late socialist period were a serious anomaly in the world economy, particularly in terms of their "over-achievements" in the area of the quality of life and "underperformance" in the realms of democracy and internal legitimacy. Two points ought to be empha-sized here. First, it is important to keep these facts in mind when evaluating these societies' popular expectations regarding their future under capitalism and the tremendous disillusionment that followed. It was extremely difficult for the soci-eties of the state-socialist bloc, socialized into a world of free basic and medium-level health care, social protection, and educational facilities, to foresee that the "simple" abolition of the imperial structures on their soil, the restoration of state sovereignty, the introduction of the freedom of economic enterprise and the like, would lead to impoverishment on such a scale.

The heart of the question in addressing the problem of the precipitous declines revealed in the transformation is, second, how to interpret the "positive" statistical anomalies that the socialist states represented. It is possible to argue – as the IMF and the various other organs of international economic pressure, as well as their experts, do with a particular vengeance – that this anomaly needs to be eliminated by bringing the societies of the region "in line" with the rest of the world by reducing their provisions in social welfare and collective consumption in general. This is the all-too-well-known, supposedly universal remedy of struc-tural adjustment.

It would be possible, however, to think about the positive comparative anomaly of the late-socialist societies in a different way. It is possible to consider their anomalously high achievements in the area of the quality-of-life as part of a historical heritage that could be transformed into a comparative advantage.

What these anomalies would mean in such a framework is that much of the large economic, political, and social institutional systems necessary for providing widely accessible educational, health care and other social welfare provisions is already in place. This results in populations that have skill levels that are greater than expected on the basis of the world-system position of the economy in which they work. In the presence of appropriate national industrial policy initiatives, those positive anomalies could be turned into economic niches for these societies. In such a scenario, the anomalous position of the post-socialist states would also be abolished – this time, instead of adjusting quality of life downward, by "correcting" national economic performance "upward." That that has not happened yet, has much to do with the highly ideological preoccupation of the system-changing elites with the task of proving themselves worthy of what they perceive as Western political "trust" by transforming their post-comprador states into auctioneer agents instead of developmental states, putting the productive assets of their national economy – hitherto under the sign of the hammer-and-sickle – now *under the hammer.*

Notes

1 This project was partly supported by a grant, entitled "Property Change and Privatization Ideologies" funded by OTKA (the National Science Research Fund of Hungary) under number T6739, various hidden and explicit subsidies by the Institute for Political Studies of the Hungarian Academy of Science, and partial research and travel expenses covered by Rutgers University. Part of this chapter was written while on a research visit at the Zentrum für Zeithistorische Forschung (ZZF) in Potsdam, Germany. Generous support from ZZF also provided for assistance in Berlin and Potsdam by Dr Brigitta Gantner. I am particularly grateful to Christoph Kleßmann and Thomas Lindenberger for their assistance while in Berlin, to Rainer Land, Ina Merkel, and Michael Brie for conversations on the post-GDR situation, to Magdolna Csizmadia of the UN Economic Comparisons project for her expert advice on various comparative indices, to Judit Bodnár and Caleb Southworth for comments on an earlier version of this chapter, to Andrea Grant-Friedman for proofreading assistance, and to the organizers of the Irvine conference for providing an initial push for this project.

2 I am using the terms "socialism" and "socialist" as markers to denote the societies of the Soviet bloc. The vexing question of whether or not they represented a "genuinely" socialist form of society (i.e., whether or not their experience conforms to an idealized image of a post-capitalist society derived from a radical critique of capitalism) is not the subject of this inquiry.

3 This is summarized after Böröcz 1992a and 1992b.

4 I am quite aware of the loaded nature of the "modernization" terminology. (See Böröcz 1995.) I use the term in this chapter to denote an ideological construct positing "catching up with the advanced societies" as the main purpose of political, social, and cultural efforts.

5 See Bodnár 1996. Rural housing remained, in striking contrast, almost entirely unsubsidized by the state, leading to the emergence of very creative, reciprocity-based rural labor-pooling practices (Sik 1986) making up for the structural disadvantages associated with rural residence. All this contributed handsomely to a deepening of rural–urban contrasts in the late state-socialist period in Hungary (Bodnár and Böröcz, 1998).

6 They also provided, through the subsidization and ideological promotion of household appliances by the state, the basic technological means for the full-time inclusion of working-age women in the labor force on a massive scale without reordering the gender-based division of labor in the family. So, the state-socialist societies of central and eastern Europe in the 1960s present us with the first historical instance of societies with virtually full female employment. This, in conjunction with increasing consumer expectations, rising female educational attainment, and continued housing shortages, resulted in such specific problems as serious drops in the birth rates that were to be addressed soon by way of generous maternity-support policies.

7 Socialist consumerism – a little-acknowledged and appropriately untheorized feature of European state socialism since the 1960s – was promoted with a particular vengeance in the GDR, whose leadership was preoccupied in overtaking the "West" (in their case, West Germany) in every possible respect. Artefacts of this bizarre cultural modernizationist project, ranging from promotion of GDR-made jeans through fiction films teaching East German audiences how to be good (demanding and conscientious) consumers of GDR-made household appliances, were displayed at a striking exhibition entitled *Wunderwirtschaft*, on display at the time of the writing of this essay at the Kulturbrauerei, an important post-state-socialist cultural institution in (former East-) Berlin's Prenzlauer Berg district (Wunderwirtschaft 1996). In Hungary, parallel developments took place in a more informalistic–metaphorized, "winking" fashion, causing serious ideological confusion among the party rank-and-file. This was duly reflected in public debates on the social advantages and ills of socialist consumerism (e.g., the "frigidair-socialism" debate, the "cashew nuts" controversy, or repeated alarmist voices raised in fear of the country's shrinking population, called the "kicsi vagy kocsi?" (kid or car?) dispute.)

8 This, amply expressed in the low correlation scores between enterprise profitability and managerial incomes in late state-socialist Hungary, is what economist János Kornai interpreted as the "soft budget constraint" of the socialist state. As a result, monthly revisions to five-year plans were not an uncommon feature of these societies, giving a new, ironical meaning to the NGO terminology referring to them as "centrally planned economies." For a clear and brief sociological summary, see Stark and Nee (1989), especially pp. 9–12.

9 This was an area of lending in which Austrian banks had a clear comparative advantage and great successes as organizers. This contributed handsomely to Austria's spectacular success in carving out a very lucrative niche between the two political–military blocs for much of the region's post-Second World War history (see pp. 83–100. in Böröcz 1996.) It could be argued that the choice of this niche for Austria had much to do with another special relationship – less binding and less emotionally loaded than the inner-German bind but clearly recognizable both in popular rhetoric and the behavior of large institutions – between Austria and those of its neighbors that were fellow successor states of the Austro-Hungarian Monarchy two generations earlier. This was particularly clear for the relations between Austria and Hungary.

10 Historian Hans-Hermann Hertle (1996) offers a breathtaking summary of the contingent, "nonlinear" nature of the East German collapse. It is captured astutely by a GDR border officer reporting by phone to his superiors after the opening of the Bornholmerstraße checkpoint in Berlin: "We are now flooding!" (*"Wir fluten jetzt!"*, Hertle 1996: 166).

11 The presence of the Soviet Army during the "unwinding" (in official German terminology, *Abwicklung*, see Borneman 1992, and Böröcz 1995) of the comprador states worked as a crucial stabilizing force during the collapse. Generalized political violence erupted in connection with the collapse of the central and east European comprador states only in those two societies (Romania and Yugoslavia) that were not under Soviet military occupation during the collapse.

12 This term is introduced, elsewhere (Böröcz 1998) to denote economists who moved, in close harmony with the perimeters of allowable political speech over the span of the last ten years or so, from arguments advocating the "market-socialist" reform of state-socialist economies through calls for the transformation to "the market," some arriving at the extreme position of advocating a highly utopian form of "pristine" capitalism without any interference in the market.

13 See, for example, Stark 1996; Böröcz 1993.

14 This is the unambiguous conclusion of a number of empirical studies on managerial elite selection in the transformation (Böröcz and Róna-Tas 1995; 1996; Róna-Tas and Böröcz 1996).

15 As a result, the property transformation process has been extremely tenuous economically. High transaction costs and poor representation of the seller's interest in the transactions has caused the net state revenues from privatization in Hungary and in the former GDR (Bródy 1996: 3) to be zero. Scandals of enormous magnitude have signaled the likely presence of corruption in the process.

16 Over two-thirds of foreign direct investment in Hungary has been showered on the capital city and its immediate agglomeration.

17 Of course, all of the region's states (as well as the vast majority of the world's states in general) are multiethnic so the practical question is to what extent their legal structures recognize that condition. This notion is introduced here to designate those states that had made explicit provisions in their constitutional order to recognize the presence of multiple ethnic groupings in their territories.

18 See UNDP 1991; 1997.

References

Bodnár, J. (1996) "The post-state-socialist city. Urban change in Budapest," PhD dissertation, Department of Sociology, Johns Hopkins University, Baltimore.

Bodnár, J. and Böröcz, J. (1998) "Housing advantages for the better-connected? Institutional segmentation, settlement type and network effects in late state-socialist housing inequalities," *Social Forces* 76: 4, June, 76 (4): 1275–304.

Borneman, J. (1992) *Belonging in the Two Berlins. Kin, State, Nation*, Cambridge, MA: Cambridge University Press.

Böröcz, J. (1992a) "Dual dependency and property vacuum: social change on the state socialist semiperiphery," *Theory and Society* 21: 77–104.

—— (1992b) "Dual dependency and the informalization of external linkages: the case of Hungary," *Research in Social Movements, Conflicts and Change* 14: 189–209.

—— (1993) "Simulating the great transformation: property change under prolonged informality in Hungary," *Archives européennes de sociologie/Europäisches Archiv für Soziologie/European Journal of Sociology* XXXIV (1): 81–107, May.

—— (1994) "The triple crisis: state, class and nation in central Europe after the collapse of dual dependency," *Political Economy of the World System Panel on the Transition from State Socialism*, Annual Meeting of the American Sociological Association, Los Angeles, August 9.

—— (1995) *Social Change by Fusion?* Paper presented at the 32nd Conference of the International Institute of Sociology, Università degli Studi, Trieste – Gorizia, July 3–6.

—— (1996) *Leisure Migration. A Sociological Comparison*, Oxford, UK: Pergamon Press.

—— (1998) "Reaction as progress: economists as intellectuals," in András Bozóki (ed.) *Intellectuals and Politics in Central Europe*, Budapest: Central European University Press.

Böröcz, J. and Róna-Tas, Á. (1995) "Small leap forward: emergence of new economic elites," *Theory and Society* 5: 751–81.

—— (1996) "Musical chairs: economic elite selection under managerial hegemony in four post-state-socialist societies," paper presented at the conference of the European Studies Association, Chicago, March 14–16.

Böröcz, J. and Smith, D.A. (1995) "Introduction: late twentieth-century challenges for world-system analysis," in D.A. Smith and J. Böröcz (eds) *A New World Order? Global Transformation in the Late 20th Century*, Westport, CT: Greenwood Press, pp. 1–15.

Bródy, A. (1996) "Az állam (tulajdonának) elhalása, avagy merre vezet az út Dublinbe," *Kritika* 12: 2–3.

Campbell, J. (1996) "An institutional analysis of fiscal reform in postcommunist Europe," *Theory and Society* 25: 45–84.

Gerschenkron, A. (1959) "Economic backwardness in historical perspective," in B.F. Hoselitz (ed.) *The Progress of Underdeveloped Areas*, Chicago: University of Chicago Press, pp. 3–29.

Hertle, H.-H. (1996) *Chronik des Mauerfalls. Die dramatischen Ereignisse um den 9. November 1989*, Berlin: Ch. Links Verlag.

Róna-Tas, Á. and Böröcz, J. (1996) "Formation of new business elites in Bulgaria, the Czech Republic, Hungary, and Poland: continuity and change, pre-communist and communist legacies," paper presented at the conference on "Democracy, Markets, and Civil Societies in Post-1989 East-Central Europe, Minda de Gunzburg Center for European Studies, Harvard University, Cambridge, Mass., May 17–19.

Sik, E. (1986) "Labor exchange of households in Hungary", in R. Andorka and L. Bertalan (eds) *Economy and Society in Hungary*, Budapest: Department of Sociology, Karl Marx University of Economic Sciences, pp. 35–66.

Stark, D. (1996) "Recombinant property in Eastern European capitalism," *American Journal of Sociology* 101: 993–1027.

Stark, D. and Nee, V. (1989) "Toward an institutional analysis of state socialism," in V. Nee and D. Stark, with M. Selden (eds) *Remaking the Economic Institutions of Socialism: China and Eastern Europe*, Stanford: Stanford University Press, pp. 1–31.

United Nations Development Program (1991) *Human Development Report 1991*, New York: United Nations Development Program.

—— (1997) *Human Development Report 1997*, New York: United Nations Development Program.

Wunderwirtschaft (1996) *Wunderwirtschaft. DDR-Konsumkultur und Produktdesign in den 60er Jahren*, from August 17 1997 to January 12 1997 im Museum in Nordflügel auf der Kulturbrauerei, Knaackstrae 97, Berlin-Prenzlauer Berg. Mittwoch-Sonntag 14–21 Uhr.

11 Globalization, sovereignty, and policy choice

Lessons from the Mexican peso crisis

Manuel Pastor, Jr [1]

Introduction

On December 20, 1994, Mexico spun into a currency crisis. Pressed by falling reserves, the government attempted a step devaluation of 15 per cent – and was soon forced into a free float of the slipping peso. Through the early months of 1995, nervous investors reacting by pulling assets not only from Mexican financial markets but also from Argentina, Brazil, and other Latin American markets. The United States, anxious to restore confidence in both the sinking Mexican economy and emerging markets in general, combined with the International Monetary Fund to produce a US$53 billion rescue package in late February 1995.[2] In return, Mexico was forced to promise a harsh new adjustment program, one that eventually produced a sharp recession and an even steeper fall in wages.

What does the peso crisis in Mexico – the Latin American reformer once celebrated as the prime example of neoliberal success – tell us about globalization and sovereignty in the global era? At first glance, the story seems to suggest a loss of "control sovereignty" (see Krasner, Chapter 2, this volume) – the unforgiving discipline of an international market punished Mexico for irresponsible macroeconomic policy and induced a dramatic change in economic policy. It also suggests a loss of Westphalian sovereignty. While hardly specific to this era – recall the numerous external interventions in Latin America and the Caribbean in the early twentieth century, including the seizure of national customs houses to force Latin debtors to honor their obligations – the heavy (and quite visible) hand of the IMF did imply a reduction in domestic authority over the macroeconomy.

Yet, the story is not quite so simple. On the one hand, giving up sovereignty was a sovereign decision: Mexican policy-makers surrendered control and authority to international capital markets both before and after the crisis because they believed that such a full opening to the outside world would impose domestic macroeconomic "rationality" and enhance investor confidence. On the other, the new "rationality" Mexico sought by increasing its exposure to global pressures was not really all that rational – after all, supposedly savvy international investors failed to anticipate the crisis and the social costs of "righting" Mexico's economic ship have weakened the political grip of the same policy-makers that made the pro-globalization decision.

From the perspective of the issues raised in this volume, three particular questions loom large:

1   Why was a financial crisis of this magnitude not anticipated by international investors whom economic theory considers to be generally well informed in their predictions concerning market behavior? That is, does surrendering control over domestic policy to global forces make sense when economic agents and market operations are less than rational?

2   Was there an alternative to both the policy that provoked the crisis and the policy response that followed? That is, had globalization eliminated the possibility of Mexican policy choice?

3   What are the implications for other countries seeking to embrace globalization as a way of restraining the rent-seeking actions or populist impulses of their own domestic political actors? That is, are there other possible modes for international integration?

In this chapter, I suggest that market rationality was not particularly rational; specifically, the international economy apparently validated an unsustainable macroeconomic and exchange-rate strategy, a result that suggests that relying on the international system and its economic actors for rational discipline may not be as promising as some neoliberal theorists believe. As for alternatives, I argue that the government could have initiated a slow and controlled devaluation soon after the real exchange rate began to appreciate above historical levels in 1992. That is, within the global environment, alternative policy choices were available. As for implications for other developing countries, I suggest that there are routes other than the Mexican prostration before the international market. Indeed, other Latin American reformers may want to reconsider the "Mexican model" and instead explore the lessons that can be drawn from the more pragmatic forms of international integration typical of East Asia in an earlier era and Chile and Colombia in the last decade. While economies can no longer be sealed off, globalization does not entirely preclude carving out the operating room to address income distribution and other long-term concerns.

What happened?

Mexico's December 1994 financial shakeout was a long time in the making. Key was the previous crisis of the early 1980s, a period in which state-driven import-substitution-industrialization (ISI) gave way, often with IMF prodding, to an embrace of neoliberal strategies of liberalization, privatization, and deregulation. Of course, the adoption of neoliberal economics was neither complete nor consistent. The first stabilization package prescribed by the De la Madrid administration (1982–8), for example, was much more focused on macroeconomic stability than microeconomic reform and leaned heavily on the usual tools of currency devaluation and fiscal tightening. The results were less than impressive: inflation remained stubbornly high and the sharp recession of 1983 was followed by an anemic recovery, then another sharp fall in 1986 as the decline in world oil prices reverberated through the economy. By 1987, inflation stood at 159.2 per cent, an all-time high for modern Mexico, while GDP limped along at a 1.9 per cent annual rate.

The revised neoliberal model adopted by President Salinas in 1988 shifted direction in both micro and macro policy. On the micro side, the Salinas administration accelerated Mexico's privatization of state enterprises, particularly the banks, and sped up the liberalization of both domestic prices and foreign trade and investment. The latter was intimately linked to a new macroeconomic strategy that sought to break inertial inflation by combining wage and price restraints negotiated with the private sector with a government commitment to tighten fiscal and monetary policy, freeze the exchange rate, and liberalize trade.[3] Mexico had been on a more gradual schedule to liberalize imports in anticipation of its 1986 entry into the GATT, but it moved ahead of its GATT commitments on the grounds that import competition, if coupled with a frozen peso, would serve as an effective brake on domestic inflation.[4] Embracing globalization, in short, was supposed to provide a new discipline on both the private sector and governmental policy-makers, with higher growth and lower inflation intended to be the happy consequences.

The combination of a creative incomes policy, sound fiscal policy, and increased trade liberalization did help restore some degree of stability to the Mexican macroeconomy. Economic growth during the Salinas years averaged 2.8 per cent, while inflation fell from the aforementioned level of 159.2 per cent in 1987 to 7.1 per cent in 1994. Real interest rates also fell from 16 per cent in 1988 to the 4–6 per cent range in 1991–2, before rising above 8 per cent in 1994; a simultaneous increase in the availability of consumer credit helped finance an expansion in domestic aggregate demand, which propelled overall growth and led to a general rise in the sense of consumer well-being.

Yet, while the Mexican government was successful at controlling inflation and facilitating short-term economic growth, the use of the exchange rate as a price "anchor" led to an increasingly overvalued real peso. The first negative consequence of this strategy was reflected in the trade figures: between 1987 and 1993, exports rose a healthy 88 per cent (with maquila sales included) but imports rose by an even larger 247 per cent, causing Mexico's 1987 trade surplus of US$ 8.8 billion to be transformed to a trade deficit of nearly US$ 13.5 billion by 1993. The trade deficit problem was compounded by the government's decision to aggressively increase personal credit for domestic spending. Imports burgeoned as Mexican consumers used their new easily attained credit cards to purchase a wide range of US goods that had previously been unavailable.[5]

To finance the trade imbalance, Mexico turned to foreign investment. In fact, the hunger for foreign capital through this period partially explains why Mexico moved so aggressively to negotiate the North American Free Trade Agreement (NAFTA) with the US: Mexico hoped that the anticipation of access through low-wage Mexico to the high-income US market would induce new capital flows even as the implicit guarantee of policy stability provided by NAFTA would entice Mexican flight capital home. Indeed, while most of the US debate focused on the possible dislocations that increased US–Mexican trade might induce, most observers acknowledge that the most dramatic shift in NAFTA was the liberalization of Mexico's treatment of foreign investors (see, for example, Hufbauer and Schott 1993). In short, NAFTA was more about investment than markets, more about capital than trade.

However, the foreign direct investment that Mexico sought was less eager to make a long-term commitment and the bulk of incoming capital during the run-up to NAFTA's adoption consisted of highly mobile portfolio investments. While foreign direct investment (FDI) in actual production facilities increased a healthy 57.6 per cent from 1989 to 1993, the more mobile portfolio investment rose by more than 8,000 per cent. By 1993, portfolio investment accounted for 86.8 per cent of total foreign investment in Mexico, compared to just 11.3 per cent in 1989.[6]

This increased influence of portfolio investors left Mexico susceptible to rapid changes in investor confidence. Of course, making the Mexican economy vulnerable to investor whims was exactly the point; Mexican policy-makers had decided to place the approbation and sustainability of their approach explicitly in the hands of the private sector. Essentially, the authorities had surrendered control in order to gain credibility; by becoming so open to volatile portfolio investment, they had created such a large potential penalty for policy shifts and thus seemed to "lock in" both current policies and investor expectations.

As long as investor confidence remained high, there was little reason to worry about rising levels of portfolio investment. However, the flow of external finance began to dry up in 1994, partly as a result of higher interest rates in the US. Equally influential were the political crises associated with the Chiapas uprising (which seems to have caused a bigger exodus of Mexican capital – as measured by the usual capital flight variable of net errors and omissions – than a reduction in portfolio investment *per se*), the assassination of PRI Presidential candidate Luis Colosio in March 1994, and the uncertainties associated with the national elections held in August of that same year.

The "rational" global investors disciplining Mexico thus began to demand higher interest rates to compensate for both the perceived riskiness of an unstable political environment and ongoing increases in US rates. Eager to calm investors' nerves and concerned that an interest rate hike in mid-1994 would provoke a mild recession as the nation headed into a presidential election, the government made a strategic choice: it converted much of its short-term peso-denominated Cetes debt to dollar-denominated Tesobonos in mid-1994.[7] While dollar-denominated Tesobonos constituted only 6 per cent of the total foreign holding of government securities in December 1993, just a year later these new financial instruments accounted for 87 per cent of the total.

The conversion to Tesobonos did not eliminate the fundamental problem, and indeed may have exacerbated the sense of risk, particularly on the part of local investors more familiar with the Mexican government's record at promise-keeping. With trade still far from balance, foreign reserves (minus gold) plummeted from a high of US$29.3 billion in February 1994 to just US$6.3 billion in December 1994, a particularly alarming turn when one realized (and some soon did) that nearly US$30 billion worth of Tesobonos were due to mature in 1995. The decision to announce a step devaluation finally came on December 20, 1994, when dollar reserves were nearly depleted. Two days later, the peso was set to freely float (i.e., sink) as capital continued to hemorrhage outward.

Why wasn't the crisis anticipated?

The Mexican case presents a striking anomaly for those who have touted the macroeconomic benefits of globalization. Both the December 20 devaluation and the forces that continued to drive the peso downward in the following months seem to have been the usual externally imposed discipline of a disapproving market: excess trade deficits were eventually rewarded with an outward stampede of capital. Yet, the rapidity of Mexico's reversal hardly speaks to the rationality of an internationalized market and seems to bode badly for those who would rather allow foreign influences to constrain the predilections of domestic policy-makers.

One key challenge to globalization theory and policy involves the failure of the markets to project the crisis. Much of economic theory is built on the assumption that rational actors should be able to anticipate such market movements and to adjust accordingly; indeed, the private sector's supposed ability to guess policy consequences and steer the economy in a more stable direction is one rationale for opening the capital account. Yet, the Mexican devaluation seems to have caught international investors, academic economists, and even many high-ranking officials in the United States (with reportedly close ties to the upper ranks of the Mexican Finance Ministry) completely off guard.[8] In short, the persistence of foreign investors in Mexican markets – and their shock at the consequent loss in their asset values – may be more of a surprise than the devaluation itself.

In the wake of the devaluation, a virtual cottage industry of explanations has cropped up, with authors' foci ranging from Mexico's unexpectedly unstable political environment to the shift from peso-financed government debt into dollar-financed government debt.[9] But while all of these explanations shed light on the timing of the crisis, they tell us little about why the crisis was not predicted by a broader group of investors and financiers. After all, the figures on Tesobono composition were widely known to investors playing in those markets and the political roller-coaster of 1994 could hardly have been a surprise to knowledgeable analysts on Wall Street and policy-makers in Washington and elsewhere.[10]

Part of the surprise may have been due to a presumption that globalization, intended for domestic discipline, had actually eliminated domestic policy choice (as argued above, such openness actually reflected a *particular* policy choice). Because of this, both the government and the markets no longer viewed the real exchange rate as a policy tool, but rather as an economic *outcome*. From this perspective, the peso's appreciation over the 1988–93 period reflected increasing levels of confidence in the Mexican economy and hence a rise in underlying asset values. As such, the ongoing massive capital inflows were not problematic. However, as Dornbusch and others insist, the real exchange rate is, in fact, a "policy-influenced or even policy-dominated variable" (Dornbusch *et al.* 1995: 251). In particular, the use of the nominal exchange rate as an anti-inflation tool can, given the lags in disinflation, produce real appreciation; therefore, the challenge of stabilizing regimes is to shift away from exchange rate-targeting and learn to live with slightly higher inflation but stronger trade competitiveness.

Interestingly, the negative outcomes of Mexico's real overvaluation could easily have been anticipated if economists and investors had compared Mexican macroeconomic policy from 1988–94 to the similar strategy employed by Chile between 1978–81; in both cases, trade liberalization was combined with a fixed exchange rate as a way to tame domestic inflationary pressures and, in both cases, the exchange rate subsequently collapsed.[11] To illustrate the parallels, I periodize the Chilean and Mexican cases along the following lines: (1) pre-reform (including a precipitating crisis, which for Chile was the socialist/populist regime of Salvador Allende, and for Mexico the impending debt crisis during the last years of the Lopez Portillo government from 1976–82); (2) monetarist stabilization (which for Chile was the initial response of the Pinochet dictator-ship that took over in 1973 and for Mexico, the De la Madrid administration's reliance on the traditional macroeconomic tool of devaluation); (3) exchange-rate targeting (which in both cases was coupled with trade liberalization to dampen inflationary pressures); and (4) the aftermath.[12] A close look at Table 11.1 and Figures 11.1 to 11.4 suggests just how reminiscent Mexico's crisis is of Chile's a decade earlier – and also suggests that the devaluation was less surprising than many have thought.

Why did savvy international investors miss the parallels? The answer lies, I believe, in three interrelated phenomena: (1) a set of ideological priors that convinced key policy-makers and private sector analysts that a country playing so strongly by the market's rules could hardly wind up getting it wrong; (2) a perception that the political costs of devaluation were so prohibitive that no rational Mexican official would even contemplate this option; and, (3) a "herd instinct" on the part of investors that caused the stampede away from Mexican assets to be more dramatic than may have been necessary.

On the first point, it is important to recall that Mexican policy-makers under-went a sharp ideological shift during the De la Madrid and Salinas presidencies. The obvious failures of ISI led to a firm embrace of the so-called "Washington Consensus," which held that markets could do little wrong and governments could do little but. While such a belief in the efficacy of the market is usually rendered in microeconomic terms – except for a burdensome regulation or inap-propriate price control, markets would clear – there is a highly relevant macro-economic counterpart: the neoliberal view that if the government budget is balanced, large private-sector-driven trade imbalances simply reflect the optimism

Table 11.1 Exchange rate targeting in Chile and Mexico

				Chile			
	GDP growth	Inflation rate	Real effective exchange rate (1976=100)	Wage share of manufacturing value-added (1976=100)	Exports (FOB) (millions of US$)	Imports (millions of US$)	Merchandise trade balance (millions of US$)
Pre-reform							
1971	9.2	26.7	105.5	156.0	1,000	927	73
1972	−0.7	149.2	110.7	202.6	851	1,012	(161)
1973	−4.8	558.6	123.1	111.9	1,316	1,329	(13)
Monetarist stabilization							
1974	2.5	376.0	107.3	83.0	2,152	1,901	250
1975	−11.6	340.7	115.0	84.0	1,590	1,520	70
1976	3.5	174.3	100.0	100.0	2,116	1,473	643
1977	8.6	63.4	96.9	119.7	2,186	2,151	35
Exchange rate targeting							
1978	7.5	30.3	112.2	122.9	2,460	2,886	(426)
1979	8.7	38.9	100.3	124.5	3,835	4,190	(355)
1980	8.2	31.2	86.2	125.9	4,705	5,469	(764)
1981	4.8	9.5	77.4	157.3	3,836	6,513	(2,677)
Aftermath							
1982	−10.4	20.7	90.6	139.3	3,706	3,643	63
1983	−3.7	23.1	95.9	116.9	3,831	2,845	986

Mexico

		GDP growth	Inflation rate	Real effective exchange rate (1988=100)	Wage share of manufacturing value-added (1988=100)	Exports (FOB) (millions of US$)	Imports (millions of US$)	Merchandise trade balance (millions of US$)
	1980	8.4	29.8	84.0	185	18,031	21,087	(3,056)
Pre-reform	1981	8.8	28.7	76.5	192	23,307	27,184	(3,877)
	1982	−0.7	98.9	113.0	191	24,056	17,009	7,047
	1983	−4.1	80.8	120.8	134	25,953	11,848	14,105
	1984	3.7	59.2	104.4	119	29,101	15,915	13,186
Monetarist stabilizsation	1985	2.7	63.7	100.8	118	26,758	18,359	8,399
	1986	−3.9	105.7	125.2	113	21,803	16,784	5,019
	1987	1.9	159.2	124.8	99	27,599	18,813	8,786
	1988	1.3	51.7	100.0	100	30,692	28,081	2,611
	1989	3.5	19.7	94.7	106	35,171	34,766	405
	1990	4.3	29.9	88.5	113	40,711	41,592	(881)
Exchange rate targeting	1991	3.9	18.8	77.6	122	42,687	49,996	(7,279)
	1992	2.8	11.9	69.3	NA	46,196	62,130	(15,934)
	1993	0.4	8.0	65.1	NA	51,885	65,366	(13,481)
	1994	3.8	7.1	66.8	NA	60,879	79,346	(18,467)
Aftermath	1995	−6.2	52.0	95.2	NA	79,543	72,454	7,089
	1996	5.0	27.7	85.8	NA	95,999	89,469	6,530

Sources: GDP growth, wage share, and Chilean trade from World Tables, 1995 (CD-ROM). December to December inflation from INTERNATIONAL FINAN-CIAL STATISTICS. Chilean real exchange rate from Ramos (1986); Mexican real exchange rate calculated using the *period average* exchange rate, domestic CPI, and U.S. WPI, with data from World Tables, 1995 (CD-ROM) and IFS (CD-ROM, Sept. 1997). Mexican Trade data is inclusive of maquila operations; 1996 Mexican trade (and GDP) is based on data from the New York Mexican Consulate Web page; 1996 inflation and real exchange rate based on IFS (CD-ROM, Sept. 1997).

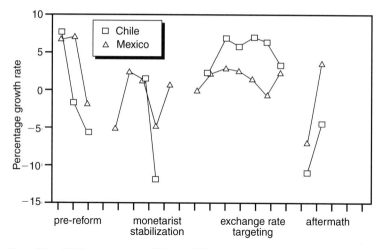

Figure 11.1 GDP growth rates, Chile and Mexico

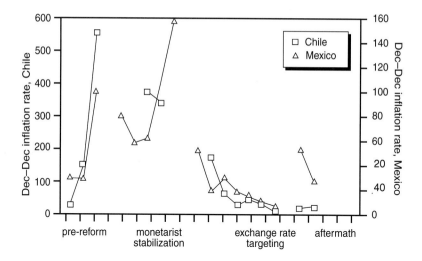

Figure 11.2 Inflation rates, Chile and Mexico

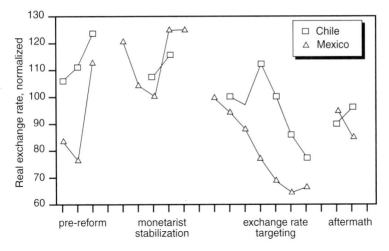

Figure 11.3 Real exchange rates, Chile and Mexico

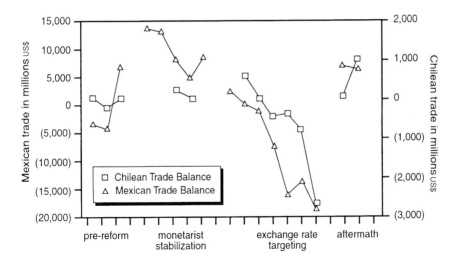

Figure 11.4 Trade balance, Chile and Mexico

of foreign investors who, after all, would only finance the imbalance if they believed it to be sustainable.[13]

This was certainly the picture projected in numerous interviews conducted with high-level Mexican policy-makers in 1993 and 1994: the budget was more or less balanced, foreign capital was clearly interested in Mexico, and the resulting overvalued exchange rate was thought to reflect a "ratification" of the country's economic policy.[14] A closer analysis would have suggested that Mexico's imbalances were actually the result of low savings and not simply high foreign investment; more wariness about the market would have sent some warning flags that the main form of foreign financing, portfolio investment, was exposing the country to some potentially destabilizing external shocks in the event of a shift in investor sentiment. Instead, both domestic and foreign decision-makers bought into the government's own confidence; like the policy-makers themselves, they believed that Mexico had yielded control to a *rational* market and did not doubt that it would deliver the appropriate discipline necessary to keep the economy on a smooth equilibrium growth path.

In addition, investors perceived that the costs of a devaluation would be quite high; indeed, maintaining the perception that there would be a high cost to policy change was exactly the point, since this helped enhance credibility for the current policy.[15] Moreover, overvaluation helped "mask" an underlying deterioration in income distribution that continued through the Salinas epoch. As noted in Pastor and Wise (1997), the upper tenth decile of households gained between 1984 and 1992; the bottom 70 per cent saw flat or negative returns, especially during the period of more intense market reform under Salinas.[16] Despite this, overvaluation gave Mexicans a general sense of prosperity – while real GNP per capita grew at a modest annual rate of 1.0 per cent between 1988 and 1994, the growth of dollar GNP per capita skyrocketed at an average annual rate of 12.5 per cent and new consumer imports were widely available. Mexicans, with newly issued personal credit cards in hand, felt richer, and there was understandably little incentive for policy-makers to remind them that they were not.

However, when reserves fell to a critical level, the government had no choice but to accept the economic and political costs of depreciation. And once the truth was out about the unsustainability of the Mexican peso, financial markets rapidly entered into the "bust" phase of a typical "overlending/revulsion" cycle: in the two-day period between the step devaluation and the decision to free-float the peso, Mexico's international reserves fell by $4 billion.[17]

In its influential post-mortem of the crisis, the IMF has made much of this "speculative attack" on the peso. In this "attack" view, currency crises result when investors, increasingly aware of "deteriorating fundamentals," decide to abandon a particular currency and cash in their gains before the inevitable devaluation.[18] This stampede naturally intensifies the economic pressure associated with deteriorating fundamentals and contributes to the overshooting of the exchange rate when it is finally devalued.

Although this explanation enables us to better understand the severity of the pesos' decline, as well as the phenomena of attacks, stampedes, and overshooting, it does *not* capture the element of nearly complete surprise that seemed to characterize investor reaction. Indeed, the difference in the rate of return between peso- and dollar-denominated government-debt instruments was not very large through most of 1994 (IMF 1995: 75), which indicates that few investors were lying in wait for a devaluation. Moreover, "catching on" to the economic fundamentals after the government's desperate measures on December 20 suggests little prescience by economic actors and hardly represents a ringing endorsement of market rationality.[19]

The failure to anticipate, then, was largely due to the belief held by both

Mexican policy-makers and their international counterparts that adoption of a more globalized approach guaranteed Mexico's success.[20] Compounding this was the perception in Mexico City that any attempt to depreciate the peso would impose prohibitively high costs, itself a key feature of the policy regime. However, once these ideological and political thresholds were crossed, the volatile dynamics of financial markets took over, propelling the peso downward. And while the anticipation of these events was entirely possible, it would have required a more realistic assessment of the Mexican strategy from the beginning, as well as a more sober comparison of this strategy with the earlier Chilean experience discussed above.

The whole story is hardly consistent with the notion of a virtuous and anonymous international market restraining local actors against the temptations of poor macroeconomic management. Instead, market participants seemed to have maintained blinders that encouraged Mexico's unsustainable path, then "revulsed" in sudden recognition of the damage their own financial support had rendered to the Mexican macroeconomy. In this sense, one is forced to question the globalization "rationality" both imposed on, and adopted by, Mexican authorities.

Was there an alternative to the Mexican crisis?

If the crisis could have been anticipated, could it also have been avoided? That is, were there alternative policy choices? Some have argued that Mexican authorities could have tightened monetary policy, forcing a peso-protecting recession that would have resulted in a temporary but small adjustment and eventually resuscitated the "Mexican miracle."[21] Yet, tightening monetary policy to defend the peso was problematic, not only because of election concerns but also because banks were carrying a large portfolio of non-performing loans, a trend that made policy-makers fear the prospect of interest rate hikes.[22]

By contrast, a more neatly executed devaluation, perhaps as early as 1992, could have promoted a surge in exports and foreign direct investment, with the latter being less problematic than portfolio flows due to its long-term and less volatile nature (i.e., it is more difficult to withdraw a plant than it is to withdraw a stock purchase). Unfortunately, devaluation was postponed partly because a key piece of Mexico's long-term strategy, the NAFTA agreement, was still being negotiated – and then, after the negotiations concluded in August 1992, the actual treaty was waiting for approval by the US Congress. Through this period, depreciation was politically delicate as this would risk reversing Mexico's huge trade deficit with the US, a phenomenon that would have "confirmed" the potential job loss US-based NAFTA opponents feared. In this sense, Mexico's own attempt to globalize its economy locked it into an unsustainable exchange rate strategy: the attempt to embrace market rationality had forced an irrational approach.

With NAFTA secured in late 1993, the government had an opportunity to consider devaluation. However, the outbreak of violence in Chiapas on January 1,

1994 – the same day that NAFTA took effect – effectively precluded depreciation, partly to avoid any air of financial panic. The March 1994 assassination of PRI presidential candidate, Luis Colosio, afforded an opportunity to shift policy: the authorities could have cast the blame on this unexpected political event without a major loss of credibility, particularly since the US and Canada immediately stepped forward with a US$7 billion swap facility to help cushion any exchange rate movement.[23] The Mexican government did manage to force through a 10 per cent decline in the peso's value, essentially by allowing the peso to float up to the top of the exchange rate band that had been established and systematically widened over the previous year, but this gesture hardly made up for the real appreciation that had occurred earlier.

After August, President Salinas could have devalued and thereby allowed the newly elected President Zedillo to take office with a more sustainable currency and little of the blame for the depreciation. Some have attributed Salinas's refusal to devalue to his desire to close his administration on a successful note, and thus clinch his candidacy for the directorship of the new World Trade Organization. Other accounts suggest that Salinas was nearly persuaded by Zedillo to devalue but then backed off when told that Treasury Ministry Pedro Aspe, architect of the earlier stabilization and a symbol of Mexican financial stability, would resign in response. If such personal motives or roles were important, this is a telling indictment, not so much of Salinas or Aspe as of an international system and domestic political structure that allow single individuals to hold so much influence over the macroeconomic policy of a major emerging market.

In any case, there was an alternative to the crisis – although it would have required some degree of political courage and the willingness of Salinas to "fall on his sword" in order to smooth the way for his successor. And the fact that alternatives were possible means that the Mexican crash cannot simply be ascribed to the effects of globalization. Rather, the Mexicans chose a particular form of international integration and policy that laid the conditions for the collapse.

This is not to say that the Zedillo administration had much room to act once the crisis began in earnest. Significantly, the original adjustment program unveiled in January 1995 did little to calm markets or stem inflation. Obviously, no program would have been credible until there was strong evidence that multilateral support would be forthcoming, something not clarified until late January and formally agreed to in mid-February by the US, the IMF, and other Paris Club leaders. With the mammoth US$53 billion loan package in place, Mexico's March 1995 program was able to halt the slide in the peso, restore some degree of voluntary capital inflows, and calm jittered nerves.

As it turns out, the subsequent economic recovery has been relatively rapid, with the 1995 recession followed by an export-driven expansion, partly because of the new exchange rate policy (see Table 11.1).[24] However, real wages fell by nearly 25 per cent between 1994 and 1996 and did not stop their decline until mid-1997. In addition, the distributional wreckage of adjustment has gone well beyond the usually suffering lower classes. As noted earlier, consumer credit had been made more available during the Salinas era and middle-class Mexicans, fresh from the deprivation of the slow growth and income declines of the early 1980s, eagerly borrowed. Predictably, the astronomical interest rates adopted to weather the recent macroeconomic storm have made debt servicing on credit cards and mortgages extremely problematic. Middle-class consumers blame not themselves but erratic government policies and have formed the so-called "Barzón" movement to seek debt relief.[25] Thus, the poor and the middle classes have been unified in economic suffering as well as doubts about the government's capacity to manage the economy. The political fallout has included a series of striking electoral losses by the government party, including the loss of a legislative majority in the 1997 Congressional elections and the consequent emergence of real contestation in the legislature over Mexico's economic policy.

The implications of the Mexican crisis

What are the implications of the Mexican peso crisis for the issues of globalization and sovereignty that are the central concerns of this volume? First and foremost, Mexico's experience casts some doubt on the merits of globalization as a way to regulate macroeconomic policy and outcomes. After all, Mexico's exposure to international capital markets was supposed to constitute a restraining influence that would keep inflation low, growth high, and the currency stable. Instead, supposedly rational investors were caught by surprise (and with balance sheets showing) at the Mexican meltdown. After the peso finally crashed, adjustment did occur: when dollars speak, developing country Treasury ministers listen. Still this sort of whipsaw discipline, replete with high unemployment, falling real wages, financial panics, and rising political conflict, is far from the smooth equilibrium path of neoliberal tales.

The second implication – and one that is quite consistent with the themes of other authors in this volume – is that globalization has constrained but not entirely eliminated sovereign control over economic policy.[26] In the Mexican case, the control the state surrendered to the international capital markets reflected a policy choice: openness to volatile capital flows was supposed to gain investor confidence. When the policy regime was no longer optimal for medium-term macroeconomic stability, alternatives were available: at several key points between 1992 and 1994, Mexican policy-makers probably could have shifted course with regard to exchange rate policy without significantly destabilizing the economy. More broadly, Mexico could have acknowledged the inevitability of increasing globalization but adopted a different route for integrating its economy into international flows of trade and capital.

Here, it may be useful to understand the lessons Chile learned when its own experiment with exchange rate targeting led to macroeconomic crisis in the early 1980s.[27] The country wisely abandoned its attachment to fixed exchange rates and learned to live with slightly higher inflation but a more competitive exchange rate; while Mexico initially appeared to be following suit, the peso appreciated dramatically through 1996 and less dramatically thereafter. Most significantly, Chile departed from a strictly "hands-off" market-orientation and instituted measures to tame the destabilizing financial surges that still torment Mexico, including taxes on capital movements and requirements that incoming capital commit itself to a minimum stay before being allowed to exit the country. This, in turn, helped the Chileans maintain their real exchange rate at a competitive level, insuring that they would lead into the world market with their products and not their financial dependence.[28]

Such interventions in international capital flows were common in East Asia before that region's own movement toward financial liberalization helped precipitate a crisis. Another key characteristic in most of East Asia was a relatively equal distribution of income, often achieved through dramatic equity transfers such as land reform. A new spate of research (including Alesina and Rodrik 1994; Persson and Tabellini 1994; Berg and Sachs 1988; and others) has suggested that such egalitarian distributions may have helped growth by reducing political conflict, securing property rights, and encouraging a wider investment in basic human capital.[29] In contrast, both Mexico's strategy under President Salinas and its recent adjustment package under President Zedillo have added salt to the wounds of long-standing inequities in the distribution of land, access to credit, and income (Pastor and Wise 1997).

In sum, the international system is not the rational market of neoliberal theory: credit market imperfections mean that financial booms are followed by busts as fickle investors help prop up currencies, then panic at the first sight of a downward drift. Sovereign choices are still possible: as noted above, those developing countries that have made the most of their opportunities have targeted trade flows more than capital market liberalization, regulated the financial side in order to maintain competitive exchange rates and real sector gains, and attempted to ameliorate existing maldistributions of income and assets, in part to cement the political and policy alliances needed for long-term export growth (Berg and Sachs 1988). There is, in short, room for appropriate state interventions, particularly if policy transparency and democratic accountability can serve as levers against the rent-seeking behavior that has historically been a part of Latin American economic policy-making.

In this sense, the cautionary tale from Mexico is not so much about failing to trust the global market as it is about trusting it too much. The peso crash of 1994 – particularly the failure of policy-makers and markets to fully anticipate the problem – suggests the weakness of policy frameworks that are excessively ideological in their free-market faith. If we are to avoid another "surprise" – in Mexico or in any other developing country – what is needed is more caution about market liberalization and more recognition of the continuing space for policy choice even within the context of a highly globalized economy.

Notes

1 This chapter draws parts of the Mexican case study from a more technical piece called, "Peso, Policies, and Predictions," in C. Wise (ed.) *The Post-NAFTA Political Economy: Mexico and the Western Hemisphere*, Pennsylvania State University, 1998. This research was supported by the Social Science Research Council and the US Institute of Peace.

2 For a review of the US rescue package and a comparison to the financial assistance rendered during Mexico's 1982 debt crisis, see Lustig (1996).

3 As Budget Secretary under De la Madrid, Salinas helped to design and implement a social "pact" (or Pacto) in 1987, which committed the government, business, and labor to price restraints. See Dornbusch and Werner (1994: 287–9) for a detailed account of the various agreements that came under the rubric of the Pacto from 1987 to 1994.

4 For example, the first Pacto halved the tariff rate and eliminated import permits (see Dornbusch and Werner 1994: 288). Exchange rate fixing was not fully incorporated into the various Pactos until mid-1988, several months prior to the Presidential elections.

5 As Oks and van Wijnbergen (1995: 167) note, real consumer credit jumped at an annualized rate exceeding 50 per cent between March 1989 and April 1992, fueling imports as well as domestic demand.

6 Calculations of capital flows are based on the International Monetary Fund's *International Financial Statistics*, CD-ROM, March 1996.

7 The reluctance to hike interest rates was also due to legitimate concern about the fragility of the banking system, a topic addressed below (see Sachs *et al.* 1995: 13).

8 As Edwards (1995: 297) reports, a "number of international investment firms were still recommending Mexican securities to their clients" right up until December 20.

9 See IMF 1995; Dornbusch *et al.* 1995; Heath 1995; Sachs *et al.* 1995; Springer and Molina 1995; among others.

10 Some investors have claimed that they were not sufficiently informed of Mexico's reserve figures. The IMF (1995: 560) notes that a decline of one-third in international reserves since November 1994 was not announced until *after* the December devaluation. However, this notion of an information gap fails to explain why money managers seemed to believe that Mexico's current account deficits were sustainable over the longer term. Moreover, as Eichengreen and Fishlow (1996: 40) point out, "the virtual unanimity that more and better information is necessary enables portfolio fund managers to find an excuse for their poor predictions. Once there is fuller information, the next crisis will fail to be foreseen for other, and also initially profitable, reasons."

11 Dornbusch *et al.* (1995) also draw a comparison with Chile.

12 The periodization scheme for Chile is drawn from the analysis in Pastor (1992) and Ramos (1986). The data for Mexican trade include *maquila* sales.

13 Some observers argue that, in fact, the Mexican trade balance was related to a budget deficit, albeit one that was non-traditional. Heath (1995), for example, suggests that Mexican authorities allowed the rapid expansion of credit via the state's development banks (amounting to 4 per cent of GDP in 1994), a policy that was obscured by the government's 1993 decision to remove such financial intermediation from public sector balance figures. Sachs *et al.* (1994: 6) counter that "most or all of such activities do not belong in an economically meaningful definition of a budget deficit," primarily because total lending is only a cost (rather than an asset) in the event of a bad loan. They also note that regulations on such development banks (in order to prevent losses) had also been tightened in 1993.

14 Interviews conducted in Mexico City, with follow-ups in 1995. See also the discussion in Heath (1995) and Edwards (1995) as well as the argument along these lines in Aspe Armella (1993: 190–3).

15 This period of Mexican policy-making conforms neatly with models of political economy, in which governments try to solve time inconsistency and credibility problems by committing to a policy which would be extraordinarily costly to reverse – and thereby convince investors of the sustainability of such policies. See Rodrik (1989; 1996).

16 Although the figures for the 1994 survey are now released, technical problems preclude a reliable calculation of the growth of real monetary income by decile for the 1992–4 period. However, the decile distribution of nominal income appears to have changed little and, making use of this and other indicators, Pastor and Wise (1997) estimate that real income held more or less steady for the lower deciles, declined slightly in the middle, and improved marginally in the top two deciles.

17 For more on capital flow cycles in general, see Eichengreen and Fishlow (1996), Dornbusch and Werner (1994: 259) and IMF (1995: 57).

18 The classic article on speculative attacks remains Krugman (1979); see also the overview in Agenor and Flood (1994).

19 Lustig's (1995) analysis is different in detail, but her insistence that the financial crisis followed (and was due to) the devaluation squares with my notion that any speculative attack came after the Mexican government's announcement and actions on December 20.

20 To be fair, US Treasury officials were concerned about Mexico's potential overvaluation problem and quietly relayed their concerns to Mexican authorities. Obviously, both sides found it easier to downplay this concern for fear of "spooking" the markets into the sort of speculative attack that eventually occurred. See D. Wessel, P.B. Carroll, and T.T. Vogel, Jr, "How Mexico's crisis ambushed top minds in officialdom, finance," *Wall Street Journal* July 6, 1995, p. A1.

21 The IMF (1995: 73) implies this possibility in its discussion of the inappropriate sterilization of reserve losses in the second half of 1994. See also the discussion of options in Council on Foreign Relations (CFR) (1996).

22 The fear of damaging the banks also helps to explain why authorities opted to convert peso-denominated government securities to dollar-denominated ones: they were concerned that the domestic interest rate hikes necessary to cover the depreciation risk on peso securities would bankrupt the system.

23 Dornbusch and Werner (1994: 285) also suggest that there were "several days following the assassination of candidate Colosio during which the nation rallied behind the official party and that could have provided the cover for a realignment."

24 For a detailed analysis of the reasons for the recovery, see Pastor (1998).

25 The Barzón movement was originally focused on rural debtors seeking to prevent bank foreclosure on their farms but soon spread to urban areas. The government eventually responded by providing smaller debtors with some degree of relief, in particular an Agreement for Immediate Aid to Debtors (ADE), which subsidized interest rates for a limited period and temporarily halted most foreclosures. See Mark Stevenson, 'Mexico's bad year for banks,' *El Financiero International Edition* December 25, 1995–January 7, 1996, p. 9.

26 Where I disagree to some degree with other authors is whether globalization constitutes a new phenomenon. While it is true that domestic economies have long been driven by international factors, today's increased volatility of capital flows – which makes it possible to punish or reward developing country policy-makers nearly instantaneously – does lend a qualitatively new character to international integration.

27 For various perspectives on the Chilean reform during the 1980s, see Bosworth *et al.* (1994). Colombia, another relative success in the panorama of Latin American economies, has thrived on a similar combination of orthodox and heterodox policies.

28 Some may suggest that another key element in this turnaround was the authoritarian ability to force through reform in Chile. It helps to recall, however, that the Pinochet regime was also responsible for the disaster of the late 1970s – and that the thick insulation of Mexican policy-makers proved to be no antidote to bad economic policy

29 Persson and Tabellini (1994) note that more equal distributions are consistent with a more widespread benefit from any innovation that raises profit and growth rates. Thus, the median voter is less likely to vote for confiscation. Rodrik (1994) offers a direct examination of the impacts of a more progressive distribution of income and human capital investment (education) on growth in East Asia.

References

Agenor, P.-R. and Flood, R. (1994) "Speculative attacks and balance of payments crisis," in F. van der Ploeg (ed.) *The Handbook of International Macroeconomics*, Cambridge, MA: Basil Blackwell.

Alesina, A. and Rodrik, D. (1994) "Distributive policies and economic growth," *Quarterly Journal of Economics*, CIX: 436.

Aspe Armella, P. (1993) *El Camino Mexicano de la Transformacion Economica*, Mexico, DF: Fondo de Cultura Economica.

Berg, A. and Sachs, J. (1988) "The debt crisis: structural explanations of country performance," *Journal of Development Economics* 29: 271–306.

Bosworth, B.P., Dornbusch, R., and Labán, R. (1994) *The Chilean Economy: Policy Lessons and Challenges*, Washington, DC: The Brookings Institution.

Council on Foreign Relations (1996) *Lessons of the Mexican Peso Crisis: Report of an Independent Task Force*, New York, NY: Council on Foreign Relations.

Dornbusch, R. and Werner, A. (1994) "Mexico: stabilization, reform, and no growth," *Brookings Papers on Economic Activity*, 1: 253–315.

Dornbusch, R., Goldfajn, I., and Valdés, R.O. (1995) "Currency crises and collapses," *Brookings Papers on Economic Activity* 2: 219–93.

Edwards, S. (1995) *Crisis and Reform in Latin America*, Oxford: Oxford University Press.

Eichengreen, B. and Fishlow, A. (1996) *Contending with Capital Flows: What is Different About the 1990s?* New York, NY: Council on Foreign Relations.

Heath, J.E. (1995) "The devaluation of the Mexican peso in 1994: economic policy and institutions," Center for Strategic and International Studies, Washington, DC, policy papers on the Americas, vol. VI, study S, June.

Hufbauer, G.C. and Schott, J.J. (1993) *NAFTA: An Assessment*, Washington DC: Institute for International Economics.

International Monetary Fund. (1995) *International Capital Markets: Developments, Prospects, and Policy Issues*, Washington, DC: IMF.

Krugman, P. (1979) "A model of balance of payment crisis," *Journal of Money, Credit and Banking* 11: 311–25, August.

Lustig, N. (1995) "The Mexican peso crisis: the foreseeable and the surprise," Brookings discussion paper, no. 114, Washington, DC: The Brookings Institution.

—— (1996) "Mexico in crisis, the US to the rescue: The financial assistance packages of 1982 and 1995," Brookings discussion paper (June), Washington, DC: Brookings Institution.

Oks, D. and van Wijnbergen, S. (1995) "Mexico after the debt crisis: is growth sustainable?" *Journal of Development Economics* 47: 135–54.

Pastor, M. (1992) *Inflation, Stabilization and Debt: Macroeconomic Experiments in Peru and Bolivia*, Boulder, CO: Westview Special Studies on Latin American and the Caribbean.

—— (1998) "Pesos, policies, and predictions: Why the crisis? Why the surprise? Why the recovery?" In C. Wise (ed.) *The Post-NAFTA Political Economy: Mexico and the Western Hemisphere*, Pennsylvania: Pennsylvania State University Press.

Pastor, M. and Wise, C. (1997) "State policy, distribution, and neoliberal reform in Mexico," *Journal of Latin American Studies* 419–56.

Persson, T. and Tabellini, G. (1994) "Is inequality harmful for growth?" *American Economic Review* 84 (3): 600–21.

Ramos, J. (1986) *Neoconservative Economics in the Southern Cone of Latin America, 1973–1983*, Baltimore, Md.: Johns Hopkins University Press.

Rodrik, D. (1989) "Promises, promises: Credible policy via signalling", *The Economic Journal*, 99, September.

—— (1994) "King Kong meets Godzilla: The World Bank and the East Asian miracle," in A. Fishlow (ed.) *Miracle or Design: Lessons from the East Asian Experience*, Washington: Overseas Development Council, pp. 13–53.

—— (1996) "The political economy of policy reform," *Journal of Economic Literature* 34: 9–41, March.

Sachs, J., Tornell, A., and Velasco, A. (1995) "The collapse of the Mexican peso: What have we learned?" NBER working paper 5142, Cambridge, MA: National Bureau of Economic Research, June.

Springer, G.L. and Molina, J.L. (1995) "The Mexican financial crisis: Genesis, impact, and implications," *Journal of Interamerican Studies and World Affairs* 37 (2): 57–81, Summer.

Acknowledgment

This is a revised version of a chapter that first appeared as "Peso, Policies and Predictions" in Carol Wise (ed.) *The Post-NAFTA Political Economy: Mexico and the Western Hemisphere*, Pennsylvania State University Press, 1998.

12 States, sovereignty and the response of Southeast Asia's "miracle" economies to globalization[1]

Richard Stubbs

One of the major tenets of the globalization literature is that globalization has undermined the sovereignty of states (Ohmae 1990; Strange 1996). The marked increase in the extent to which capital, goods, people, and ideas can in effect transcend borders by moving between widely dispersed locations very rapidly, and in some instances almost simultaneously (Scholte 1997: 431), as well as the spiral of political and diplomatic activities that has characterized the globalization process are said to limit the extent to which states can control, and speak for, the population within their territory, resist the influence of external authorities, and conduct effective relations with other states. By contrast there are those who persuasively argue that globalists have overstated and overgeneralized the degree of state powerlessness (Weiss 1998).

This chapter reviews the experience of Southeast Asia's "miracle" economies – Indonesia, Malaysia, Singapore, and Thailand (World Bank 1993) – over the last twenty-five years and demonstrates that the impact of globalization on state sovereignty varies across time. In other words, it is argued that globalization is a complicated process that does not always have the single effect of undermining or transforming or bolstering state sovereignty but rather, can be responsible for producing each of these effects at different points in time. Moreover, despite the severe economic crisis of the late 1990s, it can be argued that as a result of the impact of globalization three of the "miracle" economies – Malaysia, Singapore, and Thailand – can be said to have increased, even if by some measures only marginally, their sovereignty over the last quarter century.

Before laying out the argument in detail it is important to clear away some of the underbrush. Obviously it is assumed here that globalization is not simply a phenomenon of the 1990s. Indeed, in many ways it is difficult to decide on a definitive starting point for globalization in Southeast Asia. However, for the purposes of this analysis globalization will be assumed to have started in the mid-1970s. This date marks the onset of industrialization as foreign direct investment (FDI) began to flow into the region in rapidly increasing amounts. Certainly, from this point on non-communist Southeast Asia became a beneficiary of the "territorial fragmentation of the international economy" and highly mobile capital's search for higher profits (Cox 1997: 23). Through the late 1970s and early 1980s, the process of globalization through the spread of FDI and increasing industrialization quickly gathered strength. It moved into high gear with the rapid appreciation of the yen in the wake of the Plaza Accord of 1985 and the subsequent tidal wave of first, Japanese FDI and later, FDI from Taiwan, Hong Kong, South Korea, the US, and Europe that swept across Singapore, Malaysia, Thailand, and Indonesia in the late 1980s and the first half of the 1990s.

A crucial problem that needs to be addressed is how to deal with the terms "state" and "sovereignty." Different analysts define "state" in different ways (Stubbs and Underhill 1994: 421–2). For example, some students of international relations think of the state in territorial terms as a "geographically-contained structure whose agents claim ultimate political authority within their domain" (noted in Biersteker and Weber 1996: 2). Alternatively, many scholars, especially those with a background in comparative politics, view the "state" in institutional or Weberian terms as "a set of administrative, policing and military organizations headed and more or less well coordinated by an executive authority" (Skocpol 1979: 29). It is in this institutional or Weberian sense that the term will be used in this chapter.

Similarly, the concept of sovereignty has become increasingly contested in the literature with a number of historical analyses suggesting that the meaning given to sovereignty is continually evolving (Biersteker and Weber 1996; Camilleri 1990: 34–49; Thompson 1994: 11–18). External sovereignty, or what has been termed "juridical sovereignty" or "negative sovereignty," should be distinguished from internal or "political sovereignty" or "positive sovereignty" (Jackson 1990: 26–31; Rosenau 1995; Thompson 1994: 14–18). Juridical sovereignty refers to the notion, rooted in international law, that states are recognized by other states as members of the international community; that they are considered "judicially equal"; and that the "territorial integrity and political independence" of each state "is inviolable" (Lapidoth 1995: 10). Alternatively, political sovereignty refers to the extent to which an institutional state is capable of controlling its territory and population and maneuvering so as to gain an advantageous position within the global economy. Juridical sovereignty is, therefore, an absolute, formal condition while political sovereignty is variable and substantive (Jackson 1990: 29). Importantly, as Jackson points out, in the past states were "empirical realities before they were legal personalities" (Jackson 1990: 34) so that other states were forced to recognize them as members of the international community. However, during the post-Second World War era states have gained juridical sovereignty by virtue of being granted independence with little concern for the empirical capacity of the institutional state to claim sovereignty over its territory and population.

Yet, globalization has prompted students of international and comparative politics to focus once again on the "empirical realities" of the internal sovereignty of states. Hence, while juridical sovereignty is important in that it is assumed by the community of sovereign states that all states that are recognized as sovereign within the international system are equal and independent (Lapidoth 1995: 9–10), changes in the global economy and to global and regional politics have raised questions about the extent to which institutional states can exert control over their population and territory. This view of sovereignty is what Stephen Krasner in Chapter 2 in this volume terms "control or interdependence sovereignty" and, as he notes, specifically refers to the capacity of governments to monitor and where necessary to direct activities such as the movement of people, goods, ideas, and capital within and across borders. Importantly, then, the expectation, embedded in juridical sovereignty, that states do have ultimate authority within their borders and can control their populations may not be met in all cases (Thompson 1994: 17). Indeed, in many developing countries the empirical sovereignty exercised by the institutional state bares no relationship to what is assumed by the assigning of juridical sovereignty to the territorial state.

Krasner, in his chapter, singles out another key form of sovereignty: "Westphalian sovereignty." Here, sovereignty refers to "the exclusion of external authority." Krasner's emphasis on the extent to which states are able to restrict the influence of external authority is especially apt in the case of Southeast Asia. On the economic front, international institutions such as the World Bank and the IMF, as well as economically powerful states, such as Japan, have at times heavily influenced the economic policies of particular states. Similarly, the United States, among others, has helped to develop the security policies of individual non-communist Southeast Asian states. And, of course, a number of Western states and various arms of the United Nations have attempted to influence the policies and actions of states in the region with regard to setting labor and environmental standards and acknowledging workers' rights and human rights more generally.

The emphasis in this chapter, then, will be on what Krasner terms "control sovereignty," or the capacity of a state to control activities within and across its borders, and "Westphalian sovereignty," which emphasizes the autonomy of the institutional state within its territory. This approach – of emphasizing the degree of political sovereignty, or control and autonomy, exercised by the institutional state – is crucial in understanding the argument that globalization has at times increased the sovereignty of the state in Southeast Asia's "miracle" economies. The turmoil created by the Second World War and its aftermath, and the uncertainties generated by the Cold War and the fighting it precipitated, combined to limit the political sovereignty of the institutional state in Southeast Asia in the 1950s and 1960s. Hence, unlike in Europe or North America, where globalization has affected institutional states with a high degree of sovereignty, in Southeast Asia globalization has had an impact upon institutional states which, although relatively strong by Third World standards, enjoyed only a limited degree of sovereignty. In other words, institutional states in the developing world start at a much lower point on the degree-of-sovereignty continuum (Rosenau 1995: 195–200) than those in the developed world.

The following analysis is divided into four chronologically ordered sections. The first and third sections deal with the way in which globalization has enhanced the sovereignty of Southeast Asia's "miracle" economies. The first section outlines the formation of the institutional state in Southeast Asia and how this laid the foundation for the expansion of state capacity as globalization generated rapidly increasing government revenues. The more administratively developed the region's states became the more they were able to deal with the forces of globalization in a way that, at times, even increased their control and autonomy. The third section evaluates the impact of the massive inflow of capital, technology and information from such competing centers as Japan, the US, Greater China, and Europe on the political sovereignty of the region's institutional states. In this section there is also an assessment of the extent to which the institutional states of Southeast Asia made use of regional organizations, most notably the Association of Southeast Asian Nations (ASEAN) to counter the pressure to make policy changes from both the market and international institutions.

The second and fourth sections, deal with the way in which globalization has undermined the sovereignty of institutional states of Southeast Asia's "miracle" economies. Generally, state sovereignty is eroded through the imperatives of the market, especially the financial market; changes in technology; and the pressures that can be exercised by international governmental and non-governmental institutions. The rapid flow of capital or the increasing availability of information and the circulation of ideas may, for example, serve to handcuff a state as it attempts to manage its economy and order its society. At the same time, major powers and international organizations, such as the World Bank, the International Monetary Fund (IMF) or the World Trade Organization (WTO), can put pressures on states to follow a particular economic model and adopt a prescribed set of political practices. At various times each of these factors has been at work in Southeast Asia. The second section looks at the period in the mid-1980s when the region suffered a major recession that left it vulnerable to external pressures. The fourth section examines the 1997–8 economic crisis and the extent to which it may be argued that globalization played a role in reducing the capacity of the institutional states of the previously successful economies of Southeast Asia to exercise control over activities within and across their borders and to limit the influence of external authority within their territories.

Period I: the early years

Most of the Southeast Asian countries gained independence – and thus acquired juridical or international law sovereignty – in the fifteen years after the end of the Second World War. Like many other Third World countries, they were granted self-government in a relatively precipitous fashion. But there was also an additional problem in that the states of Southeast Asia achieved independence in the context of regional upheaval. The devastation visited on the region by the Japanese Occupation and its aftermath and the advent of the Cold War provided an inauspicious setting for the creation of independent states. Indeed, Southeast Asia's developing institutional states were faced with the enormous task of regulating their societies and economies and attempting to impose order within their territory during a time of considerable uncertainty and, in some instances, even chaos. Yet out of this turmoil a number of relatively strong institutional states emerged in Southeast Asia.

Paradoxically, a key reason for the rise of Southeast Asia's strong institutional states was the region's recent geopolitical history. In Malaya and Singapore during the guerrilla war waged by the Malayan Communist Party (MCP) from 1948 to 1960, the institutional states used windfall government revenues generated by the boom in commodity prices following the outbreak of the Korean War to expand both the military and the civil administration (Stubbs 1989: 261–3). Both Malaya – or Malaysia as it became known after 1963 – and Singapore – which became independent when it separated from Malaysia in 1965 – faced continued threats to their security even after the MCP was defeated. Confrontation with Indonesia from 1963 to 1965, the continuing threat from communism, which was presented by the expansion of the Vietnam War in the late 1960s, and the eventual success of the Vietcong and communist North Vietnam in 1975, the Vietnamese invasion of Cambodia in December 1978, and the existence of small, but persistent, communist guerrilla groups along the Thai–Malaysia border all required that the institutional state maintain a strong coercive capability. An effective administrative capacity was also found to be critical, not only in supporting the coercive aspects of the state but also in the redistribution of wealth in Malaysia so as to preserve racial harmony between the Malays and non-Malays (Snodgrass 1980). In Singapore there was the additional concern of being a very small, predominantly ethnic-Chinese country surrounded by ethnic-Malay neighbors. Survival was a major theme of the governing People's Action Party leadership. A strong, resourceful and efficient administration was also seen as a necessary prerequisite for the country's development (Milne and Mauzy 1990: 62–4).

Importantly, for both Singapore and Malaysia the globalization process that got under way in the mid-1970s helped to reinforce the strong institutional state. Increasing foreign direct investment, which was the result of capital seeking cheaper locations for manufacturing industries, expanded the economies of the two countries. The major consequence in terms of the argument being developed here was the marked increase in government revenues, which allowed for an expansion of state capacity. In Malaysia the augmented revenues helped enlarge the bureaucracy so that it could implement the New Economic Policy that sought to deal with the rising discontent within Malaysian society, especially among rural Malays. In Singapore, the increase in revenues as well as the high savings rate allowed for an expansion of the bureaucracy, for a heavy investment in economic and social infrastructure – such as port facilities and housing – and for the government itself to become "an entrepreneur in a big way" (Huff 1994: 320).

For Thailand the Vietnam War was crucial to the development of the institutional state. From the mid-1950s onwards the American government began to send aid to Thailand in an effort to shore up what was seen in Washington as an important frontline ally in the battle against Asian communism. In particular, at the height of the Vietnam War, from the mid-1960s to the early 1970s, the US pumped large amounts of money into the Thai economy and various government programs. The Thai army and police were provided with training and equipment and generally, the Thai institutional state's capacity to defend itself was considerably enhanced. Moreover, the Thai administration was a significant target of aid funding (Muscat 1990: 123–35, 256–71).

For Indonesia the key event was clearly the 1965 coup and the military's rise to power under President Suharto. Having defeated the Indonesian Communist Party (PKI) and spearheaded an unprecedented wave of bloodletting against communists and suspected communists, the military systematically consolidated its power. Threats from communism at home and Vietnamese and Chinese communism regionally provided the rationale for the primary role of the military, the centralization of power, and the interventionist policies. The revenues generated by the rapid increase in the price of oil funded the expansion of both the military and civil aspects of the institutional state (Robison 1986). Although not possessing the administrative capacity of its Southeast Asian neighbors, the Indonesian state none the less was able to develop a relatively strong central government.

Overall, then, in Singapore and Malaysia and to a lesser extent in Thailand and Indonesia, a confluence of geopolitical factors laid the foundations of a relatively strong institutional state. This development was in marked contrast to most other Third World countries, which, as Migdal has noted, had strong societies and weak states (Migdal 1988). Moreover, in each of the four Southeast Asian countries the institutional state was able to wrest the society from social chaos and abject poverty, and to initiate significant levels of social stability and prosperity. The resulting "performance legitimacy" enjoyed by the institutional states in these countries enhanced the capacity of each of the governments to regulate their respective societies and manage their economies.

Period II: the mid-1980s recession

In the early 1980s a series of global economic developments began to have an accumulative impact on Southeast Asia's economies. The end result was a region-wide recession in 1985 and 1986 that brought markedly lower growth rates for Thailand and Indonesia and, for the first time in many years, negative growth rates for Malaysia and Singapore (ASEAN-Japan Centre 1992: 8). There were a number of key reasons for the recession that were set in train by the rapid raise in oil prices in 1980 and 1981 (MacIntyre and Jayasuriya 1992: 1–3; Robison *et al.* 1987). The industrialized world responded to the sharp spike in oil prices by instituting restrictive fiscal and monetary policies to cope with inflation and rising trade deficits. At the same time many countries abandoned the fixed exchange rate regime, adopting a floating system that led to greater fluctuations in the foreign exchange market. The subsequent decline in world trade and oversupply of primary commodities had a major impact on the four Southeast Asian "miracle" economies. Dropping commodity prices and difficulties penetrating the major markets of the industrialized world produced a growing balance of payments problem. On top of this, Indonesia, Malaysia, and Thailand faced major difficulties as high global interest rates made servicing the large sums borrowed abroad during the years of high growth and low interest rates in the

1970s increasingly onerous. The rapid appreciation of the yen, in which a significant portion of the debt burden was denominated, produced by the Plaza Accord of September 1985, only served to exacerbate the problem.

The region-wide recession of 1985–6, forced the institutional states of Indonesia, Malaysia, Singapore, and Thailand to accept advice and aid from external authorities and to open up their economies to the rest of the world. Most particularly, as Jomo (1987: 146–7) has noted, the region was open to the influence of multilateral agencies such as the IMF and the World Bank. Certainly, there was a widespread recognition that new sources of capital were required and that the balance of payments problem had to be addressed by increasing exports of manufactured goods. This recognition, when combined with advice from global institutions and market pressures, forced each of the "miracle" economies of Southeast Asia to relax the terms and conditions under which FDI was allowed into their economies. In addition, other economic regulations were liberalized and privatization was introduced (MacIntyre and Jayasuriya 1992). Moreover, Thailand took such measures as devaluing the baht and reducing business taxes (Pasuk 1992). Overall, the economic down-turn of the 1980s undermined the political sovereignty of the institutional states of the region, limiting their control over the activities of groups such as multinational corporations and increasing the influence of external authorities, most notably the international financial institutions. Furthermore, domestic enterprises, in Indonesia especially, began actively to seek out joint ventures with foreign firms rather than relying heavily on government supplied capital as they had in the past. Hence, Indonesia, Malaysia, and Thailand joined Singapore in making export-oriented industrialization, rather than government-sponsored import-substitution industrialization, the primary approach to economic development.

Despite major concerns at the time, the recession of the mid-1980s proved to be something of a minor setback in the onward economic march of Southeast Asia's successful economies. Certainly, the institutional state's control over the activities within and across its borders and its ability to resist the attempts of external authorities to influence government actions were diminished for a period. However, the change in economic strategy could also be said to be evidence that the institutional state still had the capacity to transform policy and thus, the state retained a good deal of political sovereignty. Moreover, the state's political sovereignty remained greater than it had been in the 1960s and early 1970s. There were many fewer overt violent challenges to the authority of the institutional state, the government's writ extended to all parts of the country, and the legitimacy of state institutions was widely accepted. Indeed, the impact of globalization on the sovereignty of the economically successful Southeast Asian states appeared at the time to be something of a two-steps-forward, one-step-backward process.

Period III: post-Plaza prosperity

Paradoxically, one of the events that initially had caused Southeast Asians concern, the Plaza Accord, launched a period in which the forces of globalization brought rapid economic growth and a marked increase in state sovereignty to Indonesia, Malaysia, Singapore, and Thailand. Simultaneous with the economic reforms in the four non-communist Southeast Asian countries, the G-5 finance ministers, in September 1985, agreed under the Plaza Accord to give their central banks the responsibility of raising the value of the yen against the dollar. The rapid appreciation of the yen, allied to structural changes that were taking place in the Japanese economy, forced a number of manufacturing companies to relocate outside Japan. Initially, Japanese companies targeted South Korea and Taiwan, but the currencies in these economies also appreciated during 1986 and 1987. So they turned next to Southeast Asia. They saw it as a region that was geographically close to Japan and that had economies with a reasonable economic infrastructure, a cheap but relatively skilled workforce, and a bureaucracy capable of implementing programs and projects. And, of course, the region had suddenly become much more receptive to FDI. As a result, between 1988 and 1995 the flow of Japanese FDI in the ASEAN economies – Brunei, Indonesia, Malaysia, the Philippines, Singapore, and Thailand – was well over US$32 billion (ASEAN-Japan Centre 1996: 61). Moreover, in order to continue to compete with Japanese manufacturers, other companies from the US, Europe, and the Asian newly industrializing economies (NIEs) outside of Southeast Asia – Hong Kong, South Korea, and Taiwan – had to follow the Japanese lead and set up shop in one of the ASEAN states. The recipient states of most of the export-oriented manufacturing FDI were Singapore, Thailand, Malaysia, or Indonesia.

The economically successful states of Southeast Asia, then, benefited from the increased mobility of FDI that accompanied globalization and liberalization. Certainly, with the onset of globalization, the institutional state in each of the four successful Southeast Asian countries was positioned to use the increased resources generated by the inflow of FDI and the generally higher levels of economic activity to augment its capacity to govern. For example, with inflation and currency fluctuations discounted, government revenues in Malaysia, Singapore, Thailand, and Indonesia have doubled over the last ten years (International Monetary Fund 1997). This increase in resources allowed for more effective government debt management and, hence, less dependence on external public debt financing. More generally, the economically successful governments of the region were able to expand the capacity of the state so as to provide the minimum levels of economic and administrative infrastructure required for rapid capitalist development.

In addition, the massive increase in foreign investment in the late 1980s and into the 1990s, especially in manufacturing, brought large numbers of individuals and families into the cash economy and thus more directly into the orbit of the government. Equally, enhanced government revenues, and the ensuing larger numbers of trained government employees, allowed for an increase in the number of programs that could bring benefits to the people of the region and, of course, larger portions of the population that could be brought under the government's control. Similarly, increased resources have enabled governments in Southeast Asia to acquire the technology and to train and expand the number of personnel – such as the military, police, customs and immigration officers, and finance officials – to monitor and direct cross-border activities.

The economic prosperity that suffused much of Southeast Asia during this period also appeared to enhance the political sovereignty of the institutional states' "miracle" economies of the region in two other ways. First, the massive flow of capital, technology, and information into Southeast Asia over the last decade has come from a variety of sources. And along with the investment has come increased transfers of various forms of technology, management expertise, production, and marketing information, as well as business values and practices. There has also been a rise in the amount of foreign news – often from the US, but also from places like Japan and Hong Kong – and also entertainment materials – including magazines, comic books, films, and computer games from the US and other parts of Asia. These media have flooded the region and, of course, embedded within their messages are particular social and cultural values.

For Southeast Asia, then, there are multiple, competing centers driving the globalization process (Prasert 1996: 6–7). The US is obviously very important. It has traditionally been a source of FDI and since the Vietnam War has been the major market for countries such as Singapore and Thailand. With US influence comes pressure to adopt neoliberal economic policies as well as political reforms – such as emphasizing individual human rights, workers rights, and an open competitive party system – that will conform more to Western liberal–democratic practices and provide the foundation for a neoliberal economic system. But in Southeast Asia the American neoliberal paradigm has its challengers. In particular, paradigms associated with the Japanese and the ethnic-Chinese community in East and Southeast Asia have become increasingly influential (Friedman, Chapter 13, this volume). The ideas and values associated with the Japanese and ethnic-Chinese paradigms place a high priority on the group or community and the preservation of harmonious social relations. Moreover, they see the rule of law as being relatively unimportant, arguing instead that economic exchanges, just like all social transactions, are governed by the social obligations that each person has to his or her immediate and extended family and to the wider society in which they live. (Hamilton 1991: 53; Jayasuriya 1996).

The competition among these major centers of capital, ideas, values, and practices, each of which drives its own version of globalization, created a certain amount of policy space for the institutional states of the economically successful Southeast Asian countries. This latitude for action is helped by the fact that Asian, North American, and European companies sought out Southeast Asian production and export platforms as much as the Southeast Asian states attempted to attract investors. Moreover, while there was some liberalization in terms of the lowering of tariff barriers, some of the reforms that are usually associated with neoliberalism, such as privatization, were given a decidedly Asian twist. Hence, for example, some governments proceeded with partial privatization to bring in needed foreign capital or privatized so that the governing party or close business associates of members of the government were beneficiaries. In other words, the pressures to produce both the economic and political reforms advocated in the neoliberal version of globalization were not so great as to force the economically successful institutional states in Southeast Asia to adopt wholesale policies prescribed by advocates of the neoliberal paradigm. Indeed, the governments of the region were very much in control of their economies, picking and choosing their policies from the different, competing globalization paradigms that permeated the region. Certainly, they were able to maintain more control over their economies and societies than might be expected.

Second, the capacity of Southeast Asia's institutional states to deflect external influences was not simply a function of the opportunities presented by competing economic paradigms. It was also the result of the development of a regional identity and the rise of regional organizations. In addition, a growing sense of their economic and strategic importance to the world's major powers gave Southeast Asian states the confidence to stand up to Western pressure for specific changes to their economic and political practices. During the 1990s there were a rising number of references to an increasingly vigorous "Asian consciousness and identity" (Funabashi 1993: 75). This growing regional awareness was spurred on by the series of cross-cutting regional investments that characterize East and Southeast Asia and facilitate the emergence of cross-national production networks and complexes, crucial shared cultural norms – including an emphasis on community, social order and harmony – and respect for authority (Hamilton 1991; Orrù 1991). These economic linkages and common political and social characteristics have encouraged governments of East and Southeast Asia to band together in order to ward off aspects of American-style neoliberalism and Western liberal–democratic political practices associated with globalization that run counter to their views of how their society, economy, and political systems should best be organized.

Based on this growing sense of regionalism, the institutional states of Southeast Asia began to collaborate in a number of formal settings, often with the institutional states in East Asia, to manage the impact of attempts to promote a globalized neoliberalism. Foremost among the organizations that were used by the Southeast Asian states is ASEAN. In the late 1980s and into the 1990s the growing international influence of the Southeast Asian countries, as other countries sought to increase trade links with the region, combined with the increased international emphasis on multilateralism and the fact that the Association was the only regional interstate organization to give ASEAN a pivotal role in international affairs.

Perhaps most significantly, ASEAN lies at the heart of the Asia–Pacific Economic Cooperation (APEC) process. In order to assuage fears that ASEAN would be superseded by APEC, an agreement was reached, when it was founded in 1989, that the APEC annual meetings would be hosted by an ASEAN member every second year. As the APEC process is essentially driven by the institutional state that hosts the annual summit in a particular year, and with an ASEAN state hosting the summit every second year, ASEAN's influence is considerable. In essence, the individual institutional states of the ASEAN members have been able to use the juridical equality of territorial sovereignty to gain a disproportionate influence over decision-making within APEC. Despite demands by the US, backed by Australia, Canada, and New Zealand, that APEC become an economic policy-setting body with enforceable neoliberal rules and regulations, the ASEAN members, supported by other Asian states, notably Japan, have ensured that APEC remains a forum for consultation, discussion, and voluntary action that is operated by consensus. The neoliberal agenda that has been at the center of the American proposals at APEC has, therefore, been turned aside by the concerted action of ASEAN institutional states (*Asiaweek*, December 8, 1995: 21–4; Hulme 1996)

In addition, ASEAN institutional states, often collectively, have been in the forefront in criticizing efforts to extend to all parts of the globe Western conceptions of human rights, democratic governance, and environmental standards. As the Malaysian Foreign Minister, Ahmad Badawi has noted: "Attempts to impose the standards of one side on the other tread upon the sovereignty of nations" (*Straits Times* (Singapore), July 23, 1991). By mobilizing opposition to the West, in such forums as the UN World Conference on Human Rights in Vienna and the UN Conference on Environment and Development in Rio, the ASEAN members have been able to parry bids to universalize Western standards of human rights, workers' rights, governance, and environmental protection.

Hence, a number of the pressures to undertake reforms that the institutional states of Southeast Asia saw as undermining their sovereignty were countered in the post-Plaza period through international action. Rising economic fortunes resulting from globalization increased the international prestige of the states of the region. Moreover, acting collectively through ASEAN, and less formal groupings of Asian and other Third World countries, the Southeast Asian states consolidated and extended their considerable power to direct their economy and regulate their society.

Period IV: the late 1990s economic crisis

In the late 1990s the forces of globalization proved once again that they can not only provide the opportunity and means to bolster the institutional state but can also undermine the state and its political sovereignty. In many ways the good times of the previous decade carried the seeds of the economic crisis that engulfed Southeast Asia in the late 1990s. Based on the wave of investment from Japan and their rapid economic growth, the emerging markets of Southeast Asia gained a global reputation during the 1990s as a very profitable place to invest. The herd instinct among investors meant that the large capital flows into the four "miracle" economies were not always accompanied by a full appreciation of the risks involved. At the same time, the sustained and heavy investment in the region from 1986–96 fueled inflated property and stock market values, a lax approach to domestic lending practices, and an excessive reliance on short-term foreign loans (International Monetary Fund 1998: 3). Importantly, urged on by the US and the major international financial institutions, the governments of the region had attempted to respond to what were argued to be the imperatives of globalization by liberalizing, and essentially privatizing, the financial system and opening up the capital account so that a rapidly increasing number of private domestic banks and finance companies gained access to a vast pool of largely short-term offshore funds (Montes 1998: xvii).

In early July 1997 a confluence of factors, including increasing competition from China's low-cost manufactured goods, the appreciation of the US dollar, and a widening current account deficit forced the Thai government to abandon its practice of pegging the baht to the US dollar. Within weeks the baht lost over a third of its value and a contagion effect produced significant declines in the value of other currencies in the region. The currency crisis forced investors to examine more closely the lax financial practices in the "miracle" economies. The rapidly dwindling value of the assets that had been used to secure private domestic loans and the problems of debt servicing became apparent and, based on a globally disseminated negative analyses of the situation, the herd instinct once again took over and investors fled the region. The currency crisis became a full-blown economic crisis.

The economic crisis has severely undermined the political sovereignty of the institutional state. The economic ministries and the central banks of Indonesia and Thailand have come under the tutelage of the International Monetary Fund (IMF). Just as importantly, the governments of Indonesia and Thailand came under considerable pressure from the IMF to clean up the corrupt practices that have bedeviled their economies in the past. Initially, the Malaysian government also decided to adopt some of the policies advocated by the IMF before eventually seeking to restore a measure of stability and to help revive the economy of the country by implementing a policy of foreign exchange controls. And Singapore, which has suffered more because of investment in, and trade with, its neighbors than because of lax financial practices, has declared that it will meet international banking standards, especially in terms of transparency and disclosure and the use of a more risk-focused approach to bank examination. While the IMF may have to back off from some of the strict measures it attempted to enforce in Indonesia and Thailand in the early days of the rescue package, it is clear that the governments of the two countries will have to accept much of the IMF's prescriptions for restoring their respective economies. This is the only way that confidence can be restored and international capital lured back to the region.

Not only have the governments of the "miracle" economies had to bow to external pressures, they have not had the support of either ASEAN or East Asian neighbors in dealing with the crisis that they might have expected. Certainly, among their East Asian allies the consensus has been that the only way that the governments of the "miracle" economies of Southeast Asia can restore investor confidence in the region is to accept the advice of the IMF and other key external authorities. In other words, they were urged to give up some of the political sovereignty they had acquired by their active membership in regional organizations.

However, it should not be assumed that each of the four institutional states being analyzed here suffered equally in terms of their loss of political sovereignty. The weaker the institutional state and the less political sovereignty it wielded the more its political sovereignty was eroded. Hence, Indonesian institutional state has lost a significant portion of its capacity to control activities within and across the borders of the country and to exclude external influences. The riots of May 1998, the government's inability to deal expeditiously with the meltdown in the banking system, and the need to call in the IMF and the World Bank to help solve the economic crisis and the severe food shortages are all indicative of the loss of political sovereignty suffered by the Indonesian state. While in Thailand the state has not been undermined as much as in Indonesia, the severity of the economic crisis has taken a considerable toll on the government's freedom to maneuver. Similarly, in Malaysia the prime minister, Mahathir Mohamad, has had to appreciate that lashing out at speculators gave the impression that the government was losing control and that such pronouncements cost the government and the Malaysian economy dearly. External market pressures cannot be ignored.

Singapore, however, while clearly also suffering a loss of political sovereignty, has fared much better. Its currency has depreciated the least; its banking system, although much weakened, remains relatively stable; and its strong institutional state has been able to maintain control of activities within the state and keep external influences from becoming more intrusive than they were already. Significantly, Singapore, an entrepôt, which has always valued free trade and the development of an open economy, recognizes the importance of accommodating the forces of globalization and technological change. As the deputy prime minister, Lee Hsien Loong, has argued in a speech to the Association of Banks in Singapore, "It is better to embrace liberalization proactively, at our own pace, than face the prospect of one day being swept away by the floodwaters of competition" (Lee (1998: http://www.4.gov.sg/mti/assnbank.html). Overall, then, it is important to note that the stronger the institutional state and the more sovereignty it had before the onset of the crisis the better it was able to weather the storm.

Conclusion

In order to gain a full understanding of the impact of globalization on the political sovereignty of institutional states, it is important not just to look at the last year or two but to employ an historical perspective. An analysis of the sovereignty of the four institutional states of Southeast Asia's "miracle" economies undertaken twenty-five years ago would have emphasized the degree to which they were subject to both internal and external threats to their security. On the economic front all four states relied heavily on producing or trading primary commodities with all the uncertainty and limitations on a state's economic policies that such a dependency entailed. However, over the last quarter century globalization has changed both the resources available to Southeast Asia's states and the international environment in which they have to operate. Security threats have disappeared as prosperity has eliminated many of the socioeconomic conditions that bred discontent, communism has retreated around the globe in the face of an expanding global economy, and Southeast Asia's "miracle" economies have diversified as export-manufacturing FDI has flooded the region. Relatively strong states have ensured that the economic boom times produced increased revenues. These increased revenues have, in turn, allowed the institutional states to exercise much more control over their territory and population and to participate actively in regional and international affairs.

Hence, globalization clearly had positive effects on the political sovereignty of the institutional states of Southeast Asia's "miracle" economies during the boom times. As Michael Mann (1997: 494) has noted while globalization may weaken "the most advanced nation states of the north," successful economic development has served to "strengthen nation-states elsewhere." For example, Malaysia was given the political space to implement its "New Economic Policy," which sought to maintain ethnic harmony by requiring that Malays be more active participants in the economy. Singapore as a small, vulnerable state gained in "Westphalian sovereignty" as its economic value to neighboring states became enhanced with its ability to capture and redirect global capital into the rest of the region. And the Thai and Indonesian institutional states were able to use the increased resources made available by the flood of investment into their economies to provide both carrot and stick so as to sharply reduce the threat from dissident groups within their borders.

Yet, as the two recessionary periods that have engulfed Southeast Asia in the last twenty-five years have demonstrated, globalization can have as many negative effects on the political sovereignty of institutional states as positive ones. Certainly, the economic crisis of the late 1990s has forced governments to bow to international market pressures and advice from international financial institutions and make some major changes to their economic, political, and social policies. Ironically, one of the changes that the international financial community has called for is that governments in the region exert greater control over domestic financial institutions and practices. They are being asked to do this just as their resources and their political sovereignty are being drastically reduced. And, perhaps even more importantly, the reduction in resources available to institutional states has jeopardized their ability to manage their economies and regulate their societies. Economic deprivation and social upheavals will undoubtedly lead to social and political disturbances. The virtuous spiral generated by the economic prosperity of the early 1990s may well give way to a vicious spiral of disorder and unrest unless the crisis is properly managed by all parties.

Certainly, the immediate prospects for the "miracle" economies do not look good. Japan, which has led the rise of the regional economy is itself in a recession and seems unable to regain its former economic dynamism. It is possible that capital from Greater China – Hong Kong, the People's Republic of China and Taiwan – will provide some boost to the flagging economies of Southeast Asia, and hence of course a growing threat to Japanese economic influence in the region, but it seems unlikely that the growth figures of the early 1990s will be repeated in the near future.

It is also important to note that the undermining of political sovereignty can place governments in the difficult position of having to accept policies that are alien to their society and culture. Whereas before the onset of the crisis, when they were being wooed by international capital, the institutional states of the "miracle" economies could pick and choose among the economic policies advanced by the US government, international financial institutions, Japanese advisers, and ethnic Chinese investors, now, in order to regain a measure of confidence in their economies, they must accept policies that may not fit in with their social mores and cultural values. In addition, there is a fear in Southeast Asia that without the political sovereignty to make their own decisions relatively free of external pressures, the institutional states of the region will once again become battle grounds for fights over economic and security influence among the competing centers – US, Europe, Japan, and China – driving their own particular versions of globalization.

All of which is to argue that there should be no automatic assumptions made about the impact of globalization on state sovereignty. As the experience of the institutional states of Southeast Asia demonstrates, globalization can, over time, be both a positive and a negative force. Perhaps most instructively, the impact of globalization on Southeast Asia suggests that the stronger the state and the more political sovereignty it has, the more it is able to transform its society so as to adapt to, and even at times take advantage of, the globalization process.

Notes

1 Thanks are due to Kim Richard Nossal, Tony Porter, Grace Skogstad, Dave Smith, Dorothy Solinger, Steve Topik, and an anonymous reader from Routledge for their comments on earlier drafts of this chapter; Klarka Zeman for her research assistance; and the Social Science Research Council of Canada for research funding.

References

ASEAN–Japan Centre (1992/1996) *ASEAN–Japan Statistical Pocketbook*, Tokyo: ASEAN Promotion Centre on Trade, Investment and Tourism.

Biersteker, T.J. and Weber, C. (1996) "The social construction of state sovereignty," in T.J. Biersteker and C. Weber (eds) *State Sovereignty as Social Construct*, Cambridge: Cambridge University Press, pp. 1–21.

Camilleri, J.A. (1990) "Rethinking sovereignty in a shrinking, fragmented world," in R.B.J. Walker and S.H. Mendlovitz (eds) *Contending Sovereignties: Redefining Political Community*, Boulder, CO: Lynne Reiner, pp. 13–44.

Cox, R.W (1997) "A perspective on globalization," in J.H. Mittleman (ed.) *Globalization: Critical Reflections*, Boulder, CO: Lynne Reiner, pp. 21–30.

Funabashi, Y. (1993) "The Asianization of Asia," *Foreign Affairs* 72, November/December.

Hamilton, G.G. (1991) "The organizational foundations of Western and Chinese commerce: A historical and comparative analysis," in G.G. Hamilton (ed.) *Business Networks and Economic Development in East and Southeast Asia*, Hong Kong: Centre of Asian Studies, University of Hong Kong, pp. 48–65.

Huff, W.G. (1994) *The Economic Growth of Singapore: Trade and Development in the Twentieth Century*, Cambridge: Cambridge University Press.

Hulme, D. (1996) "Asia takes charge of the APEC train," *Asian Business* 26: 32–5, January.

International Monetary Fund (1997) *International Financial Statistics*, Washington: International Monetary Fund, May.

—— (1998) *World Economic Outlook*, Washington: International Monetary Fund, May.

Jackson, R.H. (1990) *Quasi-States: Sovereignty, International Relations, and the Third World*, Cambridge: Cambridge University Press.

Jayasuriya, K. (1996) "The rule of law and capitalism in East Asia," *The Pacific Review* 9 (3): 367–88.

Jomo K.S. (1987) "Economic crisis and policy response in Malaysia," in R. Robison, K. Hewison, and R. Higgott (eds) *Southeast Asia in the 1980s: The Politics of Economic Crisis*, Sydney: Allen and Unwin, pp. 113–48.

Lapidoth, R. (1995) "Redefining authority: the past, present and future of sovereignty," *Harvard International Review* 3: 8–11, 70, Summer.

MacIntyre, A.J. and K. Jayasuriya (eds) (1992) *The Dynamics of Economic Policy Reform in South-east Asia and the South-west Pacific*, Kuala Lumpur: Oxford University Press.

Mann, M. (1997) "Has globalization ended the rise and rise of the nation-state?" *Review of International Political Economy* 4 : 472–96, Autumn.

Migdal, J.S. (1988) *Strong Societies and Weak States: State–Society Relations and State Capabilities in the Third World*, Princeton: Princeton University Press.

Milne, R.S. and Mauzy, D.K. (1990) *Singapore: The Legacy of Lee Kuan Yew*, Boulder, CO: Westview.

Montes, M.F. (1998) *The Currency Crisis in Southeast Asia*, revised edn, Singapore: Institute of Southeast Asian Studies.

Muscat R.J. (1990) *Thailand and the United States: Development , Security and Foreign Aid*, New York: Columbia University Press.

Ohmae, K. (1990) *The Borderless World: Power and Strategy in the Interlinked Economy*, London: Harper Collins.

Orrù, M. (1991) "Practical and theoretical aspects of Japanese business networks," in G.G. Hamilton (ed.) *Business Networks and Economic Development in East and Southeast Asia*, Hong Kong: Centre of Asian Studies, University of Hong Kong, pp. 244–71.

Pasuk P. (1992) "Technocrats, businessmen and generals: democracy and economic policy-making in Thailand," in A.J. MacIntyre and K. Jayasuriya (eds) *The Dynamics of Economic Policy Reform in South-east Asia and the South-west Pacific*, Kuala Lumpur: Oxford University Press, pp. 10–31.

Prasert C. (1996) "Challenge of and response to globalization: The case of Southeast Asia," paper presented to the ISA-JAIR Joint Convention, Makuhari, Japan, September 20–22, 1996.

Robison, R. (1986) *Indonesia: The Rise of Capital*, Sydney: Allen and Unwin.

Robison, R., Higgott, R., and Hewison, K. (1987) "Crisis in economic strategy in the 1980s: the factors at work," in R. Robison, K. Hewison and R. Higgott (eds) *Southeast Asia in the 1980s: The Politics of Economic Crisis*, Sydney: Allen and Unwin pp. 1–15.

Rosenau, J.N. (1995) "Sovereignty in a turbulent world," in G.M. Lyons and M. Mastanduno (eds) *Beyond Westphalia: State Sovereignty and International Intervention*, Baltimore: Johns Hopkins University Press.

Scholte, J.A. (1997) "Global capitalism and the state," *International Affairs* 73: 427–52, July.

Skocpol, T. (1979) *States and Social Revolutions: A Comparative Analysis of France, Russia and China*, Cambridge: Cambridge University Press.

Snodgrass, D.R. (1980) *Inequality and Economic Development in Malaysia*, Kuala Lumpur: Oxford University Press.

Strange, S. (1996) *The Retreat of the State: The Diffusion of Power in the World Economy*, Cambridge: Cambridge University Press.

Stubbs, R. (1989) *Hearts and Minds in Guerrilla Warfare: The Malayan Emergency 1948–1960*, Singapore: Oxford University Press.

Stubbs, R. and Underhill, G.R.D. (1994) "State policies and global changes," in R. Stubbs and G.R.D. Underhill (eds) *Political Economy and the Changing Global Order*, New York: St. Martin's Press, pp. 421–24.

Thomson, J.E. (1994) *Mercenaries, Pirates and Sovereigns: State Building and Extraterritorial Violence in Early Modern Europe*, Princeton: Princeton University Press.

Weiss, L. (1998) *The Myth of the Powerless State: Governing the Economy in a Global Era*, Oxford: Polity Press.

World Bank (1993) *The East Asian Miracle: Economic Growth and Public Policy*, Policy Research Report, Washington DC: The World Bank.

13 Reinterpreting the Asianization of the world and the role of the state in the rise of China

Edward Friedman

The role of the state

Fascination with out-of-control globalization, a combination of new and volatile international finance and Keynesian macroeconomic levers that no longer work for governments as they did during the Golden Age of the Bretton Woods era when growth came with equity, can easily lead to the conclusion that states no longer have power and that "now it is the markets which...are the masters over the governments" (Strange 1996: 4). Neoliberals on the right celebrate the change; social democrats on the left decry it. The Asian financial turmoil at the end of the twentieth century may seem to prove that Asia's post-Second World War state-leveraged growth with equity is no longer possible. Yet the continuing rise of China in the last third of the twentieth century, even after Richard Nixon ended the Bretton Woods fixed link of the dollar to gold on August 15, 1971, suggests that it is important not to ignore how much governments can still do to facilitate wealth with equity (Evans 1995; Friedman 1996: 413–17). Structural adjustment programs (SAPs), which overly weaken a state, can hurt a nation's capacity to grow (Haggard and Kaufman 1995). Governments are needed to build institutions that respond to international challenges, to facilitate the rise of sunrise industries, to manage the currency, and to build needed infrastructure, including suitable support for education and research.

A strong state is not an authoritarian or parasitic state. A strong state is one with the capacity to formulate, legitimate, and implement crucial policies. South Korea under the patriotic tyrant, Syngman Rhee, in the 1950s was not a strong state. Rhee wounded the Korean people, making them what the World Bank considered a basket case. The regime was corrupt and ineffective. The subsequent Park dictatorship was, at first, brutal but capable. It built a technocratic civil service, forged government-business alliances and fostered, at least temporarily, popular legitimation for policies of all-out growth in quiet emulation of Japan, policies that could be facilitated by a new, strong state capacity.

A similar capacity existed in a democratic Japan. The issue is not democracy or dictatorship. South Korean authoritarians ignored Japan's democratic, political regime. There is no relationship between strong state capacity and form of political regime. A strong state can be democratic or not, although, over time, the accountability of democracy may make it easier to check cronyist corruption that otherwise could entrench narrow, selfish interests unwilling or incapable of responding to rapidly changing international economic forces. State-leveraging for wealth expansion must be market-regarding. In sum, strong state capacity and state effectiveness should not be confused with the very different issues of either proactive government action in the economy or regime form, that is, democracy or dictatorship.

This simple reality, the absolute distinction between state capacity and political form, means that two popular sets of ideologies are clearly not true. The pundits who claim that authoritarianism is the essence of the Asian development state are wrong. Japan was democratic (Friedman 1994; Kohno 1997). Equally wrong are the pundits who insist that only the good governance of democracy makes growth possible. A democracy is no guarantee of success. India is proof enough. Corrupt ties between top state administrators, criminal elements, and major corporate conglomerates, *keiretsu*, also made it difficult for Japan in the 1990s to come to grips with its bursting financial bubble for fear that all these groups, and their political party patrons and agents, would be discredited and possibly imprisoned. Japan, therefore, kept stagnating after its financial bubble burst in 1991.

Another claim that finds no support from the East Asian experience is that growth automatically evolves into democracy. The people of the Philippines, the harbinger of the 1980s democratic movements in Korea, Taiwan, and China, reacted against an authoritarianism that was "cronyist" and economically debilitating; it impoverished most Filipinos. The Philippines democratized when the economy declined, as did most of Latin America in the 1980s and 1990s. Much of the force that has made for late twentieth-century democratization, far from being a result of natural evolution from economic success, has, in fact, been a response to economic failure. Although Taiwan is usually considered a counter-example, in fact, Taiwan's most militant democrats in the 1970s doubted that Taiwan had prospered economically. The same is true with Korea. The fighters for democracy in both Taiwan and Korea did not experience democracy as the ripened fruit of a tree of happy and successful economic growth.

That certain kinds of wishful thinking about links between economy and polity are not true does not mean that there is no link between economy and polity. It is indeed true that when economic growth is somewhat equitable, and when the countryside is not dominated by large estates that repress rural labor, making it dependent and immobile, then that kind of mobile and equitable economy makes it easier for democrats to find a popular base, and makes it easier for dictators to leave power knowing that there are plenty of places in society in which they can still enjoy the good life (Moore 1966; Paige 1997). Leaving power, then, need not mean losing wealth and influence.

To be sure, growth can be part of these facilitating conditions. But economic developments that ease a democratic breakthrough are neither necessary nor sufficient causes of democratization. A political transition must still be won by brave people in a political struggle that, sadly, almost always produces martyrs before it produces success. The notion that free markets naturally evolve into free polities is not supported by data from the history of democratization.

Besides, markets are not free. They are, as Polanyi showed long ago, always embedded differentially by institutions, laws and policies. Each piece of embedding is a most political act. The continuing centrality of the state, of policy, and of political institutions is highlighted by the rise of China as part of a resurgent Asianization of the world, that is, the return of Asia to a global centrality that had been lost only in the nineteenth century (Frank 1998). Only then did strong, modern nation states in Europe lead the world in steel, military strength, and rising living standards.

Yet, the conventional wisdom of Anglo-American economics, running a gamut from Susan Strange to Paul Krugman (Krugman 1994), rejects this central historical fact, the persistence of Asian strength. The financial meltdown in Asia during the 1990s reinforces a misleading notion of Asia's rise as a flash in the pan. While Strange finds that post-Bretton Woods globalization (asymmetric interdependence) cripples the state and Krugman finds that the nineteenth-century globalization of telegraph and steam engine still define economic relations, both find nothing to learn from in the rise of Asia, which Strange attributes merely to luck and to American largesse, even though the World Bank in the early 1990s projected that by 2020 five of the seven largest economies in the world would be in Asia: Japan, China, India, Indonesia, and Korea. Perhaps it will prove as wrong to dismiss the rise of Asia into the twenty-first century as it was to conclude that the Great Depression meant the end of the rise of Western Europe and North America. It is not easy to see long-term forces and trends.

Krugman claims that the leveraging of state capacity in East Asia – as in Soviet-style command economies – has not led to any productivity growth. That claim ignores the quantitative data (Jefferson and Singh 1997) and the eye-witness observation of how ending Mao-era command-economy economic irrationality has led to an extraordinary rise of living standards all over China, including most of the rural poor, who were locked into stagnant misery by Mao-era anti-market policies. My own investigations in China since just before reform began substantiate the incontrovertible data on China's real rise in material well-being.

Yet, Strange and Krugman agree that governance in East Asia has nothing to teach, even though East Asia was the dynamo of the world economy in the two decades following the end of the Bretton Woods system, with European–Asian trade greater than European–American trade, as American–Asian trade was also greater than American–European trade. And intra-Asian trade was greater than any of the just-mentioned dyads. The indisputable fact of a risen Asia requires explanation.

Krugman (1994) concedes that China "in recent years posted truly impressive rates of economic growth" including "dramatic improvements in efficiency" such that a continuation of present trends means that "by the year 2010 its economy will be a third larger than ours." (Given the late twentieth-century Asian economic slow-down, economists pushed the date of China's successful catch-up back a decade or two.) Krugman then tries to discredit the numbers, arguing that one should not calculate Chinese growth from 1978 when it began but from 1964, when Mao ruled, a method showing "only modest growth in efficiency." But why calculate from 1964? In 1964–5 Mao initiated an economically irrational war mobilization known as the third front, that devastated China's economy. It was only at the very end of 1978 that post-Mao leaders reformed collective agriculture and opened up to the dynamism of East Asian policies, institutions, and spillover. No serious economist doubts China's impressive efficiency growth since 1979. Indeed, understanding the role of East Asian states in Asia's extraordinary rise is a prerequisite for seeing who will win or lose in our new age. Losers, in this volatile world, however, can include strong states that become corrupt states when power-holders care for their own bottom line rather than the common weal of the nation.

Parochial analysts elsewhere do not comprehend the growing Asian consensus that, after a short European interregnum, the great civilizations of Asia, as throughout recorded history, once again are to be the decisive factors in the world market (perhaps as an integrated Asia-Pacific and Eurasia). Rulers in Beijing, however, are committed to not permitting Japan to be the hegemon of an Asian twenty-first century. Communist Party leaders in China mean to have China on top. National pride and ambition have been central to the rise of Japan, Korea, and China. Nationalisms, as Europeans so painfully learned from the Franco-Prussian War to the Second World War, can conflict violently. Here again, the nature of the state is a central matter. How, then, has the state factored in to the complex rise of China?

Government policy

The twin crises of debt and inflation that crippled so much of the developing world in the late 1970s and early 1980s did not strike a still-isolated People's Republic. An autarkic Mao-era China also avoided the 1970s international loan fever that left East and Central Europe subsequently facing a crushing debt burden after two oil price spikes ignited a commodity cartel fervor that was followed by a painful global depression, with the combination putting socialist Europe, as the import substitution states of Latin America and Sub-Saharan African primary commodity exporters, in desperate straits. Fortuitously for the Chinese, Mao so hated money and the ultra left was so weighty that China did not take big loans, even in the era after the 1973–4 OPEC price spike.

Contingent factors, Mao's ideology, and the power balance at China's state center, were beneficial to China's later rise and carry some general lessons. It is dangerous for nations to rely overly on volatile, liquid capital. While post-Mao China has been market-oriented, it has, as the Asian states it emulates, also abjured a major foreign presence in loans, stocks and bonds.

It is close to impossible, however, to avoid the impact of globalized capital in the post-1985 era of new financial instruments and of the instantaneous movement of capital beyond government reach. The kind of state institutions and policies that had worked for East Asia into the mid-1980s had to be reformed to meet the challenges of a new age, a particular reality hidden by those who love or hate overly abstract notions such as capitalism or the free market, broad abstractions that obscure actually decisive forces. How a national entity handles money in the new age is crucial. Policies and institutions continue to be decisive. The mix of state intervention and market orientation practiced by Asian nations that historically served them so well has to adapt to a rapidly changing global reality. That quite specific new reality is not usefully captured by flabby and vague totalizing terms such as capitalism or socialism that overlook the impact of changing particular dynamics, either international finance or new technologies.[1]

China was better positioned to take advantage of the new opportunities because, both in the Mao era and in the post-Mao era, it practiced tight fiscal restraints to avoid inflation. In so doing, China was taking the path of East Asia ever since the 1880 Matsukata reforms in Japan, when the Japanese government chose to privatize state-owned enterprises in order to guarantee that state revenues would remain in balance and that inflation would be avoided (Wu 1994). In a sense, China, as all of successful East Asia, imposed an IMF-style structural adjustment program (SAP) on itself. The IMF came to consider Beijing to be an SAP honor student, although, in fact, the benefits of fiscal discipline were self-imposed. By imposing the pain of change itself, China avoided a politics of scapegoating needed reforms as alien impositions. The politics of avoiding populist nativism during institutional restructuring is a vital matter.

Yet the new forms of capital could derail a China that may be developing its own financial bubble, as did Japan, Thailand, Korea, Indonesia, and Malaysia in the 1990s (Henderson 1998). The Chinese economy cannot forever subsidize money-losing state-owned enterprises (SOEs) and allow its banking system to go bankrupt (Hughes 1998; Lardy 1998). Entrenched interests that block continual adaptation can bring an economic rise to an end. Terms like capitalism or socialism highlight industrial production with or against the market, but slight the huge independent power of finance, in addition to technology, state capacity and policy choices *vis-à-vis* the global market. An economic rise is not the result of an autonomous industrial system that operates in isolation from these many other large forces.

While I sympathize with governments that fear IMF-promoted SAPs that have no safety nets for the vulnerable, the lesson of China's rise, in particular, and East Asia's, in general, is that it is the role of government to make fiscal discipline acceptable to the nation at large. Politicians have to develop policy packages that make relatively low inflationary growth economically possible and politically palatable. A government that imagines the forces of growth as a foreign plague to be kept out of a pure nation cripples the nation's capacity to run rapidly and move ahead.

An SAP does not inevitably and uniquely make a state weak. Out-of-control inflation far more often discredits and destroys the state, as occurred in pre-Mao China. Post-Mao China was fortunate. A fiscally restrained China, a socialism very different from Gorbachev's Russia, could enter the post-Mao era of reform without the burden of debt and inflation that hobbled post-socialist states elsewhere, turning prior command economy-generated latent inflation into an explosion of hyperinflation. Such decisive and unique Chinese factors are invisible to those who only see polar dichotomies such as capitalism/socialism and state/market. Suitable government policy is a crucial ingredient of all market-oriented success. There is, to be sure, no continuing rise without a market orientation. To highlight the centrality of the state is not to ignore the importance of getting certain economic numbers right.

Another Chinese advantage in embarking on policies of reform in an age of globalization was the structure of agriculture. It was similar to that of East Asia in its post-Second World War dynamism. Mao had won control of the state by wooing villagers with programs that subverted the power of large landed interests such that, between 1938 and 1952, rural China had become (and was internally referred to as) something of a petty bourgeois paradise (Friedman *et al.* 1991). Thus, the kind of landed elites who benefit from an overvalued currency so that their luxury imports of items such as a Mercedes-Benz should be cheap, did not dominate post-Mao rural China or elsewhere in rapidly rising parts of post-Second World War East Asia. China could initiate post-Mao reforms without landed elites, which tend toward political coalitions that almost make impossible growth based on global openness and competitively priced industrial products.

Here again, one finds a complex state–market nexus that belies a stark opposition of statist socialism versus free-market capitalism. In contrast to a Philippines elite tied to old, large landed interests, Beijing could, with inflation manageable and the countryside dynamized by small proprietors, carry out East Asian style export-oriented industrialization (EOI). Successful EOI requires an undervalued currency to maximize foreign exchange earnings from exports. China could implement this policy because the socioeconomic forces that usually have the political clout to oppose that policy hardly existed in China. Government and policy, as shaped by path dependent forces, were decisive.

Export earnings could then be translated, often by corrupt elements seen as siphoning off too large a share of national wealth, into upgrading technology, infrastructure, science education and other productive areas that benefited from high-cost imports. Less important than the source of the original foreign exchange earnings is whether the state helps channel reinvestment to upgrade the economy. Too much corruption can end the flow of assets in wealth-expanding directions. The post-Mao explosion of productive efficiency, however, was overwhelming. No longer dependent, as in the Mao era, for export earnings from primary products such as tungsten and hogs, redundant rural primary producers could, in the post-Mao era, enter work that produced more value, while land could be turned to higher-value production. Wealth expanded even for most of the rural poor, although a chauvinist policy of grain self-sufficiency kept millions of farmers far poorer than need be.

This summary of policies conducive to China's rise and continuing problems in an age of globalization highlights the centrality of the state, that is, of domestic politics, of policies, and of national institutions. Scapegoating globalist forces, whose threat is quite real, can call attention away from the items within the purview of a government that it can change to the benefit of its own people. The point is not that there are no global forces that can overwhelm nations with financial volatility and income polarization (Grieder 1997),[2] but that, however crucial those factors are, they do not exhaust the arenas in which governments can act to enhance the wealth of their people.

Analysts do not agree on the relative significance of the recent extraordinary changes in lead market sectors, in the international division of labor, in the end of the Bretton Woods boom, and in the spread of extraordinarily rapid systems of communication and transportation. These new forces have altered the world. Yet, great weight in this debate on a new global political economy should go to the finding that since China, as part of a second tier of newly industrializing Asian countries such as Thailand, Malaysia, and Indonesia, could rise rapidly in the 1980s and 1990s by institutions, policies, and linkages pioneered by Japan, Taiwan, South Korea, Hong Kong, and Singapore in the Bretton Woods era, then, at a minimum, state actions have not completely lost their extraordinary relevance. Government continues to matter very much, both for the better and for the worse. Both have been seen in Asia.

The political capacity to rise

Asian success is the core of late twentieth-century globalization. The rise of most of the 1.3 billion Chinese confounds the notion that the previously poor cannot rise in the age of globalization that erupted into human consciousness beginning in the late 1960s and early 1970s. Yet globalist analysts tend to be Eurocentrists who imagine a threat "posed by East Asia economies" (Jessup 1997: 571). They do not focus on a once-stagnant China's spectacular performance that has raised the living standards of hundreds of millions of people and instead chant a chorus of global pessimism. Since China, nearing the end of the Mao era, was locked into massive poverty similar to the other absolutely poorest parts of the world (Friedman 1987), the great and recent achievement of post-Mao China, especially for the poorest of the poor (Kristof and Wu Dunn 1994) challenges pessimistic conclusions about globalism.

While global finance can treat states with large imbalanced budgets savagely and neoliberalism's formula is both one-sided and brutal, the view that the poor can no longer rise ignores the complaint of richer societies – including Japan and Hong Kong – where workers fear hollowing out because good jobs are moving and raising up once-poor people. Might this be imagined as part of a potentially equalizing global rise? Even Strange now finds that transnational corporations "redistribute wealth from the developed industrialized countries to the poorer developed ones" (Strange 1996: 54). Lipietz agrees that low-wage countries that rejected "subcontracting production" via the "internationalization of productive processes" locked themselves out of the dynamics of growth (Lipietz 1997). Even Greider grants that globalization has allowed Asia, home to most of the world's poor, to rise (Greider 1997). Globalization, then, is both risk and opportunity.

Poor people in China, whose per capita income and trade dependency ratio were similar to India's at the death of Mao Zedong, have, in the age of globalization, competed so well that China became the number one recipient of non-liquid direct foreign investment in the world from 1986 for more than a decade. China has linked into the benefits of borrowing best practices, continuous upgrading, foreign direct investment and other global dynamics such that, by 1997, China had the second largest foreign exchange reserves in the world. As with Japan, state leverage was used to facilitate a transfer – albeit, not always a legal one – of productive technologies. The Chinese increasingly face the twenty-first century with enormous self-confidence, angry at outsiders who will not acknowledge that the twenty-first century is likely to be one in which the previously poor people of China take a central role on the global stage. Consequently, it is vital to understand why a poor China, integrated into a dynamic Asia–Pacific, could perform so well in the age of globalization, especially for the poorest of the poor. The poor everywhere have a stake in comprehending China's post-Mao rise.

Yet, even China's great gains have carried costs that could threaten to eradicate success. As the opportunities should not be gainsaid, so the risks are quite potent. There is a fear that an experience of regional polarization or greed by the cronies of power-holders in China could sunder the nation or unleash an anti-openness backlash (Friedman forthcoming). Globalization, even for the successful, is painful and perilous. This contradictory reality calls for a clarification of specifics that are confused and blurred by extreme simplifications, imagining a choice only between market or state, capitalism or socialism, globalization or protectionist self-reliance. State and market are complexly entangled in a China benefiting from deep involvement with the world market.

China at the inception of globalization

In 1968, Mao Zedong called off the vigilante blood-letting of his class-struggle version of war communism. Mao's autarkic, anti-imperialist commandist socialism was bankrupt. What then exploded in China, as also in much of the similarly bankrupt socialist bloc dominated from Moscow, has been dubbed the informal sector. In China, this meant that local officials, to get around economically irrational aspects of the Leninist state, colluded with local people who produced, transported, and marketed artificially scarce items in high demand all over the land. In China, this pervasive dynamic of "informalization" was blocked not by the state, a misleadingly essentialized concept, but by a particular set of market-disregarding institutions, interests, and policies that included some of the state. Any state has contradictory forces. But certain local governments in China, from Fengyuan in Anhui to Wenzhou in Zhejiang, facilitated local entrepreneurs already in the late Mao era.

Although the Leninist center in China launched campaigns in the early 1970s to destroy this burgeoning informal economy, campaigns "to cut capitalist tails," such movements were honored only in form in areas such as Wenzhou in

Zhejiang province, regions less tied in to tight networks loyal to anti-market central leaders. Hence, political distance from a commandist state facilitated success for market-oriented societal forces tied to local parts of the state structure. It is impossible to comprehend the rise of China in terms of state versus market. Only by disaggregating the state and finding how particular parts of the state furthered informalization and pressured for an end to war-communism policies by power-holders at the state center can one find the fissures and alliances across state and market that facilitated China's rise. Between 1968 and 1970 allies of rural petty proprietors began to seize the initiative at the state center (Friedman *et al.* forthcoming).

Openness to the scum of the earth

All accounts of China's rise describe the "open policy" as its core, forgetting crucial domestic factors, such as combining efficient rural marketization with the continued subsidization out of the wealth of society of money-losing SOEs. Believers in all-or-nothing notions of a good market versus a bad state kept predicting the implosion of China's reform success if SOEs were not swiftly privatized (James Kynge, "Two-speed China emerges as state factories are shut or sold," *Financial Times*, June 16, 1998). Swiftness aside, the SOE burden is a serious matter. Reformers in China, however, could not politically challenge the elite networks of ruling-party comrades, ministries, and provincial power-holders that lived off inefficient SOEs. Reformers acted much as the Government on Taiwan had long acted, permitting new enterprises (greenfieldization) gradually to reduce the weight of the SOEs (Goldman 1994: Chapter 4). Waste seemed the price of stable progress. The state subsidized waste. It bought off potential opponents of reform. Corrupt waste, an undertheorized topic, bought political peace, a *sina qua non* to reassure long-term foreign direct investment. The state/market binary misleads. What to marketeers may seem pure waste, may be, to political leaders promoting reform, the price of elite acquiescence in a larger reform package. Yet, that political waste, often involved in criminality, could eventually delegitimate the state. In general, touters of an East Asian development state idealize the state and understate corrosive costs such as criminality and corruption. The romanticizers make East Asia seem an inimitable world of virtue and discipline that can not be achieved elsewhere (Friedman 1996). Asian success should be analyzed in all its actual conflictual complexity.

Adam Smith argued in *The Wealth of Nations* that entrenched mercantilist privileging of friends of the court with rent-taking state monopolies could impede growth, intensify economic inequality, and delegitimate the system. It has happened in South Korea. It threatens Taiwanese and Japanese power-holders. It is occurring in China, too. Yet even with corruption, one must distinguish anti-economic payoffs to political networks that bleed the economy from corruption that greases the wheels of economic dynamism. Much Chinese corruption keeps the economy going when political institutions fail.

Let me exemplify this generalization with an instance from personal experience. Local governments are ordered by Beijing to rebuild rural bridges so they can bear the weight of heavy trucks hauling containers to ships at ocean ports. Upgrading facilities brings the poor hinterland into the dynamism of China's export-oriented growth. State power promotes an infrastructure that will engender wealth expansion.

But the center does not provide sufficient funds for local agents of the state to pay construction workers. Regularly villagers are dragooned into unpaid labor service by a coercive local state. The workers lose other money-earning opportunities during their stint of corvée labor. They resent it. They blame local power-holders. The local officials have to prove to local people that the government is not ripping off the people. During or after the forced labor, the workers, often with the support of the local party, unofficially impress tolls on all out-of-region vehicles. They stop such traffic and hold up the drivers, using the threat of physical violence. They recoup from outsiders the cost of lost income.

Yet the coercive criminality could some day threaten national unity as it legitimates people in the regions seeking justice by associating with local groups capable of "protection." The regional forces only rip off those from outside the region. The political contradictions of economic reform, therefore, make it premature to dub China a case of reform success, even though there is no reason to doubt the reality of China's sustained and explosive growth. The contradictions of state policy combine with an incomplete logic of economic reform so as to infuse painful regional income gaps with a scapegoating and stereotyping logic of mistrustful regional identities.

Local identities intensify as a result of failings of the central state and the stigmatizing of outsiders. Disorder spreads. Outsiders are scapegoated. The contradictory consequence of successful growth in China, within a largely unreformed Leninist apparatus, is an explosion of outrage at "them," those up there, outsiders, those responsible for the policies which seem to treat "us," real people who labor here, unjustly. "They" are seen as alien, denounced as corrupt, imagined as profiteering by enriching themselves at the price of selling "us" out. Even as people rise rapidly, they experience polarization as a plot of undeserving rich at the state center. Virtually all opposition to the government in Beijing in the 1980s denounced ruling groups for betraying China and serving Japan (Whiting 1989). Given the weight of anti-Japanese sentiment in the legitimation of Chinese nationalism, a passion that is the heir of a war to liberate the nation from Japanese invaders, the popular experience of "them" as "pro Japanese" is a strong negative hanging over ruling groups.

Non-Asians often wrongly presume that the cultural models of modernization are invariably Western. Karaoke, a Japanese cultural creation, however, have spread. I was at a karaoke in a region that suffered the murderous slaughter of Japan's 1942 "Three All" campaign, a region full of families where multiple generations have served and sacrificed in the Chinese military, going back to the days of the anti-Japan war, when a Japanese businessman rose in the government's karaoke and sang in Japanese. Everyone had to applaud. The locals wanted the businessman to build a factory. But they hated, truly hated, wooing the business. There are great tensions just beneath the surface of China's fabulous reform success.

Young Chinese girls go to beauty parlors and survey Japanese fashion magazines to see what they should look like so as not to be a backward bumpkin. To the elders, these young women are being made immoral, made into Japanese. And if the younger generation instead takes its cues to the future from visions of Hong Kong found in popular Hong Kong movies, that, too, can be felt as the immoral fruit of imperialism by elders discombobulated by change. These elders believe that while patriotic Chinese sacrificed to fight off Americans in Korea and to fend off Russians from the north, Hong Kong people got fat off imperialism. They, the rich of the south, are imagined in the rural north as "whores" selling out to ill-willed foreigners.

While brothels in China mainly serve poor Chinese workers, as they previously served locals in early industrialization in Paris or London, prostitutes are seen popularly as the plaything of foreign exploiters, who are literally penetrating China. It seems shameful. Strikes mainly explode in factories owned by Asian neighbors. "They" are exploitative. "They" are imagined as some syntheses of the narcotraffickers of the Opium War and the brutal invaders from Japan. Feeling victimized, even as they rise, humiliated Chinese seek justice, not an aping of immoral aliens.

In a passionately reactive nationalism, many Chinese are way ahead of their government in wanting the twenty-first century to be a Chinese century, not a Japanese century. Ordinary folk feel morally superior to ruling groups who try to tamp down patriotic anti-Japanese passions such as opposition to Japanese occupation of disputed islands in the East China Sea or visits by the heirs of wartime Japanese Emperor, Hirohito. Loyal Chinese contrast themselves to rulers, who are presumed to be selfish and traitorous. China's super-patriotism of the 1990s is spontaneous and from below. Ruling groups who might wish to promote the benefits of peaceful international exchange feel compelled to stand up vigorously for China against Japan or Taiwan or America. As with a rising Europe of the late nineteenth century, a future of peaceful progress in Asia is far from certain. Passionate competitive nationalism augurs far less happy outcomes. A prolonged rise does not preclude periods of great economic deflation or international war.

The world market can seem less like a benefit to many Chinese and more like a sell-out to foreigners. The government inadvertently pours oil on this fire of chauvinism by blaming problems – AIDS, drugs, juvenile delinquency, disrespect for elders, the abandonment of the aged, divorce, prostitution – on foreigners. Despite economic success, Chinese can feel globalization as a traumatic rupture reminiscent of immoralities such as Britain's Opium War against China and Japan's Nanjing Massacre. China, a major beneficiary of globalization, is, none the less, still threatened by a backlash against globalization. A successful economic rise requires a masterful politics. It is not just a matter of getting the numbers right.

Because the creative destruction of rapid growth brings so much discombobulating change, because reform out of command economy irrationalities inevitably turns many hard-working people into losers, there is a huge potential for reactionary, nostalgic hate-filled mobilizations. The growth of so much potential for domestic and global mischief is a warning about why global forces require governance so that macroeconomic levers of policy that can bring growth with equity are again in play for national governments. If not, post-Bretton Woods growth is subject to all the strains that in earlier generations ended in mercantilist, war-prone, beggar-thy-neighbor policies that led to depression, fascism, and war. A rapid rise need not be smooth or peaceful.

Those getting wealthy in China are popularly imagined as anti-imperialism had imagined the rich – traitors devoid of authentic Chinese culture, sellers-out of the nation, frequenters of karaoke and prostitutes, paid agents of unscrupulous and contemptuous foreigners, people defiling innocent Chinese women. There is thus much to which brown–red demagogues can appeal, combining a romanticization of the past with an anti-foreign hard line. Rising through globalization is experienced by chauvinists as a privileging of the scum of the sacred Chinese earth. In this perspective, the Japanese, who launched an all-out invasion of China in 1937, are unrepentant savage invaders, holocaust deniers, and a continuing threat. Proud young Chinese males feel, much as Israeli sabras, "never again *to me*." Investors in China can seem to nativists like immoral oppressors.

To revanchist patriots, East Asia is not a model to be emulated. Taiwanese, in this backlash Chinese perspective, are the brutal and reactionary exploiters who deservedly lost the Chinese civil war, traitors who hide out on an island where their survival depends on obeisance to the arrogant and imperialistic Americans (partners and heirs of the Opium War British) and allegiance to the anti-Chinese Japanese, whose goal, official Chinese propaganda asserts, is to restore Japanese hegemony in Asia. Hong Kong is the home of the worst exploiters of the civil war era, people who fled China and got rich on China's misery (e.g., the need to get around an American "blockade"), serving as an intermediary in world trade to the long-suffering Chinese people who stayed poor because they heroically sacrificed blood and treasure to maintain independence, rebuffing threats from imperialists in Washington, Moscow, and Delhi. Thus, Hong Kong wealth is imagined as immoral. A popular image in north China is that Chinese are poor because they are patriots. It is only just, then, that Hong Kong should share its wealth with a long-suffering Chinese people.

This revanchist politics has a regional base. People in areas that once benefited from now-money-losing SOEs readily imagine further reform as serving only these alien, anti-China interests who have supposedly been fattened unjustly. Elites in Beijing who fear that reform will undermine the system that has been so good to their families and friends are still attracted by the discourse of anti-imperialism to fight against the scum of the earth, both in and around Chinese territory. Consequently, the rise of chauvinism in China, the pervasive popularity of scapegoating the beneficiaries of reform in the image of a blood-sucking, alien bourgeoisie in Europe, the Jew as money-lender and money-grubber, the emotion of racism, makes it a bit premature to dub reform in China a success (Miles 1997; Friedman 1995). China palpitates with explosive angers and tensions.

The chauvinistic faction among Chinese ruling groups rejects any open, plural, tolerant, non-centered notion of Asia. Chauvinists imagine a pure Chinese race with 5,000 years of glorious history. They imagine China as having a pure language. Even Koreans, Japanese, Tibetans, and Muslim Uighurs are imagined as part of the Chinese race, and, as Hong Kong in 1997, and Taiwan in some not-distant future, to be reabsorbed as part of one great Chinese people of a common blood ruled from Beijing. Chauvinists imagine the wealth of Hong Kong and Taiwan and Chinese elsewhere in Asia as ill-gotten imperialist plunder that should be shared with the suffering, sacrificing citizens of the People's Republic of China. Such an interpretation can make conflict among Asian nations more likely. Major wars – Pearl Harbor, Korea, Vietnam – can explode from conflicting Asian nationalisms.

In a Sinocentric vision, littoral China is almost alien. It is blamed for the income gap with hinterland Chinese, seen as suffering because a handful of traitors at the state center have unfairly fattened the undeserving, semi-aliens of coastal China who sometimes look and sound as if they have forgotten they are Chinese. I have a vivid memory of a Beijing official in Canton muttering, after dealing with a Cantonese-speaking shopkeeper, "I might as well be in Hanoi."

Regional tensions are so sensitive that all sides have been forced to make a top priority of the reversing of the income gap between coast and hinterland, city and countryside, which grew from 1985. Whether momentum in the direction of equity in China can be sustained may be a matter of large political moment. State policy and politics are decisive.

But the emotional appeal of Sinocentric chauvinism goes deeper than statistics on income distribution. There is a tremendous political struggle ongoing in China between those who invoke a future of a Sinocentric Asia and those who see China as part of an open and pluralist Asia. The chauvinists censor data on millennia of Eurasian interchange, which shows greater genetic similarity from Japan to Europe across north China than similarity of north and south China across the Yangtze River. Chauvinistic Chinese today, as imperialistic Europeans a century earlier, seem attracted by the appeals of Social Darwinist racism. They imagine their superior civilization in terms of a pure race.

Fearful of losing power, fearful that full reform would end their status and wealth, chauvinists make use of a notion of a Chinese Asia that augurs ill for those who prefer an open and tolerant Asia. The power struggle in China consequently is of import to the whole world. China is ever weightier in Asia. Indeed, with Japan's politics preventing a coming to grips with the causes of economic stagnation since 1991, rulers in Beijing responded to Asia's 1997–8 financial meltdown by trying to establish China's currency, the renminbi, as Asia's linchpin currency (James Kynge, "Renminbi seen as Asia's linchpin currency," *Financial Times*, June 9, 1998).

And yet, there actually are reform forces in China who do not fear a more open Asia. Such Chinese would end war-prone confrontations in the East China Sea, the Taiwan Straits region, and the South China Sea. They would facilitate solutions to conflicts that would allow much of the maritime wealth of the region to improve the lives of the Chinese and other Asian people. They would help lower barriers so Taiwan could be more involved with the mainland of China, an involvement that would also speed wealth expansion in China. Such a China would think of China as successful because open – a China whose wealth and glories were won since ancient times both across the Silk Road and the South China Seas. The major historical museum in hinterland Xian, once Changan, the first major city after the desert oases on the Silk Road, tells its history just that way. A Chinese rise incorporated within this kind of Asianization is a peaceful China, contributing to an Asianization of general benefit to the species. The rise of China could lead in many different directions. It so much matters how Asians interpret the rise of Asia.

The rise of China is changing Asia and the world. Thus, it matters very much who wins the power struggle in China and what project the government in Beijing will act upon in Asia and the Asia/Pacific region. Little is more misleading than the vision that growth solves all problems and that China will inevitably and peacefully evolve into a democratic and tolerant polity. The politically contested actions of the state remain decisive. It matters so much who controls these levers of power and how they interpret the role of the state in Asia's future.

Conclusion

In a neoliberal perspective where economics shape everything else, capitalism solves all problems. But the entire analysis of this study has adjured that notion of capitalism because it obscures the complex, decisive, always-changing and interactive reality of the multiple institutions, levels, and forces that infuse state–market relations. Capitalism and socialism are regularly invoked as totalizing nineteenth-century European, modernist, grand narratives. Such oppositional binaries do not clarify better future projects. Since socialism has no theory to comprehend contemporary dynamics and no program to grapple with contemporary problems (Alterman 1996: 6–77), the all-embracing binary of capitalism versus socialism in Europe and North America serves mainly to legitimate neoliberal hegemony where the free market is the solution and the state is the origin of all problems. The misleading binary capitalism/socialism prevents analysts from seeing the power of reinterpreted future projects and from disaggregating the state and disembedding the market and discovering their complex and changeable linkages as informed by newly globalized finance and revolutions in communications technology, a change dubbed globalization.

In the East Asian developmental model, the state encourages and rewards winners in sunrise industries. But how? It is the particulars that are hidden by the binary of state versus market that are decisive. And those particulars may be very different in the age of microelectronic information technologies.

Asian successes force analysts to disembed the market and disaggregate the state. Asian successes reveal that nineteenth-century grand narratives about a rise of capitalism or socialism hide Asian interpretations of past and future and obscure the diverse and complex relations over millennia among trade, technology, government macroeconomic management of fiscal or monetary policy, state capacity, tax policy, property relations, etc. Asia's success allows an analyst to abandon misleading oversimplifications that serve self-wounding political projects and obscure wealth-expanding dynamics. Asian growth with equity has had much to do with state institutions and actions, with government spending on education and skills, policies of land reform, and a commitment to a meritocratic technocracy. Asian governments have done well when they rewarded winners. But Asian societies have been wounded when their states entrenched corrupt criminality, when governments selected national champions and protected losers (Evans 1995). Seeing only capitalism/socialism and market/state blinds people to the actual and particular mix of policies and institutions, good and bad, in Asia. This mix does not heed the boundaries of state/market. It is not captured by the binary capitalism/socialism.

For "socialist" chauvinists (or fascist feudalists, as Chinese democrats often say) in a rising China, the notion of an evil, exploitative, polarizing capitalist imperialism remains central. Given China's rise through policies of openness and market-regardedness, it might seem that chauvinistic Sinocentrists have no future in China. But elites tend to be most ideological, the better to obscure their narrow, selfish interests. To be persuaded of this obdurate reality, one need only look at ideologues in America who see the Cold War as a triumph of the market over the state, of capitalism wiping out socialism. American triumphalists ignore the rise of China, which just happens to be home to most of the people in the old socialist world. The triumphalists also ignore the rise of Asia, the major transformation of the Cold War era. Europeans committed to the EU as their future can better understand the deep truth in the Japanese witticism that when America and Russia called a halt to their Cold War, Japan had won. But in a rising and nationalistic China, that outcome is unacceptable. Much delicate diplomacy may be needed to escape worst-case outcomes, to make China–Japan reconciliation a major goal.

The rise of Asia can help us subvert false generalizations and explode misleading polar binaries. The rise of China begins in the late 1960s when Mao Zedong moved away from a communist fundamentalism which had devastated the Chinese nation, leaving the people in stagnant misery. Since economic reform began in China there have been no socialist initiatives to improve the lives of the Chinese people. The self-reliant, anti-imperialist command economy was bankrupt.

Yet, the rise of Asia is not the success of capitalism, not even a so-called Asian variant of capitalism. The Japanese tell a joke about Anglo-American neoliberal economists who foolishly believe that a free market left to itself solves all problems. The Japanese ask, "How many neoliberal economists does it take to change a light bulb?" The quip retort is, "None! They just sit in the dark and wait for the hidden hand to do it for them. And they wait and wait and wait." Japanese people understand that government intervention has been decisive in their rise.

The World Bank study on East Asia's rise that Japan sought refused to grapple with the causes of Asia's rise. How is it that societies where unions are weak can be economically equitable high-income societies? What was it in Asia that has persisted that has made possible Asia's great success? After all, Europeans did not get to East Asia in strength until late in the nineteenth century. By then Japan had already begun its Meiji reforms. Japan defeated Russia in 1904–5. East Asia never was incorporated by Europe. Japan imposed itself on Korea and Taiwan in the 1890s. China's republican revolutionary Sun Yat-sen, at the turn into the twentieth century, urged joining with this already risen Japan to stave off newly threatening Europeans. Europe never conquered East Asia.

If China could be defeated by a few miserable ships from a distant Britain around 1840 in the Opium War, it had to be because a great China at that moment was unusually weak. The question is, how did China injure itself for so long that it declined so far that even the British could defeat China? Asia's rise, interpreted in this way, is a return to normality, a historical continuity. Effective Asian governments have facilitated Asia's continuing rise.

And yet the state is not the solution, either. Adam Smith's sociology of mercantilism is as apt as ever. Unaccountable mercantilism readily degenerates into corrupt deals among friendly elite networks at the expense of the general populace. These rent-taking, parasitic and corrupt forces were kept in check in Japan and elsewhere in Asia for a long time because of fears that, unless economic success was shared, the well-armed foreigners, as they did in the Opium War, would impose their will on vulnerable Asian peoples.

But once Asia became secure in its economic success, the limits on the evils inherent in unaccountable mercantilism disappeared. The evils ran rampant. Corruption and involvement with criminal gangs have become so bad that many Asian peoples can even look at Italian polities with envy. Asia needs to make its governments accountable to their people or cynicism and delegitimation will spread and the sources of Asian economic dynamism with equity will end. These forces of rot are strong all over East and Southeast Asia. This central issue is not a matter of abandoning the state and freeing the market, but of reforming rotting parts of the state so that the state/market nexus still serves the nation, and does not act as the handmaiden of greedy and unaccountable elites.

Asia is full of hope and full of problems. It matters for all humanity who wins in political combat all over Asia. It matters what policies Asians pursue. There are better and worse forces contesting. Their struggle is most palpable and most crucial in a rising China. Asianization has not yet fully defined itself. As peoples everywhere in the 1980s sought to learn from the good in Asia, the key question is, what will be the content of Asianization as Asia returns to greatness? Asia, however, should not be romanticized to hide what is not healthy.

China is the great success of the era of globalization. Not only has China grown at the fastest rate and attracted the most foreign direct investment, but it could yet grapple successfully with the problems of maintaining equity. From the launching of reform in 1978 until 1984–5, rural reform permitted the previously marginalized hinterland poor to close the income gap rapidly with the urban industrial centers that had been privileged by Leninism. But then, the trend went the other way, when further rural reform was blocked by a chauvinist state fearful of rural proprietorship.

That tendency of polarization persuaded all ruling groups of the need for the state to help the poorest of the poor rise. As elsewhere in the world, a failure to close the income gap can make globalization seem a sell-out to foreign interests because it is interests most closely tied to the foreign ones that seem to benefit most unfairly. That consciousness grew in China. The economic winners seemed ever more alien and immoral. Reformers had to worry that, as elsewhere, nativist demagogues would succeed in mobilizing popular anxieties over a loss of pure Chineseness. This would not only discredit and subvert reformers but it could also lead on to a nativist chauvinism full of war dangers for the entire region.

Since 1995, Beijing has insisted on ever greater transportation and communications investment in the poorest regions. Tax breaks for better-off regions are conditioned on investing in the poorest regions. Even though the central government controls less and less of national tax revenue, even as it conforms ever more to WTO guidelines, it has promoted an equity-oriented policy that is almost the opposite of red-lining. Thus, China has, contradictorily, been promoting movement and growth for the poorest of the poor, even as it has not negated the privileged, criminal and corrupt groups whose greedy power works in a polarizing direction.

It is far too soon to call China a success. A lack of political reform, persisting economic problems and a pervasiveness of corruption and nepotism lead many Chinese to believe that polarization will not be reversed, that the center actually is on the side of the most selfish and the most criminal. What matters is who is in power, whether the institutions undergirding decision-making can seem fair, what policies are implemented. Globalization disempowers the state and makes the social justice of equity close to impossible. But even if the reforms are reversed because of a chauvinist ascendance or a lack of political reform, that reversal still would not alter a basic fact: globalization cannot be all-defining and neoliberalism cannot be an absolute imperative of TINAism.[3] This is because China has proven there is an alternative: global economic success combined with equity at home remains possible. A poor people can rise even in the age of globalization if a government experienced as fair and capable wills it and acts wisely. State and market, government and economy are not opposites or absolutely autonomous, not if one understands how Chinese and other Asians experience their great rise.

Notes

1 In light of Asia's global centrality into the nineteenth century, it is doubtful "if there is such a thing as 'capitalism'" (Frank 1998: xix, xxiv, 15, and 330–2).

2 Greider argues that the explosion of capital that earns higher rates of profits and is beyond the reach of government tax collectors siphons money away from more productive and higher job-creating investments. The results include tendencies toward income polarization, a production glut and a financial bubble. Consequently, for the health of all nations, a global governance of the new capital is needed. Neoliberal prescriptions of leaving it to the market will prove a disaster. Even conservative American bankers can concur in a need to govern global finance.

3 TINAism means there is no alternative to neoliberal policies and a free market.

References

Alterman, E. (1996) "Left out?" *Nation* 6–7, December 2.

Evans, P. (1995) *Embedded Autonomy: State and Industrial Transformation*, Princeton: Princeton University Press.

Frank, A.G. (1998) *ReORIENT*, Berkeley: University of California Press.

Friedman, E. (1987) "Maoism and the Liberation of the Poor," *World Politics* 39 (3): 408–28.

—— (1994) *The Politics of Democratization: Generalizing East Asian Experiences*, Boulder, CO: Westview.

—— (1995) "Is China a model of reform success?" in *National Identity and Democratic Prospects in Socialist China*, Armonk: M.E. Sharpe.

—— (1996) "Intervention of the proper kind," *The Review of Politics* 58 (2): 413–17.

—— (forthcoming), "Lessons and non-lessons for India from China's Reforms," in F. Frankel (ed.) *Democracy and Transformation: India Fifty Years After Independence*.

Friedman, E., Pickowicz, P., and Selden, M. (1991) *Chinese Village, Socialist State*, New Haven: Yale University Press.

—— (forthcoming) *Revolution, Resistance and Reform in Village China*, New Haven: Yale University Press.

Goldman, M. (1994) "China as a model," in *Lost Opportunity*, New York: Norton, ch. 9.

Greider, W. (1997) *One World, Ready or Not: The Manic Logic of Global Capitalism*, New York: Simon and Schuster.

Haggard, S. and Kaufman, R. (1995), *The Political Economy of Democratic Transitions*, Princeton: Princeton University Press.

Henderson, C. (1998), *Asia Falling*, New York: McGraw-Hill.

Hughes, N. (1998), "Smashing the iron rice bowl," *Foreign Affairs:* 67–77.

Jefferson, G. and Singh, I. (1997) "Ownership reform as a process of creative reduction in Chinese industry?" in Joint Economic Committee (eds) *China's Economic Future*, Armonk: M.E. Sharpe, pp. 176–202.

Jessup, R. (1997), "Capitalism and its future," *Review of International Political Economy* 4 (3): 561–81.

Kohno, M. (1997), *Japan's Postwar Party Politics*, Princeton: Princeton University Press.

Kristof, N. and Wu Dunn, S. (1994) *China Wakes*, New York: Random House.

Krugman, P. (1994), "The myth of Asia's miracle," *Foreign Affairs* 73: 62–78.

Lardy, N. (1998), "China and the Asian Contagion," *Foreign Affairs* 77: 78–88.

Lipietz, A. (1997), "The post-Fordist world," *Review of International Political Economics*, 4 (1): 2–41.

Miles, J. (1997) *Legacy of Tiananmen*, Ann Arbor: University of Michigan Press.

Moore, B., Jr (1966) *Social Origins of Dictatorship and Democracy*, Boston: Beacon.

Paige, J. (1997) *Coffee and Power*, Cambridge: Harvard University Press.

Strange, S. (1996) *The Retreat of the State: The Diffusion of Power in the World Economy*, Cambridge: Cambridge University Press.

Whiting, A. (1989) *China Eyes Japan*, Berkeley: University of California Press.

Wu, Y. (1994) *Comparative Economic Transformations*, Stanford: Stanford University Press.

14 Hemmed in?

The state in Africa and global liberalization

Julius E. Nyang'oro

Africa's involvement in the changing world economy has been a long one, and its effects on the lives of Africans have been profound. Samir Amin and W.W. Rostow, Felix Houphouet-Boigny and Samora Machel, would hardly dispute such a statement. But the question of whether this involvement has led Africans along a road toward material and social progress or into a dead end is very much in dispute.

(Cooper 1981: 1)

From the poorest countries to the Third World to the most advanced exemplars of welfare capitalism, one of the few universals in the history of the twentieth century is the increasingly pervasive influence of the state as an institution and social actor.

(Evans 1995: 4)

Africa is in crisis and its future depends on the answers to life and death questions – on famine, food aid, the price of oil, irreversible environmental damage, the impact of the AIDS virus, arms sales, democracy. But one further question in particular stands out. Sub-Saharan Africa's total debt is US$175 billion and therefore its dependency on the international financial institutions is unusually strong. The terms on which finance for long-term economic development is provided is the most explosive issue of all. Hope for Africa and Africans depends on this.

(Brown and Tiffen 1994: 1)

Introduction

For several centuries, as Walter Rodney (1972), Immanuel Wallerstein (1986), and others have told us, Africa has been part of the global economy.[1] Perhaps the two most enduring connections between Africa and the West are the Atlantic Slave trade, which lasted roughly 400 years and the European colonial system, which lasted roughly 100 years. While the former connection has been viewed as the most economically exploitative to Africa by the outside world, the latter represented the end result of a long historical process of incorporating Africa into the global capitalist system. The end of the colonial system in Africa, which took place from the late 1950s to the mid-1970s was supposed to usher in a period of rapid modernization and economic development. The assumption here was that since Africans were now in charge of their own destiny, they would embark on a systematic transformation of the economy via state action to improve the material conditions of their citizens (Nyang'oro 1989). The state actually was expected to play the twin/dual role of developmentalism and welfarism. This expectation was natural because of the promises that were being given to the masses by the elite nationalists who were campaigning hard to dislodge the colonial state. It was also logical that any modern state would perform those functions anyway – given the example of the colonial "mother" country in its own domestic environment – in Britain, France, Belgium, etc. Most former colonial powers are leaders in state welfarism.

If developmentalism and welfarism were viewed as the natural growth of the nationalist struggle for independence, the connection between Africa and the global economy for purposes of meeting these goals was also taken to be a given, in light of colonialism and the emphasis on the export sector as an engine of economic growth (Belassa 1964). Most nationalist leaders had been schooled in the economic tradition of global trade and the "free" market as the principal engine of growth. It is indeed remarkable that now the discourse on economic development in the West, especially in the United States, is about globalization. Literature on economic development in Africa going back two decades already had a strong element of globalization (Rodney 1972; Nabudere 1977; Amin 1974; 1977). The only question was how globalization was affecting the development process. In most instances, for those with a leftist perspective, the answer was overwhelmingly negative (Rweyemamu 1973; Leys 1975; Langdon 1981). Few saw the structure of globalization and international trade as positive for Africa (Belassa 1964; Warren 1980).

By 1980 it was obvious that although Africa was an active participant in the global economy – regardless of the nature of that participation – the continent was in serious economic trouble. The dramatic nature of the collapse of African economies was captured in the infamous study by the World Bank (1981), which is popularly known as the Berg Report. Data from the Berg Report and other World Bank sources indicated that between 1965 and 1983 the average growth rate of low-income countries in Sub-Saharan African countries (i.e., the majority of the countries) was −0.2 per cent. Most of the positive growth had occurred only in oil-producing countries (Nigeria, Cameroon, Congo) due to the oil bonanza on the heels of OPEC oil prices increases in 1974. Overall, however, Africa as a region was deemed to be in serious economic trouble (Ravenhill 1986).

The Berg Report diagnosed the problem in Africa principally to be that of excessive state interference in the operation of the market. The medicine proposed was quite straightforward: African countries should remove the impediments to growth and efficiency caused by state interference in the operation of markets. Broadly speaking, the economic reforms proposed by the World Bank were intended to substantially liberalize and privatize domestic economies on the continent. As Howard Stein (1995: 1) has noted, by 1987 the economic reform programs were ubiquitous in Sub-Saharan Africa with twenty-seven countries initiating policy changes in exchange for the World Bank's structural adjustment loans. By the mid-1990s, for all intents and purposes, the whole region had adopted the Bank's reform program.[2] The adoption of structural adjustment programs (SAPs) by African countries raises a number of questions in relation to the process and consequences of globalization, questions that I will address further below. But the initial question that must be addressed is whether indeed SAPs have had their desired consequences of enhanced economic growth in Africa. As we will see below, the answer is a resounding no. Second, given the insistence by SAPs of state withdrawal from the economy, what role, if any, has (and can) the state in Africa play under conditions of globalization? How is sovereignty to be understood in Africa? The questions are relevant given the assault on the state from both internal forces (civil society moving variously toward disengagement from the state) and external forces (multilateral financial institutions and to some extent transnational corporations). Here, the discussion on state sovereignty by Stephen Krasner (Chapter 2, this volume) is instructive. In the case of Africa, there is no question that globalization has challenged the effectiveness of state control, as has happened universally. The measure for this erosion of control is the universal application of SAPs. While it may be true that globalization has not altered state authority as Krasner argues, it is clear that state authority as used by Krasner – domestic constitutional order, autonomy, and international recognition – has been severely challenged in Africa. Except for international recognition, many states on the continent lack the other two elements. In this regard, Africa may be different from other regions, which would also account for the failure of globalization to qualitatively and positively affect the region's development profile. I will come back to this question further below.

I will start the discussion on the state in Africa by examining the region's objective conditions. The argument I will be developing is that while Africa is part of a globalized (and globalizing) system, its engagement is tenuous and problematic, given the little positive effect the global system has had on Africa. Furthermore, the state, which has played a leading role in the transformation of the economies of Latin America and Southeast Asia, cannot perform the same function in Africa. Historically and in contemporary times, the state in Africa simply has not had the capacity to engage in strategic planning and to effectively insulate itself from pressures both internal and external (Evans, 1995). Fundamentally, I am in agreement with Krasner that globalization as such is not a new phenomenon if we understand it to be the increase in international flows of ideas, people, goods, and factors. What has changed over time on a global scale is the density and intensity of these flows. For someone concerned with Sub-Saharan Africa, the analytical and practical question is why these flows are either bypassing the region, or have not had an appreciably positive impact on the region.

The African economy: the reality of decline

Unlike all the other regions in the global economy today, Africa still suffers from the most acute problems of underdevelopment. After one and a half decades of structural adjustment, it is now generally accepted that the 1980s was a lost decade for Africa in terms of social and economic development. Indeed the Sub-Sahara region experienced further economic regression in the early 1990s. The annual mean rate of growth of per capita income in the region was 0.8 per cent in the 1970s; it slumped to negative 2.2 per cent per year from 1980 to 1989 (Ravenhill, 1993: 19). *The Mid-Term Review of the United Nations New Agenda for the Development of Africa in the 1990s* (UN-NADAF 1996) actually notes that many of the problems the region faced five years ago have become more acute, while most of the region's potential has yet to be realized. The elements of the continuing crisis are as follows (all data from UN-NADAF, 1996):

- In the 1990s, Africa GDP has accounted for less and less of world output (about 2.04 per cent on average) even though its share of world population has increased (to about 12 per cent in 1995). While Africa's GDP grew by 2.3 per cent in 1995, its population increased by 2.9 per cent, resulting in an actual per capita decline of 0.06 per cent.
- Africa's total external debt is now widely acknowledged to be unsustainable. It rose from US$289 billion in 1991 to over US$314 billion in 1995. Specifically, the Sub-Saharan Africa debt climbed from US$194 billion to US$223.2 billion over the same period, and from over 239 per cent to almost 279 per cent of export earnings.
- Although Africa's annual debt-service payments fell from US$30 billion in 1991 to US$22 billion in 1994, they rose to US$33 billion in 1995. Reflecting this trend, Africa was using 31.3 per cent of its export earnings to service its debt in 1991. Although this ratio fell to 23.4 per cent in 1994, it climbed to nearly 31 per cent in 1995. Sub-Saharan Africa's arrears on debt-service payments nearly doubled from US$32.6 billion to US$62 billion in the 1984–94 period. Essentially, debt service claims nearly one-fifth of Africa's savings and over 4 per cent of GDP.
- Heavy indebtedness has been identified as a disincentive to foreign direct investment (FDI). In spite of the political and economic reforms implemented in most of the countries in the region, the continent is being bypassed by the boom in investment flows. For all developing countries, net FDI inflows rose remarkably from US$22.6 billion in 1991 to US$60 billion in 1995. But the story was very different for Africa, with net FDI increasing from US$1.8 billion in 1991 to US$2.9 billion in 1994, before falling back 27 per cent in 1995 to US$2.1 billion. This confirms the continuing decline in Africa's share of total FDI to developing countries, which has fallen from 10 per cent in 1987–91 to 5 per cent in 1992–4 and just 3.6 per cent in 1995.
- Africa's continued reliance on a handful of primary commodities for the bulk of its export earnings, together with growing competition from Asian

and Latin American producers in a shrinking market for many raw materials, resulted in the region's share of world trade declining from 3.1 per cent in 1990 to 2.1 per cent in 1995 (Brown and Tiffen 1994: 28–40). In order to be competitive under globalization, it is generally held that there must be diversification of commodity exports. Yet, African countries continue to rely on the same commodities they did thirty years ago. Primary commodities accounted for approximately 75 per cent of Africa's total foreign exchange earnings over the first half of the 1990s, while some African countries relied on a single commodity for more than three-quarters of their total exports.

• While many developing countries have been able to profit from increasing levels of trade by diversifying production and trading partners, Africa for the most part has not. The region essentially has been bypassed by the conspicuous transformation in commodities traded globally (i.e., manufactures and information technologies). This can be demonstrated by the fact that between 1990–95, the region's share in the trade of developing countries fell from 10.9 per cent to 6.4 per cent, while its share with the European Union (EU) – which accounts for 70 per cent of Africa's total trade – fell from 3.3 per cent in 1992 to 2.8 per cent in 1995.

Thus, the picture that we get of Africa's economic development is particularly depressing. I borrowed the term "hemmed in" for the title of this paper from Callaghy and Ravenhill (1993), who note that considering the data coming out of Africa, and the apparent failure by the International Monetary Fund (IMF) and the World Bank to make sense of Africa's economic crisis, the economic prognosis for the continent in the foreseeable future is particularly bleak. Hence, the notion of being hemmed in:

> By 'hemmed in' we mean a situation in which the viable policy alternatives and the capacities and resources needed to implement them, available to African governments are severely constrained as a consequence of volatile politics, weak states, weak markets, debt problems, and an unfavourable international environment.
>
> (Callaghy and Ravenhill 1993: 2)

The context for discussion of state capacity and sovereignty in Africa is, then, that of severe constraint which differs sharply with what one may expect to find in Latin America and Southeast Asia, for example. Richard Stubbs in his contribution to this volume notes the constraints that Southeast Asian countries faced soon after their independence in their attempt to improve their material conditions: the legacy of the Japanese occupation, the rise of the People's Republic of China, and the advent of the Cold War. Yet it would seem that these constraints were turned into assets, especially with the increased involvement of the United States in the region as a result of Vietnam. With American support, states in the region gradually developed a credible coercive administrative capacity as well as considerable legitimacy. For Sub-Saharan Africa, however, most states were barely functioning when the colonial powers left, and in the most extreme cases such as Congo–Zaire and Sudan, civil war broke out immediately after independence, challenging the legitimacy of the state. It is no wonder, therefore, that the two largest countries in the region (Congo–Zaire and Sudan) are still embroiled in deep social conflict. In May 1997, the regime of Mobutu Sese Seko in Zaire was finally overthrown by a rebel group led by Laurent Desire Kabila. Even then, Kabila's legitimacy was still being challenged by a number of groups in the country. In the Sudan, an Islamic fundamentalist regime continues to occupy state reins, but has little *control* in terms of security and economic activity – over more than two-thirds of the country. What we see in these two cases therefore is a classic case of the continuation of the unfinished business of territorial integration during the colonial era, and a poor transition to independence engendered by the inability of the colonial state to properly prepare dependent territories for independence. While globalization may have a role to play in the undermining of state sovereignty, it is also empirically evident that internal groups in many African countries play an even more critical role in eroding state sovereignty in terms of internal control (Krasner, Chapter 2, this volume).

State capacity and strategic planning for development

No one takes seriously the proposition that states are always by nature inimical to the workings of the market and that states should at all cost be made to play a most minimal role in economic development. The history of economic development in late nineteenth-century Europe, mid-twentieth-century Japan, and in the late twentieth century in the developing world (especially Latin America and Southeast Asia) has shown that the state can and has played an indispensable role in furthering economic development, especially in industrialization (Deyo 1987; Evans 1995; Stein 1995). Evans has appropriately reminded us that

> the state lies at the center of solutions to the problem of order. *Without the state, markets, the other master institution of modern society, cannot function.* We do not spend our valuable time standing in lines in front of counters of bureaucrats because we are masochists. We stand there because we need what the state provides.
>
> (Evans 1995: 3, emphasis added)

In the case of Africa, given the low level of economic development at the time of independence, the state not only took over the task of maintaining order in society, but assumed the role of the most important economic player in the area of manufacturing and the general organization of the economy. This was universally true for the whole continent. In any case, the state was the only entity that could perform this function; Africa had no domestic bourgeoisie! While it is true that the state did a poor job of it (Bates 1981), there were not, and still are not, many alternatives to state action in manufacturing given the minimal amount of FDI on the continent.

There is an even more compelling reason for the need to continue with a strategy of industrialization led by the state. From the very beginning, industrialization as a basis and reflection of development was rooted in the mainstream analyses and theoretical insights of the modernization development literature (Rostow 1960). Africa has not been immune to this thinking. Indeed the early thrust of import substitution industrialization (ISI) in pre- and post-independent Africa was partly a result of this thinking, partly a genuine need for internally manufactured goods, and partly a result of historical lessons learned primarily from the Latin American experience of the last great depression and the postwar period. Even though ISI was accepted as the basis for industrialization for most of Africa, it is also clear that in most cases, the impact of import-substitution policies has been quite limited primarily because it has scarcely begun. Thus the whole proposition about the state getting out of the economic sector is problematic at best because it has not seriously begun. But what has been exasperating for many observers of Africa in the last decade and a half is the continuing insistence by the World Bank (initially through the Berg Report) that manufacturing must give way to increased agricultural production. The Bank's rationale has been that Africa needs to use its "comparative advantage" in primary commodity production. But as Brown and Tiffen (1994) and others have pointed out, there is a need for Africa to diversify its production profile by increasing its manufacturing capacity. Without manufacturing and industrialization, the ability of Africa to effectively participate in the contemporary global economy is doomed to failure.

The reason for diversification is simple. It is clear that prices for most of Africa's primary commodities had slackened by the late 1990s and the projection by most sources is that there would be a continued long-term decline, partly due to decreasing demand. According to the United Nations Conference on Trade and Development (UNCTAD), average annual prices for Africa's commodities in 1984–94 were down in real terms: for tropical beverages (by -10.4 per cent), agricultural raw materials (-1.3 per cent), vegetable oilseeds and oils (-4.8 per cent), and minerals, ores and metals (-1.5 per cent). It is also projected that technological progress in the production of synthetics and other substitutes for primary commodities can be expected to further depress demand and prices (UN-NADAF 1996: 6).

However, to talk about the need for diversification and its benefits to economic development is talking about the obvious. What is of analytical value is the question why so far, Africa has not been able to carry out the diversification that is required to enhance its material production. Peter Evans gave a partial answer to the question when he compared development in Latin America (a less dynamic region) with that of East Asia (a more dynamic region). He noted that the most important difference between the two regions in terms of the pace of industrialization and efficiency, is the degree of external control over the management of the internal productive apparatus, essentially the role of direct foreign investment (Evans 1987: 205–6).

As a Latin Americanist, Evans was struck by the restricted historical role played by transnational capital in East Asia whereby transnational capital became important only after the process of industrialization was well underway. Latin America, on the other hand, industrialized in a context that maximized the consequences of direct foreign investment. As an Africanist, I am struck by the inapplicability of the Evans' discussion of the two regions to the region of my concern where the discussion is on the impact of FDI on industrialization and overall economic diversification. With the exception of South Africa, direct foreign investment in Africa is minimal and industrialization has not taken root (Riddel *et al.* 1990). Indeed, in many instances, we are looking at economies that are barely functional in the conventional sense.

Thus, the role of the state in Africa under these conditions has to be viewed differently from the state in either Latin America or East Asia. While Peter Evans talks about the "embedded autonomy" of the state in East Asia (that is, the capacity of the state to insulate itself from domestic pressure), for many Africanists the talk is about collapsed and/or collapsing states. If we are to accept the notion that in a globalized economy the state principally reacts to worldwide economic forces, we also implicitly accept the idea that in order for the state to be relevant, it has to have the capacity to react (Mittleman 1996: 7). Collapsed or collapsing states cannot really react to global economic forces because they lack the minimal wherewithal to do so. William Zartman and his colleagues have captured the essence of the state in many African countries, which sheds some light on the difference between competent states in other regions of the world and those one finds in many parts of Africa: "State collapse…refers to a situation where the structure, authority (legitimate power), law, and political order have fallen apart and must be reconstituted in some form, old or new (Zartman, 1995: 1).

Zartman proceeds to show how many African states have essentially collapsed or are in the process of reconstituting themselves into images still unknown.[3] The number of African countries where states fit the characteristics outlined by Zartman are numerous. In Table 14.1, I have attempted to categorize Sub-Saharan countries into three groups to reflect the discussion in Zartman's volume. The three categories are (1) really collapsed or collapsing states that are yet to reconstitute themselves; (2) states in transition but whose legitimacy is still under question and facing severe strain in their attempt to establish political order; and (3) states that are relatively stable and do not face challenges to their central authority.

Not everyone will agree with my choices of which countries belong to what category. I, however, think that my categories reflect what is happening on the ground in light of what is being reported in reputable media (see, for example, various issues of *Africa Confidential* 1990–97). The case of Congo–Zaire will serve as an illustration of the problem of state collapse in Africa. Toward the end of 1996, the world became aware of the disintegration of Zaire in the wake of the Rwandan refugee crisis. Almost two million Rwandans had become refugees in Zaire after the widely reported genocide of Tutsis by a radical element within the Hutu ruling class (Prunier 1996). Some of the Hutu refugees in Zaire had actually participated in the genocide but the Zairian authorities could not or did

Table 14.1 State stability in Africa

Group 1 Collapsed/Collapsing	Group 2 In transition	Group 3 Relatively stable
Angola	Cameroon	Benin
Burundi	Ethiopia	Botswana
Central African Republic	The Gambia	Burkina Faso
Chad	Guinea	Côte d'Ivoire
Congo-Brazaville	Kenya	Equatorial Guinea
Congo-Zaire	Lesotho	Eritrea
Liberia	Madagascar	Gabon
Mozambique	Malawi	Ghana
Rwanda	Nigeria	Guinea-Bissau
Sierra-Leone	Togo	Namibia
Somalia	Uganda	Senegal
Sudan	Zambia	Swaziland
		Tanzania
		Zimbabwe

not want to apprehend them. In effect the Hutu militia within the refugee camps were running their own mini-state on Zairian territory. An attack on the refugee camps by ethnic Tutsi elements within Zaire, and from across the border in Rwanda, late in 1996 led to the dispersal of the Hutu militia and started a chain of events that led to the consolidation of the rebel movement in Zaire led by Laurent Kabila. It took Kabila's forces approximately eight months to march from eastern Zaire to Kinshasa, the capital. Kinshasa fell to Kabila's forces in May 1997.

What should be evident from the swift success of Kabila and his group is that the collapse of the Zairian state under Mobutu Sese Seko did not begin in late 1996. The Zairian state had actually been disintegrating for a good two decades (Nzongola-Ntalaja 1986; Sangmpam 1994; Callaghy 1984). The Mobutu regime in Zaire had survived for three decades primarily because of external support – France and the United States – and Mobutu's skillful manipulation of the realities of the Cold War. As long as the Soviet Union was busy in neighboring Angola, Mobutu was assured of US support regardless of whether the regime in Kinshasa had any internal legitimacy. For a long time Zaire had actually operated as three separate regions with the only visible evidence of central authority being the presidential guard in Mobutu's home town of Gbadolite. The case of Zaire is now better known internationally because of active reporting by the foreign press but this experience of state collapse or near-state collapse has been replicated in a number of countries in varying degrees. These countries include Angola, Burundi, the Central African Republic, Ethiopia, Liberia, Mozambique, Rwanda, Sierra Leone, Somalia, and the Sudan. It is no wonder then that most of the United Nations peacekeeping efforts have been concentrated in Africa in the last few years because of the persistent challenge to state authority and legitimacy by various groups in society. The mobilizing ideologies for such groups have taken various forms including: ethnicity, regionalism, anti-colonialism, anti-theocracy, etc.

The picture, then, that emerges regarding the state in African countries is that if indeed globalization of a positive nature is to benefit Africa, the state must radically transform itself to be an effective player in the globalization sweepstakes. As it stands now, the concern about state sovereignty in many parts of Africa is really an inconsequential one, given its incapacity to effectively influence both its external and internal environments. Thomas Callaghy succinctly put the problem of the state in Africa in the following way:

> the major issue in contemporary Africa...is the absence of central state authority and the resulting search for it. While the nature of the international system appears to maintain, with a few exceptions and alterations, the persistence of new states in their basically artificial colonial boundaries, the search for internal and external sovereignty, authority, and unity remains very incomplete in most African countries.
>
> (Callaghy 1984: 32)

Concretely then, sovereignty for the state in Africa means very little. It is true that states in Africa have the trappings of international sovereignty (Jackson and Rosberg 1982): they are recognized by other states, belong to international organizations, and have foreign representation. However, in terms of real control of their territories, that is a doubtful proposition. At the end of the 1990s decade, states in countries such as Rwanda, Burundi, Congo–Zaire, Sudan, Liberia, Sierra Leone, Mozambique, Angola, Central African Republic, to mention a few, can hardly claim effective control of their territories. Internally, the thriving informal economy effectively makes the state of less consequence to the lives of the overwhelming majority of the population (Rothchild and Chazan 1988; Fatton 1992; Harbeson *et al.* 1994; MacGaffey *et al.* 1991). This point suggests that while globalization may undermine state sovereignty generally, the African experience points to a very serious internal erosion of sovereignty and state capacity. The issue, therefore, may be appropriately framed in terms of what would be the most viable way to reconstitute the state in a manner that will enable it to be responsive both to internal and external demands – a question that is markedly different from the one that may be raised by observers of South East Asia or Latin America.

As a demonstration of state incapacity in Africa, I will conclude with an example of migration of peoples on the continent. In terms of migration, the most common reason for the movement of people on the continent is not primarily the search for economic opportunity, but rather it is because they have been displaced by civil war. Africa is home to the largest number of refugees in the world. If we take the recent case of the Great Lakes region – Tanzania, Uganda, Zaire, Rwanda, and Burundi – the ongoing crisis in Congo–Zaire,

Rwanda, and Burundi has resulted in the movement of between 4 and 7 million people. Similarly, in Angola, Mozambique, and Liberia, a further 7 million people have variously been displaced. In Northeast Africa, especially in Sudan, large segments of the population are refugees, living in horrible, squalor conditions. In short, the state in most of these countries is not the effective Leviathan that we have come to expect in modern times.

State sovereignty in Africa: some conclusions

It is obvious that state sovereignty in Africa is a fairly problematic concept. The starting point for the analysis really should be whether at the time of independence three decades ago, real sovereignty, i.e. effective control of the internal and external environments was a viable proposition. The answer of course is *no*. In the ensuing thirty years, the problem has actually become worse. In the early years of independence, one expected to find the old colonial master having substantial influence in the activities of the new state, whether in international relations or economic development. However, as the economic condition of most countries deteriorated, the chipping away at sovereignty of the state in Africa has been spearheaded by the multilateral financial institutions, principally the IMF and the World Bank. Even the conservative *The Economist* has recently remarked at the way in which the governance and economic decision process in African countries is fully within the hands of these two institutions, in spite of the difficulty in implementing their conditionality:

> SAPs remain deeply flawed; the IMF is so obsessed with price stability it doesn't think hard about anything else. The Bank, on the other hand, has hundreds of good ideas but no priorities. The Bank's standard programmes call on weak, debt-ridden countries to introduce value-added taxes, new customs administration, civil service reform, privatization of infrastructure, decentralized public administration, etc. – often within months. It was, alas, par for the course when the bank set one hundred and eleven conditions in its "policy-framework" paper on Kenya.
>
> (*The Economist*, June 29, 1996)

Why would Kenya (and other states in Africa) accede to these unreasonable and unworkable conditions? The answer is fairly straightforward: these countries are in such desperate economic condition that they have to accept all conditionality. Implementation, however, is a different matter. In a study of two countries, one praised for faithfully implementing conditionality (Ghana under Jerry Rawlings) and one condemned for poor implementation (Zambia under Kenneth Kaunda), Matthew Martin found that Ghana's record was not as perfect, nor was Zambia's as appalling. The big difference in the perception was that Ghana was able to successfully explain to the Bank why it did not fully implement the program while Zambia pretty much adopted the rhetoric of sovereignty, in which case it was punished by the withholding of funds by the World Bank

(Martin 1993). Thus, in a fundamental sense state sovereignty in Africa has been an unrealized objective from the beginning, in which case it makes current discussions about sovereignty in the global system less applicable to the region – precisely because there really has never been real state sovereignty in Africa.

In retrospect however, demanding or expecting absolute sovereignty for the state in Africa is unrealistic, indeed as it has been unrealistic for every state going back to Westphalia. As Krasner reminds us in Chapter 2, this volume, activities that in theory could be conceived as eroding state sovereignty: the demand for religious toleration, human rights, use of shared waterways, etc., have always constrained state action. We therefore should not expect anything less in terms of pressure on state sovereignty in the contemporary period given the fact that there is increased density in international interaction. Specifically in the case of Africa, it is clear that SAPs under the guidance of IFIs have clearly eroded the capacity of the state to take many independent actions including financial regulation and operation of the market. The source of the erosion of state capacity, however, goes beyond that. Internally, many African states have lacked the sovereignty enjoyed by effective states because of the historical reasons outlined in this chapter. Thus, the state in Africa is caught in a double whammy of erosion of sovereignty by globalization, and by internal forces which continue to challenge the legitimacy of the state itself.

Notes

1 In this chapter, Africa is used as shorthand for Sub-Saharan Africa, excluding South Africa.

2 The Mid-Term Review of the United Nations New Agenda for the Development of Africa in the 1990s (UN-NADAF 1996) actually puts the number of countries in Sub-Saharan Africa that are currently under adjustment at thirty-seven.

3 Zartman further elaborates on the concept of state collapse, which I find useful in understanding the dilemma of development in Africa if we accept the state as a central player:

> Collapse means that the basic functions of the state are no longer performed....As the decision making center of government, the state is paralyzed and inoperative: laws are not made, order is not preserved, societal cohesion is not enhanced. As a symbol of identity, it has lost its power of conferring a name on its people and meaning to their social action. As a territory it is no longer assured security and provisionment by a central sovereign organization. As the authoritative political institution, it has lost its right to command and conduct public affairs. As a system of socioeconomic organization, its functional balance of inputs and outputs is destroyed; it no longer receives support from nor exercises control over its people, and it no longer is even the target of demands, because its people know that it is incapable of providing supplies. No longer functioning, with neither traditional nor charismatic nor institutional sources of legitimacy, it has lost the right to rule.
>
> (Zartman 1995: 5)

4 I wish to note that the concept of the state used in this chapter is a fairly straightforward liberal/modernization usage. Arguably, modernization may lack the

sophistication and subtlety of Gramscian analysis on the nature of the state, yet, I view the two approaches as fundamentally the same in so far as they apply to the African scene. What Jean-Francois Bayart (1993) calls the "passive revolution" in describing the transition from the colonial to the post-colonial state, I view as simply the transference of fairly weak state institutions from the colonial to the post-colonial state. As I argue in the chapter, the 100 years or so of colonial rule in Africa never established the long (effective) reach of the state, which then could provide a basis for sweeping legitimacy by the post-colonial state. Indeed, in the quest to make itself more legitimate, the post-colonial state made itself an "enemy" of the citizens because of its extractive agenda. Thus, Bayart's "passive revolution" failed, which would be an extension of Zartman's and others' "collapsed" states.

References

Africa Confidential (London), various issues 1990–7, inclusive.

Amin, S. (1974) *Accumulation on a World Scale*, 2 vols, New York: Monthly Review.

—— (1977) *Imperialism and Unequal Development*, New York: Monthly Review.

Bates, R.H. (1981) *Markets and States in Africa: The Political Basis of Agricultural Policies*, Berkeley: University of California Press.

Bayart, J.-F. (1993) *The State in Africa: The Politics of the Belly*, London: Langman.

Belassa, B.A. (1964) *Trade Prospects for Developing Countries*, Homewood, IL: R.D. Irwin.

Brown, M.B. and Tiffen, P. (1994) *Short Changed: Africa and World Trade*, Boulder, CO: Pluto Press.

Callaghy, T.M. (1984) *The State–Society Struggle: Zaire in Comparative Perspective*, New York: Columbia University Press.

Callaghy, T.M. and Ravenhill, J. (1993) "Introduction: vision, politics, and structure: Afro-optimism, Afro-pessimism or realism?" in T.M. Callaghy and J. Ravenhill (eds) *Hemmed In: Responses to Africa's Economic Decline*, New York: Columbia University Press, pp. 1–17.

Cooper, F. (1981) "Africa and the World Economy," *African Studies Review* 24 (2/3): 1–86.

Deyo, F.C. (ed.) (1987) *The Political Economy of the New Asian Industrialism*, Ithaca: Cornell University Press.

Evans, P. (1987) "Class, State and Dependence in East Asia: Lessons for Latin American-ists," in F.C. Deyo (ed.) *The Political Economy of the New Asian Industrialism*, Ithaca: Cornell University Press.

—— (1995) *Embedded Autonomy: States and Industrial Transformation*, Princeton: Princeton University Press.

Fatton, R., Jr (1992) *Predatory Rule: State and Civil Society in Africa*, Boulder, CO: Lynne Reinner.

Harbeson, J.W., D. Rothchild, and N. Chazan (eds) (1994) *Civil Society and the State in Africa*, Boulder, CO: Lynne Reinner.

Jackson, R.H. and Rosberg, C.G. (1982) "Why Africa's weak states persist: the empirical and juridical in statehood," *World Politics* 27.

Langdon, S.N. (1981) *Multinational Corporations in the Political Economy of Kenya*, New York: St. Martin's.

Leys, C. (1975) *Underdevelopment in Kenya: The Political Economy of Neo-Colonialism, 1964–1971*, Berkeley: University of California Press.

MacGaffey, J. with Vwakyanakazi Mukohya, Rukarangria wa Nkera, Brooke Grundfest

Schoepf, Makwala ma Mavambu ye Beda, and Walu Engundu (1991) *The Real Economy in Zaire: The Contribution of Smuggling and Other Unofficial Activities to National Wealth*, Philadelphia: University of Pennsylvania Press.

Martin, M. (1993) "Neither Phoenix nor Icarus: negotiating economic reform in Ghana and Zambia, 1983–1992," in T.M. Callaghy and J. Ravenhill (eds) *Hemmed In: Responses to Africa's Economic Decline*, New York: Columbia University Press.

Mittleman, J.H. (1996) "The dynamics of globalization," in J.H. Mittleman (ed.) *Globalization: Critical Reflections*, Boulder, CO: Lynne Reinner, pp. 1–19.

Nabudere, D.W. (1977) *The Political Economy of Imperialism*, London: Zed Press.

Nyang'oro, J.E. (1989) *The State and Capitalist Development in Africa: Declining Political Economies*, New York: Praeger.

Nzongola-Ntalaja (ed.) (1986) *The Crisis in Zaire: Myths and Realities*, Trenton, NJ: Africa World Press.

Prunier, G. (1996) *The Rwanda Crisis: History of Genocide*, New York: Columbia University Press.

Ravenhill, J. (ed.) (1986) *Africa in Economic Crisis*, New York: Columbia University Press.

—— (1993) "A second decade of adjustment: greater complexity, greater uncertainty," in T.M. Callaghy and J. Ravenhill (eds) *Hemmed In: Responses to Africa's Economic Decline*, New York: Columbia University Press, pp. 18–53.

Riddel, R.C., Coughlin, P. Harvey, C., Karmiloff, I., Lewis, S., Jr, Sharpley, J. and Stevens, C. (1990) *Manufacturing Africa: Performance and Prospects of Seven Countries in Sub-Saharan Africa*, London: James Currey.

Rodney, W. (1972) *How Europe Underdeveloped Africa*, Dar es Salaam: Tanzania Publishing House.

Rostow, W.W. (1960) *The Stages of Economic Growth: A Non-Communist Manifesto*, Cambridge: Cambridge University Press.

Rothchild, D. and Chazan, N. (eds) (1988) *The Precarious Balance: State and Society in Africa*, Boulder, CO: Westview.

Rweyemamu, J. (1973) *Underdevelopment and Industrialization in Tanzania: A Study of Perverse Capitalist Industrial Development*, Nairobi: Oxford University Press.

Sangmpam, S.N. (1994) *Pseudocapitalism and the Overpoliticized State: Reconciling Politics and Anthropology in Zaire*, Brookfield, VT: Ashgate.

Stein, H. (ed.) (1995) "Policy alternatives to structural adjustment in Africa: an introduction," in *Asian Industrialization and Africa: Studies in Policy Alternatives to Structural Adjustment*, New York: St. Martin's, pp. 1–29.

United Nations (1996) *Mid-term Review of the United Nations New Agenda for the Development of Africa in the 1990s*, New York: United Nations.

Wallerstein, I. (1986) *Africa and the Modern World*, Trenton, NJ: Africa World Press.

Warren, W. (1980) *Imperialism: The Pioneer of Capitalism*, London: New Left Books.

World Bank (1981) *Accelerated Development in Sub-Saharan Africa: An Agenda for Action*, World Bank: Washington, DC.

Zartman, I.W. (ed.) (1995) "Introduction: Posing the Problem of State Collapse," in *Collapsed States: The Disintegration and Restoration of Legitimate Authority*, Boulder, CO: Lynne Reinner.

Index